SEEING OURSELVES

EXPLORING RACE, ETHNICITY, AND CULTURE

If I cannot see myself I cannot see others clearly;
and if I cannot see others clearly,
seeing myself becomes more and more difficult.
— Lyn

Not everything that is faced can be changed,
but nothing can be changed until it is faced.
— James Baldwin

It is what we think we know already that often prevents us
from learning.
— Claude Bernard

As hard as it may be to believe,
in Canadian society, issues of race and ethnicity are often ignored.
With so little acknowledgment of our diversity,
we will remain blind to our reality.
— Kai James

SEEING OURSELVES

EXPLORING RACE, ETHNICITY, AND CULTURE

FOURTH EDITION

CARL E. JAMES

YORK UNIVERSITY

THOMPSON EDUCATIONAL PUBLISHING, INC.
Toronto

Information on how to obtain copies of this book is available at:

Website:	http://www.thompsonbooks.com
E-mail:	publisher@thompsonbooks.com
Telephone:	(416) 766–2763
Fax:	(416) 766–0398

Library and Archives Canada Cataloguing in Publication

James, Carl
Seeing ourselves : exploring race, ethnicity and culture / Carl E. James. -- 4th ed.

Includes bibliographical references and index.
ISBN 978-1-55077-171-8

1. Canada--Race relations. 2. Canada--Ethnic relations.
3. Multiculturalism--Canada. I. Title.

FC104.J35 2010   305.800971   C2009-906309-3

Production Editor:	Katy Bartlett
Designer:	Tibor Choleva
Copy Editor:	Caley Baker
Proofreader:	Write On!
Cover Illustration:	"Globe Driver" James Turner

Every reasonable effort has been made to acquire permission for copyrighted materials used in this book and to acknowledge such permissions accurately. Any errors or omissions called to the publisher's attention will be corrected in future printings. We acknowledge the support of the Government of Canada through the Book Publishing Industry Development Program for our publishing activities.

Printed in Canada. 1 2 3 4 5 6   14 13 12 11 10

TABLE OF CONTENTS

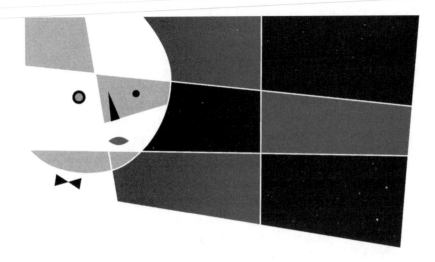

PREFACE

The materials for *Seeing Ourselves* were first put together in 1989 as a result of my desire to have a resource for the courses I taught. I wanted to bring together student essays and comments about race, ethnicity, and citizenship, so that students could "speak" to each other through their own work. I hoped that—through the works and voices of "people like them"—they would come to see that issues of race and ethnic relations were not merely my constructions or those of minority peoples. These issues are also the concern of dominant group members, including many of the students, who speak eloquently about themselves and issues in racial and ethnic terms. Since its publication, I have been using this book in many of my classes, and it has generated a number of questions, comments, and additional reflective essays, some of which have been included in subsequent editions. From these class discussions and comments, as well as those I have received from other readers—high school, college, and university students—I have gained new insights and perspectives that I am taking this opportunity to share. I hope that, in this new edition, and in the tradition of teacher as researcher, I continue to provide the reader with a lens through which to view the complexity, dynamism, variation, tension, and conflict that characterize identities and cultural relations in society, particularly in the context in which students discuss them.

The comments and essays that appear in this book and earlier editions have all been written within the context of prevailing popular discourses of identity pertaining to race, ethnicity, and nationality. And while I did not set out to capture how concepts of race, ethnicity, and citizenship are taken up and articulated by post-secondary students over a period of time, this work does just that, given that the essays now cover a twenty-year period. In the more recent comments and essays, there is evidence that students are not addressing these issues for the first time. Indeed, many of today's young people have already been confronted with increasing ethnic and racial diversity in their neighbourhoods, communities, schools, and workplaces. Some are well acquainted with the growing literature on whiteness. Moreover, issues of ethnicity, race, skin colour (or complexion), racism, ethnocentrism, and religious prejudices are now informed by the events of 9/11 and the tumultuous decade that has followed, as well as the continuous annual inflow of 200,000 to 250,000 immigrants and refugees to Canada, especially into large metropolitan cities. The events of 9/11 and the "changing faces" in Canada have made prominent the matter of racial profiling, as well as questions of immigration, citizenship, and multiculturalism.

Generally, the essays and comments in this book provide critical insights into the thinking and analytical processes of "naive" or "non-expert" individuals, who reflect on issues related to society, community, ethnicity, race, culture, and identity. I have attempted to preserve the voices of contributors, their analyses, and the ways in which they articulate their ideas. Student excerpts and essays have been reproduced with the permission of the writers, though in some cases pseudonyms have been used. It is important to remember that the student excerpts included in the text are individual accounts and, therefore, cannot be generalized to others, not even those of similar racial and ethnic background. I have also used this as an occasion to dialogue using newspaper articles and reports of local, national, and international events and issues. My attempt in this volume is, as much as possible, to engage the voices and sentiments of individuals—through essays, excerpts, etc.—and those of communities and state—through media comments and reports, and government reports, policies, and legislation—by way of examining the various dimensions of the issues.

Effective communication or dialogue requires common use of terminologies and language. Familiarity with certain terms does not necessarily translate into a shared understanding of them or agreement on how they should be used; therefore, for the purpose of discussion and by way of establishing what might be considered shared reference, the terms used in our discussion are defined, and many appear in a glossary at the end of the text. As Jackson and Meadows (1991) point out, "individuals' definitions or conceptual frameworks ... may either hinder or facilitate an understanding of the behaviours and experiences that occur in their lives and the lives of others. Often a change in the conceptual framework can open a whole new realm of understanding of these behaviours and experiences" (72). I contend that definitions are useful tools, if only as a starting point. In this regard, I recognize that terms such as *racial minority, marginalized people, racialized "others,"* and so on have particular political meanings and implications, and one term might be preferred over another; the same is true for the terms *ethnic majority* or *dominant group.* That said, I should point out that my use of the term *racial minority* is not to present those considered the minority as having an inferior position, but to convey the position of individuals or groups within the power structure of the society.

Further, in terms of complexity, it goes without saying that race, ethnicity, citizenship, and immigrant status do not exist independent of social class, gender, dis/ability, sexuality, and other such factors. Indeed, these factors are interrelated, and it is difficult to disentangle them and point to a particular factor as operating in any given situation or at one time. But the complex, unstable, and fluid relationship between the factors notwithstanding, the discussion needs to start somewhere, and race or ethnicity—or both—are valuable points at which to enter the discussion and examine the issues.

Ultimately, any discourse that deals with critical theory or anti-racism must engage people in working toward social change. This necessarily involves individuals' self-knowledge and awareness, as well as ongoing critical self-reflection. It also means getting to know others as individuals and in relation to their communities in order to engage in effective social action.

ORGANIZATION OF THE BOOK

The themes upon which our discussion is built are: identity in terms of ethnicity and race (within which immigrant/refugee/citizenship status, faith, language, generation, etc., are also taken up); multiculturalism; immigration policies and practices; mechanisms of differentiation (racism, xenophobia, etc.); educational and employment equity programs; and privileges based on identity. In Chapter 1, I set out that individuals' behaviours as well as their attitudes, values, and beliefs are structured by culture; hence, I take the understanding of culture to be an important starting point for the analysis of individuals' experiences with regard to race and ethnicity. In Chapter 2, I put forward an understanding of culture, noting the ways in which it structures the life experiences of individuals and their responses to their social and physical environments. The fact is, just as individuals' experiences and responses to their physical and social environments *are shaped by* culture, individuals themselves *shape* culture. This dynamic is part of the Canadian culture—the core set of norms, values, and expectations by which Canadian residents adhere, and into which immigrants are expected to integrate. In this chapter, I also start to articulate the complexity, variations, and fluidity of Canadian culture as it is experienced and lived by people on the basis of their differing races, ethnicities, languages, faiths, etc.

In Chapter 3, with the help of a conceptual diagram, I attempt to represent the many individual (intrinsic), community, institutional, and societal factors that contribute to identity construction. I examine the ways in which cultural identities are understood, referenced, experienced, and articulated by individuals, and in relation to the cultural contexts in which individuals live, work, learn, and play. I contend that while there are inherent problems in naming or categorizing individuals' identities, and of course, individuals' roles in constructing their identities, in terms of, for instance race and ethnicity, the fact remains that categorizations do occur, and individuals identify themselves, or are identified as, members of particular ethnic and racial groups. Clearly, socializing agents such as familial, educational, community, and social institutions play significant roles in socializing and, by extension, disciplining (or sanctioning) members into the cultural norms, values, beliefs, expectations, and aspirations of society.

In Chapter 4, I explore the interrelationship of these institutions and their significance in the construction of cultural identification. I examine the information and skills that they pass on to individuals so that they may effectively negotiate and navigate social and cultural institutions, noting particularly the contradictions, tensions, and conflicts that are inherent to culture.

Multiculturalism is a well-established discourse in Canada, and it operates to frame ideas about Canadians' openness to cultural differences, democracy, social justice, and equality of opportunity. This discourse operates similarly in many Western countries; however, as more and more immigrants and refugees come into these countries, and as ethnic, racial, and religious minority groups demand the rights and opportunities to which they are entitled, multiculturalism is challenged in its capacity—as a policy or ideology—to respond to the diversity within these societies. Some of the promises, challenges, and understandings of multiculturalism are explored in Chapter 5. I start with a review of the discussion of multiculturalism in Europe and elsewhere, then go on to explore its viability in societies where inequity, colour blindness and racism, xenophobia, Islamophobia, etc., are inherent in the social structure. I also look at how this discourse plays out in individuals' sense of cultural identification.

Immigrants are a constant in many Western countries with low birth rates that threaten economic prosperity, but inviting immigrants into the society also invites many challenges. In Chapter 6, I examine these challenges. Starting with a brief historical review of Canadian immigration, I proceed to discuss current Canadian immigration policies and practices, and what the presence of immigrants has meant for the economic, social, and political development and progress of the country. An interesting question here, which some of the essays and media reports address, is when does one cease to be an immigrant? This question is important because, within the discourse of multiculturalism, immigrants are the ones with culture who must be integrated, and often it seems (or it is perceived) that their culture never leaves them. In other words, those with accents and those who are "visible" are the immigrants and the ones with culture. This discourse has particular implications with regards to who identifies as a Canadian.

Issues pertaining to employment and educational equity are discussed in Chapter 7. As in the other chapters, student essays and media articles are used to illustrate individual experiences with equity programs and to examine the difficulties and limitations of, tensions created by, and satisfaction with equity programs. I discuss how equity programs are understood, particularly in terms of the perception that educational and occupational opportunities are already accessible to everyone—irrespective of factors such as race, language, social class, gender, ethnicity, disability—and the notion that it is therefore up to individuals to prepare themselves and take advantage of the available opportunities. This perception exists even in the face of structurally unequal barriers to access.

To conclude, in Chapter 8, I return to the theme of privilege and difference, which often surfaces in individual essays and excerpts pertaining to identity. I discuss individuals' acknowledgement of the significance of race and ethnicity in their identification and in relation to the privileges that they do or do not enjoy. I conclude by suggesting that we need a critical approach to education that will enable us to recognize the ways in which inequity operates to privilege some citizens and disadvantage others. We need to get to *know* each other as we get to *know* ourselves, our communities, and the structures that operate to afford us the opportunities and privileges we have. Ultimately, we need to act on this critical education.

Carl E. Tonge James

ACKNOWLEDGEMENTS

That this book has been written is due to the contributions and efforts of several people to whom I owe a tremendous debt. It is appropriate that I start by acknowledging the many students who contributed their essays and short excerpts, trusting me enough to share their experiences, thoughts, ideas, and feelings. To all of them I am sincerely grateful. Their individual and collective contributions, I am sure, will further debates and discussions of race and ethnic relations, as well as anti-racism education and social action.

This edition of *Seeing Ourselves* benefits from the cumulative assistance and support I have received from many individuals over the years. The research material, editorial assistance, and critical feedback and insights I received from Leanne Taylor were particularly valuable to the completion of this edition. She gave generously of her time and energy, and I am very grateful to her. I wish also to acknowledge with gratitude the research assistance and contributions of Krysta Pandolfi, Kai James, Selom Chapman-Nyaho, Kulsoom Anwer, Nazareth Yirgalem, Ansar Dualeh, and Ayderus Alawi, all of whom helped with this edition. I cannot forget the valuable research assistance that Dianna Abraham, Yasmin Razack, Kai James, Maxine Wood, and Gordon Pon provided for the previous editions. And I must continue to acknowledge Verna Frayne, Lisa Sutcliffe, and Alix Yule who were there at the initial stage of this project and encouraged me. I remain appreciative of everyone's supports, knowing that this edition builds on their early contributions that make the work what it is today.

I must again say thanks to colleagues and friends, particularly Carol Geddis for our conversation and Fyre Jean Graveline for her illustration of the Medicine Wheel, both of which appear in the previous as well as this edition, and to Kulsoom Anwer for her essay, which appears in Chapter 7, and Cristine Clifford Cullinan for her comments and suggestions particularly. The creative skill of Tibor Choleva has been invaluable in the development of the diagrams that I hope make for effective visual representation.

I am also indebted to the reviewers of this edition, whose comments, insights, and suggestions have helped make this edition an accessible and relevant resource.

I acknowledge the major editing work of Rachel Stuckey, who reviewed, commented, and edited several versions of the manuscript, helping me to make it ready for publication. Without her generous suggestions and support, I think I would still be working on the manuscript well into the next decade. She was effective in giving me deadlines and was patient when I needed more time.

Of course, this book has benefitted tremendously from the consistent support of the folks at Thompson Educational Publishing, particularly the encouragement, enthusiasm, and counsel of Keith Thompson. Caley Baker helped to put the "finishing touches" on the manuscript thereby contributing its cogent read. And Katy Bartlett in her role as editorial and production manager patiently responded to my questions and queries as we worked through the production process. Many thanks to all of you for your support and assistance.

There is always pressure when trying to produce a manuscript, but even more so while continuing to carry on with regular work activities and a teaching schedule. In this regard, the assistance, patience, and thoughtfulness of colleagues Patricia Gagliardi-Ursua at the York Centre for Education and Community (YCEC) were invaluable to me. To my other university colleagues, friends, and students who provided support and feedback about the book, I say thank you.

Finally, special thanks to Kai, Milderine, Dorne, Sammy, and other family members for their constant support, of which I am always assured. In a major way, they have also contributed to this book through our conversations, their questions, and sharing of their life experiences. I gain much insight through our personal connections—connections from which I will continue to learn for a long time to come.

INTRODUCTION

Over the years, I have worked with post-secondary education students—examining and responding to questions pertaining to equity, social justice, identity, belonging, privilege, racism, and discrimination—as they sought to understand their role, and prepared to work, in the diverse society that Canada has become. Understandably, the many issues and concerns raised by students start with their own sense of themselves and their experiences as raced, gendered, and classed citizens.

In this book, we examine the questions, comments, experiences, and perceptions of students, as articulated in their essays and other discussions. Not surprisingly, how young people understand things is heavily informed by the liberal discourse of individualism, which holds that individuals are in control of their situation and outcome. There is a tendency for students not to see the impact of economic, political, and cultural structures on their ideas, attitudes, values, behaviours, etc. My intention here is to examine individuals' concerns in relation to the cultural contexts that they inhabit. This is not to underestimate the agency that individuals exercise in structuring or constructing their interests and aspirations, but rather to note that individuals are socialized in a system in which the culture plays a significant role in structuring their identity, beliefs, ideas, outcomes, etc. My emphasis is on how culture structures all individuals' beliefs, values, expectations, and behaviours.

Individuals are socialized by and interact with institutions such as family, schools, faith communities, the justice system, social services, etc.

FIGURE 1.1 – SOCIETY/INSTITUTION/INDIVIDUAL INTERCONNECTEDNESS

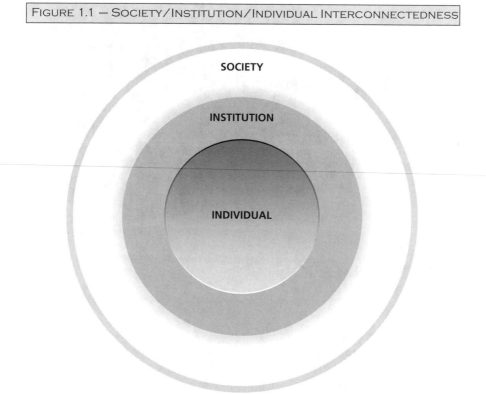

In other words, individuals are enmeshed in these institutions or social and cultural structures that mediate their lives. As **Figure 1.1** indicates, individuals, institutions, and society are interconnected. Individuals interact with institutions (such as family, schools, the justice system, political institutions, etc.) that socialize (and in the process, discipline through sanctions, etc.) them into the ways and values of society; and these in turn are influenced by global economic, political, and social structures and events.

In addition to the diversity that existed among Aboriginal peoples before Europeans colonized **Turtle Island**, ethnic and racial diversity has long characterized Canada's population. However, despite our interactions with a diversity of people in our neighbourhoods, schools, colleges, universities, workplaces, professional associations, and many other contexts—particularly in major metropolitan areas of Canada—we know very little about each other. What we do know is often what we learn from the media, in books, or in educational institutions. Sometimes, we get to learn about each other through friends and acquaintances, or through family members—if we happen to have persons of different racial and ethnic backgrounds as family members. With such limited or circumscribed knowledge of each other, we remain unaware of the issues that affect our daily lives, such as the effects of racism and discrimination, and the taken-for-granted privileges, power, and access to opportunities that some of us have, as well as the selves that we present within the various contexts in which we move.

But how do we come to know each other? Is there a point when we can say that we really know a person, or a member of a particular ethno-racial group, or the group itself? What would that mean? To me, knowing an individual or a group means having a level of understanding of the individual or group in relation to the social, political, economic, and cultural contexts in which they live and seek to realize their aspirations. Such knowing is understanding how the social construction of race and ethnicity, or how the meanings our society gives to race, ethnicity, national language fluency, and religious affiliation affect the opportunities and possibilities of individuals or groups. Indeed, human beings are complex—our behaviours, attitudes, values, and views of ourselves and others are related to the contexts, structures, and circumstances in which we find ourselves, and our interactions with others. To understand diversity is also to know about the experiences of others and, in the process, to know about ourselves.

It goes without saying that race, ethnicity, citizenship, and immigrant status do not exist independent of social class, gender, dis/ability, sexuality, and other such factors. Indeed, all these factors are interrelated; hence, it is difficult to disentangle them and point to a particular factor operating independently in any given situation or at any one time. I am aware of the problem with **essentialism**—that is, the belief that "individuals or groups have inherent unchanging characteristics rooted in biology or in self-contained culture that explains their status" (Hill Collins 1998, 277). As Saskia Wieringa (2002) puts it,

> Essentialism takes as its starting point a position that human behaviour is "natural," predetermined by genetics, biological and physiological mechanisms which are essentially the same in all humans and only need to be uncovered by science. These mechanisms are not subject to change. (8)

I am not interested in perpetuating this binary or unitary construction of identity in terms of race or ethnicity. While there are many common experiences to be found among people of the same ethno-racial groups, the experiences of group members are mediated by a myriad of other identities and constructs including, but not limited to, gender, class, sexuality, physical ability, religion, etc. Indeed, race, ethnicity, citizenship, religion, aboriginality, and other social identities are interconnected, not distinct, and are "simultaneously and differently experienced" by individuals (Kohli 2009; see also Campbell 2009). But the complexities and unstable relationships among these factors notwithstanding, the discussion needs to start somewhere, and race or ethnicity, or both, are valuable points at which to enter the discussion and examine the issues.

ISSUES AND CONCERNS PERTAINING TO RACE, ETHNICITY, AND CULTURE

The growing evidence that racialized minority immigrants face increasing barriers to integrating and succeeding in society and the growing reality that they are identifying themselves as Canadians less and less suggests that multiculturalism as practiced does not "translate" well for minorities. In the *Globe and Mail*, Marina Jiménez cites research by Jeffrey Reitz of the University of Toronto, which indicates that members of racial minorities born in Canada feel less like they belong than their parents do; a warning that Canada, "long considered a model of integration," may soon find the kind of unrest seen recently in France (*Globe and Mail*, January 12, 2007, A1).

In a recent report, Statistics Canada projected that by 2017 (Canada's 150th birthday) this country will look much different—racial minorities will make up, for example, more than half of the Greater Toronto Area's population. In 2001, the ratio of racial minorities in Canada was about one in eight; Statistics Canada predicts that in 2017, that ratio will be one in five. According to the *Toronto Star*, such predictions "paint a picture of a vibrant, globally connected culture. But they also raise questions about how prepared we are to house, educate and offer opportunities to new Canadians—especially in the Toronto area, which will be home to nearly half the land's visible minorities" (March 23, 2005, A1).

Sun Media's 2007 *Racial Tolerance Report* makes clear some of the barriers that may prevent racialized minority immigrants from succeeding in Canada (Leger 2007). Based on a national representative sample of 3,092 adult Canadians, the report found that almost half (47 percent) admitted to being at least slightly racist. Not surprisingly, those who admitted to being strongly or moderately racist (9 percent of the total) were more likely to agree with the statement "some races are more gifted than others." Fifty-seven percent of respondents feel that Canada needs to institute more strict control of immigrants before awarding them Canadian citizenship. Ninety-two percent of respondents said they had witnessed racist comments and behaviours, but only one-third said they intervened or informed authorities of what they had witnessed. Not surprisingly, the majority (66 percent) of racial minority Canadians report being victims of racism.

If Canada is to be "home" (with all that this term conveys) to racial minorities, they must be *accepted* as Canadians and understood as having all the related rights and privileges. This understanding is important particularly in cases of individuals like the governor general of Canada. So, for instance, the fact that Governor General Michaëlle Jean was born outside of Canada (as were many of our prime ministers) is irrelevant to the fact that she acquiesced to Prime Minister Stephen Harper's request to prorogue (or postpone) parliament in November 2008, thereby allowing him to avoid a vote of non-confidence.[1] Nor should the governor general's discussion of Haiti when meeting with President Obama during his visit to Ottawa call into question her citizenship and commitment to Canada. It has become too easy to fall back on, or include, minorities' places of birth in criticisms of their actions—a practice that does not reflect well on the multicultural discourse of integration.

Canada has made some progress in its attention to race, ethnicity, culture, and historical oppressions. For example, in 2008, the federal government resolved the largest number of Native land-claim disputes to date in its attempt to improve relations with the Aboriginal peoples of Canada and to stimulate economic development on reserves. During the same year, the government also issued an official apology to residential school survivors. In a speech to the House of Commons on June 11, 2008, Harper apologized on behalf of Canadians for "one of the darkest chapters in our history" (*Toronto Star,* June 11, 2008b, AA6), in which generations of Aboriginal children were forcibly removed from their families and sent to residential schools in a systematic effort to assimilate the people and destroy their communities. An editorial in the *Toronto Star* discussed the need for and significance of the apology:

> It would be difficult to underestimate [*sic*] the damage done to the estimated 150,000 First Nations, Métis and Inuit children who attended church-run residential schools from the 19th century until the final decades of the 20th century. They were separated from their families for long stretches, punished for speaking their own languages, and deprived of their cultural traditions. Some suffered physical and sexual abuse at the hands of those who sought to "civilize" them. Others died from disease and neglect before they could return home. (June 11, 2008b, AA6)

Many consider the government's apology an important step in the healing process. The apology created an opportunity for Canadians to address and recognize the reality and consequences of residential schools and their long-lasting systemic effects. These effects can be seen in Aboriginal communities nationwide, in the form of familial, social, economic, emotional, and spiritual problems. As Phil Fontaine, former national chief of the Assembly of First Nations, and also a former residential school student, said of the apology, "This is so very important. This is about reconciliation and ... about Canada coming to terms with its past." According to an article in the *Toronto Star*, Fontaine hopes that the apology "will help shape Canada for the future" (June 11, 2008b, AA6; see also M. James 2007).

But the residential school apology was not the government's first effort to recognize the past (see Gibney et al. 2007). In 2006, Prime Minister Harper made a series of important historical recognitions on behalf of Canadians. On June 22, 2006, the prime minister made a formal apology in the House of Commons for the implementation of the Chinese head tax (see Chapter 6, page 175). Later that summer, on August 6 in Surrey, British Columbia, Harper spoke of the "continuous journey" legislation that discriminated against immigrants from India and South Asia (see Chapter 6, page 176). In that speech, Harper acknowledged what is known as the *Komagata Maru* incident and announced that the Government of Canada was committed to consulting with the Indo-Canadian community in its efforts to appropriately "recognize this sad moment in Canada's history" (Abbott 2006; M. James 2007).

Earlier, the Canadian government also issued apologies to other groups, such as Japanese Canadians (September 1988) and Italian Canadians (November 1990) for their internment during World War II, and Jews (May 2008) for having denied Jewish refugees entry before the war. However, Canada and Canadians are not without our contradictions. Despite their appeal for an acknowledgement of their plight during and after World War I (1914–1920), when they were interned at Spirit Lake camp near Amos, Quebec, Ukrainians have not received an apology.[2] Also, still left unaddressed and unrecognized by the government is the historical oppression of Blacks in Canada.[3] Governments have not yet acknowledged their role in the slavery of African peoples; the immigration laws that barred Blacks, such as the homesteaders from Oklahoma, from immigrating and settling in Canada; the segregated school laws; and the destruction of communities like Africville in Halifax, Nova Scotia. If such experiences and oppression are not named, these issues will be forgotten and not taken up by Canadians.

It is important to bear in mind the ways in which individuals and communities, national and international events, and the conditions that result from these events are interrelated. This is quite evident in examinations of issues pertaining to race, ethnicity, religion, and immigration, particularly since September 11, 2001. The prejudice and stereotypes that were once revealed only in intimate settings and anonymous polls are no longer taboo, and are now freely discussed in public forums and widely reported in media. Framing incidents as acts of Islamist terrorism has encouraged uneasiness about multiculturalism and immigration. Shortly after the 9/11 attacks in the United States, five men were detained in Canada for suspected terrorism under national security certificates, which allow for the deportation of non-citizens deemed a risk to Canada. In 2007, the Supreme Court ruled national security certificates to be unconstitutional because defendants were not allowed to see the evidence against them or refute the allegations (M. Shephard, *Toronto Star*, October 22, 2007, A15).[4] Perhaps no issue has generated as much attention as the case of Maher Arar, a Canadian citizen of Syrian origin, who in 2002 was detained during a stopover in New York while waiting to board a flight to Montreal. After being questioned, he was deported to Syria as a suspected terrorist. After ten months in Syria, where he was tortured until he falsely admitted to terrorist training in Afghanistan, Arar was released to Canada. A formal inquiry exonerated Arar and blamed RCMP investigators for providing inaccurate information to American officials (see Pitter 2008).[5]

There is also the case of Canadian-born Omar Khadr who, at the age of fifteen, was arrested in Afghanistan in 2003 and transferred to the Guantanamo Bay prison in Cuba, accused of killing an American soldier in a standoff. In August of 2009, Khadr was the only Western citizen held in the Guantanamo Bay prison. Even though two Canadian federal court judges ordered the government to seek Khadr's return to Canada, the Harper government continued to fight the court's decision. While Canadians may have come to accept the Arar case as one of injustice, opinions remain split over the case of young Khadr. The possible closing of the Guantanamo Bay prison by the Obama administration raised concerns among Canadians about the release of Omar Khadr back to Canada, and what this would mean for Canadians, in terms of the economic resources required to assist him in making this transition.[6] The reactions of Canadians are influenced by the fact that Omar's father, Ahmed Said Khadr, is understood to have been a supporter of al Qaeda, and other family members have expressed support for the senior Khadr's actions.[7] For this reason, there have been calls for the Khadr family to be stripped of their citizenship. But as Janet Bagnall wrote in a 2004 *Montreal Gazette* article: "There is no legal basis for stripping someone of citizenship because of his or her views. Citizenship is a fundamental right. It is not something that can be capriciously denied on the basis of one person deciding another person's views are unacceptable" (April 23, 2004, A23).

International incidents of violence or apparent terrorist acts inspire caution among Canadians as they do in other parts of the world. When a train bombing in Madrid, Spain, in March 2004 killed 191 people and injured over 400, Canadians took notice. Originally blamed on the Basque separatist group ETA, the bombing was later revealed to be the work of an al Qaeda–inspired group. The bombings in July 2005 on the public transit system in London, England, which killed 52 people, raised further concern among Canadians. That all four bombers were residents of the United Kingdom is an important consideration. Riots in Paris, France, in October 2005 by marginalized Arab and African youths brought into focus the consequences of the poverty and discrimination faced by immigrants. The riots took place after two teenagers were electrocuted while hiding in a power-generation station after running from police. And in December of the same year, Australia also experienced its share of unrest when, after reports of violence by "Middle Eastern" gangs, thousands of white Australians gathered in a Sydney beachfront suburb to protest against immigration. The protest turned into racially motivated mob violence and retaliatory violence continued for days, including mob attacks against innocent bystanders.

In Canada in the summer of 2006, eighteen people were arrested for allegedly plotting to blow up the CN Tower, the Toronto Stock Exchange, and several other targets. The men, most of them Canadian-born and young, were said to be inspired by al Qaeda and were charged with contributing to the activity of a terrorist group.[8]

These local and international events have not only fuelled blatant **Islamophobia** in Canada's public discourse, but have also forced a reconceptualization of citizenship, multiculturalism, religious rights, and global migration as they relate to race and ethnic identities. So an incident involving an eleven-year-old hijab-wearing soccer player, which would, in most circumstances, have been considered a local community concern, took on national significance. A soccer referee in Laval, Quebec, told the young soccer player to remove her hijab to play the match because it was a "physical threat." This resulted in the player's team, and several other Ontario teams, withdrawing from the tournament (*Montreal Gazette*, February 27, 2007, A20).

According to Daniel Del Gobbo (2009), a recent Supreme Court of Canada ruling related to freedom of religion, "may signal to members of some religious faiths that their sincere beliefs and practices, incommensurate with the broad social legislation, may not be guaranteed at all." The case was the challenge by the Hutterian Brethren of Wilson Colony, Alberta, to the provincial government's requirement that they carry photographs on their driver's licences. Although all licences issued since 1974 have included a photograph of the holder, exceptions were made for members of the Hutterite community until 2003, when the government introduced new regulation that made a photograph a requirement for them.

The government claimed that "an exemption from the photo requirement would materially increase the vulnerability of the licensing system and the risk of identity-related fraud." For their part, the Hutterian Brethren, who lived in a colony of about 250 members, objected to photo identification because they, as the Court document shows, "believe that permitting their photo to be taken violates the Second Commandment: 'You shall not make for yourself an idol, or any likeness of what is in heaven above or on the earth beneath or in the water under the earth' (Exodus 20:4)."

Chief Justice Beverley McLachlin commented that individuals could claim that many of the regulations of our modern society have an effect on their religious beliefs, but that validating each claim could "seriously undermine the universality of many regulatory programs, including the attempt to reduce abuse of driver's licences at issue here, to the overall detriment of the community." She concluded that the photo requirement minimally impaired the Hutterites' right to freedom of religion, and observed: "In judging the seriousness of the limit in a particular case, the perspective of the religious or conscientious claimant is important. However, this perspective must be considered in the context of a multicultural, multi-religious society where the duty of state authorities to legislate for the general good inevitably produces conflicts with individual beliefs." The ruling suggested that claims such as the Hutterites' argument that their religious freedom had been violated must in the future be evaluated on a case-by-case basis.

In giving consideration to world and local events that seem to have Canadians rethinking the efficacy of and their commitment to multiculturalism, Allan Gregg, in a 2006 article in *The Walrus*, suggests that these international events have fuelled immigration anxiety in Canada. Less than half of Canadians think Canada is accepting the right amount of immigrants, and 40 percent believe that immigrants from some countries contribute more to Canada than others. According to Gregg, while 80 percent of Canadians think that European immigrants make a positive contribution, only 59 percent think the same of Asians. The numbers fall to 45 percent for East Indians (or South Asians) and 33 percent for people from the Caribbean (Gregg 2006, 40). Additionally, 69 percent of Canadians still believe immigrants should "integrate and become part of the Canadian culture," rather than "maintain their [own] identity." As Gregg concludes, "To some extent, it seems that Canadians, like their brethren in Europe, Australia, and elsewhere, have had their fill of multiculturalism and hyphenated citizenship" (40).

It is in this context that the town council of Hérouxville, Quebec, in early 2007, passed a declaration of behaviours they expected from potential immigrants who might consider living in that community. The items listed in the declaration included such things as no stoning or burning of women with acid, no carrying of "weapons" (i.e., kirpans) by children to school, and that women were allowed to drive, dance, and make their own decisions. This declaration was posted on the town's website and mailed to the provincial and federal immigration ministers (D. Moore, *Globe and Mail*, January 30, 2007b, A12). As a follow-up to this and other events, Quebec's premier, Jean Charest, in March of the same year, announced a commission on the subject of "reasonable accommodation" (see Chapter 5, page 141). The report on the commission's findings was released on May 22, 2008. Among other things, and in reference to Islamophobia, which had become an increasing concern not only among Quebecers but Canadians generally, Gerard Bouchard and Charles Taylor, chairs of the commission, identified that Quebec's Muslims were less stringently religious than most other immigrant groups, and the presence of so-called hard-line Islamists was marginal (*Globe and Mail*, May 21, 2008, A16).

The federal government's conscious effort to battle "the perception of Canada as a soft touch for asylum seekers" and "to play hardball" in such immigration cases (Armstrong and Ibbitson, *Globe and Mail*, October 20, 2009) also influences our society's view of immigrants. In October 2009, seventy-six Sri Lankan males arrived off Vancouver Harbour aboard "a rusty boat" called the *Ocean Lady*. As required by Canada's *Immigration and Refugee Protection Act*, these asylum seekers were detained and given a hearing. Supporters of the refugees say they have legitimate claims to asylum as members of the losing side in Sri Lanka's long civil war between the government and the rebel Tamil Tigers. Civilian Tamils were caught in the conflict, and many are now being detained in an internment camp in Sri Lanka, a situation condemned by many human rights organizations. Politicians and citizens have called for the Canadian government to acknowledge that while the civil war may have ended in Sri Lanka, civilian freedoms have not necessarily been restored or improved (Armstrong, *Globe and Mail*, October 18, 2009).

Jason Kenney, Canada's immigration minister, was quoted as saying: "We don't want to develop a reputation of having a two-tier immigration system—one tier for legal, law-abiding immigrants who patiently wait to come to the country, and a second tier who seek to come through the back door ... We need to do a much better job of shutting the back door of immigration for those who seek to abuse that asylum system."[9] The premise here is that "many refugee claims are bogus," casting asylum seekers in a negative light (Armstrong and Ibbitson, *Globe and Mail*, October 20, 2009).

Also relevant to our discussion in this text is the use of racial profiling and the role it has played in the construction of, differential treatment toward, and damaging experiences of minority Canadians. The Ontario Human Rights Commission (2003) defines **racial profiling** as

> any action undertaken for reasons of safety, security, or
> public protection that relies on stereotypes about race,
> colour, ethnicity, ancestry, religion, or place of origin
> rather than on reasonable suspicion, to single out an
> individual for greater scrutiny or different treatment. The
> Commission has noted that profiling can occur because
> of a combination of the above factors and that age and/
> or gender can influence the experience of profiling. (6)

The case of Suaad Hagi Mohamud serves as an example (M. Shephard, *Toronto Star*, August 15, 2009, A1). The Somali-born Canadian woman was detained in Nairobi airport by Kenyan immigration and KLM airline officials, who said that the picture in her four-year-old Canadian passport did not look like her—"because her lips and glasses were different." It was suggested that she was using a false passport. Canadian officials agreed and "branded her an imposter and cancelled her passport." Her other pieces of Canadian identification—driver's license, etc., did not help. After nearly three months, including eight days in jail, and a DNA test that proved she is who she claimed to be, Mohamud's passport was finally returned to her and she was allowed to travel to Canada. In the aftermath, many questions arose about with regards to whether Ottawa's failure to intervene was influenced by Mohamud's race, country of origin, and religion.

Another recent incident was ruled a case of racial profiling by the Ontario Human Rights Commission: attacks against Asian fishermen in an area north of Toronto in the summer and fall of 2007. As reported in the *National Post* by C. Offman, the Asian fishermen were threatened with racist comments, their fishing gear was often destroyed, and in some cases they were pushed into the lake. York Regional Police Chief Armand LeBarge claimed these attacks were connected to an editorial in the Ontario Federation of Anglers and Hunters newsletter that advised members to ask Asians about licenses and the size of their catch, assuming that they might not be familiar with Canadian fishing regulations (*National Post*, May 14, 2008, A3).

While racial profiling is experienced among members of the society generally, it is with members of law enforcement that its practice is particularly concerning. In the report, *Paying the Price: The Human Cost of Racial Profiling*, the Ontario Human Rights Commission (2003) tells of the stops, searches, harassments, and unwarranted questioning of racial and religious minority Canadians—especially Aboriginals, Muslims, Arabs, South Asians, African Canadians, and people perceived to be from the Middle East—by police, security personnel, immigration and customs officers, and border control officers. The commission's report followed an extensive investigation in 2002 by the *Toronto Star,* which demonstrated the existence of racial profiling by the city's police force (October 19, 2002, A1). The investigation revealed that a disproportionate number of Black motorists were ticketed for traffic and other violations, a number of which became known only after the driver was stopped. The data presented by the series of articles also showed that whites stopped for drug possession were released at the scene 76.5 percent of the time, compared to only 61.8 percent of the time for Blacks; and accused Blacks taken to police station were held overnight for a bail hearing at twice the rate of whites. The findings served to support the claim made by many in Toronto's Black communities that Blacks, particularly youth, are subject to greater police scrutiny. Toronto's police union responded with a libel lawsuit against the newspaper (P. Small, *Toronto Star,* January 18, 2003, A6).

A number of studies and reports demonstrate the existence of racial profiling in Canada, particularly by law enforcement officers (Henry and Tator 2006b; James 2004; Wortley and Tanner 2004)—an occurrence that Ontario Court judges have ruled is worthy of consideration in sentencing accused people. In one case, Justice Molloy of the Ontario Superior Court wrote that two Toronto police officers had no reasonable grounds for stopping an accused on drug charges, and that he was singled out and his car searched "because he was a Black male driving an expensive Mercedes" (Blatchford, *Globe and Mail,* September 17, 2004, A1). A year earlier, the *Globe and Mail's* K. Makin reported that in reference to a case involving an eighteen-year-old Black youth, Ontario Court of Appeal Judge Rosenberg noted that "systemic racism and the background factors faced by black youths in Toronto are important matters" to a case (*Globe and Mail,* February 13, 2003, A1). These judges underscored the fact that the perceptions and actions of police officers are not simply based on their individual attitudes, but are informed by a system of policies and corresponding practices, which are to be found within institutions. In other words, racism is not simply a reflection of individuals' negative attitudes toward racial minority members of society (i.e., individual racism), but is also a reflection of how the policies, regulations, programs, values, norms, sanctions, and practices of institutions within society inform and structure individuals' attitudes and practices toward those considered subordinate or inferior (i.e., systemic racism) (James 2004, 40).

Racial profiling by educators is also believed to affect the educational opportunities and achievements of minority students. In the case of Black students, parents and community members have long argued that their schooling and educational experiences, and related outcomes, have to do with educators' stereotypes or profile of them as "at risk," low-achieving, disinterested students who are likely to become disruptive in class and eventually drop out (James 2004). To counter the consequences of this profile of their students, Black parents and community members in Toronto and Halifax have been, for more than twenty years, requesting schools that would address the particular needs, interests, problems, and aspirations of these students and their parents. While there have been earlier (in 1986 and 1993) attempts in the Toronto area to establish such schools (Wallace 2009), recent reports that indicate that the drop-out rate for Black high school students stands at 40 percent have accelerated demands for Black-focused or Africentric schooling. The Toronto District School Board finally decided to open a Black-focused school in the fall of 2009. But this decision sparked considerable and heated debates that are observed worldwide. The reactions to the school indicate that a significant number of Canadians, including political and educational leaders, are against such a school, claiming that it is not in keeping with the multicultural ideology of integration (Brown, *Toronto Star*, January 30, 2008, A1; Wallace 2009). Many supporters of the school question these reactions to the establishment of an Africentric alternative school when in the same school board there exist a number of focused schools and programs, such as those for Aboriginal students.

SEEING OURSELVES

In his 2002 book, *The Problem of Race in the 21st Century*, Thomas Holt points out that race and racism are by their very nature "chameleon-like." Thus, describing the current state of knowledge about race and racism is difficult because:

> Neither race nor racism can live independently of its social environments, the times and spaces it inhabits. By nature a changeling, it attaches itself to and draws sustenance from other social phenomena and from racist discourse itself, like one of those insidious monsters in late-night science-fiction movies. The historian is left to examine the carcass it once inhabited before moving on to another social body, while the sociologist busily constructs diagnostic questionnaires after the disease has already mutated. (21)

Indeed, as Holt asserts, both individual identity and the significance we ascribe to race, as well as ethnicity, cannot be seen separately from the institutions and larger societal contexts that influence them. Our understanding and use of race, ethnicity, and other demographic variables in our everyday discourses and interactions is informed by institutions and cultural contexts.

Reflecting on my work with students in the 1980s, I recall the reluctance among students to explicitly name race as an identifier— they said they did not "see" it, nor did they want to be asked to name race, because doing so would mean that they were "racist." (However, ethnicity was seemingly an acceptable identifier.) But at the time, they would talk about the problems brought into Canada by immigrants. And how they could identify immigrants by their race (i.e., non-white) or accent. The reluctance to name race was also inspired by the desire to believe in and maintain the meritocratic dream and democratic ideology that Canada is a not a racist society, and that everyone—irrespective of skin colour, social class, and social networks—would be able to attain the things to which they aspire. Majority ethnic group students expressed interest in getting to "know" about minority students, but that meant me telling them about "Aboriginals," "East Indians," "West Indians," "Italians," "Asians," "Sikhs," and others—a reflection of the notion that it is possible to provide them with the necessary and sufficient information about these groups. And there were statements such as:

○ If I went to their country, I would have to adopt their culture

○ When you are in Rome, you do as the Romans do

○ The immigrants are coming and taking all the jobs

○ The immigrants are causing all the crimes

○ The minorities are causing the racism; they cry racism for everything, especially when they don't get the jobs

○ The government is just trying to please the minorities; that is why there is employment equity

○ People are getting hired because of their race, not because they are qualified for the jobs

Today's students have more interaction with minority group members and they count racialized minority group members among their friends, work and recreational colleagues, and some, among their family members; there is no longer the expectation that one class or a series of presentations can fully convey the complex and diverse realities of racialized Canada. But there is still the reluctance to name or "see" race. This is understandable since, as in all generations of Canadians, today's young people are well socialized in the belief of meritocracy, democracy, and equality of opportunity, and "officially" we do not gather race data as a means of explaining issues and trends. In this regard, students often explain the social and economic conditions, high unemployment, school failure rates, etc., of racialized Canadians as a reflection of their individual, family, or ethno-racial community attitudes, values, and actions. This orientation to the issues is to be expected given the pervasive ideology of individualism that informs the messages that the students receive. Many of today's young Canadians see the election of Barack Obama as president of the United States as evidence that a Black or biracial person—in fact, any person of colour—is able to attain the goals to which they aspire, if only they take advantage of the opportunities presented to them.

My aim in this new edition of *Seeing Ourselves* is to once again engage with readers in a reflective critical dialogue about our systems to enable an understanding of the realities of racial, ethnic, and cultural influences in our lives. Actually, these influences are so much a part of our lives that there is a tendency to take them for granted. It often seems much easier, particularly for ethnic majority group members, to see these influences operating in the lives and behaviours of "other" Canadians—immigrants and "multicultural" Canadians. And minority group members seem habitually better able to identify the racial, ethnic, and immigrant cultural influences in their own lives and in the lives of the dominant group members.

This text is not intended to force readers to identify themselves in ethnic or racial terms. Rather, the aim of the text is to have them begin to reflect critically and examine their world view, and to try to understand how factors such as ethnicity, race, and culture help to structure the ways in which we think of ourselves and others within the context of Canadian society. This text is intended to encourage individuals to begin to "paint themselves into the picture." The purpose of this book is not to study "other" Canadians—to learn about their "culture" or to study the victims of racism—but rather to encourage readers to analyze their ideas and experiences as majority- and minority-group Canadians, to reflect on their personal contradictions and challenges, and to begin to critique the various ways in which inequalities of power and privilege exist in our society.

Race, ethnicity, and culture are not abstract notions. They influence all of us personally, from how we see ourselves and others to the ways institutions in our society operate, and we must appreciate the extent to which we internalize and operate with the meanings that have been given to these factors. The challenge is to bring individuals to the understanding that culture exists with all of us, it shapes and informs the lives of all Canadians, and it is, in turn, acted upon by all Canadians. My intention here is to present the various ways in which we construct ourselves and others in terms of race, ethnicity, and culture and to share my impressions as one who has been part of this discussion for some time. The essays and comments that are included in this book were deliberately chosen to provide a picture of how anti-racism education and critical learning assists, or frustrates, our ability to move beyond ourselves to learn about each other, and to understand the complexities of learning, living, and working in a society characterized by racial, ethnic, religious, and cultural diversity and inequity. Having heard from readers about earlier volumes of this book, I am sure that there are comments and viewpoints with which you, the reader, will identify, or stories that reflect your own experiences. Insofar as these reflections provide you with additional or critical insights, this project will have been useful, for it can serve as a catalyst for personal growth that, in turn, might compel you to engage in a process of action for social change.

The inclusion of racist or prejudiced language and information or positions articulated in some of the comments and essays is not intended to legitimize these views, but rather to engage, expose, and examine them. Moreover, in presenting these ideas, I seek to include the various perspectives, ideas, opinions, histories, and beliefs that have been part of our dialogues and discussions (for more on this approach, see Howard 2002). While there is the risk that their inclusion may contribute to, or be used to validate the stereotypes, prejudices, and racist information that I seek to dispel and eliminate, my hope is that these ideas presented in this context will act as a catalyst for challenging our learned "truths," "facts," and misinformation.

LYN: "I AM A MEMBER OF A MAJORITY GROUP THAT HAS A GREAT DEAL OF POWER."

As a white English Canadian, my values, behaviours, and attitudes are influenced by my origins in direct relation to the fact that I am a member of the single largest group—racially, ethnically, and to a large extent, culturally … My experience of the class system in Britain has made me aware of how differences in origin—in this case, most noticeably defined by accent (in speech)—have a direct relationship to the position a person holds in society in terms of economic power, political influence, and control over day-to-day life. What I learned as a teenager in the 1960s in North America, when issues of civil rights and discrimination were in the news, the subject of popular books, and certainly regularly discussed in classrooms, reinforced my awareness of what influences a person's ability to be accepted in society—to succeed in the terms laid down by that society and also in terms of personal freedom.

I am a member of a majority [i.e., dominant] group that has a great deal of power; so, while I may have an awareness of racial issues, and I may condemn my society for its inherent racism, it is white culture that I experience day to day. The very fact that discrimination is rarely an issue for me personally results in my own racial identity becoming an invisible thing. The powerful people I interact with either directly or indirectly—the politician, the employer, the teacher, the social worker—are invariably white. I know that my race will not be an issue for most of the people I must deal with, as I know we will have a commonality from the start … There is a good chance that our backgrounds will be similar, in terms of culture or ethnicity, or both. Nor will I expect my values or behaviour to be an issue, because I fit into the "norm."

Racial and ethnic cultures mesh to form a powerful image of what is accepted or expected—the idea of the "norm." I see myself reflected not only in the powerful people I am in contact with, but in the books I read in school, the movies I see, the people I read about in newspapers. My day-to-day experiences reinforce all that I have learned—the language and behaviour I have been taught; the values I have been told are the most important; the attitudes of which I am or am not conscious. As a result, I begin to measure other cultures by the standards of my own without being aware that I am doing so.

It is this lack of awareness, this assumption of the norm ... that blocks my ability to understand and appreciate other values, other cultures, and to question my own. I see what is different, but I don't analyze the difference. And it isn't crucial that I do so because I do not have to adapt myself. My group has the power, and I don't have to attune myself to any other way of living unless I choose to. And choice versus necessity has a strong impact on what I see and learn.

My group, being dominant, has the power to define what is acceptable, what is most valuable about me and, in doing so, to define attitudes of which I am and am not conscious. If I cannot see myself, I cannot see others clearly; and if I cannot see others clearly, seeing myself becomes more and more difficult. The mask is never removed. In this way, the power of the majority group is maintained, as their values, behaviours, and attitudes become self-perpetuating.

USING A CULTURAL ANALYSIS FRAMEWORK

The best way to address the problems that individuals face in communities, families, schools, workplaces, etc., (and to unpack the current events discussed in this introduction) is to understand that the context for these problems or issues is culturally rooted. For this revised edition of *Seeing Ourselves*, following McDermott and Varenne (2006), we take what can be called a **cultural analysis perspective**. What such a perspective requires is simply that in our analysis of the world (and in our attempt to better understand ourselves and each other), we appreciate and respect the experiences of other people by understanding how they live, struggle, and exist in the world. A cultural analysis perspective means taking on a particular view and theory of culture that better enables us to see and understand the complex ways in which individuals lead their lives (McDermott and Varenne 2006).

Cultural analysis means asking complicated questions about our world and our interactions within it. For example, a cultural analysis pays attention to not only which students might do well in school and which may fail, but also addresses the ways in which institutions are designed, setting some students up for failure more than others. Rather than focusing solely on how individuals are expected to conduct themselves in different groups, cultural analysis unpacks the ways that people are constantly creating categories in which people are placed based on their behaviour.

For example, in exploring issues of aboriginality, race, ethnicity, immigration, citizenship, religion, sexuality, multiculturalism, and so on, a cultural analysis would question not just what Native and settlers, Black and white, male and female, immigrant and "Canadian," Muslim and Christian individuals do, but also *when* the categories of Aboriginal, Black, white, male, female, immigrant, "Canadian," Muslim, and Christian are made significant, and *why*. Of course, each of these categories is involved and important; however, they do not hold meaning in and of themselves, but in relation to other categories and in relation to how they are engaged by others. Such "identity" categories are not static and unchanging, but carry different meanings in different contexts. A cultural analysis forces us to expose these shifting meanings. Ultimately, a cultural analysis does not get bogged down with providing solutions to what we imagine are problems, but tackles the conditions that have defined problems in particular ways.

When done effectively, a cultural analysis creates more questions than answers. It is also a challenging approach because when we engage in cultural analysis, we do so as part of the culture we are studying. Thus, any cultural understanding must appreciate the ways in which culture is dynamic, shifting, and constantly interacting with other forces in society (including ourselves). Analyzing culture and asking questions allows us to expose many of the cultural practices, beliefs, and norms that we come to take for granted, but which nonetheless influence each of our daily lives. Even the process of writing this fourth edition of *Seeing Ourselves* is indicative of our interrelationship and interconnection with the culture we are in and the events that comprise it. The examples on which I draw are all influenced by a range of events occurring in different communities and social situations.

Because we are part of the culture we are exploring, investigating culture also requires that we be "reflexive." As McDermott and Varenne (2006) put it, "We have no choice but to study that which we also make. There is no privileged position from which to escape culture." Of course, some might respond to a cultural analysis approach by saying that there are a variety of different ways to analyze one's world, so why a focus on culture? Certainly, this is true. As McDermott and Varenne further explain, psychologists explore the actions "involving individual persons making up their minds," and social analysis seeks to "account for the influence of one person (or group) on others" (10). What sets cultural analysis apart, however, is that it focuses not just on individuals and their interactions but also "on the collective constructions all actors must deal with" (10).

TELLING STORIES

The storytelling approach that forms the basis of this book is, I believe, a strong and effective—though often provocative—method of learning about and discussing difficult issues. Stories or narratives, especially those from cross-cultural settings, allow us to engage in a process of critical reflection in which we question our ideas, prejudices, assumptions, actions, and privileges. We also remember the emotional significance of our own experiences and come to recognize the effect these may have had on those who we consider to be different. In this process of personal reflection and storytelling, it is hoped that individuals will come to evaluate explicitly the significance of the social, political, and cultural structures, events, and contexts that shape their ideologies, attitudes, values, and behaviours, and how these in turn operate to inform their beliefs and their construction of people they consider to be different from themselves (James 2001, 410; see also Scering 1997).

Working on this book with Leanne Taylor, who helped me as a research assistant, allowed me to engage in dialogue in a way that further enabled me to tell my stories. Telling stories enabled us to think through them in more detail and thus more effectively capture the ideas we wanted to communicate, ultimately allowing us to go into areas that we might not have thought of going. And, as Leanne would say, "we don't tell stories to ourselves;" stories require a listener and someone with whom to engage in dialogue and the telling of the story. So the idea of this book is, in part, to tell the stories of individuals who are generous enough to share them to those who are interested enough to listen (through reading). We hope that the examples that are used, and the experiences that are communicated, relate people's personal experiences and interests. As a reader, you become a listener to our stories and can talk back to these stories; because this book is ultimately a discussion, "we" is used throughout to refer to the author and readers. By writing this book, I am inviting others to hear these stories so that they too can critically reflect and gain further insights into the complexities of culture, race, and ethnicity.

Martha Nussbaum explains that the importance of storytelling lies in its ability to force us "to see and to respond to many things that may be difficult to confront [but] they make this process palatable by giving us pleasure in the very act of confrontation" (as cited in Preskill and Jacobvitz 2001, 4). Therefore, the act of telling stories and relaying personal narratives pushes individuals to face their flaws and errors as human beings, as well as shed light on the ways in which institutions and systems often mis-educate and diminish people. Errande (2000) also points out that "all narratives, whether oral or written, personal or collective, official or subaltern, are 'narratives of identity'... [and] are representations of reality in which narrators also communicate how they see themselves and wish others to see them" (16). In discussing autobiographical narratives, Conway (1999) writes:

> The satisfaction comes from being allowed inside the experience of another person who really lived and who tells about the experiences which did in fact occur. In this way ... the reader is able to try on the experience of another, just as one would try a dress or a suit of clothes, to see what the image in the mirror then looks like. We like to try on new identities because we crave the confirmation of like experience or the enlargement of transformation which can come from viewing a similar experience from a different perspective. (6)

Enabling individuals, and students in particular, to use their voices, whether through verbal and written comments, essays, group presentations and discussions, or publications such as this, helps to enable them and validate their knowledge and lived experiences as they attempt to address their needs, interests, and aspirations. Furthermore, built on subjective experience, stories are a useful "route to understanding our lives and the lives of others" and can help to legitimate the knowledge that arises from our respective social positions (Bell, Morrow, and Tastsoglou 1999, 23). Through conversations, individuals can obtain deeper insight into the issues with which they struggle as well as the emotions that contribute to the complexity of one's experience. We will begin by exploring culture and cultural identity and then hear individual stories, which will help us understand the complexity of identity and the issues surrounding race, ethnicity, and culture in our own national identity.

NOTES

1. Recall that in November 2008, the Liberal, NDP, and Bloc Québecois parties agreed to a coalition to challenge Prime Minister Stephen Harper's Conservative leadership. Governor General Michaëlle Jean's decision to prorogue Parliament sparked criticism from many Canadians on both sides of the debate. They expressed concern that an "immigrant" like Jean—who, as governor general, has the authority to dissolve Parliament and appoint a new government from elected members—was able to make decisions about the fate of Canada.

2. For a discussion of Ukrainian Canadians' appeal for their place in multicultural Canada, see Julia Lalande's article, "The roots of multiculturalism—Ukrainian-Canadian involvement in the multiculturalism discussion of the 1960s as an example of the position of the 'Third Force.'" *Canadian Ethnic Studies*, XXXVIII, No. 1, 2006, 47–64.

3. There is some debate in North American English as to whether white and black should be treated as proper nouns or adjectives, as in Whites, Blacks, White person, Black person.

While current language conventions would call for the use of the lower case—whites, blacks—when simply describing appearance, or consistent capitalization (White, Black), I would argue that individuals of African heritage are part of a cultural group, and should be treated as any other ethnic, religious, or national group; therefore, in this text "Black" is capitalized to designate a cultural group. As Cheryl Harris (1993) puts forth by using the term "Black" throughout her *Harvard Law Review* article, "Whiteness as Property," and following the reasons articulated by professor Kimberle Crenshaw, "Blacks, like Asians, Latinos, and other 'minorities,' constitute a specific cultural group and, as such, require denotation as a proper noun" (1710).

4. All of these detainees have now been released.

5. In January 2007, Arar settled a lawsuit with the Canadian government, which provided him with a formal apology and $10.5 million in compensation. The American government, however, still refuses to remove Arar from their no-fly and border-watch lists (Freeze, *Globe and Mail*, October 20, 2007, A1).

6. While Omar Khadr is now an adult—having been held in prison for over six years— many argue that since he was exposed to al Qaeda and Islamist extremism at such a young age, his actions in 2003 should be considered those of a child soldier and he should be treated as a victim of indoctrination. At the time of publication, Omar Khadr is awaiting trial at a military commission in the United States on terrorism charges. No firm date or location for the trial had been established.

7. Ahmed Said Khadr was shot and killed by Pakistani troops near the Afghan border in 2003.

8. Six of the accused were granted bail and charges were stayed for three of the five youths charged (*Toronto Star*, April 6, 2008a, A9). One of the accused was tried and convicted of belonging to a terror cell in 2008; he was sentenced in September 2009 to fourteen years in prison. Nine of the suspects are scheduled to go on trial in 2010.

9. Kenney noted that asylum claims have increased to almost 70 percent in the past two years, and that Canada's acceptance rate stood at approximately 40 percent—twice the rate of other developed countries (Armstrong and Ibbitson 2009).

10. In 1998 and 1999, two unmarked boats were found off the Canadian coast without any passengers, presumably, as Cooper writes, because "the migrants had already arrived ashore (93).

CONCEPTUALIZING CULTURE

If birds were suddenly endowed with scientific curiosity they might examine many things, but the sky itself would be overlooked as a suitable subject; if fish were to become curious about the world, it would never occur to them to begin by investigating water. For birds and fish would take the sky and water for granted, unaware of their profound influence because they comprise the medium for every act. Human beings in a similar way occupy a symbolic universe governed by codes that are unconsciously acquired and automatically employed. So much so that they rarely notice the ways people conduct their affairs in other cultures. (Barnlund 1988, 14)

According to Barnlund, "cultural myopia" (as described above) is a common characteristic of the members of every society. As such, employing a cultural analysis means recognizing that each of us, in different ways, has mannerisms, beliefs, values, and activities that are important to us— even when it may not seem like we are aware of it. As McDermott and Varenne put it, "people in culture can be made systematically inarticulate about the fundamentals of this culture" (2006, 26). Thus, taking a cultural perspective means understanding that while people may indicate in their actions the things that matter to them and the things in which they are most invested, the ways in which they do so may differ and may not be easily recognizable or as articulate as we might expect. Many experiences and understandings of life are not always easily spoken, but are often taken for granted and "understood" as part of people's lives and routines. As such, "learning from human beings is akin to reading an alien language: one must assume that what may sound like gibberish is in fact a language, and a translatable one at that. The task of translation, we all know, is not easy, not by any means, precisely because what is most worth translating cannot fit into any of the words (categories, etc.) that initially appeared available" (McDermott and Varenne 2006, 26). What is even more crucial to understand is that culture is not something that we can easily translate. It is considerably complex, and as Kallen asserts, "the most important part of culture is that it is a learned phenomenon; it is acquired, for the most part, through the ordinary processes of growing up and participating in the daily life of a particular [among others] ethnic collective" (1995, 20).

Jackson and Meadows point out that "for most people the term [culture] is vague because individuals live the culture and seldom explain it or consciously think about or evaluate it" (1991, 72). No society is without culture—a core set of values and expectations that exert tremendous influence on our lives, structure our world view, shape our behaviour, and pattern our responses. Adler asserts that "all human beings share a similar biology, universally limited by the rhythms of life" (1977, 27). We all move through a similar sequence of phases in life: from birth, to infancy, childhood, adolescence, adulthood, middle age, old age, and death. Adler continues:

> The ultimate interpretation of human biology is a cultural phenomenon; that is, the meaning of human biological patterns are culturally derived. Though all human beings are born, reproduce, and die, it is culture which dictates the meaning of sexuality, the ceremonials of birth, the transitions of life, and the rituals of death. (Adler 1977, 27)

All things considered, culture is a set of collective practices, experiences, values, and so on that cannot always be expressed in discursive form.

In this chapter, we explore culture as a *structure* that frames the life experiences and responses of individuals to social and environmental factors, and which *individuals* help to construct. The objective is to arrive at an understanding of culture—the core set of norms, values, and expectations to which Canadian residents adhere—and to explore how people living in Canada, and in particular communities within Canada, are expected to integrate into a set of cultural values and aspirations.

FIGURE 2.1 – CULTURE AND ITS INTERRELATIONSHIPS

One way of conceptualizing culture is to think of a woven tapestry, such as the one pictured above, that stretches out in all directions. The different patterns, shades, and strands can be thought of as the various elements of culture such as religion, arts, economics, sports, faith communities, education, geography, technology, media politics, resources, and industry. The elements both rely on and play off each other and make up culture (the tapestry) as a whole.

CONCEPTUALIZING CULTURE

In his exploration of the roots, meanings, and uses of the word culture, Raymond Williams (1983) writes:

> Culture is one of the two or three most complicated words in the English language. This is partly because of its intricate historical development, in several European languages, but mainly because it has now come to be used for important concepts in several distinct intellectual disciplines and in several distinct and incompatible systems of thought. (87)

In terms of its social and anthropological reference to material production, the term *culture*, as Williams emphasizes, captures the complexity of the senses and argument "about the relations between general human development and particular way of life" (1983, 91). Taking this complexity into consideration, and with reference to J. G. Heder's eighteenth-century text, *Ideas on the Philosophy of the History of Mankind*, Williams also makes the point that it is necessary "to speak of 'cultures' in the plural: The specific and variable cultures of different nations and periods, but also the specific and variable cultures of social and economic groups within a nation" (89). In this regard, then, our reference here to culture(s) is not to detract from its complexity and variations in terms of the activities, relationships, and processes that the word symbolizes, but to explore its subjective and historical dimension in the ways individuals have come to make sense of culture in their own lives and the lives of others in Canada.

In his discussion of culture, Renato Rosaldo (1993), in *Culture and Truth,* writes:

> Culture lends significance to human experience by selecting from and organizing it. It refers broadly to the forms through which people make sense of their lives, rather than more narrowly to the opera or art museums. It does not inhabit a set-aside domain, as does, for example, that of politics or economics. From the pirouettes of classical ballet to the most brute of brute facts, all human conduct is culturally mediated. Culture encompasses the everyday and the esoteric, the mundane and the elevated, the ridiculous and the sublime. Neither high nor low, culture is all-pervasive. (26)

It is this idea of the "all-pervasiveness" of culture that we wish to emphasize. Culture is not only embedded in everything that we do, it is, as Kagawa-Singer and Chung (1994) assert, "a tool that defines our reality, worldview and purpose in life" (198). Moreover, the familial and social groups to which we belong or with which we identify, and the society in which they live (or once lived) not only provide the reference for proper or acceptable behaviours, they also sanction that behaviour: "These beliefs, values, and behaviors of culture provide its members with some degree of personal and social meaning for human existence, learned through tradition and transmitted from generation to generation" (Kagawa-Singer and Chung 1994, 198). In discussing the importance of paying attention to the culture or cultural backgrounds of service recipients in a therapy situation, Kagawa-Singer and Chung go on to suggest that human beings have three basic needs for psychological well-being: "1) a sense of safety, 2) sense of self-worth, and 3) sense of belonging," and these are satisfied through the culture of the group with which individuals identify (199).

Simply put, **culture** is a concept that refers to the way in which a given society, community, or group organizes and conducts itself as distinguished from that of other societies, communities, or groups. Culture consists of a dynamic and complex set of values, beliefs, norms, patterns of thinking, styles of communication, linguistic expressions, and ways of interpreting and interacting with the world that help people understand and thus survive their varied circumstances. Therefore, members of any given society, community, or group will not only be influenced or shaped by the culture of their group, community, and that society, but will also shape it.

A culture is not merely the sum of its parts—a collection of individuals—but is created through the interactions and relationships between people. A focus on culture allows us to explore where we have been, where we are now, and where we might be heading in the future. Culture operates as the "glue" for society. It is not merely an individually constructed way of acting or thinking, nor is it strictly a collection of personal values. According to Thiederman (1992):

> Culture is informed by the existing laws; regulations of society; and world economic, social, and political structures (e.g., capitalism) and events. Without culture, society would be in disarray. Have you ever wondered, for example, who decided that it is "polite" to say "thank you" after an exchange? Some cultures consider it rude to say "thank you" because it ends what ought to be an infinite flow of give and take. Why do we think it intrusive when a stranger sits next to us in an empty subway car? In many other countries, it would be regarded as an insult if the person sat elsewhere. (3)

Culture is not defined strictly by artifacts, clothing, or food, but by how group members use, interpret, and perceive those artifacts; neither is it a fixed set of customs, languages, or rituals. These are the symbols of a culture, and they too change. Observable aspects of culture are merely surface and, in some ways, tangible reflections of a complex, interconnected set of elements that fulfill specific functions in the lives of the members of that society. Culture is what organizes our everyday lives. It gives us cues as to how we should act in given situations, it provides markers for our values, it helps organize our individual lives, as well as our families and communities. It also guides the structure of society and its institutions (government, schools, and so on). In fact, we adhere to particular ways of doing things or the rules of society or group because we place a value on them. We respond to behaviour with disgust, horror, pleasure, or disdain, not only because we consider some rules useful, but because we judge them as right or wrong. And while we continually evaluate and re-invent rules, members of society are still sanctioned, punished, or rewarded on the basis of their loyalty to the rules. The result is that people are powerfully motivated to abide by society's rules and to attempt to force others to do so.

While cultural rules are decided on informally, they carry immense value and influence our behaviour and ideas. For example, our automatic tendencies to hold the door open for someone or to say "good morning" are actions that are culturally influenced. And many of these practices, ideas, and assumptions are not even part of our conscious reality. They are often invisible and taken for granted. Schwalbe (2005) explains one way in which culture can be created:

> Someone finds a solution to a problem, other people see that it works and adopt it, and eventually the solution becomes "what everyone does." For a time people remember the idea behind the practice, but then, after a while, they forget. "This is just how we do things," they begin to say. When children come along they are taught the practice as a matter of course, perhaps with little explanation of the ideas on which it was originally based. It is as if the practice—the behavior that solves the problem—becomes part of a sediment that constitutes culture. (19)

One example of this practice is the routine of teeth-brushing. As Schwalbe puts it: "Before you were born, someone devised teeth-brushing as a way to avoid tooth decay. This was a solution (or a partial one) to a problem that existed before you did. Today almost all children are taught to brush their teeth. This is the sense in which teeth-brushing has become part of the culture. People now do it routinely" (2005, 19).

Simple actions such as boarding a bus, making a dental appointment, dropping by to see a friend, and attending classes are aspects of culture. These behaviours are governed by the shared assumptions and rules of the culture. The commonality of these values makes it possible to predict and control behaviour. For example, teachers and students with similar social histories or from the same community are likely to know what to expect from each other on the basis of commonly understood rules about schooling. Younger students know that they must raise their hand in class if they wish to speak. However, older students (e.g., those in university) understand that while raising one's hand is not always required, there are still understood assumptions about when it is appropriate to interrupt a discussion and when one should wait. We routinely operate on the assumption that all of us know the rules and will conduct ourselves accordingly. This enables us to depend on each other to behave in predictable ways.

People arriving into a new society will immediately identify the cultural ideas, values, customs, traditions, and practices in which people function and operate. These are often more clear to someone from the outside, because when culture is constantly around us, we don't even recognize its presence. We take culture for granted, even as it so greatly informs our routine activities or everyday practices. For example, it is understood what is expected of us when we walk onto a bus or hail a taxi. It doesn't seem strange to us to walk down the street and see people walking around with their hands to their ears talking into a small metal object. Nor is it strange to us to see someone sitting on a bus speaking aloud while a blue light glows in their ear. Because we understand that these individuals are speaking on mobile phones, we wouldn't consider telling the driver that there is a strange or mentally ill person on the bus, nor will we change our seats out of concern. Imagine someone coming from elsewhere who has not had experience with such devices. This is an example of how much our practices and behaviours are part of our everyday existence. This is in part because we never stop to think of them as unusual, weird, or strange—in reality these are unarticulated things that we accept.

This tendency for individuals to not see the elements or "strangeness" in our own culture(s) and all its taken-for-granted rituals, practices, assumptions, and behaviours was captured in the classic text *Body Ritual Among the Nacirema*, by Horace Miner (1956). Miner wrote a satirical work outlining the cultural practices of a group he describes as "a North American group living in the territory between the Canadian Cree, the Yaqui and Tarahumare of Mexico, and the Carib and Arawak of the Antilles" (503). Of course, "Nacirema" is "American," spelled backwards. So in presenting the Nacirema as a "foreign" culture or group, even when he is speaking of one that is immensely familiar, Miner gives readers a glimpse into the kinds of practices in which we engage, understand, and take for granted as the norm. Of interest to our discussion here is how Miner presents some of the main elements of Nacirema culture as including various rituals and rites. For example, the "private mouth rite" (teeth-brushing) and a wall shrine (medicine chest) that houses "many charms and magical potions without which no native believes he could live;" the most powerful of these items are prepared and provided by "medicine men, whose assistance must be rewarded with substantial gifts" (1956, 504).

Similarly, our taken-for-granted practices—in other words, our cultural oddities, differences, and problems—are captured in many film and television comedies, like the *Beverly Hillbillies* in the 1960s, which portrayed poor country people striking it rich and moving to Beverly Hills and, more recently, *Third Rock from the Sun* in the 1990s, about alien researchers trying to fit in as a family in an Ohio college town. One of the most famous popular culture exposés of our taken-for-granted practices is the 1980 film, *The Gods Must Be Crazy*. In the film, a glass Coca-Cola bottle thrown from a small plane flying over the Kalahari Desert is discovered by a tribe of Bushmen. The bottle, which is unlike anything the tribe has seen before, quickly leads tribe members to engage in unknown behaviours, such as violence, envy, anger, and hatred. One tribe member, Xi, sets out to throw the bottle off the "edge of the earth." On his journey, Xi meets Westerners for the first time, and the audience sees them through Xi's eyes and perceptions.[1]

The examples I have discussed thus far are certainly not unique to North Americans. Similar practices and ideas exist among people in almost every part of the world. This speaks to the universality of many cultural forms, practices, and ideas. Spirituality, as another example, takes on different forms or is expressed differently in particular societies, but in much the same way, it serves the interests and desires of people. Music, such as reggae and jazz, is yet another work of art that is shared in many societies and community. Essentially, as individuals, we each have habits, routines, and ways of doing things that might seem unique to us, but these are derived from and informed by various historical and contemporary structures and measures, as much as by characteristics such as ethnicity, social class, dis/ability, language, race, ethnicity, age, occupation, sex, organization, etc.

STRATIFICATION, CULTURAL HEGEMONY, AND ETHNO-RACIAL DIVERSITY

The structure and expressions of culture are related to power relations among groups in society (based on characteristics such as social class, ethnicity, race, language, colour, dis/ability, sexuality, religion, and gender). The term **social stratification** applies here. This term refers to the hierarchical system in which segments of the population are ranked on the basis of their power and access to wealth and prestige. This ranking or hierarchical structure is determined by a complex interplay of wealth as related to property ownership, income, education, and occupation—in other words social class, as well as factors such as gender, ethnicity, race, length of residency, and citizenship status. Given this stratification and the resultant hierarchical or social positioning of the various groups in society, the "main" culture that emerges in any given society will largely mirror that of the group with the most economic and political power. From this perspective, cultural elements (i.e., the norms, values, traditions, and expectations) of the ethnic group with the most power will be dominant, thereby informing what is considered to be the "norm" in society. Furthermore, these norms, values, traditions, mores, and practices of the dominant group are considered "invisible," hence the notion that such people are "without culture"—in terms of everyday discourse, they are the "we." The cultural elements that are "visible" are perceived to be possessed by those "with culture"—the marginalized or ethno-racial minority members of society (Rosaldo 1993, 199). Such discourse is representative of cultural hegemony, in which the dominant culture—or the taken-for-granted "white culture"—remains the definition of what it means to be "Canadian."

Often used in reference to nation-states today, *hegemony* is the dominance of one group over all others. **Cultural hegemony** ensures that certain power relations are embedded into the social order and seem so normal and part of our everyday lives that we do not question their existence or operation. And as Michael Apple explains, "hegemony is a process, not a thing. Furthermore, it is not monolithic. It does not constitute a seamless web, nor does it refer to a process whereby dominant groups exercise top-down and near-total control over meanings" (2003, 6). As a process, hegemonic power is constantly being built and rebuilt as it is contested, negotiated, and renegotiated. Moreover, according to Jones,

> "Dominant" groups within democratic societies generally govern with a good degree of consent from the people they rule, and the maintenance of the consent is dependent upon incessant repositioning of the relationship between the rulers and the ruled. In order to maintain its authority, a ruling power must be sufficiently flexible to respond to new circumstances and to the changing wishes of those it rules. (2006, 3)

The power and dominance that one group is able to exert over others is maintained through political and economic means; however, people do not willingly subscribe to overtly oppressive conditions. For hegemony to work within democracies, dominant ideologies, values, and norms must be seen as reasonable and fair, and must seem to be granting a level of freedom and rights. In other words, they must be perceived as "common-sense" (Hall 2003, 90), thereby enabling people to consent or adhere to a certain level of control because of the legal and political significance, and the economic, social, and material benefits. To quote Jones (2006):

> A ruling power that ensures that its subordinates have enough to eat, are in paid employment and have adequate access to health care, childcare and holidays has gone a long way towards winning their hearts and minds. Equally, parliamentary democracies appear to grant subordinate people a good degree of legal-political autonomy through

> granting them various rights and through allowing them
> to vote, to regularly change their government and to stand
> for election themselves. (48)

As mentioned above, social class—an arbitrary construct that signifies individual or group positions in the stratification system—is for sociologists an important means of explaining and predicting individual or group values and behaviours. It is believed that individuals' lifestyles, values, experiences, and behaviours are intricately linked to their status—upper, middle, and lower—as measured by education, occupation, and income (or property ownership). But social class culture is also mediated by determinants of race, ethnicity, gender, dis/ability, sexuality, etc. Of particular concern to us in this text is the role and consequence of race and ethnicity in defining and understanding culture and, ultimately, in the lives of individuals.

Race and ethnicity are social constructs whose meanings are derived from the historical, social, and political contexts in which individuals live and interact. Chapter 3 has a more complete discussion of the uses and meanings of these terms, however, suffice it to say here that **ethnicity** or **ethnic group** refers to a group of people who identify themselves as, or are identified by others as, sharing a common historical and ancestral origin. In Canada, one of the ways in which ethnicity is constructed is by ancestry or by national or regional origin. This understanding of ethnicity or ethnic group identity is informed by the multiculturalism discourse (see Chapter 5). **Race** or racial group refers to individuals who are identified by particular physical characteristics—for example, the colour of one's skin—which come to represent socially constructed meanings and expectations that correspond to their ascribed status within the social hierarchy. It is important to keep clear the difference between race, ethnicity, and culture. It is common to hear culture used in place of ethnicity or race—for example, "cultural group"—which is to imply that the culture of a group or individual is largely or singly a product of their race or ethnicity. This is certainly not the case.

It is true, however, that members of a particular ethnic or racial group are likely to share certain patterns of living with other members who identify themselves, or might be identified, with the group. As Smolicz (1981, 18) writes, "the actions and attitudes of individual members are therefore likely to bear a 'family' resemblance to one another." Smolicz goes on to say that

> in many ethnically plural societies, a further distinction
> needs to be made between the ethnic group that holds the
> dominant position through its numbers, early settlement or

impact upon the main political and economic institutions, and minority or subordinate groups that have much less influence on policy-making, and limited access to resources ... It must be recognized, however, that ethnic minority cultures have their own independent historical continuity, and although they may interact with other cultures in a plural society, this does not make them a mere facet of the dominant group's tradition. (1981, 17–18)

It is the case, therefore, that the culture of minority groups cannot be considered, in a reductionist way, to be a subset of the dominant culture (see Chapter 7 for further discussion). And even though they are members of particular ethnic and racial groups, individuals will not share in all of the beliefs and practices attributed to the group. They should not be expected to think and act in similar ways, for social class, family composition, citizenship status, years of residency in a country, and other factors all contribute to differences among group members.

Critical theorists remind us that culture cannot be conceptualized in terms of unified systems of meanings, but rather as conflicting, contradictory, ambiguous, dynamic, and full of contending discourses, all of which are mediated by power. Paying attention to power relations, therefore, is critical to our understanding of culture. Power relations also inform individuals' struggle over meanings and the ways in which they conceive of being in the world (Spivey 1998). And as Kondo argues, some "in the world were and are more legitimate, more rewarded, more recognized than others—as anyone in a marginal or minority position will attest" (1990, 301). Therefore, how groups and individuals construct culture will be fragmented, highly problematic, and puzzling because they do so based on "contending personalities" (Spivey 1998, 48).

DEAN: "I WAS A BIT OF A NOVELTY ..."

I was born and partially raised in Manila, the Philippines, where pretty much everyone was Catholic, everyone spoke English and Filipino, and everyone was middle class, at least those in my immediate vicinity. I had never been conscious of race because everyone around me looked the same, and any differences between the other children in Manila were relatively insignificant. Everyone was Filipino and that's all that mattered, except there was something about my physical appearance that did distinguish me from the rest of my peers at an early age—my skin complexion.

Filipinos are supposed to be dark tan in terms of their complexion, closely following that of their Malay ancestors. My father is that way, but my mother is not. Because of my mother's fair skin most people thought we were *mestizos*, the term used in those parts for those of mixed ancestry, but specifically denoting those Filipinos with Spanish ancestry somewhere in their family tree. Ironically, it was my father's lineage that included an interracial marriage back in colonial times. But regardless of where it came from, this fair skin was passed on to my sister and me.

Although I was not conscious of the sociological underpinnings of my skin complexion at an early age, it dawned on me as a young person growing up in a homogenous Philippine society that my skin complexion was an advantage. Most people with such a complexion are considered to be attractive just because they are mistaken for *mestizos*. When I moved with my family to Canada as a fourteen-year-old, I became more conscious of my skin complexion, perhaps because it was now a disadvantage.

In 1989, Markham, Ontario, was a booming suburb north of Toronto with a population of 135,000 mostly white, Anglo-Saxon Canadians. My family and I found ourselves among the first families of Asian descent to settle in this suburb. I became more conscious of my "immigrant" status mostly because of my complexion. I thought of myself as having had all the advantages over my white peers—I had more academic knowledge than they did, I spoke English quite well (something that initially astounded them, especially if they had internalized the fact that I was an immigrant), and I was culturally astute as to what was "Canadian" and not "American."

…It was not until the turn of the next decade that the influx of Chinese immigrants from Hong Kong became significant enough in Toronto for the whites to notice … I became wary of being mistaken for Chinese because being Chinese was a disadvantage in white Markham. A lot of the whites, many of them of Irish or European ancestry, were second- or third-generation immigrants themselves and had come to Canada with absolutely nothing. The Chinese on the other hand, at least the ones who had recently settled in Canada [from Hong Kong] came to this country with their money and their BMWs. It was not exactly the group of people that you wanted others to think you were a part of, at least in the mind of a fourteen-year-old. I consciously made an effort to emphasize my "non-Chineseness" and to reiterate that I am Filipino. I was still an immigrant, but at least I wasn't Chinese.

As a teacher, my initial teaching experiences were in Markham, where very little has changed in terms of demographics in the seven or so years since I graduated. There was the same percentage of Asians in the classes, but now I was in front of the class as opposed to being part of that percentage. By this time, I was "normal" to them. These students were practically infants when I came to this country, and they were accustomed to seeing and interacting with Asians, perhaps as neighbours, more likely as classmates. No one wondered why I spoke English so well, or why I knew so much, or why I was teaching history as opposed to science or math. I was just the teacher. I was a bit of a novelty to them, not because of my race per se, but because few people of my ethnic background have gone into this line of work. This was not new to me, as I got the same kind of reaction when I pursued journalism and worked in various white male-dominated television newsrooms.

When I spent a year teaching in an ethnically diverse part of metropolitan Toronto, my race and ethnicity came into play even more than I expected. I walked into a Grade 10 class expecting to teach as usual (after all, I never worried about them not having seen someone like me before, because they do all the time), and I found that my ethnicity puzzled them. "You look Asian, but I don't know if you're Vietnamese or Chinese or what exactly," queried one student. It came to the point that their constant prying into my life made me tell them that my ethnicity was a personal question and that they shouldn't be asking me about it … A few of the bright ones figured out my ethnicity when I told them about how my grand-uncle was tortured by the Japanese after the Bataan Death March and the subsequent Japanese occupation of most of Asia during World War II … The Filipinos in my own class were quite surprised to learn that I am Filipino—the chorus was utterly similar—"You don't look Filipino, sir."

I came into teaching as unconscious of race as I possibly could be. I was conscious of the race of the students I taught, but I was hoping that they would not become conscious of mine. It was a non-issue for me. I was their history and math teacher, not their Filipino history or math teacher … This process of renegotiating the "self," i.e., one's identity as the teacher in the classroom, apart from being a process in constant flux, extends far beyond race. I found that as much as I imposed a particular distance on a particular aspect of my identity that I allowed my students to be aware of, there were aspects of that same identity that were imposed upon me. I came to realize through my teaching experiences that as I was renegotiating where I "fit" within my student's lives, they were likewise renegotiating where they "fit" in mine.

CULTURAL DIVERSITY: DIFFERENCES AND VARIATIONS AMONG ETHNO-RACIAL GROUPS

All societies are culturally diverse insofar as differences based on language, ethnicity, religion, race, region, etc., exist among its population of people. And since individuals are members of a number of different cultural groups (in terms of class, gender, ethnicity, language, etc.), they possess a combination of values, customs, and patterns of thinking derived from the culture of the society in which they live, as well as from the many groups to which they belong. Also, the geography of a country—from physical region to neighbourhood, as well as rural versus urban versus suburban setting—plays a significant role in the cultures that exist in its societies. These geographic areas, with their particular resources, structure the cultures that develop among residents. For instance, the ocean surrounding Newfoundland, the oil sands and range land of Alberta, and the forests and mountains of British Columbia all contribute to the economic, social, educational, and recreational activities of residents.

In the context of Canadian society, the official policy of multiculturalism (which we discuss in more detail in Chapter 5) structures a discourse of the nation as "multicultural," promoting the idea that cultural freedom and equality of opportunity exist for everyone and people are permitted to maintain their ethnic cultural particularities. Furthermore, culture is used as the basis for defining diversity and difference, specifically with regard to the racial, ethnic, immigrant, language, and religious backgrounds of Canadians. As such, there is a reliance on the observable and ascribed characteristics of culture, particularly of minority Canadians, in terms of constructing, understanding, and naming their differences. And while race or skin colour, specifically being non-white, is employed in the identification of individuals as different (as with the term "visible minority"), the multicultural discourse conveys the notion that it is not race per se—that is, the physical characteristics of the body—that is used as identification, but the culture of the individuals or group members. Framing culture in terms of difference (and diversity in terms of culture), has the effect of rendering invisible or immaterial the ways in which race (and discrimination) operate to inform the cultural values, attitudes, and expressions of racialized Canadians and Canadians in general. To say that someone has culture because she or he is "culturally" different tends to be done on the basis of race, colour, ethnicity, or a person's name. The use of the word "different" implies a norm that begs the question, different from what?

Clifford Jansen (2005) identifies the problem of using culture as a moniker for difference by posing the following questions:

> What exactly constitutes a cultural group? What are the boundaries that separate one culture from another? To what extent are cultures the "creation" of persons or groups from outside of the so-called culture? For instance, most of the Aboriginal groups of North America are considered by outsiders to belong to one culture referred to as "Indian." Yet, within this group, there are a huge variety of specific cultures with different languages, customs and beliefs, so that probably the greatest thing they have in common is that they are considered by outsiders to belong to one group. (21)

A **subculture**, or what I shall refer to as **group culture,** is "a group of people within a larger socio-political structure who share cultural (and often linguistic or dialectical) characteristics which are distinctive enough to distinguish it from others within the same culture" (Hoopes and Pusch 1981, 3). The elements of group cultures that find expression in the society sometimes conflict with the "culture of the society" as a whole. However, as we discussed earlier in this chapter, no culture is static. Variations in cultural expressions within a society exist as a result of social and historic factors that preserve and generate differences. The region, gender, class, race, ethnicity, religion, and sexual orientation with which people identify are factors that contribute to the variances. These social characteristics help to determine the variation in-group cultures. For instance, although individuals may share the belief that formal education is related to future career success, their understandings of career success may differ depending on the norms, values, and expectations of their cultural groups. This would then determine the kind and quantity of education that they pursue or the activities in which they engage.

It is the case, then, that the cultures of minority groups cannot be considered in a reductionist way or as a subset of what can be considered the dominant culture. Even though individuals may be members of particular ethnic and racial groups, individuals will not share in all of the beliefs and practices of the group. While we are often presented with the image of subcultures or group cultures as unified wholes, the individuals identified as part of such "groups" should not be expected to think and act in similar ways, because social class, family composition, citizenship status, years of residency in a country, and a host of other factors all contribute to the differences among group members. In this sense, it is important to understand that culture cannot be conceptualized in terms of unified systems of meanings, but rather as dynamic, ambiguous, contradictory, conflicting, and full of contending discourses, all of which are mediated, in part, by power. Paying attention to power relations, therefore, is critical to our understanding of culture. Power relations also inform individuals' struggles over meanings and the ways they understand who and what they are in the world.

Accordingly, contrary to the multiculturalism discourse of Canada, cultural differences among immigrants and minority group Canadians are not merely a product of their desire to "maintain" their cultures. In this regard, the claim—often proudly articulated by politicians (for example, in Toronto's bid for the 2008 Olympics)[2]—that ethnic minority group cultures are similar to those of their ancestral home nation is misguided. Such claims negate the fact that the culture of Portuguese ethnic group members, for instance, living in Canada or Toronto, would be different from those living in mainland Portugal or the Azores. A good test of this idea would be to ask a Portuguese person or any other immigrant or minority Canadian about his or her trip back "home." He or she would likely report that in addition to changes in language and accents, the place to which he or she has felt an affinity is different—it is no longer a place with which the Canadian can fully identify. And that is how it should be, given the changes to culture over time and generations. The notion of static and identifiable cultures that remain constant across geographical spaces contradicts the idea of such changes.

That the cultural practices, values, and customs of the Italian, African, Scottish, Portuguese, Chinese, or South Asian group members in Canada differ from those in the countries in which they comprise the dominant group also has to do with the fact that they are influenced by the *invisible* Canadian culture. Furthermore, agents of socialization, such as family, school, work, and peer groups function to ensure that individuals acquire what they need to function in the society with a minimum of disruption to the established social, cultural, economic, and political structures. So, while all immigrants and ethnic minority group members do conform to the prevailing norms, values, and expectations of the society, there are differences or variations based on their population size, history,[3] perceived role in the building of Canada, and level of commitment toward maintaining their ancestral culture. In cases where a group's cultural practices are not in conflict with the dominant cultural norms and values of the society, such cultural norms, values, and related practices may persist over time and, eventually, elements of them will become absorbed into mainstream Canadian culture. But where values and practices conflict with prevailing or mainstream cultural norms in the society, depending on the outcome of conformity pressures to change and "fit in," new cultural norms, values, and practices will emerge. For example, the practice of disciplining a child by hitting him or her is against the law in Canada, hence immigrant parents and the older generation of Canadian parents who might have been accustomed to such means of punishment have to refrain from doing so and use alternative measures. Another example is polygamous marriage, which has been against the law since 1892, so faith groups or cultures with traditions of polygamy are expected to practice monogamy.

Driedger (1989) suggests that those ethnic groups that are closer in appearance and cultural practices to the dominant Anglo-Saxon ethnic group will adjust much more readily to the Canadian cultural and social context. Specifically, Northern Europeans, Driedger argues, have considerable cultural affinity with the Anglo-Saxon culture and, being white, they are subjected to little racial prejudice and discrimination. They have some level of influence and control over their situation in the society. They voluntarily integrate into the culture of the society by adopting the language, as well as by conforming and accommodating themselves. Indeed, the settlement of Europeans, and Western Europeans in particular, in North America has been facilitated—historically and contemporarily—by centuries of shared history and religion. Nevertheless, for the most part, the cultural differences between these ethnic groups in Canada generally play out in the relatively superficial areas of cuisine, celebrations, and holidays, and Christian denominations.

While it is important to recognize the differences among ethno-racial groups, it is important to avoid the trap of essentializing group members on the basis of group membership. Indeed, as Benhabib argues in his book, *The Claims of Culture: Equity and Diversity in the Global Era,* cultures are not "unified, harmonious, seamless wholes that speak with one narrative voice" (2002, 102). Using ethno-cultural background to account for, or contextualize, the actions of individuals can have the effect of imprisoning individuals "in a cage of univocal cultural interpretations and psychological motivations," reducing their intentions to "cultural stereotypes" and their "moral agency to cultural puppetry" (89). And insofar as a uniform construction of minority groups and their cultures tends to be promoted and maintained by "community leaders," as well as outsiders such as politicians, policy-makers, educators, and community workers, it is partly because of their desire to "comprehend, search for the truth, and maintain social control" (103). As well, the practice of homogenizing ethno-racial minority groups and their cultures has the effect of silencing "dissenting opinions and contradictory perspective" and produces a "dominant master narrative of what the cultural tradition is, who is in, and who is out" (194).

In any society, the cultures of the different immigrant, ethnic, and racial groups—whether deliberately, through accommodation, or naturally through organic change—will inevitably fuse and merge at some point. Cultures cannot be totally distinct. The culture of African or Black people in Toronto cannot be distinctly different from that of European or white people, as there are places where the two merge and where we see evidence of similarities. All groups will need to find ways to negotiate and survive the economic and political contexts in which we all live. Black people will likely respond to economic, social, and environment crises in many of the same ways as white people. However, Black people will likely have to also deal with racism and discrimination, adding another layer to how they may respond. So while there are similarities and commonalities, there are also some key differences that must be taken into account. By understanding and paying attention to differences and how such differences contribute to the culture that emerges, we can understand cultural variations that exist in society.

CULTURE IS ALWAYS CHANGING

If we think back to the culture of 1998—before iPods, before smart phones, even before Google and the Web 2.0 revolution—it would not take much time to think of how much our culture has changed in such a short amount of time. Today, we are operating in a cultural context that is technologically and digitally mediated. BlackBerrys and iPods are the norm in many parts of the world. Many devices are now equipped with GPS (global positioning system) capabilities so that we can always know where we are; and virtually every place on Earth can be found on Google Maps or MapQuest. But a decade or so ago, imagine how we all found our way without such aids. Recently, while travelling outside of Toronto's city limits, I found myself having to ask for directions. While I had the address and believed I knew where I was going, when I arrived at the building, I realized it wasn't the correct location. When I stopped to ask for directions (something that was once commonplace), the store cashier looked at me strangely and seemed surprised that I would even ask for directions. Where we once gave explicit instructions for how to reach a place, we now give complete addresses for use in online map programs. This is a perfect example of a cultural shift.

As culture evolves, we grow accustomed to changes (as with the technological changes discussed above), so much so that we never realize or take note of these changes—we are caught up in them, and they become "normal" to us. They are changes in which we engage and to which we contribute—such as civil rights, the women's movement, and advances in art, music, design, and architecture. Consider the changes in our culture around environmental issues; not so long ago, people who recycled, composted, and refused plastic bags were considered to be unusual; now in major cities across Canada, such practices are expected, if not required. The place of smoking in our culture is another example of how culture and cultural habits have changed. Since its height of popularity in the 1950s, smoking cigarettes has progressed from a "must-do" to a virtual taboo in our culture, and we largely agree with the idea that smoking is bad for our health and environment. This is not the case everywhere; smoking is still commonplace in many parts of the world, while in Canada it is becoming increasingly difficult to find a place to smoke legally.

Similarly, our attitudes toward sex and sexuality have changed to the extent that now—some forty years after Pierre Trudeau, then justice minister, famously remarked that the "state has no place in the bedrooms of the nation"—Canada is one of six countries in which same-sex marriage is legal.[4] But this does not mean that there is widespread acceptance or tolerance of public discussion about sexuality and sexual practices. Indeed in every society, community, or group there are bound to be variations in terms of what is perceived as acceptable. In December of 2008, listeners to the CBC Radio show Q hosted by Jian Ghomeshi weekday mornings at ten o'clock, heard programs that addressed different elements of sex in today's society, including stories about a woman who auctioned off her virginity, a photographer's book about the swinger lifestyle, and a suburban mother who wrote a biography about an adult film star. Conscious of the different tolerance levels of members of our society, I wondered how listeners would respond to this show's content on public radio at that time of day. Sure enough, criticism flowed in. While the posts on the Q blog were mixed, this post by "Julie" reveals a visceral response to the perceived changes in content. As she put it: "I have ceased listening to the radio during the Q show, and others. With kids at home, and my own desire not to be exposed to vulgarity, it is never safe to listen anymore. Q is NOT in an adult time slot, and it is increasingly preoccupied with beyond the norm sexuality." (Q blog, December 12, 2008).

Changes in cultures are influenced, not only by local and national events, but also by world events. We are well aware of how the events of 9/11 have changed people's lives the world over, and we are reminded of this every time we go to the airport. And many of us participate in the March "Earth Hour" initiative by turning off our lights for an hour as a symbol of our commitment to the environment. Also, the devastating effects of Hurricane Katrina, not to mention the political and social after-effects, has forever changed how we think about hurricanes, just as the 2004 tsunami in South Asia has influenced how we think about earthquakes and their consequences. Both events gave particular significance and meaning to the term "natural disaster." For some of us, they were reminders of the devastation that might result from earthquakes and hurricanes; for others, they provided new understandings. While the 2004 tsunami did not reach North American shores, people everywhere took note, especially people residing in places where these natural occurrences might take place. For Canadians, particularly older residents of Newfoundland, for whom the effect of the November 18, 1929, tsunami was a distant memory, the South Asian tsunami was a reminder. We now think about how hurricanes, earthquakes, wildfires, floods, and ice storms, as well as human-made disasters such as extended power outages, might affect us, and we prepare for these events. Witness for example the government's "72 Hours" campaign encouraging Canadians to be prepared to survive for seventy-two hours before rescue in the event of a disaster.

The United States election of 2008 is significant to our discussion in many ways. The election of Barack Obama, widely promoted as the "first Black president of the United States," is serving to change the discourse on race in the United States, Canada, and undeniably, the world over.[5] The idea that a Black man can become president of the United States, coupled with the fact that his election was celebrated around the world, would have us believe that race no longer matters, and that everyone has opportunities irrespective of race.[6] Similarly, the fact that Hillary Rodham

Clinton was a serious presidential candidate for the Democratic Party is believed in some circles to be evidence that we have evolved to a culture in which gender, like race, is no longer a barrier to success.

Obama's success is held up as a testimony of the American Dream—anything is possible if you work hard enough for it. Such successes function to maintain the notion of meritocracy, thereby reassuring members of democratic societies that it is through individual efforts, hard work, and determination that their successes will be realized. On the basis of these cultural values, Americans, as well as Canadians and those residing in other professed democratic societies, live with the belief that their society is open and democratic, and therefore race, gender, and other differences are not likely to function as barriers to their success. Obama's election as president of the United States therefore seems to serve as reassurance to people everywhere, sending the message (although some might say it is a deceptive message) that equality is a foundation of today's culture. We cannot deny the significance of the 2008 presidential election, particularly the effect of Obama's role as president on the existing economic, political, environmental, welfare, and health agendas and conditions worldwide and, by extension, local, national, and international cultures. And from observing Canadians' overwhelming responses to having a "Black man in the White House," it is highly possible that just as the voting practices of Americans have changed, so too will those of Canadians.

RETHINKING "MAINSTREAM"

The tendency to use terms such as Anglo-Saxon or Anglo-Celtic to identify the basis of "mainstream," and assert the invisibility of Canadian culture, misses the fact that Aboriginal people lived in this territory for hundreds of years before Europeans, Africans, Asians, and South Asians came. These new settlers, starting with the British and the French, have contributed to and modified the "taken-for-granted" mainstream Canadian culture. It is true that the cultural identity of a society is, to an extent, defined by its dominant group, which "is usually quite distinguishable from the minority sub-group with whom they share the physical environment and the territory they inhabit" (Adler 1977, 26). However, the fact remains that ethnic and racial minority group cultures—as much as they are set off as different from the "dominant culture"—do contribute to changes within the larger culture of the society. As accommodations are made, cultures emerge with new dimensions.

Consequently, despite the historical European origins of what we see as Canadian culture, what is understood to be mainstream culture is not based entirely on one particular group. The dominance of the culture of English ethnic group Canadians is maintained, as discussed earlier, through pacification of minority groups in response to their demands, contestation, and struggle for rights, justice, and recognition. Furthermore, insofar as culture is dynamic and not enclosed, whatever *mainstream* culture exists in any society is going to be something that emerges from the existence, traditions, practices, ideas, and contributions of *everyone* in that society. It cannot be otherwise, since residents of a society living in the same space and being subjected to the same legal-political structure must negotiate an accommodation of their cultural diversity, differences, and expressions, thereby producing relative stability within the society. Essentially, then, the culture of any society or community that emerges will result from the contributions and ideas of everyone in that society.

Mainstream Canadian culture, then, is a complex combination of the values, symbols, expressions, etc., of all ethno-racial groups. As we have already indicated, cultural attributes are both visible and invisible, and they become a part of our existence, seeping into our everyday existence often with little or no conscious effort. For instance, Aboriginal artifacts and symbols (e.g., soapstone art and the now ubiquitous inukshuk) are generally taken to be Canadian. And it is common to see people wearing green on St. Patrick's Day, to hear the evening news anchor say "Gong hei fat choy" in recognition of the Chinese New Year, to see Hanukkah menorahs in public areas alongside Christmas trees, or to observe Black History Month celebrations in schools, workplaces, and communities.[7]

CONCLUSION

When we approach an issue or problem with others and find that our approaches to solving it are similar, we are in part helping to create our social reality. When the approach we choose to solve a problem or to economically, legally, politically, or otherwise sustain ourselves is embraced by others in a group, organization, or community and then becomes a routine course of action for everyone, culture is being created (Schwalbe 2005). If this approach is adopted by or becomes a reference for members of the society and is used to organize their behaviour and actions, then this helps to create the mainstream culture. Culture is all encompassing. It shapes and is shaped by the intersecting relationships of, among others, economic, political, and social systems. Hence, it is problematic to include "cultural" in the list of "economic, political, and social" factors, as if suggesting that they all share the same characteristics.

Culture also refers to a general style of behaviour, etiquette, values, tastes, and preferences; language, traditions, and customs; food, dress, and musical tastes; as well as belief systems and world views. Variations in culture are inevitable within and between ethnic, racial, and other groups. Culture is not exclusive to minority people—people different from the taken-for-granted "invisible" dominant ethno-racial group—because of their race, ethnicity, or foreign birthplace. Yet given the stratification and power relations in society, for minority group members, culture serves as a means of providing a sense of community, strength, and stability, and mediating the integrating and assimilating ways and hegemonic demands and expectations of the dominant ethno-racial group. The fact is, everyone has culture, participates in cultural practices, contributes to the construction of culture, and is shaped by cultural values, norms, aspirations, etc.[8] Indeed, as Lum affirms, cultural differences "are not limited to simply differences in ethnicity, nationality or region; they refer to patterns of thought, attitudes and behaviors, which vary according to the 'sameness' shared by distinct groups" (2006, 113).

Of course, we do not blindly follow everything dictated by the culture(s) to which we might belong or feel affiliated. The degree to which individuals identify with their group culture varies depending on place of birth, geographical residence, social class, abilities, education and occupational status and achievements, interaction with members and non-members of their group, and their willingness to adapt to dominant cultural norms, values, etc. The fact that culture is dynamic and often contains contradictions, opposition, tension, and conflict means that changes within a culture are natural. These changes result from such things as local and global events, movement of people from one country or region to another, and the interaction of various racial, ethnic, and social groups. Changes also result from the tensions and conflicts that occur as groups agitate for space, resources, recognition, and survival. An example of acontradiction in Canadian culture has to do with the notion that we are a benevolent country that values multiculturalism, cultural democracy, and equality, yet these ideals are not always practiced or upheld.

A cultural analysis enables us to adequately understand the actions, beliefs, and practices of a group and why people do the things they do by taking into consideration the cultural norms that exist in all groups and societies. An appreciation of culture allows us to see that while the actions and beliefs of some groups may seem strange or unacceptable to outsiders, to insiders of the group they are likely to be seen as normal and acceptable. This recognition does not mean that all behaviours are acceptable just because they are a group's traditional way of doing things. Clearly, culture is not static and unchanging. It moves and shifts as it is continually being influenced by key structural factors such as geography, history, political context, economics, religion, language, etc. Culture is the context in which things are happening and it is a product of how these things play out. Culture creates and culture is created all at the same time. If we think of culture as shaping all of our needs, aspirations, behaviours, and interactions, then we can understand how thinking about culture as strictly about race, ethnicity, or as something possessed by a foreign person, or merely as traditions, festivals, and food, is a distortion of the word.

NOTES

1. Thanks to Leanne Taylor for introducing me to the film *The Gods Must Be Crazy* as an example for cultural study.

2. Claiming that Toronto is home to people from all over the world, it was suggested that athletes and visitors to the Olympics would be able to culturally relate to Toronto. Further, in response to the United Nations 2004 annual Human Development Index, which listed Canada as the fourth-best country in the world in which to live, the mayor of Vancouver boasted that "immigrants aren't expected to assimilate when they move to Canada, but rather to add their culture into the mix. I am sure that the [Toronto mayor] would say the same thing; the reason we are great cities is because of our diversity" (as quoted in James 2005, 12).

3. For example, the colonization of Aboriginal peoples particularly, through forced residential schooling; the enslavement of African peoples; the internment of Japanese people during the war; the head tax charged to Chinese immigrants; and continuous journey legislation applied to South Asians. The ways in which such groups understand their history in this nation influences the ways in which they come to understand, negotiate, and feel a sense of belonging in Canada. See Chapter 6 for more detail on these topics.

4. As of 2009, the other countries are the Netherlands (2001), Belgium (2003), Spain (2005), and Norway (2009). In the United States, marriage is considered an issue of state law, and the states of Massachusetts (2004) and Connecticut (2008) allow same-sex marriage. Canada made same-sex marriage legal in 2005.

5. Some people insist on referring to Obama's mixed-race background. For example, mixed-race organizations such as Project Race and the MAVIN Foundation have drawn on, referred to, and celebrated Obama's mixed background and his capacity to be a role model for mixed-race youth. Similarly, in the election-night discussion, a white, female CNN reporter said that she was proud to witness his election because Obama represents the change that her bi-racial child is longing for—a mixed-race person in a position of power who can provide an important role model. See Chapter 3 for a further discussion of mixed-race identity.

6. Interestingly, a Stanford University study found that white Americans who voted for Obama use their political stance as leverage for defending their actions or statements that reflect racism or discrimination. For instance, compared to those who did not express their support for Obama, respondents who did indicated that they would hire a white over a black officer in a police department that has had a long history of racial tension between officers. Similarly, they were more likely to give greater amounts of money to white-controlled community groups, compared to those that are black-controlled (Effron, Cameron, and Monin 2009).

7. The national celebration of Black History Month was established in 1996 after the Honourable Jean Augustine, an Ontario Member of Parliament, won an all-party motion that made the Black history celebration not only something that was held in Ontario, but across Canada (see K. Smardz Frost, "The Birth of Black History Month," in *Heritage Matters*, Vol. 4, Issue 1, p. 17.)

Of course, the celebration takes different forms in different regions and communities in the country depending on a number of factors, not the least of which is the existence of an African Canadian community in that area.

8. Often, those Canadians who claim that "there is no Canadian culture" are the ones who go on to suggest that "people who come here should be expected to adapt to our way of life." In some cases, those "people" are Canadians who may have lived here all their lives or who have ancestry dating back generations. The reading of these Canadians' "cultural differences" might have to do with skin colour, accent, or ethnicity. I have also experienced cases in which individuals claim that they are "without culture," nevertheless they will

identity those people who "have culture" as the same people who do not behave "like Canadians." The irony here is that while denying that there is a Canadian culture or saying that they as Canadian individuals do not have culture, they are still able to rely on particular signifiers that identify a person as *not* behaving like a Canadian. Of course, this suggests that there is indeed a cultural pattern that is "Canadian"—it simply goes unarticulated and unrecognized.

CONSTRUCTING CULTURAL IDENTITY

In this chapter, we examine the ways in which cultural identities are understood, referenced, experienced, and articulated by individuals in relation to the cultural contexts in which they live, work, learn, and play. As a product of both group and individual struggles over meanings, legitimacy, recognition, and resources, culture is complex, contradictory, inconsistent, ambiguous, and dynamic, and fraught with tensions and conflict. Lodged in this dynamic cultural web of intersecting relationships with various groups and institutions (modelled in **Figure 3.1**), individuals perform, construct, and negotiate their respective identities so that they are able to fully participate in a multicultural Canada, and have their contributions acknowledged and their aspirations realized.

The narratives of students in this chapter, as in others, illustrate the multiple, ambiguous, relational, inconsistent, and performative character of cultural identity.[1] And, as will become evident in the student accounts, identity is fluid, incomplete, and always in process, embodying both possibilities and limitations in terms of how individuals understand themselves and each other, and how they experience and live their lives. As Gross-Stein (2005) puts it, identity is "the way in which a person is, or wishes to be known by others; it is a conception of self in relation to others" (366). And as Hall (1990) writes,

> Cultural identities come from somewhere, have histories.
> But like everything which is historical, they undergo

FIGURE 3.1 – IDENTITY DIAGRAM

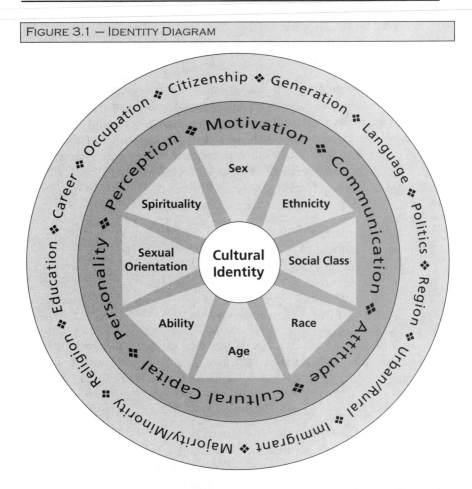

This figure represents the interconnectedness of factors that contribute to an individual's cultural or social identities which altogether contribute to lifestyle, behaviour patterns, worldview etc. Moving outward from the cultural identity circle, 1) **Personal** factors or characteristics are those intimately connected to an individual's personal being; 2) **Social psychological** factors are interrelated to personal characteristics as well as 3) the **Social structural** factors that are shared by group members or members of the society. Through societal institutions socialization or learning takes place, cultural norms, values etc are transmitted and informed, and behaviour patterns developed. Essentially, individuals' lives are mediated by the social and cultural structures in which they are enmeshed. It is worth noting that spirituality, identified as a personal characteristic, refers to, in the words of the Dalai Lama, "those qualities of the human spirit—such as love and compassion, patience, tolerance, forgiveness, contentment, a sense of responsibility, a sense of harmony—which bring happiness to both self and others." And religion is "concerned with faith in the claims to salvation of one faith tradition or another, an aspect of which is acceptance of some form of metaphysical or supernatural reality, including perhaps an idea of heaven or nirvana. Connected with this are religious teachings or dogma, ritual, prayer, and so on" (cited in hooks, p. 178).

constant transformation. Far from being eternally fixed in some essentialized past, they are subject to the continuous "play" of history, culture and power. (225)

Therefore, shaped by life experiences, histories, geographies, and encounters, as well as racial, ethnic, class, and gendered locations—and mediated or influenced by socializing agents such as family, school, etc. (as discussed in Chapter 4)—identities are always in flux, and constructed and negotiated by individuals who are incomplete subjects in a perpetual process of becoming (Hall 1996, Yon 2000). Pointing to the inherent instability of identity, British scholar and professor Ali Rattansi questions the value of delving into these issues. If all identities, he asks,

are decentered and driven by contradiction, ambiguity, ambivalence, and so forth, what is the point in exposing and exploring the instabilities of black and Asian British identities? Are they not bound to be unstable and shifting anyway? What is so special about these or indeed any other particular forms of identification? (Rattansi 2005, 54)

Regardless of the contradictions and the constant shifts and changes, individuals often still derive a sense of being, of community, and of belonging from the identities they adopt or that they are assigned.

In Chapter 2, we briefly outlined the difference between *culture*, *race*, and *ethnicity*. In this chapter, we will explore in more detail how the constructs of race and ethnicity operate in individuals' construction of cultural identities. While both demographic characteristics play an equally important role in the formulation of cultural identity for members of dominant and minority ethno-racial groups, there is the tendency to identify members of ethnic and racial minority groups only by ethnicity or race, or for them to identity themselves in ethnic or racial terms; the official "visible minority" classification helps to ensure this. According to Smith (1991), while the ethnic identity development of the majority or dominant group individual is continually being validated and reinforced by his or her group membership, and by the structure of the society's institutions, such is not the case for members of many ethnic minority groups. Positive reinforcement frees the majority individual to focus on aspects of his or her life other than ethnicity (183). Arguing that identity is a site of power difference and power relations, Dei and Calliste (2000) proffer that it is crucial to give attention to how identities are used and engaged by individuals, for while some identities and discourses of difference are privileged, others are resisted, negated, and rendered oppositional. In Chapter 5, we will discuss the role dominant and minority group membership plays in people's experiences;

in this chapter, we discuss specifically how (a) race and (b) ethnicity are understood and accounted for in individuals' identifications, and then how religion, gender, biraciality or mixed-race identity, and being Canadian (hyphenated and otherwise) are experienced and taken up in individuals' constructed identities.

Critics have argued against categorizing people by race or ethnicity because doing so could lead to essentialism. Essentialism is the notion that certain traits or behaviours of racial, ethnic, cultural, or even gendered groups are both fixed and universal, hence not allowing for variations among individuals, within groups, or over time. While many refute essentialism, some scholars indicate that despite its risks, not essentializing to a certain extent could result in leaving unchallenged the "the undiminished power of racism," and ignoring the reality that minority group members "continue to comprehend their lives" in terms of what such power does to them (Gilroy 1993, 101; see also Martin 1994). However, scholars also warn against becoming trapped in the essentialism binary—or as Martin puts it, "false difference, and other dangerous traps" (1994, 646). Such a binary can lead to the politics of authenticity, which would lock us in, as Gilroy describes, to a "fruitless exercise of social practices," and distract us from what is required to address issues of oppression. As Martin writes:

> No two individuals and no two circumstances are alike in every respect, no two are different in every respect …
> In the interest of political mobilization for social change, "strategic essentialism" (Spivak 1993) or "anti-anti-essentialism" (Gilroy 1993) are necessary, expedient and indeed critical. (1994, 646)

RACE AND THE SOCIAL CONSTRUCTION OF IDENTITY

Race is an arbitrary term that is employed in the classification of human beings. Over the years, it has been used to refer to many categories (Elliott and Fleras 1992, 28; Li 1990):

- ❍ lineage (groups of people connected by common descent or origin)
- ❍ subspecies (populations of people with distinct genotypes)
- ❍ ethnic groups (e.g., British, French, Anglo-Saxons, Italians)
- ❍ religious groups (e.g., Jews, Muslims, Christians)
- ❍ nationalities (e.g., Irish, Chinese, Ghanaian)
- ❍ minority language groups (e.g., French Canadians, Cantonese)
- ❍ blood groups (e.g., Black, white)
- ❍ people from particular geographic regions (e.g., Mediterranean, South Asia)

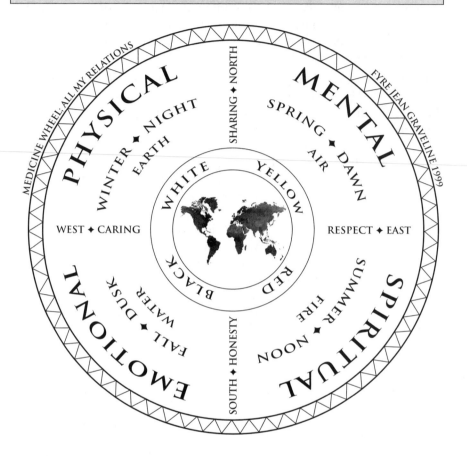

FIGURE 3.2 — MEDICINE WHEEL: ALL MY RELATIONS

To some degree, underlying these varied usages is the belief that race is an inherited biological or physical characteristic—hence a scientific or social fact[2]—that operates independently to shape individuals' personalities and as such is an important (for some, the most important) individual and group trait.[3]

But obviously, the meaning of the term race is not "fixed"—it is related to an historical understanding, as well as the political, cultural, social, and geographic context of today. The question is: Who really belongs in which categories? Many persons do not fit into any of the five colour-based racial categories (brown, black, red, yellow, white) in use today.[4] Where would we, for example, place Arabs, or people from the Middle East or Latin America, or those with a mixed racial background? A list of all such exceptions would be quite long, but one thing is evident—there is no clear, indisputable definition of race. From this perspective, then, do racial characteristics really play a role in people's lives? It is true that we have long put aside Linnaeus's classification system, which was used in the eighteenth and nineteenth centuries among European scientists to rank "the 'races' of the world in hierarchical order of innate inferiority and superiority ranging from primitive to highly civilized," with the white race of Christian Europe at the top of the hierarchy (Kallen 1995, 24). It is worth noting how this hierarchical interpretation of race diversity among humans differs considerably from that of the teachings of the medicine wheel in Aboriginal communities. As the medicine wheel indicates, there are four races of people, each equally responsible for different aspects of maintaining the four elements (water, fire, earth, and air), the four seasons, and the four states of human existence—all of which help to maintain a healthy Earth, without which we would all suffer. Important here is the interrelationship among human beings and the role that we all must play in maintaining a healthy Earth that will ensure our survival.

Omi and Winant (1993), who have been especially influential on scholarship of race and racism, proffer that race is an "unstable and 'decentered' complex of social meanings constantly being transformed by political struggle" (55). They also make the point that the concept of race "operates neither as a signifier of comprehensive identity, nor of fundamental difference, both of which are patently absurd, but rather as a marker of the infinity of variations we humans hold as a common heritage and hope for the future" (1993, 9). Albeit, race, as an identification, is so deeply woven into the fabric of society that as Winant (2000) further suggests, an inability to identify others by race can lead to "a microsociological crisis of interpretation" and that to be "without racial identity is to be in danger of having no identity. To be raceless is akin to being genderless" (184). Even gender, as Schwalbe (2005) opines, is not something we can take for granted; while sex is scientifically determined through genetics, gender is in fact a social construct. Accordingly, Schwalbe maintains that all identities are derived "from invented categories; they are not part of nature ... All your ideas about who and what you are come from the social world in which you were raised" (23).[5]

In taking up the question "Does race exist?" in a 2003 *Scientific American* article, Michael Bamshad and Steve Olson contend that if race is defined as a genetically distinct characteristic, the answer is "no."

> Can genetic information be used to distinguish human groups having a common heritage and to assign individuals to particular ones? Do such groups correspond well to predefined descriptions now widely used to specify race?

And more practically, does dividing people by familiar racial definitions or by genetic similarities say anything useful about how members of those groups experience disease or respond to drug treatment? In general, we would answer the first question yes, the second no and offer a qualified yes to the third. (Bamshad and Olson 2003, 80)

In elaborating on their "qualified yes," Bamshad and Olson maintain that groups do "differ genetically" from each other, "but how groups are divided depends on which genes are examined" (80). Some of the differences among groups are particularly significant in treating certain diseases, such as sickle-cell anemia, cancer, hypertension, and diabetes.[6] However, neither genetic composition nor a person's genetic background can be predicted from the mere self-reporting of ancestry or common notions of race (Bamshad and Olson 2003). In a 2007 study of the genetic makeup of Afro-Brazilians conducted for the Brazilian service of the BBC, the DNA of individual volunteers in the southern cities was analyzed.[7] It was found that more than half of individuals who self-identified as "Black" in the city of Porto Alegre carried the targeted genes associated with European origin, while only 8 percent of self-identified "whites" carried the same genes. In the case of singer Neguinho da Beija-Flor, even though his stage name and skin colour would mark him as Black, his DNA analysis showed that his targeted genes were about 67 percent "European" and only 31 percent "African." A surprising result as, according to the singer, "People will think I'm joking if I tell them this." In fact, according to the news report, "The results of the DNA tests surprised many by showing that skin colour does not necessarily reflect the ancestry of a person's genetic make-up" (Salek 2007; see also Bamshad and Olson 2003).[8] Such scientific evidence merely illuminates the social variety in the ways race is viewed across the globe; take into account that someone identified as "Black" in Canada might be considered "white" in the Caribbean and "coloured" in South Africa.

Even so, in everyday discourses, physical characteristics—skin colour, hair texture, and other facial and bodily features—serve not only to categorize and represent differences among people, but also, according to Stuart Hall (1996), act as "symbolic markers" to socially differentiate one group from another (617). For the purpose of our discussion, race is understood to refer to the socially constructed classification of human beings based on the historical and geographic context of individual experience. An individual's race is determined socially and psychologically, rather than biologically. It is often the basis upon which groups are formed, agency is attained, social roles are assigned and status is conferred. Consequently, individual and group identities and behaviours are products of these factors. In effect, race affects how individuals are identified, identify themselves, interact with others, and understand their place in society. Race is significant as long as groups are identified by their physical traits, and attributes are assigned as a result of these traits. It is significant as long as groups and individuals suffer consequences because of race. The social meaning of race, though problematic, is well understood by members of society, even though it is racialized "Others" who most often name race as a force within their lives.

The case of British twin girls who were born to parents of mixed race (both their mother and father had one Black parent and one white parent) is instructive. One of the twins, Remee, was "blond and fair skinned" and the other, Kian, was "black." The *Daily Mail Online* reported that "according to the Multiple Births Foundation, baby Kian must have inherited the black genes from both sides of the family, whilst Remee inherited the white ones" (Laing, February 21, 2006). As they got older, the colour differences between the girls became more apparent. In response to their physical difference, their mother made a point of saying: "There are some similarities between them … They both love apples and grapes, and their favourite television programme is *Teletubbies*." However, the biology of the case continues to fascinate.

> The odds against of a mixed race couple having twins of dramatically different colour are a million to one … Skin colour is believed to be determined by up to seven different genes working together. If a woman is of mixed race, her eggs will usually contain a mixture of genes coding for both black and white skin. Similarly, a man of mixed race will have a variety of different genes in his sperm. When these eggs and sperm come together, they will create a baby of mixed race. But very occasionally, the egg or sperm might contain genes coding for one skin colour. If both the egg and sperm contain all white genes, the baby will be white. And if both contain just the versions necessary for black skin, the baby will be black. (Laing, *Daily Mail Online*, February 21, 2006)

Even though these genetic twins, Remee and Kian, will have similar cultural experiences inside their home, their cultural identities will also be influenced by people's reading of their "race." Their similarities aside, Remee will develop a cultural identity mediated by the privilege that her blond hair and fair skin afford her, while Kian's cultural identity will be a consequence of having to navigate the barriers created by race inequities.

This story points to the limits of a biological definition of race and the significance of the social definition.

A further illustration of the "nature versus nurture" debate regarding the role of race in identity construction and behaviour is the controversy surrounding transracial adoption, in which there is a tendency to tie children's "biological origins" to "membership in a nominal community of descent" (Lal 2001, 154). Barbara Lal suggests that when advocates call for children to be placed in homes that share their racial locations and ethnicities, it implies "not only inherited physical characteristics but an inherited culture" (156). She explains that children who are adopted by families of a different "race" find they are seen as representatives of the particular culture that they were "born into," which ultimately clashes with the culture they are learning in their adoptive families and communities (Lal 2001). So, when it is suggested that "Black children must not lose their opportunity to develop an appropriate cultural identity by being reared in a white home" what is ultimately being implied is that "black and mixed-race children ought to develop a black cultural identity." This presumes that even when children are adopted at an early age, they still have a primordial attachment to a "community and culture of biological descent" that cannot be changed (Lal 2001, 156–157).

Related to this widely held notion are the rulings pertaining to the custody case of a mixed-race child in British Columbia, in which the justices gave consideration to the role of race in deciding custody of a child named Elijah. Writing on behalf of her Court of Appeal colleagues, and reversing the decision of the Supreme Court of British Columbia— which had granted custody to the child's white mother— the Honourable Justice Madame Mary Newbury, noted:

> [49] … E. F. Carasco has observed ("Race and Child Custody in Canada: Its Relevance and Role" (1999) 16 *Can. Fam. Law* 11), a child's sense of self, the child's well-being and future in our society are "inextricably related" to the colour of his or her skin. Carasco continues:
>
> If a child's identity is influenced by its racial background … and categorization of the child by skin colour plays a significant role in influencing the child's future—then "race" surely matters in a child's life. It is not a detachable factor that can be added on or ignored at will. "Colour blindness" in these situations is not helpful to the child as it ignores or denies the political and social significance of "race" and therefore ignores or denies the realities of that child's life. (*Van de Perre v. Edwards* 2000, para. 14; see also Patricia J. Williams, *Seeing a Colour-Blind Future: The Paradox of Race* [New York, 1997].)

In the end, the justices of the British Columbia Court of Appeal, agreeing with the claims of the father's wife, reasoned that in North American societies, such as in Canada, where race matters, racism is something from which children must be protected since it affects their development of healthy identities. As such they ruled that Elijah's white mother would be unable to help him understand what it means to be Black, and granted custody to his African American father (and his wife) who lived in the United States. But Canada's Supreme Court placed this reasoning aside in their ruling on two questions presented to them by the mother's lawyer: (1) What role should race play in decisions regarding custody of children of mixed race? and (2) What principles ought to be applied when such cases appear before the bar? The Supreme Court of Canada justices maintained that they had "a lot of trouble" with race being raised as an issue in the custody case (see Taylor et al. 2007, 153).[9] We return to this reasoning and decision in our discussion of mixed race, and of Canadian cultural identity.

Clearly, race is not an objective condition and we cannot speak of it as something that just "is," or as something predictable and easily determined and classifiable. Despite the lack of scientific significance and the claim that "all human lineage descended from a small group of ancestors in Africa around 60,000 years ago" (diCarlo 2006, 10), the historical interpretation of race as a concept remains structured in our existence as human beings. Hence, as we discuss in the following section, race is part of the construction of all people, as much as it is with racial minority group members in a society.

CONSTRUCTING WHITE RACIAL IDENTITY

The tendency for white individuals to ascribe race or skin colour to racial minorities (or to think of race as mainly an identifier of racial minorities) is well documented (Kendall 2006; Carr and Lund 2007; Simpson et al. 2007; Tilley 2006). As the dominant racial group, whites tend to see their colour as the norm—hence, "colourless"—while identifying non-whites in terms of colour or in terms of attributes related to skin colour. This popular conception of racial identity was evident in an exchange in which students were asked to talk about how their race and ethnicity might be factored into their constructed identities and experiences. One white student insisted that he was Canadian, and therefore his racial and ethnic identities were irrelevant. When asked if he would accept a Chinese or Black person saying the same thing—insisting that they are Canadians, and in doing so, refusing to identify themselves by their race or ethnicity—the student responded by saying he would not be satisfied with their answers because, to him, Canadians are people who look like him: "Chinese and Blacks are immigrants—they do not look Canadian."

It's important to recognize that this is not an isolated response. In the same class, another student said to me, "I feel when you mention race, you're talking about people of different ethnicities [not British or French] and from different countries." In addition, there is the perception that talking about or naming race constructs white individuals as being prejudiced or racist; hence, in such discussions white participants tend to become defensive. In this regard, they would by say: "I never see race," or "I see the person, not her race," or "I don't feel uncomfortable with Black people," or "Every time I've talked about race, it's been about stereotyping or prejudice."

Along the same lines of not seeing, or denying, "race" or claiming to be raceless, yet ascribing race to "Other" Canadians, other class members asserted:

> **Greg:** As for my race, I am white, but I never really had to think about it before. I don't feel that it ever affected the people with whom I associated or talked to. My two best friends are Black and Indian. I was brought up in a family that didn't believe in prejudice and I'm proud of that. If I don't like a person, it is because of their personality, not their race or heritage.
>
> **Henry:** Concerning my race, which is Caucasian, I really don't believe that it has contributed enormously to my identity or behaviour. I feel this way because my culture is basically all Canadian.
>
> **Laurie:** I cannot see how my race influences or affects me. I have always been aware of how my ethnicity influences my ideals, morals, values, and beliefs, and these personal elements have not changed. For me to say that race affects me would either show that I feel inferior or superior to other races, and this is incorrect.

Why are Greg, Henry, and Laurie able to give so little or no thought to their race or "whiteness"? How can they claim that their race has not "contributed enormously" to their identity, values, beliefs, and behaviours? Is their denial of race, or their racelessness, an attempt, as Laurie hints, not to "show" their feelings of "superiority to other races"? Is it likely that those who identify themselves racially are people who "feel inferior or superior"? And what about when someone, like Greg, does not think of himself in racial terms yet identifies others, such as his "two best friends," by their race or ethnicity? Is he, as Kallen (1995) might suggest, alluding to his superior status? Or is Greg merely stating the obvious, that he represents the "norm" as Carr and Lund (2007) would suggest? In identifying the race and ethnicity of his friends, Greg seems to be signalling that he is not prejudice. In essence, the comments by Greg, Henry, and Laurie indicate their attempts to avoid naming their whiteness, for to do so would require them to also acknowledge their race privilege—that "invisible package of unearned assets," as Peggy McIntosh (1995) puts it—and surrender the myth of Canadian society's racial neutrality. It is quite possible that when individuals attempt to deflect discussion about their whiteness or refuse to make their own racial selves or identities explicit (as in the case of Greg, Henry, and Laurie), they are attempting to hide their knowledge of their location and the ways in which they socially, culturally, and politically produce relations of domination. Further, because of their locations within the dominant racial group, they tend to take their racial identities for granted.

Taking their race or colour for granted fosters the notion that race does not influence their behaviour, especially in a context where their "culture," as Henry professes, "is basically all Canadian." What does it mean to be "Canadian," and what does being white have to do with being Canadian? Katia, in the following comment, speaks to this. She indicates that being white is not all that it takes to feel connected to Canada.

Katia: The application of the "white" label to all those who exhibit the physical [characteristics] of the white privileged norm is problematic for me and the manner in which I understand and speak of my identity. As I feel identified by others as "white" because of my skin colour, I reject that label, for I do not identify with the privilege associated with whiteness. The whiteness I understand to exist entails a historical connection to Canada, which has allowed one to build a bank of cultural capital from it and within it. This cultural expertise then allows them to navigate the societal and educational system with ease and understand the reasons for their actions. This applies to both the parents and the children, as they are able to communicate and operate within the dominant power system in which they were born. I have felt like an outsider with respect to this dominant culture and by virtue of that exclusion, I do not feel I can be labelled as belonging to the white dominant class as marked by my skin colour and my European descent.

My rejection of the white label, in my past experiences, has only been validated when those identifiers find out about my residence in communist Romania during an oppressive time period during the mid-to late-1980s. Those knowledgeable about the living conditions under the final stages of a failing communist regime are able to understand my family's experience as not one exhibiting signs of white privilege in North America, [which is] associated with high SES, power, and educational and occupational opportunities. The "new life" in Canada that I experienced as a young immigrant is also not one which brought my family privilege, for any privilege our white skin colour extended was cancelled out by our immigrant identity. This was especially felt settling in as a resident in a white neighbourhood where families exhibited characteristics of the dominant culture, having a multi-generational established history in the country and neighbourhood with accumulated resources. In academia, those validating the rejection of the white label by European immigrants are few, and thus my ability to "see" myself in academic research has been hindered. My identification has been at times with the experiences of those who belong to a visible minority group, for they most closely parallel my own and that of my family.

Is it really that Katia's experiences parallel those of "visible minority group" members, or the experiences of immigrants? While it is true that Katia might share with racial minority members of society the sense or experiences of being an "outsider"—not having been born in Canada— her experiences will be different from those of racial minorities whose race helps to construct them as outsiders. In fact, having experienced the "very real, very political historical realities that have affected racially mixed individuals" Adebe D. A. (2008), writing in her university newspaper, *Excalibur*, asserts that the "whole 'race is a myth' idea doesn't work" for her because: "I'm still expected to choose an agreeable classification for myself to ease the minds of those taken aback by my racial ambiguity. Of course, I've never considered myself to look ambiguous" (5). Adebe D. A. goes on to say that she is often asked: "Where are you from?"—a question which, in the Canadian context, invites the person being asked to locate him or herself, usually inferring that he or she is read as a "non-white" person, hence not from Canada. In the case of Katia, it is not whiteness that operates to determine the construction of her Canadian identity, but her immigrant status, which should not be conflated with race.

According to Frankenberg (1993) whiteness is related to "a set of locations that are historically, socially, politically and culturally produced" (6). And as Twine (2000) says, being white also means being neutral, colour-blind, or "invisible;" having a modicum of "purchasing power" and access to privileges, including a middle-class lifestyle; and feeling familiarity and comfort with the social expectations associated with "being" white and "acting" white. Therefore, the social construction of whiteness is not merely about physical attributes, but is about locations, opportunities, and material relations. While Katia might lack the "bank of cultural capital and privileges" that her white skin should have made possible in Canada, it is possible that with time she will come to enjoy the privileges of a "white," university-educated Canadian. The fact is, Canada is not colour-blind society, and being white counts for something.

The belief that one can be colour-blind informs individuals' assertions that they "do not see race," or that their lives are not affected by race. It also underlies individuals' assumptions that because they are colour-blind, they are able to cultivate friendships and even have "best friends" of colour. The notion of colour-blindness is in part advanced by Canada's multiculturalism discourse, which holds that Canada is a tolerant and pluralistic nation in which race does not matter. But Darren Lund and Paul Carr challenge this notion in their 2007 collection, *The Great White North? Exploring Whiteness, Privilege and Identity in Education*. In their introduction, they make the point that despite official multiculturalism, colour operates in Canada to affect individuals' opportunities. And in questioning the assumed racelessness among white Canadians, they write—"as two white males from Canada … who have been involved in anti-racism education"—that

> it is crucial that we understand not just the racialization of others, but our own whiteness, both as a marker, and a constituent element of our own privileged cultural, national and class location. We need to understand how our own biographies and experiences shape and limit our identities and consciousness, and the path we must take to transform them. (6)

But colour-blindness is not a claim specific to dominant group members. Indeed, like whites, schooled in the discourse of multiculturalism, racial tolerance, and democracy, racial minority members of society also use colour-blindness as a framework to understand their experiences and the social world. This is evident in statements such as "I am human," or "We're all human beings," or "It's not about colour," or "It has nothing to do with colour." For instance, racialized individuals sometimes attempt to minimize the effects of the racism they face by positioning acts of racism as random and "isolated incidents of individual prejudice" (Korgen and O'Brien 2006; Rockquemore et al. 2006). The fact is, colour-blindness makes it possible for individuals to overlook and negate the reality of race and racism in their own and other people's everyday lives. Colour-blindness reflects their inability to understand, or an unwillingness to acknowledge, racial differences (and the range of differences) which would enable them to address the experiences of racialized individuals (Essed 1990; Gotanda 2000; Williams 1997).

The Significance of Race in the Social Identification of Racialized Individuals

It is certainly an oversimplification, even in the case of racial minority members of society, to say that race is an all-encompassing identifier in the face of other categories of identification, including ethnicity, gender, class, religion, sexuality, language, and citizenship (see **Figure 3.1**, page 47). And like these other categories, not only is race a heterogeneous category, the same can be said of any one racial group category. Nevertheless, as Sefa writes, compared to all the demographic identifies that could be ascribed to him—Canadian, mixed-race—it was his race, specifically his Black identity, that stands out for him, yet it is not something that he can "take for granted."

> **Sefa:** I'm always intrigued when I read accounts of race or ethnicity that centre on Canadian-ness. For me, being Canadian was something I could take for granted. I never questioned it and never felt it was legitimately questioned. My identity was far more influenced by being "mixed-race/biracial/half-caste/etc." Belonging and identity to me didn't revolve around nationality (Canadian, African, British) but race … No, what I remember more was feeling black and wanting to be seen as black.
>
> Looking back, there were two reasons for this. First, in my generation and location, blackness was cool. Hip hop was increasingly popular and more blacks were appearing in television and movies and for young people, popular culture was black. The second reason was that there is a historical legacy and a certain morality based on the "black experience" that I identified with and wanted others to identify with me. Being frequently mistaken for being Arab, Lebanese, North African, etc., blackness was never something that I could take for granted, but something that I had to constantly assert and claim. This profoundly influenced choices such as where to go to university, what to study, what activities I became involved in, and the friends with whom I would associate.
>
> With the combination of my age, my new location, what I was studying in school, and my increasing sophistication, I became more aware of the structural and systemic manifestations of racism. Still, these were less things that affected me than things I felt the need to challenge based on my relative privilege and identification with "the black struggle." While with age the militancy is less intense, my identification of racism with the structural over the personal is still influential.

In saying that his social, educational, and cultural worlds were all informed or mediated by his blackness, Sefa is indicating the significance of blackness and its "legacy," especially in a society where the culture promotes essentialist ways of thinking about Black people. But what does it mean to identify as "Black"? Is Sefa merely subscribing to an essentialized notion of blackness with his reference to hip hop, movies, and Black popular culture? Does this mean, as a Black university student, Nerissa Martin (2008) writes, that Sefa subscribes to the idea that "To 'be black' in western culture, a black person had to have a general understanding of hip hop"?

As mentioned earlier, it is important to avoid the pitfalls of essentialism; nevertheless, as Sefa demonstrates, it is identifying as "black" that helped him develop a sense of belonging as well as agency to challenge, through his militancy, "the structural and systemic manifestations of racism." In discussing some of the inherent problems of essentialism with a friend who identifies herself as a Black Caribbean woman, I asked for her response to the suggestion that in racially categorizing herself she was being essentialist. She acknowledged that she has been called essentialist. However, while her construction of herself might seem "unitary and fixed," she hoped that it would be understood that "this identity does not capture all of who I am, nor does it foreclose the contradictions and omissions that are intrinsic to any kind of categorization." There are, as she stated, other factors, such as being working class, immigrant, educated, and so on, that are part of who she is. Still, she has chosen to name herself in ways that she feels capture her "essence," her "way of knowing and way of being" in Canadian society.

ETHNICITY AS PART OF CULTURAL IDENTITY

In Canada, the terms *ethnic population*, *ethnic community*, *ethnic food*, and *ethnic music* are often used to describe cultural groupings and affiliations, cuisines, music, and other art forms pertaining to such people identified as Italians, Indians, Chinese, Ukrainians, Jamaicans, and others. The term *ethnic* is often used interchangeably with *race*, *immigrant*, and *culture* to try to socially define or locate people based on their perceived "difference." For instance, cultural group is used when what is meant is *ethnic group*. A typical view among many Canadians is that ethnicity is an identity marker of "Other" Canadians—people not of British origin. Take, for example, Leslie's comment:

Leslie: To me, ethnicity was something that belonged to people who differed from the so-called average white Canadian—differing perhaps because of language, accent, or skin colour. Thus, I believed ethnicity was something noticeable or visible. I believe my ignorance regarding my ethnicity is because I belong to the dominant group in Canada. Because I am white, English-speaking, and have British ancestry, I have thought of myself only as a Canadian. In essence, I didn't realize I had ethnicity, because I did not differ from the stereotypical image of an average Canadian.

Ethnicity is not simply a matter of individual choice—members of society play a role in defining it. Simply put, ethnicity refers to the groupings of people who are identified or identify themselves as having a common historical, cultural, and ancestral origin. Like race, ethnicity is a social construct based on historical, social, and political elements. As such, it is subject to the ambiguities, inconsistencies, and contradictions that are to be found in societies with meanings that change over time, and in relation to context. So, for example, a person identified, or who identifies her or himself as Portuguese in Canada, has a different meaning than a person in Portugal or Brazil or Angola in terms of group membership, status allocation, and role expectations. The fact is, ethnic categorization or affiliation is based on perceived identification with others, rather than on physical characteristics (race), economic position (class), or spiritual beliefs (religion). Basically, ethnicity, as Elliott and Fleras (1992) write, "refers to a sense of identity and belonging among those who share identification or affiliation with a common set of symbols pertaining to birthright, homeland, language, culture, and heritage" (133).

Individuals adjust their identification with the symbolic components of an ethnic group according to needs and the contextual demands of the situation, suggesting that, as Elliott and Fleras (1992) note, "the retention of cultural content is less relevant when compared with the sense of felt identification" (134). Stefan is a case in point. In his early schooling context, he reasoned that identifying as Polish would limit his chances of being a part of the "in crowd," hence he skipped language classes—a symbol of Polish identification—but returned later to participate in "Polish" activities.

> **Stefan:** My ethnic identity is Polish. My parents were born in Poland and came to Canada in 1967. I was born in Toronto, Ontario, a couple of years later. I saw my ethnicity as an advantage and a disadvantage during my lifetime. When I was younger, I didn't want to admit that I was Polish. Even though I was born here, I felt that admitting my ethnicity would be a barrier to joining the "in crowd" or the "cool group" at school. I even skipped the Polish language classes my parents sent me to after school. As I became older, I realized I couldn't change my ethnicity. I was who I was. I became more proud of my Polish background. It felt good to be part of a Polish community where I was able to participate in ceremonies and activities based on my Polish background. It gave me a sense of belonging to a group, a sense of identity, a sense of security.

This sense of identity, belonging, and security that individuals achieve through their ethnicity is dynamic and based on a perceived difference, sometimes constructed in relation to a constructed sense of Canadian identity and culture. The following excerpt by Damian captures this idea and demonstrates the inherent contradictions and inconsistencies attendant to such a sense of identity.

> **Damian:** My cultural and ethnic backgrounds are very much Slovenian. More specifically, they originated in a northern province called Slovenia. My parents emigrated from there twenty-two years ago and I was born here in Canada. My parents brought with them all of their beliefs, values, and traditions. A big part of their life was, and is, a dedication to hard work and their religious faith. Throughout my life I have been taught to respect those values and accept those religious beliefs...
>
> The work ethic is very important to me. I feel that I always make an attempt to do things well and with enthusiasm. This is one of the main

cultural differences. Canadian culture dictates a more relaxed attitude towards work. One of the strange things that I tend to do is slack off when in an environment of long-time Canadians, simply because of this attitude. In a predominantly Slovenian environment, I tend to work faster and a lot harder. In this way, I am more Slovenian than Canadian.

A central focus in my life is my religious faith. My parents and most who live in the province they come from are Roman Catholic. My faith has always been a basis for my attitudes, actions, and beliefs. With respect to sex and morality, the church dictates a lot in my life. This causes many nagging conflicts. I am, I feel, a little more open-minded than many of the older-generation Slovenians in my community. That is part of their general character, which comes from that deep-rooted faith they grew up with. The fact that I grew up with the many different viewpoints from my friends and their respective backgrounds means that I have a broader outlook. In conclusion, I can say that while I was born here in Canada, my roots are very much embedded in the Slovenian way of life.

Damian sees a difference between Canadian culture and Slovenian culture. But is the "hard work" that he perceives to be part of his Slovenian culture really so? Is hard work related to his "ethnic culture" or the immigrant values, expectations, and aspirations that his parents and members of that community have passed down to Damian? We know that immigrants come to a new country to better themselves and because of their determination to fulfill their immigrant dream of making it, they tend not to, to use Damian's words, "slack off" (see Chapter 6). Damian also mentions the role that his religious faith plays in his life. Yet he did not attribute his fast and hard work to his faith, but to his ethnicity; to his religious faith he attributed his moral values, attitudes, beliefs, convictions, and actions. But can the things he attributed to ethnic culture be separated from his religious culture? Are they mutually exclusive? Certainly not; so his approach or "attitude towards work" is not only mediated by his immigrant background, but by his religious beliefs as well. And the fact that Damian is able to "slack off" when he is in an "environment of long-time Canadians" is reflective of his Canadian existence and values—after all, he was born here and grew up here—which also help to foster his "more open-minded" views. The fact is, cultural values, attitudes, behaviours, and other attributes cannot be reduced to ethnicity alone, but are interconnected to other identifiers. Furthermore, Damian's construction of his Slovenian ethnic identity is one informed by his Canadian cultural life, and the decisions he makes in negotiating the conflicts, tensions, and contradictions he experiences as he seeks to be identified or accepted as a Slovenian.

We have established that for some people religious faith or spirituality is an integral part of the ethno-cultural identity and related value system, especially for individuals with orthodox affiliation. More generally, however, religious faith or spirituality cannot be reduced as only linked to ethnicity; it is linked to national origins as well. Religion, or more generally, spirituality, informs the morals, values, ideas, norms, and behaviours of societies and groups and their members. However, with the increase in secularization and religious diversity in many of today's societies, the influence of formal religion seem to be diminishing; yet its influence can still be felt and seen in the many practices that were established long ago and have now become cultural norms. In the following essay, Mark, a Jewish Canadian, explains the connection between his ethnic identification and the role of religion in his life.

> **Mark:** "Yes, I am Jewish. Is there anything wrong with that?" I cannot remember how many times I have said that sentence, but I know it has been far too often. I believe this problem arises because too many people classify others into groups based on their ethnic backgrounds ... I would not consider myself a religious individual, nor would I consider my family religious. As the generations progress, the emphasis on religion decreases. When I was young, I was given the opportunity to learn about my ancestors, my heritage, and my religion. My parents provided me with the guidance to learn what being Jewish is all about. I must admit I am glad to know my background, yet I feel I place little emphasis on it.
>
> Although I am not a religious person, nor do I come from a religious family, some attitudes and values remain of great importance to me. The one that stands out above the rest is to continue the Jewish religion by marrying within my own ethnic group. Even though my religion may not be of great importance to me, I believe it is important to keep the Jewish faith alive so that following generations may learn of their heritage as I did. By providing children with a definite religion at birth, they are able to know and understand where their ancestors came from. It is through this understanding that people are given a certain sense of belonging and are pointed in one direction. Because I am of the Jewish religion, that is the direction I hope my family will maintain, although I do not feel that my methods are superior to those of others.

Mark establishes that there is a definite link between his ethnic identity and religion—something he thinks is important for children to learn from birth. Implicit in this idea is that teaching children about religion will not only to ensure ongoing commitment to their religion or religious faith, but will also ensure that they develop the moral virtues needed to live honest and respectable lives in society—something that not only benefits their ethnic or religious group, but society as a whole.

Evidently, there is no clear link between ethnicity and religious affiliation. For instance, not all Italians are Roman Catholics, not all

Russians are Russian Orthodox, and not all Japanese are Buddhists. The variation in religious affiliation in any one ethnic group is illustrated in Bethlehem's story. Bethlehem identifies as Christian, but despite her obviously Christian-related name and because, as she says, she is a Black woman from the Horn of Africa—the region that includes Ethiopia, Sudan, Somalia, and Djibouti—she is often assumed to be Muslim.

Bethlehem: So, daily I must set aside my frustration with people's ignorance and clarify my identity for them, and these incidents seem to rise exponentially during religious holidays. For example, during Ramadhan—a Muslim religious observance during which believers fast during daylight hours—I'm asked almost daily, "Why are you eating? Aren't you supposed to be fasting?" not by strangers, but by friends or acquaintances because, of course, up until that moment, they had assumed I was Muslim. Or, during Christmas, I have had to be armed with witty responses to annoying questions like, "You don't celebrate Christmas, right?" I've been asked this question so often during Christmas—sometimes by the same people every year—that it's become an annual Christmas tradition.

In the post-9/11 context, I've experienced the continued general suspicion that accompanies being "Other" in the West, which could at any time be due to a specific aspect of my identity or my complete personal profile, depending on where I'm at and who I'm with. I suspect that I have not experienced overt Islamophobia though, not because it does not exist or that it's not overt but because I cannot be physically identified as a Muslim woman—definitively anyway—since I do not wear a hijab.

I am acutely aware, however, that when travelling outside of Canada I will likely be questioned, maybe even interrogated, because I'm Eritrean and presumed to be Muslim, and was born in Saudi Arabia—which further complicates my identity for Westerners. My Canadian citizenship will not save me from the barrage of questions aimed at resolving the discrepancy that is my racial identity, Black, and Saudi Arabian birthplace. I'll have to explain each and every time that my parents are Eritrean, and that I was born in Saudi Arabia because there was a war in my homeland … that forced my parents and many other Eritreans to take asylum in Middle Eastern countries. It must be noted though, that there are plenty of Black Saudi Arabians (who are considered nationals) who were brought over during the Arab slave trade centuries ago; so contrary to popular belief, it's not an oxymoron to have a Black Saudi Arabian.

To make matters even more confusing, I am not Saudi Arabian by nationality because I was denied status due to my racial and religious identity at birth … So, at this point, people either give up trying to apply their inflexible methods of reasoning to make sense of my identity and instead decide to let me name myself, or they hold on dearly to their frameworks of understanding and insist that I must be wrong, at which point I walk away. It's quite fascinating to witness the aggressive manner in which some people fight to keep others from realizing their right to name their own reality.

I've always thought identity to be a fluid and complex substance that cannot be contained or effectively understood using inflexible paradigms and/or partial definitions. Rather, identity is complicated by herstory, circumstances, choices, and lack thereof. My relationship with pervading systems of classification and marginalization has been one of resistance. I resist societal classifications and expectations in Babylon's spaces—as some of my friend's call it—and take refuge in the corners and pockets of resistance that exist in this city. And there, I breathe and rejuvenate and continue to refashion my values, my identity, and my reality according to how my friends and I believe this world can be.

Bethlehem explains that she understands identity to be "fluid and complex" and as such she seems to expect that people will accept her Christian identification without question. But her experience tells her otherwise; hence, she lives her life resisting the attempts to label her as Muslim. Interestingly, there are likely other "ethnic" Eritreans or Ethiopians who, like Bethlehem, live with a culture of resistance because of religion affiliation. But while theirs might be based on the fact that they are Muslim, Bethlehem's resistance is based on the fact that she is a Christian and has to assert herself and educate those who subscribe to homogeneity among ethnic groups. Clearly, as Bethlehem's story demonstrates, it is problematic to identify groups as static, homogenous, or singular.

A notable aspect of Bethlehem's experiences is how essentialism and racialization operate to affect her life as a minority Canadian. By racialization, we mean a process by which personality traits, behaviours, and social characteristics are ascribed to minority people because of their race, and are seen as permanent and inalterable (Tanovich 2009, 157). In such a context, as the following excerpt by Shakti illustrates, while gender is sometimes a contributing factor to differentiated experiences, it is difficult to disentangle gender from race. As Shakti's experience shows, this leaves her with questions.

Shakti: I struggled with feelings of "not belonging" and trying so hard to "fit in" but always falling short of my goal. I began to question whether this was because I was a South Asian, or a woman, or was it the combination of being an ethnic female. I always felt intimidated by some of the other students, and felt powerless to respond or defend myself, or complain to my teacher if something was bothering me. Could that have had anything to do with the fact that I am a female? My South Asian upbringing demanded that I unquestioningly accept whatever situation was presented to me. The expectation that I remain passive and quiet, as is expected of an Indian girl, ensured that I would not disturb the structural routines and expectations of the school system and home.

Shakti's feelings of intimidation, powerlessness—indeed, her overall experiences with trying to "fit in"—and hesitation to "defend herself" are all indeed related to her identities of race, ethnicity, and gender, as well as others, such as age and generation in Canada. All together they operate to influence Shakti's socialization, expectations, and experiences as a young South Asian female living in Canada. Obviously, given the complexity and interrelatedness of all identities, it is never clear which of the many identity characteristics is operating to affect your experiences.

Ethnicity, like race, is socially, politically, and historically constructed. It is dynamic, having meanings and interpretations that are constantly shifting and being shaped and reshaped over time in relation to expectations, experiences, and contexts. So there is no list of behaviours, attitudes, clothing, lifestyle, cuisines, art, music, family systems, values, sexual mores, religious beliefs or affiliations, etc. that can adequately distinguish people as members of particular ethnic groups. "Cultural features" as Marger and Obsermiller write, "are only symbolic ... [and] may disappear with little or no damage to the continuation of ethnicity" (cited in Elliott and Fleras 1992, 134). That is why individuals with two or more ethnic identities, especially given the fluidity and ambiguity of ethnicity, are able to identify with one or more depending on their experiences, family situation, and community in which they were brought up. However, individuals might identify mostly with the ethnicity of the parent, family, peers, or community group into which they were socialized by these significant others; or they may identify with or take on the ethnicity that seems acceptable or to which they are ascribed because of factors such as names (i.e., having a first or last name that indicates the ethnic group to which they belong or are presumed to belong). What is significant is how people define themselves and are defined by others. I remember chatting with a young man, Shane, who looked to me to be of mixed race or possibly Black. In our conversation, he said that he is "biracial" and identified as Italian. He revealed that he had grown up in an Italian community and spoke Italian fluently. He further stated that people often doubted his Italian heritage. However, it was the only one he "knew," since he grew up with his Italian mother and did not have much interaction with his Jamaican father. In the following section, we explore further the identification and experiences of mixed-race individuals.

MIXED RACE? BIRACIAL? HALF-BREED? OR SIMPLY CANADIAN?

We have already noted there is no uniform way in which individuals of mixed race or biracial background identify. On the one hand, Shane mentioned the ethnic background of his mother (Italian) and the national background of his father (Jamaican, implying Black), but he identifies as Italian without mentioning race as an identifier. Sefa, on the other hand, said that his "identity was far more influenced by being mixed-race/biracial/half-caste" than being Canadian and "feeling black and wanting to be seen as black" was more important to him. And Adebe (2008, referenced above) writes that "from personal experience, being mixed race is not simply an easy proclamation of challenging difference by claiming everything." In her experience, her "racial ambiguity" elicits questions about her origins, and an expectation that she chooses "an agreeable classification." She goes on to write that her "complex racial background" aside, what she would "really" like to say is: "I'm just from Toronto" (5).

Adebe D. A. and others argue, as we will see in the coming discussion, that they should not have to choose an identity. They wish to be recognized for the mixed-race persons they are. According to Parker and Song (2001), the term "refers to distinctive experiences which cannot be accommodated within existing frames of reference. These experiences may be too diverse to share a name for too long, too dynamic, and dispersed to hold still for sustained political action, but they are undoubtedly too important to dismiss" (17). Even so, the seeming weight of the demands for mixed-race individuals to account for their identity claims or to "choose" one identity, appear to inspire some to maintain their claims and use the questions about their identities as opportunities to "educate," as Vanier (introduced below) does. Some others insist on their "mixed-race" or "biracial" identity, and at the same time, also identify as Black (for those with Black parents) or gesture toward that identity to the extent that it is, as Laura Mae reveals below, echoing Sefa, "where I feel most comfortable, where I do not feel so different." In the following two essays, we meet Vanier (who titled her essay, "Coming Out") and Laura Mae, who present two different perspectives.

Vanier: My name is Vanier. I'm 5'2". I have short black hair, and dark brown eyes. I have a pale, glowing complexion, and I tan well in the summer. This is what my friends see when they meet me. When I meet someone new and we start to get to know each other, and they find out that I'm a visual arts student at university, they would ask what kind of courses I'm taking. I answer with my favourite course, the Art of Colonial America and Twentieth-Century Aboriginal Art. The conversation goes on; I learn about them. I'll probably end up talking about my favourite visual artists, Rebecca Bellmore, Gerald McMaster, and Kent Monkman.

If these friends are good friends they will soon end up meeting my mom. We'll sit around the kitchen as I introduce my mom to my friends. But most times my mom can't stay long because she has to go to a research meeting. "What's the research about?" my friends might ask my mom. "Aboriginal girls in Ontario," she answers. From here, perhaps they begin to notice the sweet grass sitting on the table, and the books by Thomas King, Janice Acoose, Ruth B. Phillips, and Charlotte Townsend-Gault. They start to put things together … Maybe they begin to notice the pronouns, we, us, ours. Later on they will ask me, "Vanessa, are you Aboriginal?" I smile and answer yes. That is usually how I come out as Aboriginal.

I don't tell people when I meet them. I don't tell them when they're coming over to my house, where it may become more obvious. I don't tell them when a group is discussing a land claim that has recently been in the news. I don't tell people unless they ask. Why don't I come out sooner, why do I always wait until asked? The reason is to avoid the questions that inevitably follow my "disclosure."

I described my physical appearance at the beginning; I don't look very Aboriginal but I claim the identity for myself. The next question: "So umm, how … like … umm how Aboriginal are you? I mean like … what…?" My response: "Both my maternal grandmother's parents were Aboriginal." Here I give people the benefit of the doubt. I don't think that they are questioning how I see myself; I don't see their question as a form of disbelief, even if that is how it feels. Instead what I think they are asking is, what does it mean to you, in your life, that you claim this identity? Sometimes, the answer that both my maternal grandmother's parents are Aboriginal is enough. Sometimes people are more interested. And they start to ask another question, along the lines of, "So both your mother's grandparents on your mother's side?" At this point I am quite nervous. I take the opportunity to explain some of the inner workings of the *Indian Act*. This is where they really get confused and amazed. "You mean your great-grandfather lost his status because he joined the army?" "Yep, you couldn't be a soldier and Aboriginal at the same time." I go on to list the multiple other reasons that Aboriginal people lost status [as Indians].

Of course, I am always sure to mention the part of the *Indian Act* that said when an [Indian] woman married a non-[Indian] man she immediately lost her status, but when an [Indian] man married a White woman, not only did he not lose his status, but the woman gained his status. In 1985, when Bill C-31 was introduced [which changed the Act], my grandmother and mother did get their status back. But here is the important part … because my maternal grandmother married a White man and my mother married a White man, in the governmental terms then, I am two generations removed and therefore don't have status [as an Indian]. I retreat to this answer almost every time I am asked this question, because it is the didactic answer, the impersonal answer, and it's a good opportunity to educate people on this little-known bit of Canadian history. Is this the answer that people want to hear? It's definitely not the answer they were expecting. But it's the only answer I know how to give.

Essentially, through the questioning of friends and acquaintances, I am dealing with two questions: the first, are you Aboriginal? and the second, how are you Aboriginal? As you can see from above I try and avoid both. Part of my trepidation in answering the questions comes from the plethora of misrepresentations of Aboriginal people. I feel that once I come out as Aboriginal, I then have a responsibility to disrupt those representations. If I answer [the question of] "how I am Aboriginal" with "Well, we sometimes go to powwows," what are they going to see? What are they going to assume? I can explain that I have been to powwows, but I can't explain what it feels like when I go. I can explain that I don't speak my language (Leni Lenape), but I can't explain what it means to me not to speak my language. I can tell you that I was the only person in my Grade 11 class to burst into tears when reading "The Tree" by Grey Owl, a story about the genocide of a group of Aboriginal people, and about the characters of the Indian Princess and the Noble Indian told from the perspective of the tree, but I can't say that it was necessarily because I am Aboriginal and the other students in the class weren't.

A few years ago a PhD student interviewed me. The interview was focused on my family history and my relationship to my family history. In the interview, I focused my answers on my maternal (Aboriginal) family history. The interviewer asked me about my paternal family history. I told her what I knew wasn't very much. The interviewer asked me why I knew more/took more interest in my Aboriginal history rather then my European history. I answered that I was unsure of why, but that it seemed more important.

I'm read as white. The history I was taught in school was a European-focused one. Identifying and being identified as the descendent of European immigrants in Canada takes no effort. It is passive. If I want to be identified, and to identify myself as a descendent of the Lanope and Pottawattamie people, I have to be an activist. I choose my classes, read my books, ask my questions, and listen to my stories as a way of actively claiming and being Aboriginal.

Laura Mae: Time and again, I have been asked, "What are you?" I am a person! I understand the need to categorize people; it would be the same if someone's sex appeared ambiguous. It is human nature to figure how similar or different a person is to you.

I have been blessed with the looks from my Polish Canadian mother and the colouring of my Bermudian (black) father. I say blessed, because I no longer have the fortune to look in my mother's eyes, but [I am] still able to see them in my own. Nevertheless, my blessing has been a curse as well. Biracial people, especially those who are black and white, seem to have developed their own race category. [Many] appear black, but perhaps their hair texture is softer and their skin is lighter, but there is no doubt they are black! But I present doubt! I have the texture of my mother's hair and my nose is not completely flat. Neither of those characteristics alone would be enough to make me ambiguous, but together: "What are you?"

Growing up, I was very lucky as most of my neighbourhood friends were mixed. Out of eight of us, only two were not. Some of us would talk about which race we preferred to be. Perhaps because of the time (Michael Jackson was at the peak of his career), we preferred to be black.

We all had white mothers who were, usually, the only parent in our lives. Yet we "rejected" our white heritage to a certain degree.

Since then, I have learned to accept myself for exactly what I am: a Polish-Bermudian Canadian. While I do not have a choice in my race, I lean towards the black community. It is where I feel most comfortable, where I do not feel so different.

Not until adulthood did I have a significant number of friends that were not black. Given this, as an adult, there are times I feel alienated among my white friends, especially when it comes [to] my choice [in] men. I have only dated black men. We have the most in common and I feel comfortable when I am with them. However, my choice in men seems to be of interest to people. Many times, I have been asked why I do not date men from other races. I find it curious, because I never think to ask my friends why they have not dated black men. It is an excellent retort to a brazen question. Yet, I choose not to make them "uncomfortable." I choose not to have them face the questions of race I face, sometimes daily.

Perhaps this is why I feel comfortable within the black community. Race will always be an issue for me. I will always be the "Other." For the most part, I am accepted in the black community. Nevertheless, there is still the initial impression or inquiring look when I speak to the black community: "What is she?" I am mixed!

I understand the struggles and joys of being a café-au-lait child of a white mother. I am ambiguous. I can choose the box in which I belong, even if that means choosing more than one box or none at all. Regardless, I am exactly who I want to be, despite the fact it took me twenty-eight years to reach this point.

In the following essay, Shane declares that it is not easy "being mixed in Toronto," for no matter how much he tries to avoid "labels," he is still stereotyped as Black based on his tanned skin tone, his dress, and his "enjoyment of both basketball and hip hop."[10]

Shane: Being mixed in Toronto isn't always the easiest thing. People here are extremely concerned with labels and feel it is necessary to place one on pretty much every person they encounter. Colour and ethnicity have a lot to do with this labelling process, and me being of both Italian and Jamaican descent complicates this usually straightforward labelling process for many people. Growing up, classmates would find it hard to acknowledge that I was technically neither white nor black and found comfort in simply labelling me as black because of my tanned skin tone as well as my enjoyment of both basketball and hip hop. While growing up, my "black" label was tested numerous times, a common example being that I did not always dress as a stereotypically "black" teen or talk using the latest hip hop slang (as many black kids in my high school did).

Throughout high school I would occasionally receive comments, such as "you're looking washed out today," meaning my appearance was more stereotypical of a white teen, than of the black one I was labelled as. Throughout Grades 9 to 11, I defiantly walked a "thin line" of either acting, dressing, or talking too black or too white and kids would be quick to remind me about this. However, by Grade 11 I learned to not let the "you're acting too black" or "you're dressing too white" comments bother me and I simply allowed kids to label me as they wished. I figured I'd just continue being "me" and let them worry about whether I'm more white or more black; surely this debate will continue until they can comfortably accept the fact that I'm neither completely white nor completely black, but mixed.

It's funny that even though I have "white" in me most people simply choose to treat me as if I didn't. There have been numerous cases where people have talked to me a certain way or treated me differently because of my skin. At university [in southwestern Ontario], it is not uncommon for many kids to talk to me differently than they talk to their other white friends, and for professors or TAs to assume that I am on a sports team (usually basketball or track and field). Even when I point out that I am half Italian, people still seem to only see the black and treat me accordingly.

Referring to himself as "biracial" (obviously, these term have particular meaning for these individuals), Andrew weighs in with some important insights into what it means to be the "source of endless fascination" for many who expect him to decide on one racial identity. He recounts the struggles he has had with members of society and his parents on issues of race.

Andrew: I am given multiple names, told I am tragic, and made to feel that I must choose to be either Black or white or exist somewhere in the centre, in the benign "happy medium." I am biracial and frustrated, because the pundits of mixed-race children, who are usually not mixed themselves, believe in such a thing as "having the best of both worlds." At the same time I would not be stupid and naive enough to say that I live with the "worst" of both worlds, although in many ways I find this reasoning to be the easiest to rationalize when both my "worlds"—Black and white—look at me as some sort of aberration in a society governed by what W. E. B. Du Bois called the "colour line."

My father is white, my mother is Black, and I am Black. For some, this logic doesn't make much sense—"You could pass for white, you know"—and it seriously troubles their minds, [such] that they want to probe my mind to find out how I cope with my fissure. Being seen as a "tragic mulatto" seems to be a perennial problem and a source of endless fascination for some white and Black folk, who want to ask, "Is it possible for mixed-race people to be Black?" It seems that there must be a designated camp that I must call home, to be Black or white, or is "bi" the answer? In a world of television talk show mentalities, I know that people want to ask, "Aren't you confused?" Of course I'd answer "yes," but who isn't in this world?

As a child, it is easy to take what you see for granted, so it didn't seem like such a big deal to have parents who were not the same colour. But there was something that I didn't understand until I started to seriously think about my father's world, the Eurocentric male one, presenting itself as the centre of all of that is correct and normal, and my mother's, as a sort of bastardization of the norm. Being a product of the centre and the periphery has a funny way of playing with your head, and there's definitely not enough love in the world to save you from that sort of trauma.

When growing up, I negotiated the world on the politically conservative white side and the liberal Black side. My mother—who I once cussed in public and called "nigger"—reminded me at one and the same time that I was not white, but to always remember that my father was white. In the past couple of years my mother's reminders have seemed to come more frequently as I speak more openly about the social and political lives of Black people. To me, her reminders are supposed to serve as some sort of inhibitor to expressing a part of me that I believe she has chosen to ignore.

My father, for the most part, chooses to remain silent on the issue of colour. Sometimes I'll receive a book or an article from him where the subject or author is a Black person, which is some sort of acknowledgment that I am, to some degree, Black. We have never had any open discussion about the politics of race or identity; it is not an area that I feel comfortable dealing with, so we just continue talking about jazz, Black athletes, and jerk chicken.

Some people who are biracial are caught in a sort of world cut in two, an either/or scenario about who they are, how they should be, and what they should do. I would be a hypocrite if I said that I have eclipsed this sort of difficulty in my navigation through the mazes of the white and Black worlds. However, it is necessary to understand that hybridity creates a new space, and I am a part of this space for which there is no set archetype. If I say I am Black, it does not mean that I am everything that is not white. It is, at the same time, so simple and so complex: I love that.

Andrew refers to himself as "being a product of the centre [white] and the periphery [Black]," a person whose racial ambiguity has contributed to his struggles to negotiate a racial identity in a society (Canada) that, as he puts it, quoting W. E. B. Du Bois, is governed by the "colour line." He proffers that he occupies a space of "hybridity ... for which there is no set archetype;" like other biracial/mixed-race people, he struggles to negotiate the difficulties between the white centre—with its social, economic, political, and cultural power —and the marginal world of Black people. And despite his angry, frustrating, and baffling confrontations with his parents, and in spite of his parents, Andrew says that he has come to terms with his "biracial" identity, something that neither his parents nor society has allowed him to live with comfortably.

Similarly, Julian recounts his experiences as a mixed-race young adult negotiating his identity between his Black mother and his white Jewish father, both of whom had much to say about his decision to "lock" his hair. Let us examine his constructed identity. Interestingly, Julian says what he is "typically referred to," but does not explicitly name how he refers to himself. He seems almost defensive, starting with and repeating that he is "very secure in his skin." This seeming defensiveness might not be due to an "identity crisis;" it might be due to him being denied, questioned, and challenged in his bid to live his identity as he wishes.

> **Julian:** First of all, let me establish the fact that I have no misconceptions or confusion in regards to who I am. Although, we are ever-evolving, I firmly believe that I have a very strong understanding of who I am and how I fit in this world. I am currently twenty-three years old. I am the son of a Jewish father and a Black mother. During slavery times, I would have been referred to as a mulatto, referring to the fact that I am the offspring of a white parent and a Black parent. Nowadays (in these presumably more enlightened times) I am typically referred to by the more politically correct terms "biracial" or "mixed." In any event, I simply want to first address that I have a firm grip and understanding of who I am as a person. I am very secure in my skin, and extremely proud of both my Black Canadian and Jewish ancestry. In the same vein, I am certainly not going through any sort of identity crisis due to the fact that I am the product of two different ethnic groups.
>
> I have recently made the decision to lock my hair. I am not intending to make any profound social or political statement. Nor is it an attempt to help me "get in touch" with my African ancestry. My decision to lock my hair is simply based on the fact that I have always admired the look from an aesthetic point of view.[11]

The interesting irony here is that while Julian suggests that "locking" his hair is simply for style, it is a style that would accentuate his Blackness. This can be seen as an example of the complexity of identity and the corresponding variation in cultural taste.

The final essay is that of Luis whose mixed-race identity is mediated by his experiences as a child of immigrant Portuguese-speaking Brazilian parents.

> **Luis:** The essence of a person comes from all of their distinct features, inherited by their ancestors. I am a mix of so many [ethnicities] that I have lost count. My mother is half Polish, and half German and French. My father's family is half Italian and half [indigenous South American] with Portuguese. To top it off they were born in Brazil, giving me one more

country to [add to] my family tree. I consider myself to be a typical Brazilian: tan skin completion, I listen to samba, and speak fluent Portuguese, [but] I've been raised in Canada since the age of two.

Throughout my life people have [had] a hard time believing that I am my mother's son. She is 5'7", blonde with blue eyes—not exactly a match. My sister is almost a clone of my mom. When I was around five years old, a boy saw her pushing me on the swings and asked me where my mother was. I did my best to explain, but he continued a little skeptical. What gets me annoyed is when I get treated differently than my mother or sister. When we go on family vacations outside of Toronto, my sister gets much more attention from sales clerks. I either get ignored, or constantly followed every step. However, I don't blame them; they may have met a person who had my traits that didn't represent my kind very well. My father has the same skin complexion as myself …

I have grown up in Canada, yet haven't really integrated into the culture. I listen to very little music sung in English, and have few real friends that aren't Brazilian … People sometimes call me an immigrant, and I answer back, "damn right." When I was ten years old I wanted to be a typical Canadian. I tried, by playing American football and imitating all of my school friends. However, I looked at the mirror one day, and noticed that as much as I did change I would always be me. My kryptonite of being Brazilian has also turned into my strength.

Although I have not become a full Canadian, I am aware of all the things Canada has done for me. I've gained a deeper understanding of other cultures that I would never have received anywhere else …

There are two certainties that I have in life; that I will die and that I'm Brazilian. Life has brought me to Canada, and taught me the greatest lessons. Appearances can be elusive, especially now that there have been so many mixes in race and culture. The world has become a sort of melting pot, which I am an example of.

Like Sefa, who said that Blackness gave him the sense of self and belonging that he needed, so to does Luis's Brazilian identity. Luis tells of listening more to non-English songs, having more Brazilian friends, and at the age of ten years wanting "to be a typical Canadian"—something that he tried to do because, given his "foreign look," he was not read as Canadian (because he was not white). He admits that in response to his experiences, he took a "striking back" stance, suggesting that "since I can't be Canadian, I might as well be a full Brazilian." But to complicate matters, and show that there is no essential way of being Brazilian, Luis also notes: "Unlike most Brazilians, my passion is for volleyball and not for soccer." However, in the above excerpt, Luis also mentions that he was treated differently compared to his sister, who looks more white. This issue of treatment due to colour difference is something that many mixed-race individuals experience (Taylor 2008). It is reflective of colour stratification, which is explored in studies by Margaret Hunter. With reference to the history of racism and biases around skin colour, Hunter (2005) showed that women and men with light skin, while not exempt from experiencing racism, often end up with more educational and occupational privileges than similarly located dark-skinned individuals. She also showed that beauty and notions of ethnic authenticity are bound up in questions of colour and skin tone.

Clearly, mixed-race or biracial identities are real, particularly in the experiences of individuals who identify as such, or are ascribed such identification. These identities are dynamic and their interpretation or meaning shifts as contexts and time bring new and additional experiences. For instance, in her study of the account of biracial women of African descent, France Winddance Twine (2000) found that their identities moved in and out of whiteness throughout their lives; those who grew up in white, middle-class neighborhoods identified as white while growing up, but started claimed non-white identities as they became adults. Their shifts to non-whiteness resulted from experiences in dating or as students at multiracial universities and through their social interactions with peers and co-workers. A number of the students in this chapter—Sefa, Shane, Andrew—also cited such shifts in identity. But a number of them also give accounts of the lack of space, recognition, and respect in Canadian society for their mixed-race or multiracial and ethnic identities, through their experiences with peers, teachers, and even parents.

Earlier, we discussed how the British Columbia Court of Appeal ruled that the interests of Elijah, the child of a white mother from Vancouver and a Black father from the United States, would be best served by living with his father. Here is what the Honourable Justice Madame Mary Newbury penned for the Appeal Court decision:

> [48] Finally, there are the matters of Elijah's race, or ethnicity, and the possibility of racial difficulties he may encounter in either family environment. These issues are not referred to specifically or otherwise in the Act, (cf. the Child, Family and Community Service Act, R.S.B.C. 1996, c. 46), but they are clearly relevant to the "paramount consideration" of the best interests of the child, in particular to his health and emotional well-being. As noted earlier in these Reasons, the trial judge referred to the "heritage and culture" of Elijah briefly, but reached no resolution because of what he regarded as the evenly balanced competing claims in this regard. Perhaps because of the sensitivity of racial and cultural factors, counsel made very little reference to these matters, although

Mrs. Edwards [wife of Mr. Edwards] was asked in cross-examination whether she agreed that Elijah's "heritage" was a "complicating issue" between the two parents. She replied that Ms. Van de Perre "couldn't teach him what it's going to be like to be black, and how he is going to be seen in the world as being black, so no, she couldn't teach him that. And reading books won't help." She continued:

> All I am saying is that Elijah should have an idea where he comes from, his background, his heritage, he should have that. He should have that fundamental. And I'm not sure if he's going to get that with Ms. Van de Perre.

[49] When Dr. Korpach (who had lived in North Carolina) was asked whether "in terms of social culture" living in the southern United States would be different from living in Vancouver, she noted the larger proportion of blacks in southern United States and opined that Elijah was likely to be regarded generally as a person of black race.

Particularly curious is the identification of Elijah both as a mixed-race and Black person at the same time. He was identified as a child from a "mixed-race relationship" by his mother's lawyers, and as a "black" child by his father, his father's wife, their lawyers, and the Appeal Court judges.[12] "Such double identification," writes Taylor et al.,

> speaks not only to the precariousness, complexity, and variation of race and racial identification, but also to the role that family, judges, and members of society play in assigning the place, station and/or location that individuals will likely come to occupy in the society. (2002, 154)

Minelle Mahtani (2002), a scholar on mixed-race identity, argues that the complexity of mixed-race people's identities is frequently overlooked in Canada because of our multiculturalism policy's claims of unity, inclusion, and respect for diversity, as well as the policy's over-focus on ethnic allegiance, its creation of dichotomies of Canadian versus non-Canadian, and the problematic sustaining of "hyphenated identities." As a consequence, identifying as "Canadian" within Canada, regardless of the country's racial and ethnic diversity, becomes impossible because "when one questions national borders, one also questions the boundary markers of race and ethnicity. As such, it has been repeatedly revealed that hegemonic national discourses are not kind to those who live within marginal spaces," such as mixed-race people who may be viewed as doubly different, doubly strange, and doubly foreign (Mahtani 2002, 20). Further, Lee and Lutz (2005) contend that

> white national ethnicity compels those of non-phenotypical "whiteness" to adopt hyphenation as a response to their ambivalent citizenship identity in white settler and colonizing nations. National identity formation is a flexible process that works to stabilize the nation by destabilizing those on the frontiers of the hyphen-blackness, -brownness, -redness and all the mixtures inside and between. (18)

In the context of Mahtani's and Lee and Lutz's assertions, in the following section, we explore further what some students had to say about what it means to be Canadian or to call to themselves Canadian.

BEING CANADIAN

With the exception of the white Canadians, the above essayists did not reference being Canadian as playing a significant role in their constructed cultural identities. In fact, Sefa and Luis specified that their race and birthplace, respectively, provided them that sense of identity and feelings of belonging. However, as Sophia reveals in the following essay, identifying as Canada is not simply a product of race, but likely a combination of race and ethnicity—and not just any ethnicity. For in the case of Sophia, being bilingual and born in Quebec to a French-Canadian mother seem not to be sufficient for her to be considered a French Canadian. Her story illustrates well the role of context and people in the construction of Canadian identity. In English Canada, she is perceived to be French Canadian, and in French Canada, she is seen as English. So she is left with "getting people to accept" her "multiple identities," which she believes makes her a "quintessential Canadian"—a similarity she believes she shares with many "Other" Canadians.

Sophia: The first time I was asked to identify myself was for a graduation book that my Grade 6 class was making to mark the end of the elementary school. Each student was told to write one page in which we had to identify ourselves, say who our friends were, what was most memorable about elementary school, and name the secondary school we would be going to the following year. This task proved to be difficult for me as I could not find a simple way of identifying myself, nor could I easily name the school that I would be attending the next year.

Several of my friends identified as "Quebecois, pure laine, 100%," but this identity did not suit me even though my parents and I were born in Quebec. I also did not identify as an immigrant or refugee, as most of my other friends did. I was neither French nor English; "Quebecois" nor "Canadien;" neither a German nor an Irish immigrant. I felt odd because I didn't belong in any one category. This feeling was compounded by the fact that the following year I would not be starting secondary school in Montreal; I was moving to Vancouver, where high school begins in Grade 8. I would, in essence, be repeating the rituals of finishing elementary school in a strange new place.

In the end, with the encouragement of my family, I identified myself by explaining the multiple identities, layered one on top of the other, that describe who I am. I wrote, "I am half German, one-quarter French Canadian, one-eighth Irish, and, possibly, one-sixteenth Aboriginal." To this day, I think this might be the best way for me to identify. In some respects this multi-layered identity appears to indicate a "quintessential Canadian." One might say, as many have, that here is a person whose identity fits perfectly in Canada's bilingual and multicultural identity! Yet, in reality, these so-called indicators of "Canadian-ness" are more acceptable on a Heritage Canada poster than they are in the minds of most Canadians. People often want to put me into a simple, recognizable category, but I categorically refuse.

I am not Quebecoise because that identity is bound with nationalist aspirations that I, as of yet, do not share. Also, in Quebec, I am always perceived as representing English Canadians, while in the rest of Canada I am perceived as being French Canadian. People have often told me, "We hate all Quebecers, except you, Sophia!" or "On déteste les Anglais, sauf toi, Sophia." Just a few months ago, a friend of twenty-two years identified me as an anglophone, even though we have communicated in French for the duration of our friendship. Somehow, by refusing to have one identity, I always represent the "Other." As if there were just one "Other" identity …

I think that many Canadians have a complex and fluid identity like my own; the problem is getting other people to accept you, and figuring out which boxes to fill on the census questionnaire. In recent years, I have come to identify as a "white," urban, bilingual French Canadian, with strong German and Irish immigrant stock. "Urban" is central to my identity because my culture and values are largely the product of growing up in Canada's three largest, multiracial, multi-ethnic, multilingual, and multicul-tural cities. Also, I now identify as "white," because even though race is a socially constructed category, my race has played a significant role in shaping my experiences and opportunities in this country. Explaining how I identify is not an easy task, but I am not convinced that explaining one's identity should be "easy."

Anita, for example, said that she felt a greater "sense of Canadian pride" and appreciation of her "Canadian-ness" when outside of Canada. Not surprisingly, she identifies herself as "Canadian," while giving significance to the fact that she is half Guyanese and half Dutch. She does not identify herself as mixed race, but infers that she is, because she is the daughter of a white, Dutch father and a mother who is described as being of "mixed-race descent."[13] Anita's constructed cultural identity represents not only the complexity of her identity, but the many identities that are to be found in individuals who identify as Canadians.

> **Anita:** I am born of immigrants—one from Guyana, South America, the other from the Netherlands—who left their respective home countries in the 1960s under tragic circumstances, and met in Toronto while pursuing higher education. Their parting of ways before my birth led to my being raised in a single-parent home by my mother and her family, all relatively fair-skinned women of mixed-race descent. Having inherited much of my father's DNA—skin colour being no exception—I am a green-eyed, white-skinned woman who often gets asked if I am Italian or Eastern European. Despite being half Guyanese and brought up surrounded by Guyanese culture, I have never once been asked if I am Guyanese, and have distinct memories from my teenage years of when people would ask me what I "was" (Toronto-talk for: "What is your ethnic background?"), and I would tell them; more often than not they wouldn't believe me.
>
> That said, I can't honestly say that I identify with being Guyanese (on a somewhat related aside, I [do not really] identify with being "White," although that is perhaps a whole other issue within itself). While I have travelled to Guyana several times, know some of the political and social history of the country, can tell you the taste of and difference between pepperpot and metemgee, cassava cakes and callaloo soup, garlic pork and souse, sugar cake and pine tarts, and butter flaps and pone, and can mimic the accent with surprising accuracy, I don't feel any sort of particular attachment to the country itself. It is the birthplace of my mother and my aunt and my grandmother and cousins. My ancestors lived there. My family is buried there. But it is not my home. My home is Canada. I am Canadian. I am at home in Canada. And proud of it. Although—am I really?

What we have observed in these stories of identification is that "difference"—particularly racial and ethnic difference—contributes to the kinds of experiences and social relations that affect individuals' development of a Canadian identity. The stories indicate that parents have a special role to play in assisting their children, whose difference is likely to contribute to their alienation from Canadian society due in part to experiences with stereotyping; for, as we have already observed, Canada is not a colour-blind society. We have already read about the experiences of mixed-race and biracial children; the experience of adopted African American children is also illustrative. In a 2005 episode of the CBS program, *60 Minutes*, on the search for adopted parents, it was presented that white Canadian people, particularly from British Columbia, were increasingly adopting African American children from the United

States—and were getting approved quickly, in a matter of a few weeks. Walter Gilbert, chief executive officer of The Open Door, argued that the adoption of Black American babies (in Canada and abroad) is a "win-win" situation for the children: "Especially in Canada, people are just colour-blind. That's been our experience. We would tend to tell them [birth mothers] that our experience has been there's less prejudice. They know what they experience here" (Leung 2005).

Yet the same program showed that the experiences of Canadian adoptive families contradict the characterization of Canada as colour-blind. One adoptive parent, Juanita Alexander, speaks of her experiences with her adopted Black son: "The first time we walked into school with Elias, the comment was made, 'Your basketball program just got a big shot in the arm.'" And as her husband, Dave, added: "The assumption is that he's got rhythm and he's a great musician." Interviewer Lesley Stahl asked the parents if they considered those comments to be racist. Juanita Alexander responded by saying: "We can't necessarily always blame them (their community members) for the comments, and the curiosity that they have, because, you know, families like ours aren't that terribly common here." Even so, as the program also revealed, these Canadian parents took steps to deal with the issue by doing such things as inviting Black adults to be mentors in their children's lives, sending their children to all-Black summer camps, and participating in support groups to educate themselves. It is in these ways, then, that Black children might develop the values, customs, and behaviour patterns that may perhaps help them to identify as Black. But there is no escaping the fact that such cultural attributes will be mediated by those of their white Canadian parents, who tend to be considered "real Canadians;" people who likely have never been questioned about their identity as Canadians. Can these children then be Black in the same way as the children raised by Black parents? In essence, the racializing and stereotyping of the Alexanders' Black son is reflective of the "biological" paradigm which holds, as noted earlier, that minority children will more likely present the inherited cultural identity and related behaviours and needs as their minority birth parents (Lal 2001).

This assumption was evidenced in the notable custody case of Elijah—a case discussed earlier in this chapter. We return to this case to draw attention to how the justices' ruling contributed to a construction of Canada, compared to the United State, as a country unable to provide "a less difficult" environment for the "healthy and emotional well-being" of a Canadian-born child of a Canadian mother. I again quote at length the writing of Honourable Justice Madame Mary Newbury of the Appeals

Court, because it is important to follow the articulation of the issues and the reasoning presented.

[50] If it is correct that Elijah will be seen by the world at large as "being black," it would obviously be in his interests to live with a parent or family who can nurture his identity as a person of colour and who can appreciate and understand the day-to-day realities that black people face in North American society—including discrimination and racism in various forms. It would certainly be naive to assume that Elijah would not encounter problems of racial prejudice at some point in his life in this country. The Supreme Court of Canada has found that there is: "systemic discrimination against black and aboriginal people" in Canada: see *R. v. R. D. S.* [1997] 3 S.C.A. 484 at 508; *R. v. Williams* [1998]1 S.C.R. 1128; and also *R. v. Parks* (1993) 84 C.C.C. (3d) 353 (Ont. C.A.). This fact makes it impossible to accept the argument made by Mr. Mansfield that there is no racism in Canada.

[51] It would also be naive to think that Elijah would not encounter racial prejudice growing up in the southern United States where Mr. and Mrs. Edwards plan to settle in the long term. However, it seems to me likely that being raised in an Afro-American family in a part of the world where the black population is proportionately greater than it is here, would to some extent be less difficult than it would be in Canada. Elijah would in this event have a greater chance of achieving a sense of cultural belonging and identity and would in his father have strong role model who has succeeded in the world of professional sports.

[52] Canadian courts have adverted to the interrelated factors of culture, ethnicity and race in the context of child custody, although with little analytical rigour. An early case of note is a decision of Mcintyre J. when in the Supreme Court of British Columbia, *Hayre v. Hayre* (1973) 11 A.F.L. 188 (app. dism'd at 21 R.F.L. 191). Reference may also be made to *Anderson v. Williams* [1988] A5 B.C.J. No. 1428 (QL) (B.C.S.C.); *White v. Matthews* [1997] N.S.J. No. 604 sel (N_S. Fam. Ct), and *Maier v. Chiao-Maier* [1990] S.J. No. 531 (Sask.Q.B.) I do not propose to try to introduce greater rigour through an extended analysis of the interrelated strands of culture, race and

racial prejudice in the case at bar. It is sufficient to say that these subjects should have been considered by the court below, and that they weigh in favour of Elijah's living with the Edwards. They are not, however, determinative. (*Van de Perre v. Edwards* 2000)

Interestingly, the court that took account of race, suggesting that racism and discrimination are likely "problems" that Elijah would encounter in Canada, ruled that "being black," Elijah's interests could be best served by him living in the United States with his Black father in a community where his reality would be understood. The other courts—the Supreme Courts of British Columbia and Canada—however, put aside race, seeming to suggest that Elijah's difference is not an issue in Canada. How could the courts view this so differently? What is implied when judges signal that Canada is not as conducive to the raising of a "Black" child as the United States? Is the United States more appropriate simply because of the number of Black people living there, so a "Black" child is better able to learn about "Blackness" among "his kind"? What might be inferred when Canadian-born children of colour are informed that their white parents, their community, and their society generally are incapable or unable to "protect" them from racism and discrimination and ensure their development of healthy identities and lives in Canada? Why put aside their "difference"? What then is citizenship or nationality worth?

Conceiving of race, race difference, and consequently, racism, as factors that affect the lives of Canadians, continues to be problematic, particularly for some members of society; hence, the tendency to overlook race, preferring instead to place emphasis on ethnicity, which is consistent with the multiculturalism discourse. And as Mahtani (2002) suggests, Canadian multiculturalism helps to create "hyphenated" cultural identities in which "one is seen as not solely 'Canadian' but 'Canadian and fill-in-your-ethnic-background'" (19). In the following section, we look at how this "hyphenation" operates in the lives of Canadians.[14]

TEJAL: "WHERE ARE YOU FROM?"

Born and raised in Toronto, I should technically be considered Canadian. I do not have a foreign accent or use a marked dialect. But what I do have is a brown complexion, with dark hair and brown eyes. I am always asked, "Where are you from?" For this question, I have no answer. If I say I was born in Canada, the next question is automatically, "No, but what's your background?" to which I have to answer that my parents are from India. This finally satisfies the questioner. To my surprise the question does not only come from the dominant ethnic group, but also from minority group people.

I remember I was working at the Bay about three years ago when a lady working at the perfume counter in front of me asked me where I was from. I gave her the usual answer, I was born in Toronto but my parents are from India, to which she answered, "Oh, that's why I noticed that you have an accent." I was thinking, "Hello, did I grow up in Toronto? I went to school in Toronto, I work with 'Canadians,' and she's telling ME that I have an accent." I was very insulted. How could this woman make such a remark? She explained to me that she used to work as an airline attendant and many of the trips that she made were to India and that's why she could pick up a slight accent from me. I have to say I was quite annoyed. For one, there are hundreds of different dialects in India, and all of those accents come out in various ways. What exactly is an Indian accent? Is it an Indian accent if the spoken word is coming out of an Indian (Southeast Asian)? And does this mean that all people that look Indian automatically have accents?

I am Indian: I have dark hair, brown skin, and brown eyes, and I take great offence at being presumed to be Sri Lankan, West Indian, and, yes, in some cases, even South American. I was raised in Canada, I wear "Canadian clothes," I speak English fluently without an accent, I follow Canadian laws, and am mostly affected by Canadian society. I watch English movies and listen to music that is produced in English. I wear Indian clothes when I am at home, go to weddings and other special events, and I prefer Indian food. I know the Canadian anthem and have no idea what the Indian anthem is. I know the Canadian political parties and who is the Canadian prime minister, and not who it is in India. I know Canadian history and learned only some very little bit about Indian history in summer school this year in Canada. I will never be Canadian though, and I will never blend into Canadian society the way in which those of European decent are able to. This is because of my physical features and nothing else; for to be Canadian means being white and Christian, neither of which I am.

I do not know what I am or where I fit in, because neither of the two societies will ever fully accept me. As is the dilemma of "half-breed" or "mulatto" people ... I do not fully belong to either society. I am not Indian, nor am I Canadian, but a little bit of both. To this day I do not know how to answer the question of who I am with a definite answer of either Indian or Canadian, because I will never fully be either. I do not feel fully Indian nor do I feel fully Canadian. Perhaps with the growing immigration and the growing diversity in Canadian society, non-whites may yet come to be seen as Canadian about a hundred years from now. Perhaps I will live to see my grandchildren accepted in Canadian society one day while they still retain their Indianness culturally and physically.

HYPHENATED CANADIANS

Some Canadians, largely ethnic and racial minorities and immigrants, will use both their ethnic origin (e.g., French, Irish, Dutch, Somali, Middle Eastern) and their citizenship or nationality (i.e., Canadian) to identify themselves. For these Canadians, their identity is hyphenated— they might be more or less of one than the other, or neither: meaning that they regard themselves as equally Canadian and whatever ethnic or racial identity they claim. Individuals constantly cross these categories in ways that prevent easy or simple identification or definitions. This sentiment is articulated by Katie in the following essay.

Katie: Racially, I am white. My ethnic background is Ukrainian. Three of my grandparents were born in the Ukraine. They immigrated to Canada in the years prior to World War I. My maternal grandmother was born in the United States, and her parents were born in the Ukraine. They moved to Canada from the United States at the turn of this century and were part of the group of Ukrainians involved in opening up the Canadian West.

Culturally, I consider myself to be a hyphenated Canadian: Ukrainian Canadian. My parents and my brother and I were all born and raised in Canada. We practice Ukrainian culture as it was passed on by my grandparents. In Canada, when someone asks me what ethnic group I belong to, I say Ukrainian. However, when outside of Canada, I consider myself a Canadian.

How have these backgrounds affected me? I take my white colour for granted since we live in a predominantly white society. I am only conscious of it if I am with a group of Blacks or Asians and I would be if I were to travel to a part of the world where there are few whites (e.g., Congo) or where it is an issue (e.g., South Africa.)

Canadian culture is more deeply ingrained in me as evidenced by the clothes I wear, the language I speak (English), and the everyday Canadian foods I eat. I have been influenced by the Canadian rat race for affluence and success and the possession of various material goods that are part of the "good Canadian life," such as a television, computer, a car, and furniture and so on. I use my Ukrainian culture as a reference point from which I can observe other cultures and look for similarities ... As a second-generation Ukrainian born in Canada, my family and I have assimilated well into Canadian society and, fortunately, no longer experience the discrimination that our great-grandparents did upon first arriving here...

I did not know until recently how much my Ukrainian Orthodox background influenced me. We did not attend church regularly except for Easter, and I left the Orthodox Church during my teen years. After attending different Protestant churches over the years, I decided to adopt the Anglican Church. Its liturgy more resembles that of the Orthodox Church, and it feels more like "home" to me. It was interesting to discover how much even my small church involvement in childhood influenced my current religious practices in an almost unconscious way. I celebrate our Ukrainian Christmas as well as December 25, and Ukrainian Easter with my family every year. There are many other Ukrainian influences [in my life], such as music, crafts, foods and other religious practices.

My cultural influences have made me more open to the differences in other cultures, especially European. I can feel more a part of them and assimilate a little more easily into Polish or Greek cultures, for example, whereas my WASP[15] friends feel more awkward and different in comparison. However, I do feel different when exposed to non-European cultures, such as [South Asian] or Central African and so on. I can understand why so many have immigrated to this country, especially when it has been for political and religious reasons.

Katie illustrates how both her ethnic identity (Ukrainian) informs her ideas, values, and practices within the Canadian environment, where she is also exposed to other ethnic groups and their cultures. She talks of practicing Ukrainian culture and at the same time says that she and her family "have assimilated well into Canada." If this is the case, how can she be practicing Ukrainian culture? Or is it a question of either/or? Individuals or families do not lose the cultures that they or their families came to Canada with—their cultures do not just dissipate and they are not replaced immediately by what we might want to think is a "Canadian culture." Indeed, some kind of assimilation process has taken place, as Katie's family would have had to adjust to life in Canada and over time it will be inculcated with the values, ideas, norms, and practices of the society. These new and sometimes different practices will be reflective of the reality of a Ukrainian in Canada or Ukrainian Canadian. We might think of the hyphen, then, as representing the interlocking ethnic and national identities or the bridging of her Ukrainian identity and her Canadian identity, constructed in a society with a mixture of ethnic groups that contribute to the Canadian culture she experiences every day and by which she lives.

In contrast to Katie, Sue-Anna writes about having parents who are more recent to Canada. Hence, the assimilation process is in the early stages, evidenced by language and cultural differences, which contribute to "feelings of resentment, and embarrassment about being Portuguese." But as she relates, visiting the birth country of her parents helped to instill in her an appreciation of her hyphenated Canadian identity. Furthermore, Sue-Anna's story illustrates that, while an individual might go to the society from which their parents or ancestors migrated, they are unlikely to identify fully with that place or the people of the culture— the same would apply to immigrants who "return" to their birthplace— for ultimately they are Canadian. As Sue-Anna put it: "In Portugal I did not feel completely Portuguese, because I wasn't like the local people."

She has to continue to think of herself as "Portuguese–Canadian," always having "Canadian tendencies along with my Portuguese mannerisms."

Sue-Anna: For most of my life, I have tried to understand what identity really means. As a child I was always confused about who I was. My parents were born in Portugal and moved to Canada when they were fourteen years old. They moved to Canada separately but eventually met and were soon married. My parents struggled to learn English and can speak it fluently, but they prefer to speak in their native tongue.

Growing up, we attended an all-Portuguese church and participated in Portuguese festivals. I always felt different than my schoolmates because while they brought peanut butter and jelly sandwiches for lunch, I usually brought some sort of fish or meat dish. I began to feel different from the rest of my friends in my early teens. Furthermore, I began to feel embarrassed about being Portuguese. I remember in high school a friend of mine called my house and my mother answered the phone. After speaking to my friend briefly, she handed me the phone. The first thing my friend asked me once I answered was, "Does your mom even speak English? Seriously, how long has she lived in Canada for?" At that moment I began to resent being Portuguese. I just wanted to be Canadian and have parents who didn't have an accent and could speak and write in English. For years I hated being Portuguese. I would often tell my parents this and they would be angry with me and could not understand why I didn't embrace their culture.

It wasn't until recently that my feelings of resentment turned into feelings of interest. Everything changed when I visited Portugal this past summer. I was a little nervous to speak Portuguese, because growing up I refused to speak another language besides English. I didn't want others to know that my parents weren't born in Canada, even though they were Canadian. The first few days in Lisbon were overwhelming because everywhere I turned, I could hear people speaking Portuguese and every bakery I visited had Portuguese food and desserts that reminded me of my childhood. My trip to Portugal made me understand my parents and it allowed me to appreciate how interesting their culture was. I wanted to embrace this new culture because for years I had distanced myself from every aspect of it. I no longer wanted to be Canadian, rather I wanted to be both Portuguese and Canadian.

After I returned home I talked about my trip to anyone who would listen. I talked about how friendly Portuguese people were, how beautiful the language was, and [about] the excellent food. However, when I was in Portugal I did not feel completely Portuguese, because I wasn't like the local people. Lisbon is a very laid-back city and being a North American, I wasn't used to the slow-paced environment. I wanted things done and I wanted them done quickly.

Cultural identity is a difficult concept because I do not identify myself as a Portuguese person, yet I do not fully identify with being a Canadian as well. I guess I like to think of myself as a Portuguese-Canadian. I will always have Canadian tendencies along with my Portuguese mannerisms. I'm fortunate because I get the best of both cultures because being Portuguese has made me identify with other cultures. When I watch films or read books with European characters, I can identify with them because there are so many cultures and countries that are similar to Portugal. However, being Canadian has made me accepting of other cultures and religions as well. I think being Portuguese and Canadian is a perfect combination. Although I cannot fully identify with either, I am lucky to be a part of both.

In Chapter 6, we will discuss the assimilation or acculturation process of all immigrants. Katie and Sue-Anna indicate the assimilation process of their families. One point that is worth mentioning before ending this discussion is: What happens when hyphenated Canadians "return" to their country of origin? Do they lose the hyphen? My friend Lois is an interesting case. In Canada, Lois considered herself a "TrinCan"— Trinidadian Canadian. And now that she has returned to live in Trinidad after living in Canada for more than for thirty years, she would like to consider herself as Trinidadian. But, as she explained, her values, expectations, behaviours, and speech patterns mark her as foreign, or "not from here." Given her differences, her friends see her as "Canadian." In terms of her use of words, she pointed out that in Trinidad New Year's Eve is referred to as "Old Year's Day." When she uses the term New Year's Eve, she is immediately asked, "Oh, you're not from here. Where are you from?" Evidently, that sense of Canadian-ness does not really go away. She tells of missing Thanksgiving and the other traditions that marked her Canadian life. So even though Lois was born and grew up in Trinidad, she is no longer Trinidadian or "Trini" (as the people refer to themselves). While members of a particular diaspora may believe that they are able to return or "go back home," the reality is that they can return to the geographic space that was once their physical and emotional home, but the place they left behind changed and developed without their experiencing it, and they too have changed along with their cultural identities.

Conclusion

In this chapter, we explored cultural identities in terms of how individuals see themselves, how others see them, and how they negotiate and navigate the challenges of living and surviving in a society structured by unequal relations of power and concomitantly unhelpful constructions of ethnic and racial minority groups. While individuals exercise agency in terms of their constructions of identities, often these identities are based not only on individuals' preferences or experiences, but also on how others construct, identify, or categorize a person or group. Critics have argued against categorizing people by race and ethnicity because doing so often leads to essentialism. While this can be true, the problem of naming and categorizing individuals does not detract from the fact that people are categorized and categorize others as a way of making sense of the world, as well as to control the large amount of information or stimulation that they have to process. Also, particularly for minority members of society, claiming a particular identity can serve as a means of gaining (or providing) stability, comfort, and camaraderie, thereby mediating or counteracting the negativity and alienation they experience in society. Nevertheless, the fact remains that the degree to which individuals identify with a particular ethnic, racial, or national group (or a particular heritage) varies depending on their place of birth, social class, abilities, educational, occupational, generational status, interactions with members and non-members of their group and their willingness of adapt to the dominant cultural norms.

We have observed that in making sense of their own and others' complex, multiple, ambiguous, inconsistent, and sometimes contradictory existence, individuals usually resort to categorizing. In doing so, particular signifiers are employed. The problem, it would seem, is not so much categorization or essentialism or the use of signifiers such as skin colour, race, ethnicity, or physical appearance to construct themselves or others as different. Rather, the problem seems to be what individuals do with the signifiers and "difference" in a society where categorization is prevalent and inescapable.

NOTES

1. It is important to remember that the student excerpts in this text are individual accounts and therefore cannot be generalized to others, not even to those of similar ethnic and racial backgrounds.

2. Todorov (1993) notes that in 1684 François Bernier of France was one of those who "first used the word 'race' in its modern sense" (96). But it was Carl Linnaeus who, in his seminal work on biological classification *Systema Naturae* (1740), classified human beings in terms of *Europaeus albus* (white), *Americanus rubescens* (red), *Asiaticus fuscus* (yellow), and *Africans niger* (black). Later, in the nineteenth century, Gustave LeBon equated the human races to animal species using "anatomical characteristics such as the colour of the skin, and the shape and volume of the skull" (Todorov 1993, 107). Based on "civilization" and "culture," European being the norm, LeBon also placed human beings in a hierarchy in the order of white, yellow, black, and red (Todorov 1993). See also Satzewich's (1998) discussion of race, racism, and racialization.

3. On the question of the biological basis of race, scientists agree that, while genetic variations between human beings do exist, these variations do not occur cleanly along racial lines. In fact, as Spice (2002) writes, "scientists calculate that there is an average genetic variation that occurs within racial groups. That's why most scientists say race is a social construct, not a biological one. In other words, social rules determine what races are and what they mean" (3). Because cultural groups have been passing their genes on to their children in relative isolation (either physical or social) for most of human

history, today certain genes—such as the genes for some diseases—are more common in some groups than in others. Research into population genetics—or the frequency and distribution of genes—and the role such research plays in public health is often reported in the media in terms of "race." However, population genetics should not be confused with a scientific definition of race, and in fact many of the correlations between "race" and health or well-being found in our society have recently been attributed to social and cultural factors. For example, it is now understood that in the case of African Americans, the stress of living in a racist society (as discussed in Chapter 7), combined with low socio-economic status (which often results in a poor diet), strenuous working conditions, and lack of access to health care will negatively affect their well-being, leading to higher rates of conditions such as heart disease.

4. It is only in recent times that we have begun to use the term "brown," particularly in Toronto, to refer to people of South Asian origin. In the United Kingdom, South Asians are sometimes referred to as Black; and in the United States, brown often refers to Latin Americans. In his book, *Brown: The Last Discovery of America* (2002), Richard Rodriguez, an American writer of Mexican origin, uses the colour brown as a metaphor for in-between states of being—a mixture of racial and ethnic identities.

5. Schwalbe (2005) writes:

> Just as some people think they can see race when they see a person's skin, others think they can see gender when they see an infant's genitals. "Ah, this one has a penis—it's a boy. And this one, with a vagina, is a girl," people say. But it is a mistake to equate genitalia with gender. While penises and vaginas are plainly part of human bodies, gender is something that humans must be taught … If we did not assign the meanings we do to penises and vaginas, if we did not have the cultural habits of treating the possessors of these organs differently, we would not produce girls and boys, women and men. Such creatures are the results of many people embracing and acting on similar ideas. Other ideas and behaviors would produce different kinds of people. Men and women, as we know them, are just one set of possibilities. (23)

6. In a 2005 feature story in the *Globe and Mail*, Carolyn Abraham discusses the scientific community's understanding and application of race in research and its broader implications. She notes that scientists are attempting to scientifically understand "race" in order to explain a variety of phenomena, in particular medical needs, and as a result find out ways to develop drugs for certain ethnic and racial groups. Doing so, she argues, needs "careful consideration and communication" in order not to "set race relations back decades" (*Globe and Mail*, June 20, 2005, F1).

7. The study in question analyzed saliva swabs of each person, looking at the mitochondrial DNA (mtDNA) that is passed down by the maternal line and the Y chromosome passed through the paternal line. With minor mutations, both show in which parts of the world a person's ancestors originated. It is said that these only tell one twenty-third of a person's genetic story, since there are twenty-three chromosomal pairs in each person's cellular DNA (see Salek 2007; also Bamshad and Olson 2003). For example, consider that examining only a man's Y chromosome effectively ignores the origins of all the female ancestors on the paternal side, as well as the male ancestors of those female ancestors, all of which have contributed in some way to the man's chromosomal makeup.

8. Lewontin (2002) observes that gene frequencies of the Kikuyu and Masaai—East African neighbours—and the Japanese are all different, and "although the extent of the differences might be less in one case than in the other, it is only a matter of degree. This means that the *social* and *historical* definitions of race that put the two East African tribes in the same 'race,' but put the Japanese in a different 'race,' were purely arbitrary" (2). Geographic proximity also contributes to the arbitrary designations of race.

9. Taylor et al. (2007) also make the point that the federal Supreme Court justices' decision was certainly not colour-blind in and of itself, for "in their reluctance to address difference," they ignored "the fundamental issues of subordination" related to race and racism that the justices of the earlier courts ruled were not "detractor factors" (153).

10. That Shane is seen as Black is reflective of the notion of hypo-descent, originating in the United States where it was often known as the "one-drop rule," meaning that a single drop of "Black blood" makes a person Black. It is also known as the "one black ancestor rule" and some American courts called it the "traceable amount rule." But anthropologists call it the "hypo-descent rule," meaning that racially mixed persons are assigned the status of the subordinate group. This concept of hypo-descent emerged from the American south, beginning in the early colonial period to become the nation's definition, generally accepted by whites and Blacks (Davis 1991).

11. Locks, also known as dreadlocks or dreads, is a hairstyle common among Black people.

12. See note 10.

13. This is somewhat common in Guyana, a former British colony on the South American continent, which, like Canada, is a multiracial and multi-ethnic society made up of migrant settlers from Europe, Africa, India, the Middle East, and other areas.

14. The term "hyphenated Canadian" refers to a person who identifies his or her ethnic origin as Canadian, along with the ethnic origin of his or her ancestors, for example, Chinese Canadian. (Commonly—and throughout this book—these references are symbolically, but not actually, hyphenated.)

15. See Chapter 6, note 17.

CHAPTER 4

GRAPPLING WITH FAMILIAL AND SOCIAL INFLUENCES ON IDENTITY

In this chapter, we will orient the discussion of identity to explore how the culture of society—as communicated through family, educational, and community institutions—structures our identities, values, attitudes, behaviours, and so on. Identity and culture are not merely individual or family matters. Our discussion thus far has made evident the role played by family, peer group, community members, and educational personnel in the social construction of cultural identity. In their comments and essays students often indicate that from childhood to adulthood they were constantly negotiating their sense of identity—racial, ethnic, or otherwise—in relation to the responses and information they were obtaining from their parents, siblings, peers, teachers, communities, and society at large. Particularly significant in the process of identification are the growing-up years, when individuals are trying to make sense of their relationships with those around them, and with the society whose social, educational, economic, and political structures they must navigate. As the comments and essays in the previous chapter indicate, and as we will see in this chapter, individuals have at times been enabled, frustrated, or even in some cases, inhibited by the structures that both collectively and individually—separately and simultaneously—produce these varying results. This speaks to the complexity, fluidity, and dynamism of the relationships that do and can exist among individuals.

In this text, individuals' reflections on their families, the neighbourhoods or communities in which they were raised, the schools they attended, and the peer groups with which they associate are used to further examine the role played by these various socializing agents. In doing so, we will demonstrate that the contexts in which individuals have lived their early lives speak, to a considerable degree, to what they have become, to the social selves that emerge, and to the identities they construct. This is why, when students were asked to write about how ethnic and racial identities might explain their values, ideas, aspirations, and sense of place (or "belonging," in terms of identifying with Canada as "home"), they wrote about their years of growing up in Canada.

The first section of this chapter sets out the interrelationship between the varied levels and elements of influence; see **Figure 4.1** for a theoretical model of this interrelationship. The second and third sections are students' accounts of the role of their families, communities, and schooling on their growing-up years. The fourth section presents students' experiences of trying to fit in during these years, and beyond. For some, these experiences were attempts to fit into a society that continually constructed them as "outsiders," while demanding that they adapt, integrate, and become "Canadian." For others, these experiences meant fitting in in order to take advantage of available opportunities. As indicated in Chapter 1, the essays are mainly those I received from students for this and the previous editions of *Seeing Ourselves*. That is to say, the essays represent the experiences and thoughts of students over the past ten years. I reference the essays of some earlier contributors, as they provide useful and additional information or insights that help to set a context for our appreciation and understanding of some of the more recent and younger contributors.

FACTORS THAT INFLUENCE HUMAN BEHAVIOUR

Figure 2.1 in Chapter 2 (page 24) demonstrates the factors that contribute to an individual's cultural identity. In Chapter 3, we explored the various ways in which race and ethnicity, among other factors, contribute to the ways in which individuals construct their identities. But this process of construction, as noted earlier, is also informed and influenced by socializing agents, contexts, and events—as shown in **Figure 4.1**—which are navigated and negotiated at all levels of an individual's life cycle. Specifically, **Figure 4.1** portrays an individual existing in relation to various socializing agents. These agents operate within the contexts of communities, society, and a world predicated on particular ideologies, values, and expectations. All of these elements collectively structure an individual's sense of self, and of his or her possibilities and limitations within society.

Furthermore, within these contexts, historical and contemporary structures and events affect individuals and groups differently—in terms

FIGURE 4.1 – FACTORS THAT SHAPE HUMAN BEHAVIOUR

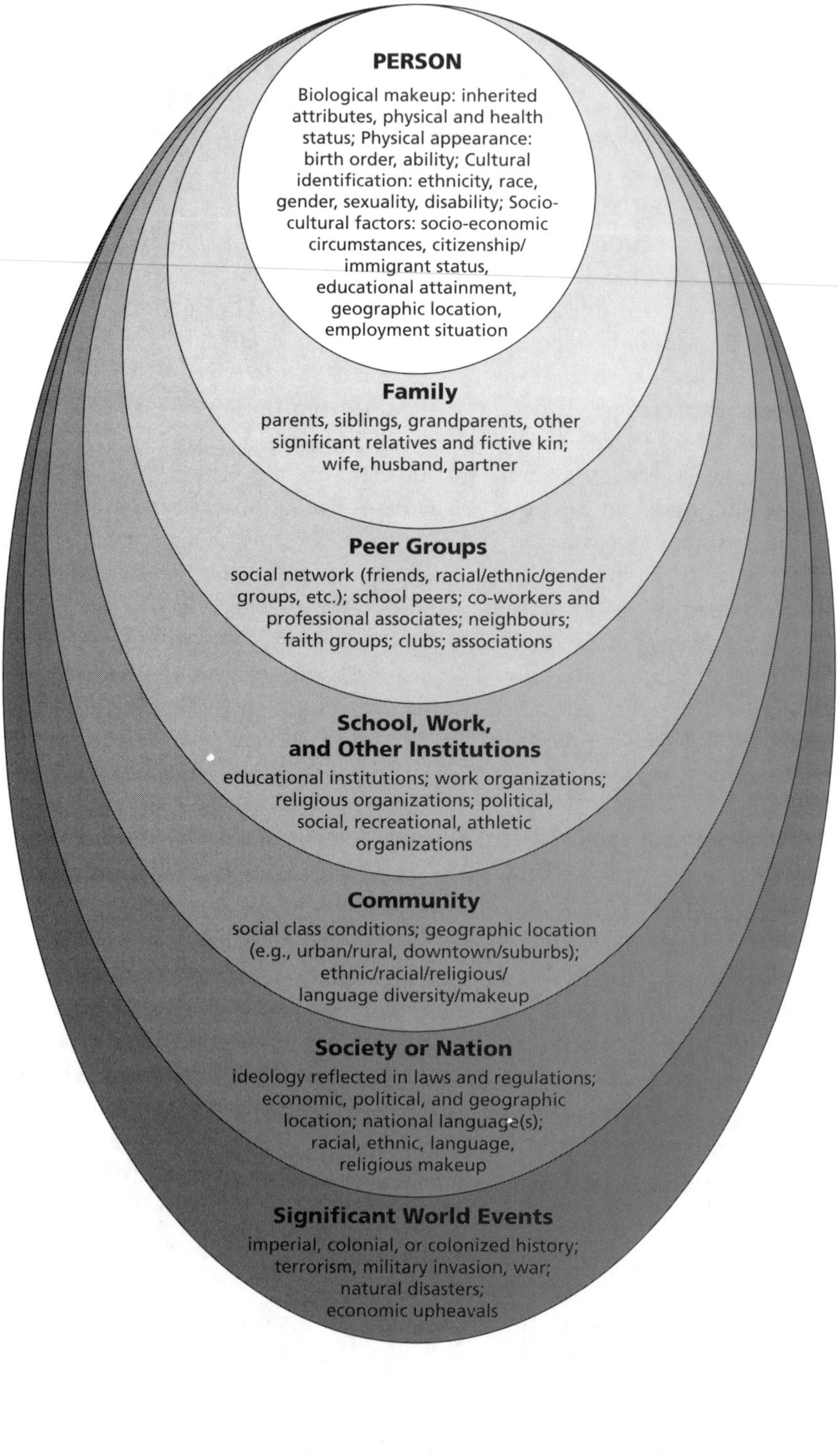

PERSON

Biological makeup: inherited attributes, physical and health status; Physical appearance: birth order, ability; Cultural identification: ethnicity, race, gender, sexuality, disability; Socio-cultural factors: socio-economic circumstances, citizenship/immigrant status, educational attainment, geographic location, employment situation

Family

parents, siblings, grandparents, other significant relatives and fictive kin; wife, husband, partner

Peer Groups

social network (friends, racial/ethnic/gender groups, etc.); school peers; co-workers and professional associates; neighbours; faith groups; clubs; associations

School, Work, and Other Institutions

educational institutions; work organizations; religious organizations; political, social, recreational, athletic organizations

Community

social class conditions; geographic location (e.g., urban/rural, downtown/suburbs); ethnic/racial/religious/language diversity/makeup

Society or Nation

ideology reflected in laws and regulations; economic, political, and geographic location; national language(s); racial, ethnic, language, religious makeup

Significant World Events

imperial, colonial, or colonized history; terrorism, military invasion, war; natural disasters; economic upheavals of factors such as social class, race, ethnicity, gender, and language—and contribute to the situations, conditions, or circumstances in which people find themselves and in which they must exercise agency.

GROWING UP: THE ROLE OF FAMILY AND COMMUNITY

While not asked to do so, student writers in this identity exercise often identify where they were born and then proceed to explore the role and significance of their peers and early neighbourhoods in their understanding of themselves as racial and ethnic persons. They talk about their family lives and values, their parents' aspirations for them, and how their parents attempted to pass on their cultural values. Evident in their stories are the issues, tensions, and conflicts with which they struggled during the process of coming to recognize their raced and ethnic selves and the corresponding privileges or lack thereof. Often missing from their accounts is the role that school played in helping them to understand their respective situations and deal with challenges. It seems regrettably true, as Peggy McIntosh (1995) has pointed out, that these young people did not receive schooling that helped them make sense of their own and others' privileges or, alternatively, their own oppressive experiences and those of others.

We'll begin with the stories of John, who "was born in Toronto, Ontario, to a mother of English nationality and a father of Canadian nationality," and Sarah, who identified as "Jewish" and "was born in Montreal, Quebec," like her parents, whose own parents (Sarah's grandparents), were "from Russia, Poland, and Romania."

Unlike Sarah, John simply mentions the birthplace and ethnicity of his parents without explicitly stating his own.

John: My mother's ethnicity is English. My father is of Scottish and Irish heritage, so my roots are completely centred in the British Isles. These roots and the values, ideas, thoughts, and beliefs passed on to me from my ancestors have helped to shape me into the person that I am now.

John also mentions that he "was raised in a predominantly white neighbourhood" with "one Japanese family and one Black family," both of which were "Canadianized" and were considered to be merely different-coloured white families." This was because they "spoke English without a trace of accent, were involved in all the community affairs and functions, and therefore did not pose a threat to the conservative, upper-middle-class lifestyle." John goes on to suggest that if they had "spoken differently or exposed their racial or ethnic rituals publicly, I believe that they would not have been so readily accepted." John also illustrates the contradictory message that he received from his parents and neighbours about race:

When a Black family moved onto his street, his parents and neighbours reacted with "there goes the neighbour[hood]"—a common lament during the social and economic changes of the 1970s. Nevertheless, the contradiction was not lost on John; after noting that there was a firm belief that "more Black families would soon follow, and the area would be considered undesirable," he went on to say: "Although my parents were raising me to believe that God loves everyone, that racial minorities had suffered great hardships, and that we must try to understand them, it still wasn't right that they were moving into our neighbourhood."

John said that he started to break away from the beliefs and values instilled in him by his parents after an experience he had at a party when he was fifteen. At the party he met "a young South African boy at school" with whom who became "inseparable" friends. Interestingly, John wrote that although his best friend's skin was "much darker" than his, he "wasn't white" until he attended a family party with his friend.

> **John:** I was the only non-African attending, and I felt like I glowed in the dark. Suddenly all the jokes … I had heard (and told) in school, all the prejudices I had acquired from family cocktail parties and all the snide remarks I had heard about "undesirables" came crashing down and confronted me. These people were friendly, polite, funny, and, most of all, caring. I enjoyed their company and they enjoyed mine.

And yet, despite the positive relationships and learning, John admitted that he is still affected by stereotypes he was exposed to when he was young.

> **John:** I still find myself occasionally thrown back to my upbringing and the ideas to which I was exposed when I was young. One example is the night in Los Angeles when I broke into a cold sweat after I was asked the time by two young Black men on a deserted street. My old stereotypes came racing back, and I had to deal with them instantaneously. Another example is the time I knew I had won a job only because I was white, male, and of British heritage. I felt a certain smugness in feeling that I belonged, rather than that I deserved the job. This situation again illustrated to me how deeply I had been influenced by my racial and ethnic origins and how, although my heritage is important to me, it is not necessarily the best, but merely one of many.

John's story illustrates that individuals do not necessarily always forget the messages, or unlearn the stereotyping they learn in their early years; hence, they have to constantly work at maintaining an anti-racism perspective. John's story also demonstrates the extent to which his identity as a white person is tied to that of racialized "others" or racial minorities, a phenomenon explained by Lund and Carr (2007) and

Weis and Fine (1996). It appears that it is only through these encounters with the "other" that John is able to talk of a racial identity; but in his conclusion, he asserts that his heritage is "merely one of many." Might this be an attempt to retreat to his "raceless" cocoon, so that he does not continue to "see" his privileges?[1]

Sarah, on the other hand, illustrates how her white identity is mediated by her Jewish identity. She was "surrounded" until the age of thirteen by her "grandparents and two sets of great-grandparents." And while she did not learn to speak Yiddish—the language spoken at home—she did have an understanding of it, particularly "the Yiddish humour," which she says, "was an important part of my life." Sarah was "exposed to the French language and culture," but "regretfully" she did not learn the language. According to Sarah, being white meant that she was "easily accepted and not subjected to prejudicial stereotyping," although her Eastern European background sometimes resulted in people changing their attitudes toward her. However, she suggested that being a white person in Canada made her feel "confident and comfortable."

Reflecting on her Jewish ethnicity, Sarah wrote:

> **Sarah**: My ethnicity is Jewish, and this plays a very strong and important role in my life. Family ties have always been strong. I was brought up in a large extended family ... Perhaps this bond is the result of the years of persecution in other lands, which forced Jews to realize that the only real thing that mattered was the family. We could lose our homes and possessions—they could be replaced. But our families couldn't be replaced...
>
> As a Jew, I have had to live with anti-Semitism. I must face the incomprehensible fact that six million Jews were slaughtered by Hitler simply because they were Jewish ... My behaviour is also greatly affected by Judaism. I celebrate all Jewish holidays. I believe this is a link to the past and to the future...
>
> My cultural background is Canadian. As a Canadian, I value my freedom. I can choose which neighbourhood I live in, which school I attend, and where I work. I am also free to practice my religion. As I have previously stated, there are discrimination and prejudices in Canada, but we have a legal system to protect us. I consider myself to be a very proud Canadian, but one who will always treasure my unique ethnicity.

Sarah's story is illustrative of the negotiation of a white identity and how her corresponding privileges were mediated by her Jewish ethnicity and related minority status, which in turn helped to shape her experiences, encounters, and opportunities. Sarah's story also illuminates the role that language (in her case, Yiddish) and the presence of grandparents play in helping to build strong family ties and relationship to community.

These ties contributed to her understanding of herself, her identity, and her strong sense of Canadianness. And yet Sarah's beliefs, practices, and identity also suggest that, while there are commonalities and overlap with other individuals, there is never "one" way of being white, or in Sarah's case, Jewish, or any other identity.

In what follows, we look at what Michelle, Hillary, and Ayanna have to say about the role and influence of their parents and their respective communities in structuring their racial and ethnic identities. A significant issue for Michelle is coming to appreciate her Aboriginal heritage; for Hillary, it is growing up as a Black child with white adoptive parents; and for Ayanna, it is having to negotiate the cultural values and expectations of her parents and ethnic community. All three tell of the struggles they experienced growing up as racialized individuals with parents and in communities who did not fully understand their situations.

Michelle describes her mixed heritage, and how it influenced her childhood experiences.

Michelle: My name is Michelle Green. I am the daughter of a Jamaican man and a First Nations woman. My name itself tells the story of slavery and massacre. Green, I believe, was my [ancestor's] slave master's name, and Michelle reflects the influence the French had on the Cree nations of Saskatchewan. Nonetheless, I take great pride in this name, as it reminds me of who I am and where I come from. My people (both Black and Native) have come a long way, and to this very day we struggle for equal opportunity and equal justice...

I was an ignorant child. As I grew up living separately from my mother, I did not really understand where she was from. I visited her only two times a year, and when I saw her, she appeared white to me. My father would tell me that she was a Métis Indian and that the reason she was so light in complexion was because her father was French. All this Indian "stuff" made no sense to me. I dared not admit that my mother was Indian; it was bad enough that I was Black. I was not even sure what an Indian was. Was she the Indian that I saw in the old western movies? Or was she the Indian that so many made fun of at school and called such names as "Paki" and "Coolie"? I did not really care which Indian she was. I decided that she looked white, and that is what I told everyone. For many years I was happy with this story. Some people actually thought I was special or unique—or so I believed...

I began school in Toronto, where my family and I lived for a short period of time ... Then we moved to [a suburb west of Toronto], where I had to make quite an adjustment ... In Toronto, there had been all kinds of people ... [My new home] was very different from this. It seemed like a whole new world. For the first time, I think, I began to feel different—I felt isolated.

This new community (environment) my family and I became a part of was predominantly European … and consisted most of middle-class people. These factors alone affected my perception of the world; coming as I had from a poor working-class environment where we had been surrounded by government housing and high-rise buildings. I was just not ready for new "habitat." Unlike the friendly, warm community that I had been forced to leave behind, the people [in this new community] were very private, and they all seemed to share an agenda that was in many respects different from those in my old community. I was immersed in a totally different cultural setting…

[Everyone] shared a common language or dialect, they acted the same, they even began to look the same! I could not figure out where exactly I fit in. Thus, I yearned to be just like "them." My desire to become a part of this community was so great that I became two different people. At home I lived through cultural expressions that had been "handed down" to me from my parents. However, when I was outside of my home I expressed the adopted culture that was dominant in my community. I saw that my parents were also doing this. For example, at home my father spoke with a very strong Jamaican accent, but when dealing with people on the "outside," his language became "distorted" (it sounded strange, unreal). He tried very hard to sound "proper." In fact, several times he commented on my own "broken" English. "Speak properly!" he demanded…

As I was raised in a Caribbean social environment, I seem to have taken on more of a Black identity than a Native one. This is not to say that my Native identity is less important to me (in fact, this year I am taking a Native history course), I am only saying that I can more easily identify with the [Black] culture. I do not, however, disregard the Native in me, as its spirit has shown me good things about the way one should live. Most importantly, though, I struggled with my identity, and it took me years to figure out where I belong.

In the section that follows, we look at what Michelle has to say about her schooling and its impact on her experiences growing up as an Aboriginal-Black person. For now, we turn our attention to Hillary as she tells about her of sense of exclusion, belonging or non-belonging, and growing up as a Black child raised by white adoptive parents in largely white communities. She writes of how her family and community played a significant role in shaping her identity and influenced her now close relationship with Black cultural expression. But at the same time, her movement to appreciate and understand her "Blackness" is framed in a way that refuses to exclude her white family, which she loves.

Hillary: To my knowledge, I was born in Montreal, Canada, and was adopted by a white couple while I was an infant. As far back as I can recall,

I noticed the difference between my family and myself. I was Black, they were white—it was an obvious difference.

In our neighbourhood—which was white and French—it was a setback to be English, and having a Black child living among a white family, willingly, was a major strike. There was no worse a household could do, it seemed. My family endured black cats in our swimming pool, broken windows, and many ignorant comments and questions … from ignorant people who had trouble seeing a human being behind skin colour.

I also encountered many racial slurs, but learned to be thick-skinned and quick-mouthed. I also realized that only an uneducated person voiced such ignorant and foolish things. Therefore, I ignored them. This was another trait I developed; ignoring people quickly and easily. My brother also taught me how to defend myself. He said he didn't want me coming home beaten up because someone didn't like the colour of my skin.

After many years we were finally accepted, since we posed no visible threat to the community. But by that time we had had enough and were ready to move. We moved to Ottawa when I was twelve years old. There weren't any Blacks in the neighbourhood, so obviously I hung out with white individuals in my age group. But I always knew and was proud to be Black. I was never ashamed of the colour of my skin, my heritage, or my cultural background. Nor did I ever want to be white in order to fit in better with my family. If anything, I wished that they were Black.

Growing up in a white family has been in a sense a growing experience, as well as a strange and difficult experience for me. People ask me frequently, "What is it like, growing up with whites?" How can I answer that? I've never known anything else. Growing up among whites has taught me to be open-minded. It has taught me about cultural diversity and about trust…

As a youth, most of my friends were white, and I developed a broad interest in music. Now most, if not all, of my friends are Black, and my interest is centred on traditional "Black" music, such as R & B, hip hop, rap, reggae, soca, jazz, and the like. I have tried to know and understand all aspects of my culture.

At times I wished that I knew and lived with my natural family so that I could be enveloped by people that I could compare myself to inside and out … and relate to culturally. But I didn't. My family is white, and I love them.

Unlike Michelle and Hillary, Ayanna is a first-generation Canadian who immigrated to Toronto with her Somali parents. She speaks of the clashes between the first, 1.5 and second generations—her peers and their parents—and how this has influenced her development and understanding of her identity as a Somali Canadian.[2] Ayanna discusses the differences between what she terms "Western culture" and the practices of her own family and ethnic community. With reference to peer friendships, she explains how her experience growing up was a "classic example of old meeting new"—"old" being the culture of her Somali parents and "new" being that of young Somalis like herself and her sister. With reference to friendship among young Somalis, Ayanna reveals how much these friendships, and young people in general, are monitored by parents. To Somali parents, friends "represent drugs, sex, alcohol, sin; they represented everything bad ... [and are] seen as brainwashers to their young, impressionable children"—something that their parents were not accustomed to "in the old country." Ayanna explains that "this makes immigrant parents uneasy" because they feel that they are losing control of their children, especially since they do not know what "their children are experiencing and learning." Ayanna contrasts Somali parents' understanding of teenage friendships with that of "Western" people. She writes that in Western society, "friends are seen as wonderful companions"—people with whom "you can share everything ... [and] have long talks over the phone." Nevertheless, in time she comes to accept the value of parents monitoring their children closely: "I now see they were right, even though at the time I thought they were wrong; I would never say it, but I thought it. It is true [that] you are who your friends are—if I would have stuck with my acquaintances, who knows where I would be now." The following excerpt encapsulates her story of friendships, parents, and what it means to grow up in Canada as a Somali Canadian female.

Ayanna: Fun! For an average Canadian teenager this word consists of a movie, "chilling," and a birthday party here or there. For a Somali parent "no way, Jose,"—the more isolation the better. This is where all the activities happen, as a kid I did not bother, why put myself in that uncomfortable situation of rejection. At the time you feel like an outsider when people invite you and you constantly have to decline, coming up with elaborate excuses. When you would like to go somewhere, you have to pitch them an idea; they [parents] only hear the main words like "get together" ([as though this description is a] tactic [to] make things seem mild).

My sister was the sneaky one who always wanted to go out. My mom would always say to her, "When you are eighteen you can do whatever you want." When she turned eighteen, the new one was, "When you are twenty you can do whatever you want." She turned twenty. My mother now says, "When you graduate school you can do whatever you want." My sister and I now say when she completes this new standard my mother will say, "When you have your own house and you are married with two kids you can do whatever you want."

Our family and cousins joke about our limitations. We were all talking recently and my sister asked my cousin, "So, how is your break so far?" expecting a mundane response like "good" or "alright;" he calmly answered, "Still on lockdown." We all started rolling with laughter. It was so funny because it is difficult to admit this in public. Being on "lockdown" seems like a weakness to others—how can you not possibly run your own life? We are comfortable enough with each other to tell it like it is. This is a huge part in the two worlds clashing. You are not able to go places with your friends because having a relationship outside school is what seals the deal, or legitimizes the friendship. When you are constantly depriving your kid from overrated "fun," they will think it is something amazing and will go to any lengths to experience it. It is extremely hard for parents to let us into the real world thinking we may start drinking or—their worst nightmare—get pregnant. I agree with their methods, but at a certain age parents should trust in the morals they have instilled in their children.

As expected, parents, as well as siblings and other family members, play a significant role in the development and construction of the ethnic and racial selves of individuals. As evident in the accounts of all the contributors, the influence of parents was mediated or compensated—or sometimes counteracted—by the communities in which they resided. Sometimes the people in the community, as in the case of John and Hillary, gave messages that were not the most helpful in providing individuals with a positive sense of themselves or others. Michelle shows how much individuals value the good feelings and sense of belonging that they get from their communities. In addition to their communities—both the geographic and ethno-racial communities—schools also play a crucial role in the lives of young people as they are growing up. This idea comes through in the above essays; every one of the contributors mentions something about their schooling. For the most part, parents expect that the cultural values, expectations, and aspirations that they try to pass on to their children will be reinforced by the schools their children attend, through their teachers, principals, and even their peers. As we see in the case of Michelle, her parents moved from a working-class, urban neighbourhood to the suburbs with the hope that Michelle would receive the schooling and education that they felt would be right for her. In the following section, we present what contributors had to say about their schooling.

ABOUT SCHOOL: THE ROLE OF THE EDUCATION SYSTEM

The narratives of contributors reflect the inevitable link between the socializing agents, contexts, and events (see **Figure 4.1**, page 94), reminding us of how teachers and school peers structure and influence not only the educational experiences and outcomes of young people, but also their social, cultural, and economic lives. In the following excerpts, Daniel and Dayna tell of the effects their teachers' lack of understanding and sensitivity had on their academic and religious experiences. And, as Daniel indicates, when teachers take the time to know their students culturally and intellectually, the results can be rewarding for all concerned.

Daniel: I am a first-generation[3] Canadian born in Halifax to Hungarian Jewish immigrants. My family moved to Toronto [when I was entering] Grade 1. My initial experience in the school system in Toronto was difficult due to language constraints—Hungarian was spoken in the home with my parents, not English. Since I had difficulty understanding English, I became a "class clown" and tuned out the education process. My Grade 2 teacher, Ms. L., wanted to fail me due to my disruptive behaviour. She did not look for reasons for the disruption, only that I had failed to understand part of the "hidden curriculum" that calls for discipline in the classroom.

It was only in Grade 4 that I began to become engaged with the education process. Part of the reason is that my language facilities had developed, but more importantly, Mrs. J., my Grade 4 teacher, took an active interest in my lack of academic success, instead of typifying or tracking me into a lower group. Mrs. J. used social learning theory constructs, such as positive reinforcement (e.g., a sticker, candy, verbal praise) in addition to making learning a game to engage me. Mrs. J.'s [efforts were] important, as now not only my parents but also my teachers viewed me as capable, and I began to see myself as capable and intelligent. Without a doubt, Mrs. J.'s methods of critically examining the reasons for my lack of academic success and not just accepting the "fact" that a student should be in the lower stream, played a role in the development of my respect for the importance of teachers in the development of today's youth.

Dayna: As a student, I was definitely the minority. I grew up for the most part in a very white, Anglo-Saxon, Protestant neighbourhood. My family is Jewish. Although there may have been diversity in my school, it was overpowered by the large, white, Christian population. We always had Christmas plays and decorations that celebrated the Christian holidays. I always felt left out and different from my friends. We would have door-decorating contests at Christmas and the entire school would look like a Christmas pageant, but [we] never seemed to celebrate other holidays. I remember in Grade 11 math, I had a test on a high holiday that I couldn't be at school for. It really irked me that a teacher could not look past her calendar to see that her test was on a day that Jewish people viewed as one of the holiest of the year. My cousins lived in a more predominantly Jewish area, and at their high school, the cafeteria served matzo bagels during Passover. It always bothered me that my school barely acknowledged other religions at all, especially mine.

The call for teachers to be sensitive and attentive to the ethnic and religious backgrounds of students is also echoed in Kulgit's comments about Christmas activities. Paradoxically, she admits to liking Christmas—the singing and the celebrations in school, but it did cause her some inner turmoil and, years later, resentment over the insensitivity of her teachers.

> **Kulgit**: I knew I was a Muslim very early on because of religious instruction from my mother, but also because it was a site of difference that made itself known often in school. For example, when I was in Grade 2, after winter break, we all had to write what we got for Christmas. Of course, I hadn't gotten anything. I had to improvise and write about what I got for my birthday, which was conveniently close to Christmas. No one else in the class had my problem … I think that the others were just unwilling to admit they hadn't celebrated Christmas or their parents were less adamant about keeping Christmas rituals out of the house. Even at that age, I resented that my teacher wasn't asking me something I could answer. I was a very good student, completing everything asked of me easily and well. But I could not do this.
>
> In elementary school, the emphasis on Christmas was enormous. Crafts, baking, tree decorating, carolling, and other Christmas traditions were undertaken with enthusiasm throughout the grades. The entire school would gather in the library and sing carols, some kitschy ("Rudolph") and others clearly religious ("O Come All Ye Faithful"). I liked carols because they were fun to sing together, but my older brother always refused to sing. Even I would be silent went it came to the parts that directly called Jesus the Lord. In those days, anti-racism didn't really exist and we were taught by immigrant parents to do all the accommodation necessary to do well in school and not get in trouble. But we still knew who we weren't and enacted our own small rebellions to preserve that. Not to say there wasn't some confusion. After all, I really enjoyed all the Christmas hoopla that paused regular classes and lessons to have fun and play games. I liked the Christmas lights and the decorated trees, colourful cookies and gaily wrapped presents. My mother though, always criticized the Canadian system as not rigorous enough and [said] that all we ever learned the first few years of school was "how to draw Santa Claus," a claim she still makes to this day. Frankly, she has a point. Christmas activities are one of my most coherent memories of my schooling from kindergarten to Grade 5. Today, that early, confused fondness for Christmas festivities has turned into resentment over the enforced onslaught.

Although her teachers seem to have paid little or no attention to the fact that she is Muslim, Kulgit was well-socialized by her immigrant parents to be obedient and respectful of her teachers, and "to do all the accommodation necessary to do well in school and not get in trouble." This idea of conforming to gain the support of teachers, evidently, often puts students at odds with the cultural values of their parents and ethnic or religious communities. This led the students to not only question their parents and cultural community values or to deny their ties to their ethnic group/community (in Michelle's case, and as we'll read, Bina's as well), but also to wish to be like "the most important people in the universe"—as Michelle did, expressing her perspective of white people.

In the above excerpt by Michelle, we learned that she was a mixed-race individual with a First Nations mother and Jamaican (Black) father. In the following excerpt, Michelle talks of her life in school and how she navigated and negotiated the schooling structures and built relationships with her teachers and peers, and eventually came "to understand her 'real place' in society."

Michelle: When we moved to [a predominantly white suburb] … I slowly got used to things in the public school I attended, and I even made new friends. My closest friend was an Irish girl named Susan, whom I admired greatly. I loved her curly blonde hair, her white skin, and her perfect family—I loved everything about her. In fact, I can even remember wishing that we could trade places. Just about everyone and everything at school was representative of all the things Susan was and I was not. All my teachers, whom I liked very much, were European or Anglo-Saxon; all the people in the storybooks I enjoyed reading were European or Anglo-Saxon; all the pictures hung around the school were of people who were of European or Anglo-Saxon descent. For goodness sake! Columbus was European, and he discovered Canada—or so I was told. The dominant culture that was taught and displayed in my school played an increasingly significant role in the formation of my identity. Tell me, what person in their right mind would not want also to be white? After all, whites seemed to be like the most important people in the universe. I realize now that the relationships I had with Susan and others (teachers, friends, mentors) undoubtedly caused me to question who I was, as I was not satisfied with just being me. I would have been a lot more content being a "pretty little white girl" with a nice family.

My feelings of difference and isolation, I believe, compelled me to form an identity that was untruthful. In fact, this identity became very real for me. When my peers asked me why my skin was so much lighter than other Black people's skin, I would tell them that I was a "half-breed." This somehow placed me closer to "them" (white people). Well, at least I thought it did. I thought that maybe if they believed I had some of the "good" colour in me, they would like and accept me more. However, I was wrong. Instead they called me "Oreo cookie," "caramel," and even "nigger."

…I recall one of my elementary school teachers saying, "We don't have many of your kind around here." To this day I wonder if she was being nice or if she was being rude about my "difference." I have learned that whites often use the term "your kind" to mean that you are separate and inferior to them.

Every day in school I listened to the lessons. I believed what the teachers taught, and I abided by their rules. I was a "good" student. Unconsciously, I was proud to have assimilated so successfully as it made "them" happy, and it also made me acceptable. It did not bother me at all that my cultures were not represented in the school curriculum. Never once did I say I was bored with their Eurocentric material. Never once did I think that something was wrong with what I was being taught. I never consciously noticed that every "good" person we talked about was European or Anglo-Saxon. In fact, I was never taught to think critically about my "place" in school. I was learning to be content with being a part of the "norm."

It was not until my later years in high school, in Grades 12 and 13, that I began to realize who I really was. My friends and one particular teacher opened my eyes to a "Black-Native" consciousness. I began to understand my "real place" in society, and for the first time, I began to tell people that my mother was Native. Still, I was ignorant about many things, and the learning process seemed to begin all over again.

University has provided me with the opportunity to learn more about myself. As I am majoring in history, I have made it my personal goal to find out more about "my people."

Building on Michelle's comments, Bina relates how race mediated her schooling experiences. Like Michelle, Bina highlights the inescapable impact that her teachers and peers had, not only on her educational engagement, but also on her social, religious, and cultural life and identity. As marginalized young people, they both indicate how much they would have liked to avoid their conflict–ridden experiences; however, they were unable to take "flight" since racial signifiers operated, not only in terms of their own construction of cultural identity, but in how others constructed them.

Bina: I was born in Canada and attended an elementary school in North York [in Toronto]. My parents both immigrated to Canada from India and England. Like most people, they came to Canada in order to make a better life for their children. Most of my friends were Christian, and the students in the school who were of other nationalities could probably be counted on one hand. While growing up, I never really considered myself different from the rest of the people at the school. I enjoyed my years there, from junior kindergarten to my Grade 6 graduation…

[In] Grade 4, and until Grade 8, racial slurs and nasty comments were what I got to hear. I had great friends who, by the way, were of all nation-alities. I enjoyed being with my circle of friends, but I did not like how the rest of my peers treated me. My parents never really knew about this, because it wasn't something that I discussed openly. I went to school, had a good time, and that was it. I can't really say for sure if the teachers were aware of this, but how could they not be? Maybe they just ignored it, because they didn't know what to say or do. I guess that is something I will never know.

After Grade 6, I went to a junior high school for two years. I can honestly say that it was here that I had my worst experiences. The guys were horrid, and the things they had to say about my ethnicity and culture were disgusting. The worst part of all this is that they didn't even know who I really was. They just assumed, and then went on from there ... My experiences led me to ignore and retaliate against my own religion and culture.

I am not an immigrant to Canada and I was born in Canada, yet I could never make people understand I was "Canadian." I didn't look "Canadian" to them, so how could I be? I began to deny my ties with any other ethnic group. My response was always, "I'm Canadian, a Christian. I celebrate Christmas, and I don't speak any languages other than English." Of course it was all a lie, except for being Canadian. My name was also a dead giveaway. Bina Patel; a Christian? After a while, I thought I had successfully convinced everyone. Even at home, I tried to distance myself as much as possible from my cultural roots. I wouldn't watch movies in which Hindi was spoken, and I wouldn't dress up in my cultural clothes.

As a member of a minority group, I was forced to conform to the existing cultural norms of the white majority group. It wasn't that they forced me directly; it was all the things they said to me and the teasing that I couldn't stand. I disassociated myself from India and any links I might have had with it.

It wasn't until high school that my perceptions changed. High school was a completely new experience for me. I met many people who belonged to the same ethnic group as I. I had a great time learning different things about my religion and culture. As I had avoided learning anything about it in the past, it was neat to have friends who knew so much. I started to identify myself as both South Asian and Canadian and had no problems with either one. I had always enjoyed school, but it was the treatment and comments that I was subjected to while growing up that made me hate everything about my culture. However, at high school, I came to accept my difference.

While many children experience difficulty in the middle-school years with teasing and becoming comfortable with their identity, it is important to note Bina's reactions. She did not tell her parents what she experienced in school, particularly in middle school. This is likely a result of what she perceived to be her parents' cultural and educational expectations of her, and their capacity to assist her. It is also possible that Bina was protecting her parents from worrying about her. And while Bina states that she is not sure if her teachers were aware of what was happening to her, it is quite likely that they were, yet were unsure of how to respond or did not wish to get involved in the situation.

In light of their alienating experiences and the lack of educational programs and information that speak to their needs, interests, and aspirations, some parents have involved their children in alternative programs that they hope will help to address their educational, cultural, and social concerns. Luel tells of how the Saturday school program he attended helped to "fill in" what was missing in the mainstream curriculum to which he was exposed while attending school in Edmonton, Alberta. He illustrates the importance and "benefits" of learning about the cultural and national background of his family, and what made his parents want to leave their country of birth and immigrate to Canada.

Luel: I went through the Edmonton public school system, from kindergarten to Grade 12, and when I look back on it, I think of it as a most positive, broadening, enjoyable experience, which prepared me well for post-secondary. Teachers were inspiring, committed, and fair, students were motivated, the classroom was exciting. (I was lucky enough to be in the AP [Advanced Placement] and IB [International Baccalaureate] programs, but most of my friends in other programs had the same positive experience as I did.) My experience in school instilled in me an appreciation of and a taste for social and intellectual diversity. As a student of African heritage, whose parents hail from east Africa, every module covered in social studies, whether it was the history of the fur trade in Canada, the modern history of the industrial rise of Japan, or the history of the world wars and the Cold War was valuable because it broadened my perspective, gave me an understanding of my role in this land that my parents immigrated to. In short, I was a real keener in school.

However, there is also a less positive side to my educational experience. To understand my role in this land, in addition to all of the things I mentioned, I also have to understand how and why I got here in the first place. I have to ask certain questions: How and why did their country of birth become a place that they would want to leave? And where and what the heck is their country of birth in the first place? What are the people there like, in terms of language, religion, politics? These are very huge questions. In order to answer them you have to study African history, the history of colonialism; you have to study African languages, literature; you have to study religions. But above all, I think, history. You have to know where your people come from, in order to know how you fit into today, and how you will proceed in the future.

These were things and educational interests which were not met in the mainstream system. I do not remember learning any African or Caribbean history in my educational experience, although I'm sure there were snippets here and there. The world history course that I took in high school was really a course in the history of Europe in the nineteenth and twentieth centuries. So I had to go somewhere else to learn these other things, which were important to my development, and it was to a Saturday school program that I went. I was lucky enough to attend weekly language classes in my parent's native language, and I was lucky that my dad forced me to read newspapers in his language, no matter how much I hated it. The benefits of this were that educational gaps were filled, a curiosity developed; and what happens is that when you start to learn and become curious about your own roots you start to become curious about other people's roots, and the more you can understand your personal history, the more you can relate to and empathize with other people's history.

Let me present an example: World War II. From my social studies classes I had the impression that this war was a European affair, with brief interludes in Asia and northern Africa. I believed that the war, despite how it shaped the Western world in which I lived, had absolutely zero relation to my personal history. And as a child, every Remembrance Day was an empty day for me; despite what teachers taught me about the sacrifices of earlier generations, I just could not connect it to earlier generations in my own family.

My attitudes would change drastically as I started to discover things on my own, outside of what was taught in high school, when I started to ask questions about my family. You see, Eritrea, my parents' country of birth, had been an Italian colony from 1890 to about halfway through World War II, when Italy was defeated in northern and eastern Africa by the Allies. I remember the moment when I discovered, in talking with my father, that my grandfather had been an *askari*, an Eritrean native who was conscripted into the colonial Italian army during the reign of Mussolini. In fact, to his death, my grandfather was called by his military rank and received a small pension from the Italian government. His relationship to Italian colonialism was an ambivalent one. On the one hand, he liked many Italians personally, and Italian became his beloved second language. Like many Eritrean peasants conscripted into the Italian army, he benefitted financially, I hesitate to say, from this. But, of course, all of this was tempered by his negative experiences under the apartheid-like system in Eritrea, which intensified when, under *Il Duce*, Mussolini, Italy became a fascist nation.

This knowledge fed back into and enhanced my social studies curriculum. Playing the roles of Poland and Israel in high school debates was greatly enhanced by my knowledge of Eritrean and Ethiopian history (struggles for independence, warfare, mass migration). This knowledge gave me a personal context to which I could relate what I was learning in social studies. My new knowledge and curiosity enabled me to bend the rules and study Africa in my world history course by researching and writing about the Italian invasion of Ethiopia in Grade 12.

The details may bore you and may not matter so much. My point is that these facts and contexts, which were not taught in the mainstream system, would become so important to my growing understanding of myself and my role in this land. First of all, cultural education in my own roots provided me with common ground from which I could relate my history to that of others, thus enabling me to empathize. Secondly, this cultural education allowed me to carry myself with confidence and grace in diverse settings, instead of with confusion and alienation, knowing that my history—in all of its ugliness and beauty—was a part of world history. It existed. I was not a little black boy who accidentally found himself in Edmonton, rootless, solitary, and exceptional. There was a background and a context, historical forces, which put me and others like me here. I carried this background, not as a burden, but as a source of guidance to consult whenever I encountered someone different from me. Finally, this cultural education paved the way for a new relationship with other older members in the African Canadian community; I came to see them as educators who knew things that I didn't know and who thus had something to teach me. Before this, and like many other youths in the African Canadian community, I had the attitude that there was nothing to learn from older members in my community, and that thus there was no point in caring or contributing to the community. Learning about my history changed this attitude.

Luel contends that his Saturday school was "part of an inclusive system," which not only enhanced and supported the education of Black students and exposed them to the resources of the African Canadian community.

Luel: [The school was] necessary for the sane and healthy emotional development of students, students who can define themselves by more profound terms than just "the only black kid in class," and without resorting to American definitions of blackness, for lack of a Canadian alternative.

This point about using American representations is important, for it is too often missed in educators' attempts to be inclusive of their students' images and experiences. The fact is, the children of African and Caribbean heritage are Canadian, and they need to know about their Canadian existence. Also noteworthy is Luel's illustration of how he came to relate to Remembrance Day not simply as an event for "Canadians" or Europeans, but also for people like him, who also had relatives who fought in the wars. Indeed, by bringing students' stories into the mainstream curriculum they can become fully engaged in their schooling. Abdi, in the following essay, further demonstrates that when the school curriculum is not inclusive of students' experiences, it can lead to disengagement from the schooling process. Abdi argues that, despite his "multicultural school" and its claims of inclusivity, there was no acknowledgement of the diversity of the student population that would foster the awareness necessary for students to get along with each other.

Abdi: My personal understanding of the various layers that make up my identity in a multicultural society did not truly happen for me until after I graduated from high school and began to work as a youth worker in a safe schools program run by the Toronto District School Board. Prior to this, I had never really questioned or critiqued what it meant to be Black, Muslim, and male in a society that can be quite suspicious and at times downright hostile to someone who looks like me; nor could I articulate what was occurring. I grew up in a part of Toronto that is considered very multicultural and went to a high school that was also viewed this way. This notion of a diverse and multicultural school was something that was constantly repeated from my very first day of high school. I remember being told on multiple occasions that what made us a multicultural school was the fact that our school had one of the most diverse student populations of any school in the city.

This diversity was celebrated by holding a UNESCO event every other year. I remember accepting this notion of multiculturalism without putting much thought into it. Looking back at things now, however, I would argue that this school environment that I accepted as being so inclusive was not an accurate reflection of a multicultural school. I say this because while it is true that there were multiple ethno-racial/cultural groups represented at my high school, these identities were rarely acknowledged in a manner that fostered inclusion through the curriculum or through other avenues that were available to the school. Furthermore, the UNESCO celebration, while entertaining, was nothing more than a superficial display of these multicultural identities. It was done in a manner that lacked substance and provided little opportunity for learning.

The lack of learning opportunities only furthered what I saw as tensions inside and outside of the school. The clearest example of this was the way in which students separated themselves into various sections of the school. There was a door that led to a certain part of the school that was known as the "Black Doors," while another door opposite was known as the "Hippie Doors," and finally one that was known as the "Gino and Asian Doors." Students who did not identify with one of these groups could attempt to integrate into one of these groups or, if that failed, could go and find their own space. While this composition may not have been intended to be a racial issue it clearly became one for me. What I found to be most interesting about the labelling of the doors was the absence of racial descriptors to identify the white students [who were] the group most represented at both the "Hippie Doors" and the "Gino and Asian" doors. This, of course, as I would come to learn some years later, was a reflection of the notion that white is representative of the status quo and all other racialized groups are viewed in relation to it.

It may have seemed a normal part of growing up to me at the time, but these divisions at my so-called multicultural high school along racial lines were never challenged by the school administration, who I am sure was aware of what was going on. All one had to do was walk into the school from any one of the above-mentioned doors to see this racial divide. Yet it was never addressed, even when fights broke between ethno-racial groups, something that occurred about once a year during each of my five years at this school…

I remember one incident in particular where a Black student who was a year younger than me got into a fight with a Vietnamese student in my grade. The Vietnamese student decided to retaliate by calling a number of his friends at other schools the following day to assist him in beating up this Black student.

As with most schools, news of a fight broke out very quickly. Like my other friends, I ran outside after school and stood on the steps in front of the "Black Doors." As I waited to see what would unfold, two Vietnamese youth who had come to assist their friend approached me. I knew them from my part-time job at a movie theatre and considered them to be my friends. They placed me in a very difficult situation by asking me if I knew the Black youth who had beaten up their friend. What made this situation so difficult for me was that I had to make a choice between continuing my friendship with them, or staying loyal to the Black youth who had beaten up their friend—someone I did not consider to be my friend but felt obligated to defend due to the fact that we were both Black. With everyone watching I made the decision not to point out the youth they were looking for, who just happened to be standing one step above me to my left. In the end, I lost two friends to protect a person that I did not consider a friend. Looking back at this situation, I can take comfort in the fact that I avoided playing a role in getting someone beat up, although in truth this was not something that concerned me at the time.

These are the memories I think of when I look back at my teenage years and the role that multiculturalism has played in shaping my identity. In my opinion, multiculturalism has created an environment where nothing of substance is ever discussed, nor are we as a society ever challenged to question how we view and interact with one another. We are instead made to falsely believe that everything is okay so long as we tolerate the diversity of our city by acknowledging the various festivals and holidays that members of ethno-racial communities celebrate.

What becomes clear in the above narratives, particularly Daniel's (see page 103), is how students can become more productive when educators develop an understanding of their cultural situation. Luel also speaks to this issue: Learning of his parents' African roots at his Saturday school and from his father allowed him to "translate" his history into text that would be relevant to him. Kulgit, Michelle, Bina, and Abdi also draw attention to the relevance of school activities and indicate that school would have come alive for them if only teachers were more culturally sensitive and aware. And as they point out, it is unfortunately only after they leave school or pursue post–secondary education, and do some of their own work to find out about themselves, the ethnic groups to which they belong, and communities in which they live, that they manage to become the successful children that their parents expected. Further, these reflections illustrate that the meaning and understanding that individuals have gained through their life experiences seem most crucial to them. As one young man puts it, when asked to account for his dismissive behaviour toward school, "I have to search deep in my background and culture, my childhood and upbringing, my old and new surroundings, in order to find reasons for my behaviour, and to search for answers."

Ultimately, what is expected of young people through their socialization and teaching from parents, family, school, and communities is for them to fit into the society and become productive citizens. Their experiences in fulfilling this expectation are discussed in the following section.

FITTING IN: COPING WITH DIFFERENCE

Part of the reality of negotiating identity is coming to terms with belonging and difference. As we have learned from the student narratives, questions that often arise include: Where do I belong? How do I fit in? What does it mean to be a racial or ethnic minority in Canada? Social institutions, experiences, schools, teachers, friends, parents, and general day-to-day living make individuals aware of who belongs and who may be excluded. While these forces are structural and operate on all of us in some way, they are also differently understood and interpreted by individuals depending on their own varying experiences, contexts, and locations. Avinder, for instance, explains that he is considered a "minority" living in Canada because of his religious beliefs, which are important to him and his family, but lead to disrespect from others.

> Avinder: I am seen by others as a minority. Some people tend to see me differently because I am of a different race. But what they do not know is that I am not so different from them. I speak the same language, eat the same food, and do the same activities. Just because I am of a different race they think that I do different things. I try to fit in with other groups and try to learn what others can teach me. All I would like is the same respect back. Religion is important to me and also very important to my parents. This does not mean that everywhere I go I take my religion with me, because this is not so. Since I was brought to this country, I try to do what others do, and I practice my religion in my own home. I believe that my family and I carry out our responsibilities as Canadians ought to. We should have our religion inside us somewhere, but practice it on your own time.

Evident in Avinder's comments, and in the comments of many whose essays appear in this section, is the distress they experience as they try to "fit in" with their peer groups, their schools, their communities, and Canadian society as a whole. This distress persists despite their concerted efforts to negotiate their identities and their presence as responsible Canadian citizens. For the most part, many seem to accept their "difference"—be it race, ethnicity, language, faith, religion, immigrant status—but are determined to retain that which is important to their cultural identity or self. Like Avinder, a number of the writers articulate the lengths to which they have gone to fit in and de-emphasize their "difference." In fact, what emerges is their emphasis on "sameness." As

Avinder notes, "I speak the same language, eat the same food and do the same activities." Seemingly exasperated, he goes on to say, "Just because I am of a different race they think that I do different things." In other words, he is asking, have I not done enough to show that I am the same? Shouldn't this be enough to "fit in" and receive the "same respect" that others do?

While Avinder and others, such as Moran and Cindy (see below), did engage in the cultural integration or acculturation process (Kallen 1995, 154)—a process of learning those cultural ways of the dominant Canadian "ethnic collectivity" to which they do not belong—they were doing so within an established system of ethnic stratification. So while they were taking on the norms, values, and patterns of the dominant group in society—and attaining some level of proficiency in utilizing these cultural attributes for effective participation in the public institutions of the society at large (Kallen 1995, 154)—they remained, as many of them so painfully admit, different, minorities, foreigners, outsiders, immigrants, individuals with accents, non-English speaking, half-breeds, biracial. Comparatively, white participants in the same classroom discussions and exercises, particularly Anthony (see page 119), often understood that race and ethnic privilege would help them to get by in society.

Here Moran and Cindy relate their attempts to fit in with the cultural expectations of society, but it has not been easy for them to do so.

Moran: I am a twenty-five-year-old, second-generation Chinese Canadian female. My name means "Admired Lotus Lily." I was born in Belleville, Ontario. My parents are naturalized Canadian citizens originally from the People's Republic of China, who met in Hong Kong. Because we relocated to Toronto when I was approximately two years old, I remember little of small-town Ontario. Practically my entire life has been spent in the big city [and] I have never left North America. And luckily for me, there is a stable community of my own ethnic background [in my city]. I take great comfort in this.

The term Chinese Canadian, in my opinion, describes a person of Chinese descent living in the Western society of Canada. It has been difficult for me, and I am sure for many others of my culture, to assimilate into some of the dominant Canadian values. Take, for example, the family. My family is very important to me, but no one actually realizes the obligations that I happily take on. Few of my friends and co-workers who are not Chinese Canadian know that I am expected to support my parents in old age (and definitely not put them in an old age home!). It is a time in my career when moving [away from] Toronto may be advantageous, but I could never move out. Some people think it's because I am insecure, but they just don't understand. I worry about my parents a great deal and moving out [of the family home] is not culturally encouraged for reasons other than marriage (if that!). But before I finish making my point, it should be noted that I take on these duties and responsibilities willingly. I would feel tremendous guilt and pressure if I upset everyone in my family.

I can hardly communicate to my parents in their native tongue, and I am not literate in Chinese. I do not see this as a liability, but my mother does. She is concerned about the preservation of the Chinese culture. For this reason, she also frowns on intermarriage. My mother still complains that my third cousin married a white man. She argues that it is because the culture will be lost within a generation, but I do not see the difference between me and my third cousin's children. I must disappoint her greatly.

It has been hard for me to fit into the Canadian culture and be accepted by other Chinese. I sometimes become paranoid and think that my cultural peers perceive me as a "wacko." This is probably because they may think of me as over-assimilated and assertive beyond their comfort zone. I don't fit the stereotype of the submissive East Asian woman. My dress and accent do not give me away. In fact, I am probably not living my culture in many ways, because I have assimilated much more than first-generation immigrants. On the other hand, even though I do not readily mesh with my own culture, I do not possess the privileges that many Canadians of European descent possess. They can mix right into the predominantly white culture at their whim; I will always have my skin colour and physical characteristics to set me apart. Metaphorically I sit on a fence and cannot be categorized or ordered into any group. First-generation, lower-income immigrants naturally assume that I am totally Westernized, and whites think that I am totally Chinese in my ways of thinking. In some ways, both points of view have grains of truth. But where do I fit? And where do I belong?

For a substantial part of my life I grew up in a predominantly European-Catholic neighbourhood. It was hard to make friends because I was different, specifically because I was from a different race. That was the first time that I experienced racism. Not only was it among students from school who sadly picked it up from their parents, but also from neighbours who did not like Chinese people. You see, our family was one of the first non-white families to move into the lower-middle-class white neighbourhood. Many of those families have moved to the suburbs now. In fact, my neighbourhood is quite "yuppie-ized" and has a greater East and South Asian population now, but I will never forget the feeling of being ostracized and the isolation that I felt then.

As a law student (yes, there are Chinese law students!), I experienced a more subtle racism. During my articling interviews, many potential employers asked me if I could speak Cantonese, because they had many commercial law clients from Hong Kong. At a bar admission presentation, I was told that I had an accent. In fact it was another woman who had the accent, but who incidentally was white, and I was the only visible minority present. After the seminar, a fellow law student noted that I did not have a Chinese accent, and that it was in fact a distinctly "Toronto" accent.

Often people will ask me "What are you?" or "Are you Filipino?" It really bothers me. I guess you could rationalize that I get mad because people are prejudging me. But it goes deeper than that. Much deeper. I get angry because I expect people to know that I am Chinese and not Filipino. The differences are vast and I perceive myself as more culturally Chinese. Sometimes I reflect and wonder what kind of Chinese I am. Am I a good person? Am I a bad person because I do not have the burning desire to go back and visit the lands of my ancestors? A lot of friends want to do this, but I do not need to see "Mecca." Am I in denial about my ethnic roots?

I often did and still do have problems telling people what professions my parents were in. My mother used to be a garment worker in Toronto. It might be a mixture of shame of being from a lower-class family. It could be the fact that I don't want people to stereotype my parents or people of my race as people who work only at low-paying, backbreaking work. The image of the immigrant garment worker and immigrant restaurant worker are classic Canadian stereotypes. It could be because I want to disassociate myself and leap into a better class and I think that knowledge of my family background would hinder my chances. So many East Asians are ghettoized and fall into a vicious cycle.

Cindy: Born and raised in Toronto and accustomed to the North American culture, I can relate to Moran's experience. It was also hard for me, like Moran, to make friends when I was in elementary and high school. I went to a predominantly Italian Catholic school. I felt isolated from my classmates because I was a visible minority, and I just didn't seem to "fit in" with the crowd. The students in my grade were not all that welcoming either. I also went to Vietnamese classes. The teachers and students also looked down on me. I had an English accent when I spoke Vietnamese. I couldn't pronounce the words correctly and my reading and writing skills were very poor. I battled with an identity crisis. I was not "white," nor was I "yellow" enough to be accepted by either culture. This affected my self-esteem and confidence during my childhood years and especially my adolescent years.

Moran talks about how people prejudge her nationality and that this disturbs her. I get this all the time from people who ask me, "What are you? Are you Chinese, Japanese, Korean?" They would name all the different Asian countries they could think of and then at the end apologize for not being able to tell me apart from other Asians because we all look the same. This comment really annoyed me because it made me feel like an outsider, "different" from "them." It emphasized the differences between Asian and Caucasian culture, making me feel unaccepted by them.

Moran and Cindy share similar struggles over trying to fit into Canadian society, as well as into the ethnic group with which they identify. A product of both their Canadian and Asian cultures (Chinese Canadian and Vietnamese Canadian cultures to be more precise), they admit to having "assimilated" some of the dominant cultural ideas, values, norms, and aspirations of their families, communities, and the various societal institutions in which they have participated. Nevertheless, they are not protected from the stereotyping and racism that Moran attributes to not being white—meaning that her "skin colour and her physical characteristics" will always set her apart in society. It is this idea of being set apart that likely adds to Moran and Cindy feeling "bothered" when asked: "What are you?" It is true that Asians are not the only group that experiences the problem of being misidentified—Europeans, Africans, and South Asians would say the same. But for Moran and Cindy, who are trying their best to "fit in" and "not feel like an outsider," their misidentification has different implications than it would for people of European origin. For instance, in the following essays, Joe and Anthony demonstrate that language was not an obstacle to fitting in, and their white skin allowed them to take advantage of opportunities. Joe writes, "[I could] do a pretty good job of disguising myself as part of the dominant group." Anthony was able to join with his "exclusively 'Canadian' friends in ridiculing the 'Wops' and 'Ginos' and other immigrant kids."

Joe: My parents emigrated from Italy and lived in Hamilton, where the family was raised. I am the youngest of four children. I grew up in a decidedly non-Italian neighbourhood. The kids in the neighbourhood were a mix of Canadians, that is, second-, third- and fourth-generation British, Scottish, and Irish descendants; first-generation Eastern Europeans; and perhaps one or two first-generation Italians. This ethnic profile was, however, simplified according to the distinctions we used at the time. As far as my parents were concerned, the populace was divided into two: English and Italian. Anyone who didn't fit into either one of these categories (say, for instance, my Lithuanian friend) was viewed as innocently irrelevant to the basic societal dichotomy of English and Italian.

The ethnic mix became somewhat more complicated in elementary school, because the school was at a distance from our immediate neighbourhood. Ethnic origins and ratios were altered. It became a little more problematic to cram all those non-Italians into the English camp, but it was even easier to entrench ourselves into the Italian camp because we were readily identified as such by both the school administration and other students. We were perceived as Italians. The predominant authority of the school was Irish and Catholic. The nuns and priests were Irish and Catholic, and we were the rather difficult, but redeemable, Italian Catholics. Belonging to such an identified and identifiable group gave rise to varied perceptions of identity. My "Italian-ness" could be causing me to suffer silent embarrassment one moment and defiant satisfaction the next. One thing was abundantly clear: I was outside the cultural norm.

The tables were turned rather dramatically in high school. The elementary school had been in a predominantly non-Italian area, but the high school was in an area where many Italians lived. Many of the students were from immigrant Italian families. It seems that the old English or Italian distinction wasn't quite relevant anymore. It was time to start making much finer distinctions. We, my immediate clique and I, chose to carve out a new, unique identity for ourselves. We began to distinguish ourselves as the more advanced, sophisticated, anglicized Italians. Our group tended to deride the excesses of our less genteel compatriots, while at the same time negotiating diplomatic relations with the English. The negotiations were fruitful, and permanent relations were established with a number of English cliques.

It is rather facile to proclaim that I always sensed something was wrong with this perception of who I was in relation to my world. During high school, however, I did develop a distinct dislike at being categorized as Italian or anything else. University was a welcome relief. Few of my peers went to university, and though I still lived in the same city, I lived in a different world. I consciously avoided anyone who dragged me back to the English or Italian characterization of my identity. I sought refuge in the company of foreign visa students. They knew nothing of this—or did they? I suppose my friends from Singapore had their own notions of what it was to live in a former British colony.

My ethnicity has been a significant factor in shaping my notion of self. Societal pressure has imposed its interpretation of who I am from the outside, and unexamined internal acceptance has reinforced this view. But all this is water under the bridge, isn't it? Surely this nonsense is buried in the past.

I have found that the insidiousness and subtle harm of ethnic and racial categorization is persistent. I can still feel the ghosts of "silent embarrassment" when British people reminisce about times gone by. Do they know that I feel uncomfortable? Are they conscious of the institutional baggage of their dominant position?

Until very recently, I denied this whole issue and held to the opinion that all of it was, in fact, buried in the past. I rejected my own unease and dismissed suspicion of the cause of this unease.

As an ESL (English as a Second Language) instructor, my association with recent immigrants has been instrumental in reawakening my sensitivities to the issue. I can see the same type of ethnic and racial categorization being applied to the learners in my classroom. I can see them being constantly reminded that they are somehow inadequate in their present form. If they don't change, they'll never move from the periphery of society. I am white and, despite any "Mediterranean" features, can do a pretty good job of disguising myself as part of the dominant group. I can fit; I can move in closer than the periphery. What, then, is a "more visible" visible minority to do? Will an African or Southeast Asian ever be adequate? Will they ever fit in enough to move closer to the centre of society? … Ethnic identification can be a psychological touchstone; ethnic categorization can be an unwelcome burden.

Joe, like Anthony (see below), suffered "silent embarrassment" because of his "Italian-ness." While Joe and his peers attempted to distinguish themselves "as the more advanced, sophisticated, anglicized Italians," Anthony seemed trapped by his Italian and Polish heritage, not only because they indicated that he was non-English, but also because they represented the fact that he was an "immigrant." Joe attempted to "fit in" by "anglicizing" himself, and Anthony distanced himself as much as he could from his family and the "marks of the lonely immigrant."

Anthony: I was born here in Canada. I am white, and have no trace of any accent. The language that is spoken in my home is English, and my family does not practice any religious customs other than status quo Christianity. Yet I think I can still empathize with the way in which many new, non-Anglo-Canadians must certainly feel.

My mother emigrated from Poland at a young age. My father, although born here, is Italian and was socialized in Toronto's large Italian community, which thus preserved many cultural traits. My name is obviously Italian, and my physical features seem to make it easy for everyone I meet to assume that I am Italian, a fact that brought me much grief while I was growing up.

I was very aware of the stigma attached to the word immigrant while growing up in Toronto. Although the word simply means a person who was born in one country and has moved to another one, it carried other connotations as well. I didn't want to be called an immigrant; I perceived it to be an insult. Although I was somewhat aware that the stereotypes of immigrants who were racial minorities were much more harmful and negative, the stereotypes of Eastern and Southern Europeans were still very much present. While playing down my Italian background as much as possible, I flat out denied being Polish.

Most Italian and Polish people I have known have been very proud of their heritage. Yet, as a youngster I did not feel this way. There was no single incident that brought these feelings on. I was never singled out in front of a large group in order to have my ethnicity ridiculed. I was not taught to hate myself the way native Indians or Africans were. I had never known first-hand the dehumanizing racism that people of colour must go through everyday. But, as far back as I can remember, I thought that the word "immigrant" meant stupid, unclean, strange, outsider.

I can remember when my grandmother … had dealings with authority figures—they were exclusively Anglo, native-born Canadians—she became immediately apprehensive, telling me always to watch what I said around those people, to make sure never to insult them. Many of these people were polite, but I remember the ones who were rude and insulting towards her. She was just another dumb immigrant who couldn't speak English.

Besides learning to be intimidated by authority figures, these situations reinforced for me the idea that immigrants were second-class citizens and that native-born Anglos were the ideal Canadians, who were to be revered and respected. To me, being other than Anglo meant being an immigrant. It meant being a janitor or a cleaning woman. It meant dressing in strange attire and speaking peculiar languages. It aroused images of my grandmother being scolded and humiliated by a cop, as if she were a child. It brought images of the leering immigrant, who both steals jobs and drains the welfare system.

There were many days I went hungry because I could not bear to be seen eating the ethnic foods my mother made me for lunch. I often avoided having friends over for fear that they might hear my mother speaking Polish. Those were the marks of the lowly immigrant that I desperately wanted no part of. I wanted blonde hair, blue eyes, and a cool "Canadian" name, like Brett Smith or Jay Johnson. Those were the marks of the Canadian.

Throughout high school I never dated girls who weren't Anglo. I joined in with my exclusively "Canadian" friends in ridiculing the "Wops" and "Ginos" and other immigrant kids at school. After twenty years of this, I systematically self-destroyed a very important part of who I was, a part I can never get back.

Joe and Anthony relate what it has been like as ethnic minority young adults trying to fit into a society in which the colour of their skin was not a marker of "difference," but opened up social and cultural possibilities for them. The following essays by Joanne, Shaun, and Ronnie, all of mixed-race background, provide insights into what their "ambiguous" identities made possible and what they limited. As well, they relate how context or geography—as in, moving from one community or neighbourhood to another—operated to help them define themselves in order to fit in.

Joanne: I am a Black, white, "mixed-race" woman of colour. This is the identity I have chosen for myself. However, this wasn't always the way I identified. How I got to this identity of "mixed race" was a long and curious journey, one shaped by various experiences of context, relationships, frustrations, and feelings of inclusion and exclusion based on colour.

I grew up in a very small town where the majority of the population was white. All the kids in my school were also, for the most part, white. And because, I believe, my friends were unable to deal with the point of "difference" that my looks created, they felt it easier to classify me as white and told me as much. I suspect that embracing me as white wasn't an extremely difficult task, as my "looks" are what people would describe as ambiguous, vague, and even "passable" at times. So, although I have always been aware that I am "mixed," by virtue of being the daughter of a Black father and a white mother, in the community where I grew up, and against the backdrop of whiteness in the town, it became perhaps a necessity that I also felt racially neutral and virtually "colourless" in order to fit in.

Interestingly, it wasn't until I went away to university—which was located in a much larger town than the one in which I had grown up, by major city standards—that I started becoming interested in questions of race and ethnicity. I aligned myself with the "people of colour" on campus and joined various anti-racism groups. It was here that I first took on a Black identity. Thinking back, I think I felt I had to be Black because it seemed clear to me that there was no other "in-between" option if I wanted to be racially political. The books and articles we read, and the racial discussions we had, left no room for mixtures. So, I became Black.

In an attempt to find my "place" and to assert my newfound "Blackness" in university, I attended numerous lectures on race and racism and sat through those token classes on women of colour found in women's studies [programs] and engaged in various debates on race. But I still couldn't help feeling disconnected from the material and from those conversations. Towards the end of my undergraduate degree, it started to become quite obvious to me that the theories of race, ethnicity, and racial identity with which I was engaging did not apply to my own experiences. They only seemed to apply to "people of colour" in a really general sort of way and lumped those who were assumed to be "Black" (specifically) or "of colour" (more generally) into one racialized and homogeneous category that ignored the fundamental differences between and among us. I think it all started coming together for me when I saw the film *Waiting to Exhale* [about the lives of four Black female friends and their relationships with men and each other]. I remember hating this film and resenting these Black women who, at various points in the film, bashed, criticized, and condemned white women for having relationships with Black men. At the time, I felt hurt because it seemed that they were indirectly attacking my own white mother, and I didn't quite know how to react, except to think that I needed to re-think my position as Black and what being Black means. It soon became clear that the experiences I had embraced in university, as well as the things I was reading and seeing, could not sufficiently account for the complexity of my own "mixed raceness" or my position as someone whose parentage, appearance, and history cross racial and ethnic lines.

When I had completed my undergraduate degree, I moved to Toronto to pursue graduate studies and immediately became more deeply aware of the nuances of my own racial difference and ambiguity, both in relation to white people and to other people of colour. It was in Toronto that I really found myself frequently experiencing "race" in ways I could not always explain or understand. I found that as I moved through Toronto's multicultural landscape, I could fit in or blend in to several different communities. However, this feeling was not always of fitting in, as I eventually realized that I was often put "on display," endlessly questioned and approached by strangers, friends, and peers, and asked who and what I was. "Could you explain your ethnicity? Where are you from? You really look like a ... Excuse me, but are you ... [fill in the blank]?" Of course, I didn't immediately consider these experiences to be "racist," just annoying, really. I didn't see them as suggesting that I "go back to where I came from," but more as questioning out of curiosity, "where are you from?" But now I see the two as inseparable—as highly indicative of the perception of my otherness and of my questionable Canadianness. The more I was faced with these questions, the more I realized that the reasons behind such questioning, as well as how I chose to respond, were not simple. I often found myself making up racial identities depending on whom I encountered, where I was or what mood I was in—sometimes to avoid confrontation and other times to fuel it. But what is most significant is that these experiences led me to start identifying myself as "mixed race" and embracing the politics associated with it.

Through my encounters, race became more than an abstract "thing" that I had been studying and criticizing. Race, and particularly mixed race, was something much more complex as it is also lived, experienced, personal, communal, and everywhere. It was my mixed raceness, combined with my embodiment of racially ambiguous features, colouring, physical appearance, gender, and location that mediated my interactions with others and played a role in how I negotiated my identity. Today, my years of postsecondary education, including my current graduate work, have provided new lenses through which I am able to continually rethink and reconstruct my sense of identity and who and what I am. Most of all, I have renegotiated my mixed raceness beyond the labels of Black and white to embody a politics of identity that accounts for my evolving experiences.

Unlike Joanne, Shaun speaks explicitly about the "privileges" and "double-edged sword" of being "mixed." His account reveals the ways that people in society understand the meanings of Blackness and whiteness, which have led him to claim a "neither-nor" identity of "mixed." His claim of a mixed-race identity is also made with an awareness of the fact that, being light-skinned, he may not face the same kinds of racism as other Blacks (privilege), but that this light skin simultaneously excludes him from full membership in Black communities (challenge). Another reason Shaun does not claim a Black identity, despite his recognition that others often assume he is Black and apply that label to him, is because he grew up with his white single mother. As Shaun puts it, "to adopt an exclusively black identity requires me to reject my mother's contribution to my genetic makeup. I am not willing to do that."

Shaun: As a mixed-raced individual, I feel privileged in some ways. And yet, [connected] with that privilege is the uncertainty and exclusion of identity. This double-edged sword has not always been obvious to me. To be clear, my mother is white and my father is black. I am mixed.

Nobody told me that I was mixed. In fact, I have been labelled "black" for most of my life. I imagine that in another life I would have adopted that identity. But I was raised by my mother. And to adopt an exclusively black identity requires me to reject my mother's contribution to my genetic makeup. I am not willing to do that.

So I told myself that I was mixed; this is my self-identity. In certain environments, however, I concede to the general opinion of who I am. And generally speaking, I am black. I am black because I am not white. I doubt that society consciously relies on the "one-drop rule," but it is the de facto standard.[4]

Since I am light-skinned, I do not conform to the prototypical white paradigm. I am defaulted, therefore, to the non-white category. This has usually relegated me to being identified by others as black. Curiously, my "black" membership has never been seriously challenged by black people. This holds true even where a black person knows that my mother is white. There does not appear to be a reverse "one-drop rule."

But I have never felt black enough. First, my mother is white and I cannot ignore that fact. Since my mother raised me, I have always explored my identity with reference to her. So I am mixed because I am not fully white. And this incomplete racial identity is complemented by my genetic black heritage. It is an analysis that begins with my mother and finishes, only out of necessity, with my father. So my blackness, while not an afterthought, is borne out of an incomplete white identity. And this is directly tied to being raised by a white mother.

Secondly, my circumstances have allowed me to downplay the importance of a racial identity. My blackness has never defined me because my mother anchored me to my mixed identity. And since I was neither white nor black, I was only partially privy to the benefits and detriments of the respective group stereotypes, prejudices, and inequities … So being mixed partially mitigates against a presumption of criminality, lower intelligence, and even the ability to dance. And while it is tempting to assume that my white mother has afforded me a certain degree of privilege through her whiteness, my encounters with society generally occur absent the knowledge of her race…

According to some people, I am black. According to me, I am mixed. Never have I been labelled white. At times, my blackness is even rejected. When I am amongst black people, it becomes clear, at least to me, that I am not fully black. Perhaps it is because I am light-skinned. Perhaps it is because one of my parents is not black. Perhaps it is because I do not face the plight and privilege of black people. Or perhaps, as I understand it, it is because I do not feel fully black. Even when I identify myself as black, it is an identification made out of convenience. Generally, being mixed means being black. And while I do not subscribe to that presumption, I also do not feel the need to correct it. Being mixed is a personal identity. And since my race is not a fundamental component of who I am, the efforts required to rebut the presumption are not proportional to the benefits that I would gain.

Ronnie adds other dimensions to the mixed-race identification. As "Native, Black, and Irish" and adopted by a white Scandinavian family living in an Alberta city, he speaks, unlike Joanne and Shaun, of feeling isolated and unable to connect to any one group; hence, he considers himself an "outsider looking in." Spirituality is an attribute that Ronnie raises, likely thinking of this as an important aspect of Aboriginal identification.

Ronnie: I believe my perceptions of my identity are skewed, due to abnormal socialization of cultural, ethnic, racial, political, and religious influences during my childhood [and] in my adulthood experiences.

From a cultural and ethnic standpoint, I attribute this to my adoption into a white family in a predominantly rural community. Biologically, I am Native, Black, and Irish. Socialization within my family [led me to perceive] my identity to be white, from a cultural and ethnic standpoint. I was treated as Caucasian in my interactions with my family, and practiced Scandinavian (white) traditions and cultural values; the result is that I identified heavily with white culture. Outside of my family [and] within the rural community, I was treated as a visible minority and often labelled as Native or mistakenly, Pakistani or East Indian. When labelled in such a manner by outsiders I would often experience racism or discrimination in my interactions in social institutions such as school. "Paki" or "Fucking Indian," was how I believed others outside my family perceived my identity to be. This caused confusion within me, as at home I was treated respectfully as white, while in the community I was treated with discrimination. Outside the home I was defined as inferior genetic stock due to ... rural attitudes on equality and equity.

Later in life, when I moved into a more urban environment, I found discriminatory attitudes towards minorities to be less apparent, as the cultural makeup was more ethnically diverse and, therefore, more open-minded and accepting of other ethnicities. When I tried to interact with Black or Native individuals or groups, however, I believed I was often perceived as white, due to my [background]. Whether this was my perception of the interactions or the reality of the interactions is irrelevant, as I felt distant and separate from my biological ethnic and cultural identity. I felt as though I was Indian and Black enough to be treated negatively, but not Indian and Black enough to be accepted within any social group; this lead me to several long years of social problems. A personal sense of [cultural and ethnic] identification seemed to elude me. I sometimes feel distant from my family based upon these feelings, as I do not believe they can associate with, or experience, the world in the same way I do.

From a religious standpoint, my view of God and faith has been skewed as a result of my cultural and ethnic socialization. Black and Native spiritual traditions and practices hold no weight with me, as I was raised in a [white] Christian environment. The result of this is that while I attempt to be open-minded and hold others' faiths valid, I cannot practice rites such as Aboriginal sweats in good faith, as my Christian values always seem to influence my perceptions—I see their meaning in a Christian context.

... While in the developmental stages of my life I did not put much thought into political affiliation. Later on in life, being exposed to differing political doctrines and reminded of [my grandfather's] beliefs and perhaps my innate admiration of him, directed me to identify with a more socialist—and to a degree, communist—perspective on how nations should be organized. As I live within a capitalistic country and governmental system, I often come into internal conflict with my actions ... and I believe that I am further marginalized for my beliefs as they do not adhere to the system in place.

Overall, I would say I do possess a good sense of identity; however, its meaning in relation to society as a whole often leads me to feel isolated. I cannot seem to connect to any social group entirely on the grounds of cultural, ethnic, racial, political, and religious identity. I often view myself as an outsider looking in, and tend to isolate myself on these grounds ... I perceive myself to be inherently good and [therefore, I believe] I should be able to judge for myself what behaviours and practices to indulge in and endorse. While this may seem to be a "holier-than-thou" approach, it seems to allow me to function and socialize with others in a context where I am able to maintain a valid existence and identity.

In varying ways, all three contributors underscore, as did Michelle earlier, the social, familial, and communal influences on their identities, and the work that they have done or must do to gain the ethnic or racial group membership they wish to have. The complexity, ambiguity, and contradiction of their mixed-race identities can be summarized in Ronnie's words: "I felt distant and separate from my biological, ethnic, and cultural identity. I felt as though I was Indian and Black enough to be treated negatively, but not Indian and Black enough to be accepted within any social group." Shaun makes the same point about not being Black enough.

All of the contributors relate their experiences of fitting into the society as several-generation Canadians or Canadian-born children of immigrant parents. Rolie who immigrated to Canada as a young adult, provides the perspective of someone who is a "first-generation" Canadian. Despite doing her "best to acquire the 'Canadian' accent so as not to sound like a foreigner," and taking on what she believed to be Canadian cultural attributes—i.e., "blowing my own trumpet during job interviews"—she concedes, like Moran, that skin colour is something she "could do nothing to change."

Rolie: Race and ethnicity are terms one rarely uses or prefers as a topic of discussion among friends, acquaintances, or fellow workers. They seem to be taboo in Canadian society. And yet, when people see each other, their first thought is, "This person is yellow or brown or mulatto or black or white." It is known that visual data have a far greater impact than those produced by any of the other senses, and hence the impact of skin colour or general features cannot be underestimated. As an individual, and being a first-generation immigrant, I have been rather fortunate [to not have] the nasty experience of "culture shock" after [moving] to Canada. My knowledge of English and previous experiences in dealing with people from different countries around the world during work and travel made my adaptation and integration into Canadian society easier than it might otherwise have been. Growing up in a large cosmopolitan city, awash in Western influence, was also a major contributing factor in my familiarity with Western culture.

Before arriving in Toronto I had never really given much thought to the importance of race, ethnicity, and culture. In fact, I rarely thought about my own culture, probably because I lived it daily. However, after being here for a few days, I realized that knowing the language and wearing Canadian-style clothing was not enough to make the transition to being a Canadian. Also, initially I wasn't sure if I wanted to be one. When asked what I was, my immediate reply was "Indian." I began to wonder if I was the target of discrimination and was going to be judged on the basis of my skin colour. I did my best to acquire the "Canadian" accent so as not to sound like a foreigner, and even became rather good at blowing my own trumpet during job interviews (which is very much against my nature), but I could do nothing to change the way I looked. It was also very frustrating to know that my long years of education in India meant almost nothing here. I began to perceive discrimination in every rejection. Yet I did manage to get a job and thought I'd won a great victory. One hurdle had been overcome, and I felt nothing could stop me from becoming a successful Canadian. However, when at work, white Canadian fellow workers would ask me, "How come you speak such good English?" I could not take it as a compliment. In fact, I always felt insulted and angered that they thought only whites could master the English language. Unfortunately, I felt I was in no position to counter their perceptions except by making an exception of myself.

The individuals in this chapter indicate that they attempted to "fit in" in a wide variety of ways. For some, fitting in meant dissociating themselves from their ethnic group. For others, it meant symbolically identifying with selected aspects of their ethnocultural traditions, while adopting those cultural attributes that enabled them to attain that to which they aspired. Still others, particularly racial minority group members, attempted to fit in by maintaining some degree of commitment to preserving aspects of their ethno-racial cultural heritage while participating, to varying degrees, in the culture of the society (see Kallen 1995).

WINSOME: "I WOULD HIDE THE FACT THAT I WAS JAMAICAN CANADIAN ..."

I am a Black female, and I consider myself Canadian. "Canadian"? I often get this question after identifying myself, followed by "What is your background?" I dread this question because it makes me feel that I do not belong, especially when asked by white Canadians. When I am asked these questions by minority group members, however, I feel that they only want to find out if we share the same background. As a result of the treatment that I receive from white Canadians, I have noticed that I avoid the latter question. For that reason I feel that white people have not accepted me as Canadian because I am Black. They don't recognize that I am Canadian like them. As a result of my rejection, I started thinking that I was inferior and did not belong.

During my early years in Canada, I would hide the fact that I was Jamaican Canadian mainly because of the negative attitudes towards Blacks in Canada and mostly Jamaicans. I would therefore tell everyone I encountered that I am Canadian ... When I was in Grade 9, I was determined to belong. I can remember trying to talk like "Canadians." I always speak proper English, and regardless of what Canadians may think of Jamaicans, they do speak English. Because I was brought up speaking English, this was not a problem for me. However, when I compared myself to other Canadians, I thought I sounded different. Therefore, I tried to sound as they did, and as a result everyone believed that I was Canadian with no hyphen, but thought that my parents were Jamaicans, again because I am not white. For that reason, this part of who I am was successfully hidden unless I felt the need to reveal my full identity.

In the early years, I mainly associated with Black people because I felt that people of other races had no idea how to relate to me. But as I went through my senior years in high school, I began to associate with members of other races, and my school, being very multicultural and welcoming, made it easy for me to feel that I belonged. For this reason, as I entered my late teenage years, I had a more positive self-concept. I was always willing to talk about racial issues, as I was experiencing racism daily.

I am now more outspoken about who I am and what I am about, and I have begun to see my accomplishments not as they relate to other races, but as a result of my determination and perseverance to accomplish my goals. I no longer hide my Jamaican background as I did when I was younger. At times I say that I am "Canadian" and get the puzzled look and the question about my background, which still annoys me.

Conclusion

The essays in this chapter demonstrate the role that families, community members, teachers, and peers play in individual construction of identity, specifically racial and ethnic identities. Their narratives illustrate the multiple, shifting, alterable, conflicting, and relational aspects of identity and the significance of history and contexts (e.g., physical or geographic and educational space) in the construction of identity. The fact is, and as the diagram indicates, whatever role the respective socializing agents played, the writers' identifications are mediated by their experiences (or struggles) negotiating the educational, economic, social, cultural, and political structures and events operating in their respective communities, in society, and in the world generally.

Despite their aspirations for their children, parents may have to weigh cultural expectations against the education and outcomes that they wish for their children and consider what will enable their children to become academically successful and able Canadian citizens. Indeed, parents expect that schools will reinforce the values and expectations that they have for their children and, if they are able, often choose specific schools for this reason. Parents who are unable to select their child's school, however, sometimes become super vigilant in monitoring, and even policing, their children's school activities—both the academic work and their friendships (as in the case of Ayanna)—knowing that friends and non-academic activities can be a distraction to their children's success.

Geography plays a significant role in the construction of identity (Haig-Brown 1988; Pon 2000). For some individuals, moving with and into difference means coming to settle for a particular identity in one context and abandoning it in another—all in the hope of fitting in. Michelle and Joanne each claimed a Black identity, but they also admit to being mixed-race. And Shaun, who uses the term "mixed race" to refer to himself, seems to eschew the Black part of his identity, claiming "my race is not a fundamental component of who I am, the efforts required to rebut the presumption are not proportional to the benefits that I would gain." It seems that being raised by a white mother and having an absent father has something to do with this identification. The opposite is true for Michelle, who was raised by her Black father. Is it possible that Shaun was trying to distance himself from the stereotypes, or essentialist notions, of Blackness—including, as he says, the "presumption of criminality, lower intelligence, and even the ability to dance?"—by attempting to argue for non-permanence, alterability, and self-definition unaffected by others? Smith (1991) points out that the development of identity by members of minority groups entails dealing with the initial sense of rejecting one's ethnic group, followed by the process of moving "from an early stage of unawareness and lack of differentiation to one of ethnic awareness, ethnic self-identification, and increasingly ethnic differentiation on the basis of contact situations" (183).

It is logical that individuals would want to distance themselves from the essentialist notions of their "difference," and as such, would work hard to be seen as average or ordinary. However, they also understand that skin colour, citizenship, religion, spirituality, language, accents, and other characteristics operate to inform their difference and their possibilities in society. Therefore, no matter how hard individuals try to fit in, perceived differences will continue to mitigate the process. As Sun-Kyung Yi, a self-identified Korean Canadian, writes in a 1992 *Globe and Mail* article entitled "An Immigrant's Split Personality," she went through the process of acculturation into the host culture, aware that only by doing so could she enjoy the benefits that Canada has to offer. Even so, she declares that it is "difficult to feel a sense of belonging and acceptance" when you are regarded as an "other" (A20).

Interestingly, some individuals, like Michelle, Hillary, and Cindy, seem to want to present their identities as unitary, static, and uncomplicated, although the stories of their experiences reflect the complexities, contradictions, and ongoing process of identity construction. The reactions of Moran, Cindy, and others, who are "bothered" that individuals are unable to "tell them apart from other Asians" or other members of their group, speak to the desire for recognition of diversity within their ethnic, racial, religious, and national-origin group. As pointed out earlier, of course, individuals might be conscious and aware of the diversity within groups, but evidently, telling people apart based on "sight" or physical features does not always work. Indeed, while outsiders might be unable to distinguish between members assumed to be Asians, Africans, Muslims, Christians, Jews, Europeans, Italians, German, Scandinavians, Swedish, Caribbean, etc., "insiders" may also be unable to do so. Hence, we attempt to use accents and names to make distinctions; however, it is not that easy to distinguish between people, whether insiders or outsiders, and we will always have problems doing so.

How might individuals, especially people of colour, cope with this? It will take sensitivity and cooperation on everyone's part to negotiate the apologies that will flow from our mistakes. Nevertheless, the fact remains, minority group members experience the "sameness" differently from racial minority group members. So sensitivity to the reactions of minority group members needs to be taken into consideration.

It seems that over time, minority group members become less preoccupied with the consequences of marginalization and more determined to get on with their lives. It is possible that this is the result of having come to terms with their existence as racialized "others" in Canadian society and developed strategies to cope and fit in to society.

However, as Kallen (1995) writes, it is possible for ethnic, compared to racial, minority group members to break out of their identification as minorities by aspiring to and mimicking the racist attitudes and behaviours of the dominant group (19). This might explain Anthony's behaviour (see page 119) in taking advantage of his race-related privilege and power in order to escape the temporary consequences of ethnic identification. Obviously, it should not be this way, for Anthony or any other person for whom white skin might operate to make them "non-visible." Until all Canadians (including all ethno-racial group members)—parents, peers, educators, community members, and others—completely acknowledge and accept the diversity of Canadians, full participation in society will be an ongoing struggle for those whose races operate as identifiers of "otherness" or "foreignness."

NOTES

1. See Kendall 2006; McIntosh 1995; Phoenix 1997; Rosenberg 1997; Tilley 2006; and Sleeter 1993.

2. When *first generation* is used to refer to Canadians who immigrated as adults, and *second generation* denotes the Canadian-born children of first-generation immigrants, *1.5 generation* is used to identify those who immigrated to Canada before starting high school.

3. While Daniel's use of the term *first-generation* is commonly understood, note that in current usage, Daniel's parents would be considered first generation and he, second generation.

4. See Chapter 3, note 10.

Examining the Limits of Multiculturalism

Multiculturalism has come to represent the understanding that society's diversity is based mainly on the race, colour, ethnicity, language, citizenship, or immigrant status differences that exist among members of the population—in other words, it is based on the presence of the "visible other." Responses to this diversity typically take one of two forms: (a) that the society is democratic and meritocratic, and the laws, policies, and regulations that exist provide members with sufficient freedom and opportunities to achieve their aspirations regardless of race, ethnicity, gender, social class, etc., or (b) that multicultural policies, legislation, and programs are useful to complement society's democratic principles, and thereby facilitate the integration and/or accommodation of immigrants and minorities. In the first context, special measures that might help to address individuals' failure to participate fully in the society or attain their aspirations are considered superfluous or unnecessary, for it is individual effort that counts and not structural or systemic factors. In the second, the creation of multicultural policies and legislation is often in response to demands or agitation by minority or immigrant groups as they seek recognition of their presence and correspondingly full participation and equality of opportunities, while striving to resist assimilation by the hegemonic group in the society.

In this chapter, we explore Canada's multiculturalism policy,[1] noting its promises, assumptions, and limitations, as well as its effect on the integration and accommodation of immigrants and minority members of the society. Questions relevant to this exploration include the following:

○ To what extent does having a multicultural policy and legislation make possible acceptance—and not just tolerance—of cultural differences among diverse members of society?

○ Given Canada's ethnic hierarchy and the history of assimilation by the British ethnic group—particularly with regard to Aboriginal peoples and the early French colonists—what does multiculturalism make possible for ethno-racial minorities in terms of the coexistence of these cultures?

○ Are such groups able to "maintain" and support their cultures while fully participating in society and, in the process, benefit from equal opportunities, as multiculturalism promises?

In addressing these questions—and in fact, in any discussion of the efficacy of multiculturalism in today's societies—we need to consider the challenges that stand in the way of its success in affording peaceful coexistence and positive integration of immigrants and minorities. In this regard, we start our discussion with a review of incidents in Europe that have focused attention on multiculturalism as problematic and regressive for modern Western nations. We then examine how multiculturalism is defined in policy and legislation in Canada and, with reference to students' comments and media sources, discuss how it is understood and taken up in practice.

DISQUIET IN THE DIVERSE POPULATIONS OF EUROPE: A REFERENCE

It is fair to say that the general attitude toward the amicable and harmonious coexistence of diverse ethnic, racial, and religious groups in Western countries has become increasingly strained since the attack on the World Trade Center in New York on September 11, 2001. Consequently, the benefits that it was once thought might be accrued from having immigrant and minority group members "maintain" and "celebrate" their cultures in Western societies have been called into question. Much of this has to do with subsequent acts of terrorism that occurred in London and Madrid, riots in France and the United Kingdom, and unjustifiable attacks on religious and racial minorities in many European cities. These events have informed the tone of the discourse of multiculturalism not only in the countries in which these incidents occurred, but also in countries like Canada. In what follows, we examine the incidents, noting the varying responses of the respective societies in which they took place to racial, ethnic, and cultural difference.

On March 11, 2004, three days before Spain's general elections, a series of organized train bombings were carried out during rush hour in Madrid, killing 191 people and wounding 1,800. In Spain, the event is known as M-11. In the *Guardian* (October 31, 2007) Paul Hamilos called the attacks: "The worst Islamist attack in European history." In a look back at the attacks and the aftermath, Hamilos explains that the perpetrators were young men, mostly from North Africa, and that they had been inspired by an al Qaeda website calling for attacks on Spain to upset the upcoming elections and ensure "the victory of the Socialist party and the withdrawal of Spanish forces" from Iraq. The attacks in Madrid were followed by nationwide protests and demonstrations in response to the bombings and Spain's involvement in Iraq. After the election, and once Spain finally withdrew from Iraq, another bomb plot was intercepted, raising questions about the real motives for the initial attack. The official investigation that followed indicated that while the accused had links to Morocco, they were residents of Spain; and though the perpetrators were inspired by al Qaeda, they had no direct connection to the terrorist organization.

More than a year later, on July 7, 2005, the public transport system in London, England, was attacked in a series of suicide bombings during the morning rush hour, now referred to as the 7/7 bombings. The bombings were a response to Britain's involvement in Iraq and other conflicts. Fifty-two commuters were killed and seven hundred injured—the four suicide bombers were also killed. The attack was the largest in London's transit system history. In his opening remarks in the "Report of the 7 July Review Committee" (June 2006), Greater London Authority Chairman Richard Barnes stated that: "What happened in London on 7 July 2005 could happen in any country, in any city, at any time. Ordinary people going about their everyday lives, were suddenly swept up in a maelstrom of extraordinary events over which they had no control" (5). That the accused bombers were born in Britain and prided themselves on being British Muslims was a matter of concern for many Britons. In his 2007 book, *Multiculturalism: A Civic Idea*, Tariq Modood captured the mood of British society by examining the media's response:

> The fact that most of the individuals involved were born and/or brought up in Britain, a country that had afforded them or their parents refuge from persecution, poverty and freedom of worship, led many to conclude that multiculturalism had failed—or, worse still, was to blame for the bombings. The multinational commentary in the British media included William Pfaff who stated that "these British bombers are a consequence of a misguided and catastrophic pursuit of multiculturalism" (Pfaff 2005),

> Gilles Kepel observing that the bombers "were the children of Britain's own multicultural society" and that the bombings have "smashed" the implicit social consensus that produced multiculturalism "to smithereens" (Kepel 2005), and Martin Wolf concluding that multiculturalism's departure from the core political values that must underpin Britain's community "is dangerous because it destroys political community ... (and) demeaning because it devalues citizenship. In this sense, at least, multiculturalism must be discarded as nonsense. (12)

The Paris riots of October 2005 also brought into sharp focus the tension and conflicts inherent in diverse societies, and what happens when disadvantaged members seek fair and equitable treatment and opportunities. The riots in the housing projects in the banlieues of Paris, were triggered when one youth was injured and two youths died while trying to avoid "identity checks" conducted by police. The young men were of Turkish, Malian, and Tunisian backgrounds. They were electrocuted when they entered a power substation to hide from police, who had been called to investigate possible trespassing on a construction site. According to T. Crampton in the *New York Times*, the teenagers were trying "to avoid the lengthy questioning that youths in the housing projects say they often face from the police. They say they are required to present identity papers and can be held as long as four hours at the police station, and sometimes their parents must come before the police will release them" (November 7, 2005).

The riots in France continued into November and soon spread from Paris to cities across the country, leading to a state of emergency, which was extended for three months by the French Parliament. Commenting on the riots, the social conditions of minorities, and "France's indecisive and problematic response to the larger question of how to maintain a stable and diverse society," Gereluk and Race (2007, 115) write that "issues of racial discrimination towards immigrants and particularly towards Muslims," as well as "allegations of police brutality and harassment" underpin the issues that brought about the riots in France. The unrest was also inspired by the reality that obtaining employment is difficult for individuals with "Arab-sounding" names and immigrants, whose applications are "systematically discarded." Whether this is a matter of individual perception or not isn't the issue—the fact remains that Muslims believe that other French citizens are hostile to them. Gereluk and Race explain that contributing to this perception is the fact that

> France's stance on pluralism has always been forthright in its protection of the civic republican tradition. The

legislative ban on conspicuous religious symbols in schools highlights their starkly different approach to multicultural values and tensions as compared with other countries, such as Britain and Canada. (Gereluk and Race 2007, 116)

At about the same time, Birmingham, England, saw fights between African-Caribbean and Asian (or Pakistani) youth, highlighting the "social problems and divisions" between these communities (Gereluk and Race 2007, 114). More importantly, the race riots in Birmingham demonstrate enduring and simmering tensions that exist among the disenfranchised, specifically racialized, members of society.

That racism-related incidents were occurring in many European countries speaks to the situation of non-white members of these societies—immigrants and citizens alike. In a 2006 article, Obi O. Akwani outlined a growing trend of racism across Europe, which makes "life far more difficult and hazardous" for people of colour "than for the average citizen in any of these countries" (n.p.). In some cases, people of colour (seen as foreigners) are attacked or beaten on the streets (as in Russia and Germany), resulting in long-term injuries and death.[2] While the situation for non-white citizens and immigrants in these countries is difficult, it is often further compounded by the conflict over perceived differences in values based on religious beliefs.[3] The potential for tragedy as a result of this ongoing conflict can be witnessed in relatively recent events in the Netherlands.

The killing of filmmaker Theo van Gogh in November 2004 precipitated retaliatory violent acts and arson attacks on mosques and Islamic schools, and counterattacks against Christian churches across the Netherlands. Van Gogh was a Dutch filmmaker, director, and producer who, working with a script written by Ayann Hirsi Ali, a Somali-born Muslim woman,[4] created a ten-minute movie telling the stories of four abused Muslim women. The filmmaker's death and resulting actions evidence the complicating and problematic role of religious diversity since 9/11, particularly with regard to Muslims in Christian societies. In this case, the murder of van Gogh by a young, Amsterdam-born, Muslim man with Dutch-Moroccan parents, and the related death threats against Hirsi Ali point to the tensions that adherence to religious dogma sometimes produces. Further contributing to the tensions in Dutch society was the fact that Hirsi Ali, a member of a conservative political party in the Netherlands, spoke out against the religious and cultural freedom afforded by the society. She argued that multicultural practices in the Netherlands and other countries, like Canada, which unquestioningly allow immigrant cultures to be protected and discourage assimilation, contribute to the negation of the rights of Muslim women in ways that

Sharia law affords (Hirsi Ali 2005). Recently, the Netherlands has begun making cultural orientation part of the immigration process, making it clear to newcomers that they are expected to respect the liberal values of Dutch society.

Like European societies that have struggled with the various demands of their ethnically and racially diverse populations in the last decade,[5] North Americans have similarly struggled to deal with minority and immigrant disenchantment and dissatisfaction over racial profiling, high unemployment, disadvantages in education, and other such issues related to systemic racism. In the United States, African Americans, Latin Americans, and other minority group members have been dealing with long-standing problems of racism and now Islamophobia, particularly since 9/11. And in Canada, with its official multicultural policy, the events in Europe, particularly the Paris riots, not only had Canadians asking whether such violence could "happen here" (Valpy, *Globe and Mail*, November 12, 2005, A1), but also signalled

> a warning that Canada, long considered a model of integration, won't be forever immune from the kind of social disruption that has plagued Europe, where marginalized immigrant communities have erupted in discontent, with riots in the Paris suburbs in the fall of 2005. (Jiménez, *Globe and Mail*, January 12, 2007, A1)

In the following section, we reflect on Canada's definition and assumptions of multiculturalism, noting the ways it seeks to accommodate Aboriginal peoples as well as immigrant and racial minority populations.

CANADA'S POLICY OF MULTICULTURALISM: INTERPRETATIONS AND PRACTICES

Canada's **multiculturalism policy** is rooted in the understanding that diversity is a source of strength and resourcefulness for Canada and Canadians, and that civic participation is possible if immigrants and ethno-racial minorities are able to maintain their cultural identities and are encouraged to take pride in their ancestry. The *Multiculturalism Act* states:

> [T]he Constitution of Canada ... recognizes the importance of preserving and enhancing the multicultural heritage of Canadians...; the government of Canada recognizes the diversity of Canadians as regards race, national or ethnic origin, colour and religion as a fundamental characteristic of Canadian society and is committed to a policy of multiculturalism designed to preserve and enhance the

> multicultural heritage of Canadians while working to
> achieve the equality of all Canadians in the economic,
> social, cultural and political life of Canada. (*Canadian
> Multiculturalism Act*, July 1988)

In 1971, Pierre Elliott Trudeau announced the official policy of
multiculturalism within the framework of bilingualism, for the purposes
of assuring Canadians of all backgrounds equal position within a nation
still working to break free from its identity as a British colony. The official
multiculturalism policy was legislated under Prime Minister Brian
Mulroney with the passing of the *Act for the Preservation and Enhancement
of Multiculturalism* in Canada in 1985. The official policy, and later the
Act, helped to promote a belief among Canadians that, in contrast to
the policies and practices of assimilation in the United States, "we are
multicultural."

The discourse that emerges is that Canada is committed to the
integration and not the assimilation of racial and ethnic groups and
immigrants. The Standing Committee on Multiculturalism (1987)
defines **integration** as "a process, clearly distinct from assimilation, by
which groups and/or individuals become able to participate fully in the
political, economic, social and cultural life of the country" (87). When
introducing the original multicultural policy in 1971, Prime Minister
Trudeau assured Canadians that neither assimilation nor conformity was
an objective of the federal government:

> There cannot be one cultural policy for Canadians of
> British and French origin, another for the original peoples,
> and yet another for all the others. For although there are
> two official languages there is no official culture, nor does
> any ethnic group take precedence over any other ... A
> policy of multiculturalism within a bilingual framework
> commends itself to the government as the most suitable
> means of assuring the cultural freedom of Canadians.
> (Palmer 1975)

Trudeau further explained that the government would assist "cultural
groups" to grow, develop, acquire an official language, and overcome
barriers so that they could contribute to Canada; and that the government
would "promote creative encounters and interchange among all Canadian
cultural groups in the interest of national unity" (Palmer 1975).

The underlying assumption of the multicultural policy, then, is that
by engaging in "creative encounters and interchanges," and having the
freedom to express their own ethnic cultures, Canadians will develop
respect for the cultures and cultural expressions of others. It is believed

that discriminatory attitudes and cultural jealousies will be avoided or overcome; so too will the tensions and conflicts that are often present in societies that are racially, ethnically, and religiously diverse—for example, the tensions coming from the demands of Aboriginal peoples and French Canadians in our own society,[6] and America's history of racial unrest. It is worth noting that the introduction of Canada's multicultural policy was not unrelated to the social justice and human rights movements of the 1960s and 1970s, which highlighted the demands of minority group members in North American and elsewhere: women's rights, civil rights, Red Power, Black Power, and anti-colonialism movements. And with the increase in immigration from the Caribbean, Asia, Africa, and other non-European, non-Christian countries—many of them former European colonies—it was important for Canada during this period of change to not only attract immigrants,[7] but to develop a means of accommodating the resulting diverse population of people.

In fact, research shows that the accommodation that immigrants experience—in other words, the support they receive—in Canada, contributes to favourable integration,[8] and ultimately to their success in the society. Simich and others (2005) found that social supports play a significant role in the health, settlement, and success of immigrants who are routinely faced with systemic challenges, limited resources, and inadequate policies and programs addressing integration. Generally, accommodation— providing immigrants with opportunities and access to needed resources—was shown to have an overall positive effect, and the result is the development of a more cohesive and productive society.

Leaving aside the concern of integrating a newcomer population, consider the Aboriginal peoples—a minority group in Canada with a long history of cultural struggle, forced assimilation, and perhaps undesired integration. Is there an expectation that they too would be "integrated" into a society largely identified with the European colonists and other settlers? At the beginning of the multiculturalism policy debate, Aboriginal peoples took the position that, since they were not part of the "foreign" constructed "other," the policy of multiculturalism did not apply to them. However, the *Multiculturalism Act* of 1988, in assenting that the policy and practices of multiculturalism apply to "all Canadians," indicates that, as "Canadians," Aboriginals are indeed included. The 1991 document, "Multiculturalism: What Is It Really About?" points out that "many of the issues to which multiculturalism responds—racism, understanding different cultures, and preserving culture—concern aboriginal peoples" (18). Nevertheless, as the document concedes, the political, social, and economic concerns of Aboriginal peoples go beyond the scope of multicultural policy, and "other federal government departments have policies and programs designed to deal with these issues" (19). We cannot ignore the fact that the *Indian Act* of 1876, land cessation treaties, and unresolved land claims remain in play in the lives and experiences of Aboriginal peoples, as does the assimilation-informed assumption among governments and citizens alike that the longer an "individual native resides in an urban area, the more likely integration into the dominant society becomes" (Frideres 1993).[9]

In considering multiculturalism as a policy that set out to integrate minorities and immigrants, it is worth noting the role that education serves in socializing students into the multicultural ethos. Multicultural education was introduced in the various provinces in the mid- to late 1970s to encourage students to learn about their own and others' heritages or culture, with the belief that doing so would reduce prejudice toward groups that were different from their own. It was expected that such a program would inspire academic performance, enhance self-esteem, and foster sensitivity to and respect for ethnocultural differences among students. It was thought that it would also promote the integration of racial, ethnic, and linguistic minority students into the existing schooling structures, helping them to overcome problems of otherness (James and Wood 2005, 99).

Within this schooling and community context of multiculturalism, it is not surprising that young people—in particular, those primarily of dominant ethno-racial group background—would come to believe in and thereby articulate the notion that Canada is indeed multicultural. This means that immigrants and minority group members can and do "hold on" to "their culture" from elsewhere even after generations of living in Canada, as Susanna wrote.

> **Susanna:** Taken as a whole, Canada is a good country to reside in. You are not forced to forget where you came from, but encouraged to continue with the cultures and traditions of your homeland. Multiculturalism is encouraged and there are many rights an immigrant has once he or she becomes a citizen, and although they may not always be followed, they do exist. It is important to appreciate where you live and the opportunities this country offers, but it is just as important to recognize where you came from, embrace it, and represent … by succeeding!

But the question is: does the belief that Canada is multicultural translate into acceptance or mere tolerance of the cultural expressions of minority members of society? Kim, a twenty-something Anglo-Canadian, offered a viewpoint that I found to be typical among students.

> **Kim:** Canada is a multicultural nation. Each individual holds on to their ethnicity. Every Canadian looks at another and assumes their roots are in another culture. Your roots are firmly planted in another country and

or culture. We celebrate diversity and acknowledge cultures, traditions, and customs that are not of this country. For example, one current tradition is the FIFA World Cup. Canada is not in the World Cup. Yet, [in Toronto] you walk down College Street, you're in Italy; you walk down Roncesvalles, you're in Poland, and you walk along Jane and Bloor, you're in Ukraine. As you walk down these neighborhoods [and you see] the national pride these people display as they wave their flags and sing their national anthem, it is clear their roots are embedded in another country or culture. Yet they are born, raised, and live in Canada. Ask any Canadian, "what is your nationality?" and their response will be their nationality, rather than Canadian. Canada is a multicultural nation; however, we lack that national pride.

And as Nancy indicates, the fact that ethnic group members "cling together" by living in ethnic enclaves serves to "trap" them inside these communities, thereby preventing them from learning English so that they may communicate and integrate into the wider society.

Nancy: When people of the same ethnicity cling together they become so involved in their own culture that they are not willing to open their eyes and experience what other cultures have to offer. It becomes impossible for them to do so because they have spent so much time in their own community that they cannot communicate with anyone outside of it. For example, I knew someone who had been in this country for sixty years. He could hardly speak a word of English, and therefore how was he supposed to communicate with anyone outside his ethnic community? He had trapped himself inside it.

For Kim, Nancy, and many others, the promotion of multiculturalism comes at a cost—the lack of a "national pride" and language proficiency, which they feel are necessary if Canada is to prosper economically, socially, and politically. To this end, such people would insist that individuals should be socialized to identify with Canada, learn English or French, and take pride in Canadian identity. This perspective suggests that, contrary to the promise of cultural democracy, immigrant and minority groups are expected to conduct themselves in a manner consistent with the established legal, political, economic, linguistic, cultural, and social structures if they are to be "accepted" or even "tolerated" members of the society. This being the case, we might ask, what then does multiculturalism in Canada make possible in terms of accommodating "difference"? What beliefs, customs, and practices of immigrants and minority group members, signalled by their "difference," will be accommodated?

ACCOMMODATING "DIFFERENCE": ADJUDICATING WHAT CAN (AND IS TO) BE ACCEPTED

Just as immigrants and minority members have to accommodate other members and existing structures of the society if they are to be tolerated, gain a modicum of acceptance, and participate fully in society, so too must other members of society and its structures be accommodative of their needs, interests, beliefs, values, and practices. **Reasonable accommodation**, a concept in labour law initially developed to address questions of equal rights for persons with disabilities and later extended through the *Canadian Charter of Rights and Freedoms* to address religion and sex (Brydon 2008), is relevant to our discussion of the accommodation of immigrants and minorities in Canadian society. In fact, the concept was central in the debates generated by the Bouchard–Taylor Commission's "extensive consultation" of "accommodation practices" in Quebec in 2007. Perhaps what is most telling about these debates is that they focused national attention on the complications, contradictions, and conflicts that result from living in diverse communities, even in a society with an official multiculturalism policy.

THE BOUCHARD-TAYLOR COMMISSION

The Consultation Commission on Accommodation Practices Related to Cultural Differences (or the Bouchard-Taylor Commission) was appointed by Quebec Premier Jean Charest in February 2007, in response to events in Hérouxville (a town of about 1,300 residents). The Municipality of Hérouxville published a standards of behaviour statement, which stated that new arrivals would be expected to leave behind the "lifestyle" of their birth country and adapt to their new environment (1). The publication includes the following:

> We consider that men and women are of the same value
> ... We consider as undesirable and prohibit any action or
> gesture ... such as: killing women by lapidation [stoning]
> or burning them alive in public places, burning them with
> acid, excising them, infibulating them or treating them as
> slaves ... In our hospitals and CLSC's women doctors can
> treat men and women and the same for the men doctors.
> (Municipalité Hérouxville, Publication of Standards)

Also, according to Hérouxville's publication, children do not carry weapons to school; prayer rooms are not made available in workplaces for "incantations;" people may not hide their faces; the town decorates Christmas trees, and displays crosses in recognition of history and "patrimony;" and residents listen to music, dance, and drink alcoholic beverages, and when they eat meat, they needn't know where it came from or how it was killed.

Signed by the mayor and six councillors, this description of the "social life, habits and customs" of Hérouxville's residents and their expectations of "new arrivals" reveal their assumption that potential "new arrivals" would likely be locked into a belief system that has them abusing women and children, rejecting Christmas, alcohol, and pork (thereby ridiculing those for whom these are acceptable practices), and mired in religious practices. As Brydon (2008) points out, the "Hérouxville declaration translates the legal language of 'reasonable accommodation' into the moral sphere, setting a 'them versus us dynamic'"(9). The declaration also seems to take the position that culture is fixed and new influences pose only a threat.

This representation of their own, and other cultures, as static is certainly not unique to the residents of Hérouxville—it was also evident in the discussion of secularism, public expressions of religious beliefs, racial discrimination, and national or cultural identities in which the Bouchard-Taylor Commission engaged. Indeed, as Jacques Beauchemin, an advisor to the commission, commented, the debates about reasonable accommodation not only provided new insights into "nationalist sentiment," they also provided the opportunity to ask: "Who are we? How do we want to live together?" (D. Moore, *Globe and Mail,* November 26, 2007a, A19).

From their hearings in various parts of the province of Quebec, the Bouchard-Taylor Commission produced a report in 2008, *Accommodation And Differences: Seeking Common Ground: Quebecers Speak Out,* in which they scrutinized the conditions of immigrants and minority members. In response to their observations, it was recommended that immediate action be taken to address unemployment among these members of the society, and that institutions must strive for more intercultural dialogue in an effort to promote cultural diversity. Other recommendations were that Quebecers demonstrate more openness toward immigrants, and that immigrants should also be responsible for their integration into French-speaking, secular society.

The report also demonstrated that the integration process was influenced by generational differences that exist between older and younger Quebecers. Older Quebecers seem to be more fearful and uneasy about accommodating minorities, believing that such accommodation would mean a decline in the French language—something that Bill 101, the French-language law passed in the late 1970s, sought to protect. Having lived through the Quiet Revolution of the 1960s and 1970s, Konrad Yakabuski writes, this generation remembered religion as a means of social control, hence they were less protective of religious tradition than they were of Quebec language and culture, and were generally suspicious of organized religion (*Globe and Mail*, November 3, 2007, A19). The younger generation, however, which "never felt the church's claws, don't carry the same baggage toward something their own parents never showed or taught them: faith" (*Globe and Mail*, November 3, 2007, A21).

The report paid significant attention to what the commission referred to as "open secularism" in provincial institutions. Among the recommendations on this subject were that

○ public officials, including police officers, be forbidden from wearing religious symbols

○ other state employees, such as teachers, should not be prevented from wearing religious symbols such as hijabs, crucifixes, or kirpans municipal councils eliminate the practice of saying prayer before sessions

○ the cross, a Christian symbol, that was displayed in the House of Assembly be removed.

Quebec's history notwithstanding, the commission wrote:

> Catholicism has left an indelible mark on Quebec's history. Traces of it are all around us. Under the principle of the neutrality of the State, religious displays linked to the functioning of public institutions should be abandoned. Thus, we do not believe that the crucifix in the National Assembly and the prayers that precede municipal council meetings have their place in a secular State. In both instances, public institutions are associated with a single religious affiliation rather than addressing themselves to all citizens.[10] (Bouchard and Taylor 2008a, 49)

However, after much discussion, the government chose not to go along with this particular recommendation.

RELIGIOUS ACCOMMODATION: THE BELLWETHER OF CULTURAL ACCEPTANCE

As the Bouchard-Taylor Commission demonstrates, government practices and uses of symbols set a model or pattern for accommodations. As such, the recommendation that governments should eliminate prayer from their sessions not only comes up against long-standing "tradition" and practices, but also challenges the very ethos of Christianity that many Canadians might expect from our elected politicians, particularly as they prepare to undertake important governing tasks and decisions. The practice, then, of *not* saying prayers is something with which legislatures have struggled, and often the decision to maintain "tradition" tends to gain support. While Quebec, for example, marks its legislative opening with a moment of silence, and British Columbia rotates between five ecumenical prayers, Nova Scotia, after evaluating established practice of reciting the Lord's Prayer at the beginning of each legislative session, decided in 2001 to continue with the practice (Sweet 2005). Similarly, in 2008, four months after Premier Dalton McGuinty announced that prayers would no longer be read before Ontario's legislative sessions, Members of Provincial Parliament voted unanimously to maintain the tradition of daily prayer (Benzie, *Toronto Star*, June 13, 2008). However, as a concession to religious accommodation, it was agreed that the Lord's Prayer would be rotated with prayers from other faiths, and that a moment of silence would be included in recognition of atheists.

Clearly, the cultural beliefs and practices that contribute to the most noticeable tensions and conflicts for Canadians—and people living in diverse societies in general—have to do with religion. Ron's statement is indicative of the negative views some Canadians hold toward accommodation of religion differences:

> **Ron:** The idea that Sikhs are allowed to wear their turbans while on duty for a Canadian police force makes me very, very mad. I know that everyone in Canada has freedom of religion, and there is nothing wrong with that. However, the *Charter of Rights and Freedoms* is like rules and regulations. The police force has rules and regulations, and under those, there is a uniform rule that states that every police officer must wear a hat. I don't think that it is right that a Sikh may change that rule. It is not fair to the rest of the police force. In fact, I think that it is an insult to this country. If I went to their country, there would be no way in hell that I or any other white man would be able to change any of their rules. I do not have any prejudices against the Sikhs or any other nationality or skin colour, but people from other countries are treating Canada like garbage and they are taking advantage of Canada and its people. I think that in order to change this problem, Canada has to take away some privileges and change the *Charter of Rights and Freedoms*.

Ron's seeming frustration with multiculturalism demonstrates his ignorance of the fact that the Sikh community has been in Canada for generations and that many Sikh Canadians died for Canada in twentieth-century wars while wearing turbans. He sees them as new, maladaptive interlopers, and views their religious symbols, ethos, and practices as a threat to Canada as he knows it.[11] Ron, who was studying to become a police officer, believed that the tradition of policing was threatened by the variation in uniforms. Observing Ron's reaction through a cultural analytical lens, it can be said that such variation challenges what the uniform stands for to him and the wider Canadian community; that is, the uniform is a symbol that elicits respect from society and signals a fraternity that provides cohesion and discipline to group members. Hence, from his perspective, such changes should not be tolerated and, even more so, not accepted. However, the reality is, the constitution gives Sikhs, like all other Canadians, the right and freedom to practice their religion. Uniforms have always been modified to accommodate changes in style, job role, technology, and safety, so why not faith?

Like the Royal Canadian Legion, which had to revisit its rule that men remove their hats out of respect for the dead, Ron should consider that head coverings mean different things in different cultures. In recognizing that the Sikh turban does not belong in the same class as a Western man's hat, the legion had to reconcile the idea that such a requirement was unnecessary for men with religious headgear. In the early 1990s, the Royal Canadian Legion's decision to institute an exception to their strictly enforced "hats off" policy, was precipitated by a Sikh-Canadian veteran who wrote to Her Majesty the Queen to explain how he had been barred from attending a ceremony at a legion hall because he would not remove his turban. Nevertheless, since officially amending its dress code to permit religious headgear, there have been similar incidents at legion halls across the country, suggesting that such rule changes do not necessarily change public perceptions, nor do they significantly change the position of minorities within Canadian society.

As mentioned earlier, schools play a significant role in socializing students in the process of accommodating diversity, particularly in terms of religious objects and practices among students. Recognizing or "celebrating" Aboriginal History Month, Black History Month, Chinese New Year, Asian Heritage Month, and other ethnic events, or referencing the literature, history, and geography of other countries (particularly non-European countries), seems less problematic than allowing students and teachers to wear their kirpans or hijab to school, or providing space for prayer or programming around religious celebrations or events. A number of cases have been taken to the Human Rights Commission and to the courts, appealing for recognition of religious beliefs and expressions (see James and Wood 2005; Lenk 2000; Sweet 2005). One early example took place in 1994, when a young Muslim girl was suspended from school in Quebec for wearing her hijab because, according to the principal, she risked marginalization because of her "difference" (Lenk 2000). A few years earlier, in Ontario, a baptized Sikh teacher, who had worked in the Peel Board of Education for more than four years, was asked to stop wearing his kirpan to school. The case was taken to the Ontario Board of

Inquiry, which in July of 1990, ruled that the policy of the school board "has an adverse impact on Sikhs, who cannot teach or attend school in the Peel region and at the same time honour the requirements of their religious faith." Contrary to the school board's argument that the policy is necessary to avoid any violent use of kirpans, the Board of Inquiry further stated that there was no support for this argument, as there has been "no evidence of violent use of the kirpan by Sikhs in Canadian schools" (James and Wood 2005, 101).[12] This decision was appealed, but the appeal was dismissed by the Ontario Divisional Court.

Since these early cases, there have been many examples of such struggles. In 2006, Muslim students at École de technologie supérieure at the Université du Québec, one of Canada's largest engineering schools, were obliged to use the stairwells for their daily prayers. Quebec's Human Rights Commission ruled that the institution "failed in its duty to accommodate Muslim students by denying them a place to pray in dignity." And contrary to the institution's claim to secularity, Marc-Andre Dowd of the commission, explained that "the secular nature of an institution doesn't remove its obligation to accommodate students in their religious needs" (I. Peritz, *Globe and Mail*, March 23, 2006, A13). While institutions may want to be seen as culturally and religiously neutral, and moreover, secular—leading many to believe that religious faiths do not matter—constitutionally, the religious faiths of citizens do matter and must be acknowledged.

Significant to this discussion of accommodation is the role of our commissions and courts in helping to maintain and uphold religious freedom, equity, and inclusivity as guaranteed through Canada's *Constitution, Charter of Rights and Freedoms, Human Rights Act, Canadian Multiculturalism Act,* and *Immigration and Refugee Protection Act.* We have already mentioned some of the rulings of commissions and courts that have adjudicated on cases involving violation of religious and human rights. But one would expect that as long as diversity exists there will be ongoing cases, and appeal after appeal in which members of our society will demand legal judgment or remedy to their situation.

Take the case of Avtar Singh Dhillon of British Columbia, who filed and won a discrimination complaint on religious grounds when he was denied a motorcycle license because he was unwilling to remove his turban and wear a helmet. Dhillon won the right to take the driving test without his helmet. This ruling was in keeping with British Columbia and Manitoba helmet exemptions for Sikhs, which are similar to those in countries such as the United Kingdom and India. These exempt drivers are not required to sign waivers and are not subjected to inflated insurance rates. In contrast, Baljinder Badesha of Ontario, who in 2008 challenged a $110 ticket he received for not wearing a helmet while riding a motorcycle, lost his case. Even though the Ontario Human Rights Commission supported Badesha, many Ontario newspaper columnists, particularly those in the mainstream press, agreed with the court's ruling against Badesha on the basis of their belief that helmets represent a matter of life or death.

These cases, in which Sikh Canadians are appealing for the right to wear their turbans, come almost two decades after the federal government changed the restrictions that prohibited Sikhs in the RCMP from wearing turbans. This decision enabled Baltej Singh Dhillon to become the first RCMP officer to wear his turban on the job. Hard hats on construction and other work sites continue to receive attention. As in the Badesha case, many argue that religious rights should not trump safety,[13] especially in Canada, where public health care has to pay for treatment of head injuries. Some argue that if Sikhs wish to forego protective headgear, they should sign waivers or take out additional insurance.

Another notable case is that of a Toronto woman, who in October 2008, was ordered by Justice Norris Weisman to remove her face-covering niqab when testifying against her assailant in a sexual assault trial. The reasoning behind the decision, which the judge admitted was "difficult," was that the complainant's religious convictions were "not that strong" and were more a "matter of comfort." It was reported that the judge took into consideration the fact that the woman had unveiled her face for a driver's license photo, although she explained to the court that the picture was taken by a female photographer with a screen blocking male potential onlookers from seeing her (B. Powell, *Toronto Star*, February 2, 2009).[14] Putting aside for a moment the important question of whether one should be able to exercise her or his religious practices in a court of law, a cultural analysis requires that we ask other equally important questions: what processes, norms, and traditions have structured our legal process in such a way that requires a person to show his or her face when giving evidence? Why is the niqab seen as disrupting the carrying out of justice? What would an accommodation of the niqab in this instance mean for the case and trial? And, accordingly, what might it mean religiously and personally for a woman who might derive comfort from wearing it, especially in a case dealing with sexual assault? Furthermore, is it up to the courts to determine how strong one's religious conviction is? What does it mean, or what evidence would be required, for a judge to determine the strength of a person's religious conviction?

It is important to critically examine or interrogate the conditions and foundation on which this case of the wearing of the niqab, as well as those involving wearing the kirpan or turban, are built. In doing so, we must acknowledge the structural and powerful role of law and the legal system—founded on particular norms and ways of operating—that effectively excludes and does not account for a range of differences. The debates on reasonable accommodation are evidence of the state having to reconcile, or come to terms with, managing differences that may seem to threaten the hegemonic structure.

In the cases mentioned above, the courts were required to adjudicate civil and criminal matters. But if matters before the court are believed to be related to religious tenets, should the courts intervene? Many governments permit family court issues to be handled through mediation or arbitration by religious institutions. What would it mean for the state to accommodate religious principles and practices that appear contrary to the state's ethics of human rights and freedoms, particularly in relation to women?

The debate in Ontario over whether to certify Sharia law comes to mind. In 2004, following the formation of the Institute for Islamic Civil Justice, which was intended to train arbitrators for family law tribunals, the province decided against certifying such tribunals. While family law cases had been heard for years by certified Christian and Jewish tribunals, this decision was influenced by strong public opposition, particularly from women's groups, who feared that such tribunals would threaten the rights of Muslim girls and women in Canada. Initially, the approval for Islamic family courts was considered a matter of equality: if Muslim families wish to use religious arbitration to govern their divorce and custody issues, they should have the right to do so, as other faiths do. However, Natasha Bakht (2005) of the National Association of Women and the Law, an organization dedicated to promoting human rights among all women in Canada, argues that all religious arbitration is inappropriate in family law because "gender dynamics, unequal power relations between men and women and systemic discrimination are always at play. As currently practiced, arbitration allows people to pick and choose the law that will apply to them" (Bakht 2005, 63).

With reference to the argument made by supporters of religious tribunals that women should be free to "live as they choose" and that a universal application of laws was not appropriate for the "private sphere," Bakht goes on to argue that this

> neo-liberal vision of "choice" disregards not only the painful dynamics of divorce and separation, but most importantly, the overall social and economic context of the lives of many women: susceptibility to homelessness upon the breakdown of a marriage, the precariousness of immigration status, abject poverty and persistent racism. Given the inability of most women to afford legal counsel and the fact that ideological and religious groups may

> offer free mediation and arbitration services, women's free choice remains dubious … The notion of free choice in the context of family arbitration is gender-insensitive as it does not take into consideration the real power dynamics at play and the collective rights at stake for women."[15] (Bakht 2005, 64)

To resolve the issue, the Ontario government decided to put an end to all religious-based family law arbitration. Despite the long-standing and apparently successful religious-based family law tribunals run by Jewish and Christian groups, in September 2005, the premier announced an end to the debate over Sharia laws, as well as an end to the existing programs.

> There will be no Sharia law in Ontario. There will be no religious arbitration in Ontario. There will be one law for all Ontarians … Ontarians will always have the right to seek advice from anyone in matters of family law, including religious advice … But no longer will religious arbitration be deciding matters of family law. (Leslie 2005)

The debates over Sharia law and the role of tribunals in dealing with issues of family law reveal the inevitable problems that must be addressed in religiously diverse and secular societies. In such cases, the judiciary has a critical role to play to ensure that religious differences are accommodated, while protecting the rights and freedom of individuals.

Essentially, while there has been some accommodation of certain cultural beliefs and practices of immigrants and minorities, particularly with regards to cuisine, cultural festivals, styles of dress, and celebrations, most often what is accommodated tends to fit within the context of European Christian tradition or does not stray too far from prevailing practices. For instance, to accommodate French Canadians, the federal government allows employees to forego the August long weekend, based on the Commonwealth tradition of the bank holiday, and instead take their holiday on Saint-Jean-Baptiste Day, Quebec's national holiday (which was popular in New France), which is celebrated on a traditional Catholic feast day. However, Biles and Ibrahim remind us that a similar opportunity is not allowed for employees to choose between Christmas Day and the Jewish holy day of Yom Kippur. Generally, the more contentious issues surrounding accommodation tend to be related to religion.[16] But, as Biles and Ibrahim (2005) write, "religious diversity is not a bogey (wo)man that Canadians should fear. Just as Catholics and Jews have become important components of Canadian society, without we might add, society coming apart at the seams, so too can other faiths take their rightful place in Canadian society" (Biles and Ibrahim 2005, 70).

ADDRESSING RELIGIOUS FREEDOM IN THE COURTS

No case exemplifies the delicate balance between religious freedom and civil rights better than the case of Bruker v. Marcovitz. Stephanie Bruker and Jessel Markovitz were married in 1969 and granted a civil divorce in 1981. At the time of the divorce, the couple agreed that Markovitz would grant Bruker a *get*, a Jewish divorce. Under Jewish law, if a woman wants to remarry, she must obtain a *get* from her first husband. Markovitz refused to grant Bruker a *get* for fifteen years, despite repeated requests and the initial divorce agreement. In 2007, Bruker sued Markovitz for breach of contract. The lower court ruled in favour of Bruker, and found that her claim for damages was within the domain of the civil court. Markovitz appealed on the argument that the court should not dictate religious practice. The Quebec Court of Appeal found that, as the obligation was religious in nature, it was a moral issue and not enforceable by the court, therefore Markovitz was not in breach of contract. However, the Supreme Court of Canada upheld the original decision of the lower court, on the basis that an agreement being religious in nature does not make it outside the realm of the civil court. The dissenting judges argued against the ruling on the grounds of religious freedom. While granting a *get* is not a civil act, promising to do so as part of a civil divorce proceeding is, and Canadian divorce law was amended in 1985 to prevent the use of religious barriers to remarriage and custody to influence civil proceedings. By refusing a *get*, Markovitz effectively prevented Bruker from remarrying within her faith, thereby infringing on her religious rights. The Supreme Court argued that Markovitz could not use freedom of religion to avoid paying damages for breaching his contract with Bruker.

In the face of the issues and problems that multiculturalism seems to generate, it is not surprising to hear young people like Ed express strong opposition to multiculturalism:

Ed: I was never a fan of the *Multiculturalism Act* and, if anything, I find myself even more opposed to it now. Although many people would like to say that this makes me a racist, I believe that I am not. A racist is someone who hates or discriminates against a person or people because of a difference (or perceived difference) in colour or religion. While I have never been like that, it sure makes my blood boil to hear that Sikhs can wear their turbans in our police forces or that schools are required to remove all symbols of Christmas from the classroom. Just because I do not like to see these events happen doesn't mean that I dislike the person for succeeding in his or her quest. I am developing a strong discriminatory attitude towards the government ...

Not only does Canada open its arms and borders to accept immigrants from all over the world, which is something that doesn't bother me, but it also willingly changes Canadian traditions and customs to accommodate them. In essence, what the Canadian government is doing is saying, "Hi! Welcome! Don't worry about learning one of the two official languages of the country. In fact, if there are any traditions that have been around in Canada for a long time that you do not like, let us know. We will either exclude you from them or change them all just for you."

What the *Multiculturalism Act* has really done is given everyone a chance to change Canada and make it more like the country they left in the first place. If you want to inspire a feeling of Canadian pride, leave Canada's laws and customs as they are and encourage people to assimilate and contribute to the country in a positive way. As John F. Kennedy so eloquently put it, "Ask not what your country can do for you, but what you can do for your country!" Although this was an American president, I believe this country needs to do some real flag waving to wake [itself] up.

In responding to Ed's comments, we might want to ask who exactly can be a "flag waver"? Can a person whose ancestry goes back generations, is a racial minority, insists on his or her religious rights and freedom—with permission to carry his or her religious symbols and take time off work for religious observances—be recognized as an "authentic" or legitimate flag-waver? When does someone become recognized as a "true" proud Canadian?

"ARE YOU CANADIAN?": NEGOTIATING "DIFFERENCE" IN MULTICULTURAL CANADA

In a *Toronto Star* article (December 8, 2007b), Bob Hepburn—in his response to the question "What exactly does it mean to be Canadian?"—noted that Canadians have been asking this question for generations. But until recently, the question was always framed in relation to being non-American; today, the question is informed by the increasing number of immigrants and ethnic and racial minorities who live here and expect their cultural values and religious beliefs and practices to be accommodated and supported. It is within this context that young people—majority and minority group members alike—are trying to construct their identity as Canadians, and make sense of and negotiate the promises, questions, contradictions, tensions, and conflicts that characterize our diversity as Canadians.

As you have read, Kim seems to appreciate the idea that "Canada is a multicultural nation" and that we "celebrate diversity and acknowledge cultures, traditions, and customs that are not of this country," but laments the fact that some people seem to have their "roots firmly planted in another country and or culture" even though "they are born, raised, and live in Canada." This, according to Kim, is evidence that we lack "national pride." Similarly, for Ron and Ed there is an unease with the way that multiculturalism has brought about changes to Canada as they know it (or the way they wish it to be). Some young people, like Kim, seem ambivalent or conflicted about multiculturalism. Others, like Ron and Ed, seem troubled or frustrated, and perhaps even angry (Ed explains how his "blood boils"), that multiculturalism legitimizes changes to the culture of Canada and permits newcomers and minority Canadians to maintain their identity.

Evident in these young people's comments is the discourse of difference that Canadian multiculturalism promotes. This discourse positions culture as something that is primarily carried out and exhibited by "foreign" people who are linguistically different, have "foreign" names, and do not look and sound "Canadian." In other words, Canadians with "culture" are from elsewhere, and their "foreign" cultural values and practices are viewed as static and based on their past experiences in other countries. This popularly held notion of "Canadianness" is also strongly related to the idea of Canadians as visibly white with "Canadian names" and without "accent;" in other words, those of British descent, and those European peoples who have assimilated sufficiently.[17]

Katalin Szepesi's (2001, 33) experience is illustrative of the struggles and hurdles to identifying as Canadian, especially when her name gets in the way. She writes:

> **Katalin**: I want to call myself Canadian, but I'm not allowed. My name is Hungarian by origin, so therefore I am Hungarian. It doesn't matter that on my mother's side I'm seventh-generation Canadian [with] family from Great Britain. It doesn't matter that I can't speak Hungarian and have only a marginal understanding of the culture. It doesn't matter that I was born and raised in Canada. It doesn't matter that I'm white. Katalin Szepesi is not a Canadian name.

Maria, who emigrated from Poland as a child, is someone for whom language initially operated as a barrier, but with time her fluency in English and "white race" helped her "blend" into society and be seen as a member of the dominant racial group—thereby making her "readily accepted."

> **Maria**: When I first came to Canada, I realized that I was different from the people around me. Mainly because the language I spoke was Polish, not English. At that time I felt inferior because of the language barrier, but as my English improved, I was readily accepted by those around me. Since I spoke English, I was seen as a Canadian and no longer as an immigrant. Then, and only then, was I able to say that I was Polish. At the present time, I feel very strongly about my ethnic background ...
>
> I feel that being a member of the white race enables me to blend much easier into the Canadian society. My major barrier was being unable to communicate with the language of the dominant culture. Given the fact

that I was white, I was no longer considered as an outsider once the language barrier was removed.

This understanding or conception of "Canadian" and "culture" is further evident in the following comments, which represent what happens when some "Canadians" are questioned about their taken-for-granted identity or "culturelessness." In some cases, they experience feelings of difficulty in trying to reconcile, rethink, or broaden their understandings.

> **Andrea**: Call me naive, ignorant, or sheltered from the real world, but I thought in order to have a culture a person had to be of a different racial group. Since I was born in Canada, I thought I was just "Canadian." Now I am told I have a culture.
>
> **Richard:** As far as my culture goes, I am at a loss. I am Canadian. Period. There are no special traditions or attitudes that have been passed on to me by my parents or grandparents. My parents have taught me what they think is important for me to know. I have no traditional food or drink, no cultural costume. I am Canadian.

Andrea and Richard's comments illustrate the feelings of many white Canadians who, when asked to identify themselves in terms of ethnicity and race, tend to refuse to say anything other than "Canadian," and usually insist they have no "culture." For these individuals, Canada has a cultural vacuum—others might say that Canadian is culturally neutral, that people from elsewhere and even non-white people who have been living here for generations are able to "maintain their culture." This is why even after years of living in Canada, non-white Canadians—or to use the uniquely Canadian term, "visible minorities"—tend not to be given the privilege of identifying themselves simply as "Canadian." When they do, they are usually asked, "Where are your parents from?" and then, "Where are your grandparents from?" As one white student explained to me, he would not accept that single descriptor, "Canadian," from a Black or Chinese person because "they do not look Canadian." Is it any wonder then that Canadians who are not white would claim, or resort to, a national identity related to their ethnic origin, country of birth, or ancestor's country of birth?

In the following comment, Aasha makes explicit the role of race in the construction of who is Canadian—until she came to know better, she thought of white people as "real Canadians." She also suggests that the claims of multiculturalism are false, especially when only some Canadians are able to enjoy the privileges that multiculturalism promises.

Aasha: If I was asked ["Are you Canadian?"] while I was in high school I would have said that white people are the real Canadians. However now that I am a bit knowledgeable as to how this country was stolen, I would say that there is only one true Canadian and that is Native Aboriginals. So everyone else is a Canadian citizen, unless they are Aboriginal. I am half Ethiopian and half Somali, but now I am also a Canadian citizen ...

This notion that I held earlier in my life attributing whites as the real Canadians, is a conception that is held by many people. For example, although black people have been here since 1608, they are still asked where did they originally come from. (I just want to say, "Well, ask your ancestors, who stole me from Africa.") But when a white person comes from anywhere in the world, be it even South Africa, they are never asked twice where they originated from, unless of course they have a foreign accent. Even when you go on the Canada Revenue website, where it says "Are you Canadian?" they have a picture of white people and where it says "Are you an Immigrant?" they have a picture of a black person. What is it insinuating? ...

All in all there is no such thing as multiculturalism in Canada—it is something they use to cover up their subtle racism by putting a front up as though they accept all people regardless of culture, race, age, gender, ability, or sexual orientation.

Aasha exposes, and at the same time challenges, the veiled racism that is inherent in the construction and naming of who is Canadian. And as she indicates, this naming is not merely a result of individuals' independent ideas, but learned through historical omissions, miseducation, and misrepresentation by institutions such as schools and government departments or agencies. It is worth noting that the representation of Canadians through websites, posters, brochures, postage stamps, magazines, etc., communicates to Canadians and non-Canadians the message of who belongs to Canada or who is Canadian. When Canadians go abroad and their identity as Canadians is questioned, it should be seen as a signal that the multicultural ethos is not effectively communicated in our messages to the outside world. Consider, for example, the experience of Katia and her university peers, who were visiting students at a university in Germany. As Katia said, the "nine Canadian girls were Romanian Canadian, Indian Canadian, Trinidadian Canadian, Pakistani Canadian, British Canadian, Muslim, and Jain," but "since it was perceived that we all have non-Canadian blood, we were not deemed true Canadians." She went on to say that their "believability" as Canadian was complicated by their countries of birth.

Going abroad or travelling in other countries sometimes brings out a person's Canadian identity or makes the "Canadian culture" clear—

values, customs, and practices by which we live, or the behaviours we present. Take for example, Norma, who writes:

> **Norma:** I was born in Mexico City and immigrated to Toronto in 1989 … and even though I am a Canadian citizen, when someone asks me where I'm from, I always say Mexico. I'm proud of my Mexican heritage, but I'm also proud to live in Canada. When I go and visit my relatives in Mexico, they always tell me that I'm not "Mexican enough." When I ask why, they say that it is because of my attitude and personality …
>
> When I go to Mexico, people whom I do not know right away ask me where I'm from. When I tell them that I was born in Mexico, they say that I don't "act" like a Mexican. I end up telling them that I live in Canada, and this answer seems to be satisfactory to them. This bothered me because I consider myself Mexican; in my house, we cook Mexican food, follow some Mexican traditions, and I speak Spanish. My parents say that I'm a mix of both Mexican and Canadian. Mexican comes first because I was born there, and Canadian, second, because it is my home. To this day, I consider myself to be Mexican Canadian yet consider Canadian history as my history. I also consider Mexican history to be my history as well.

Amber, who spent time teaching in South Africa, explains how her understanding of what it means to be Canadian was experienced as she engaged her students in dialogues about individual rights, privileges, and cultural beliefs and practices. These interactions, which included hearing views that she found unacceptable, helped Amber to appreciate the opportunities and freedom that Canada has afforded her. But while, as she says, all Canadians fly the same flag—hers is the "small flag" she carries on her baggage—she is careful to acknowledge the individual differences, as well as regional differences and cultural variations that characterize Canada, like all other modern societies. But as she says, she is a "proud" Canadian, and her patriotism is renewed when she is "away from home soil."

> **Amber:** Current geographical location and cultural differences aside, however—what does it really mean to be Canadian? Is it to drink beer, watch hockey, eat maple syrup, go to cottages in the summer, skiing in the winter, be really nice, tidy, friendly, punctuate your sentences with "eh?" and be enormously proud of not being American? Because I do and am all those things (aside from the hockey and skiing and being tidy—I'm a basketball fan, I hate the cold, and am hopelessly messy). But what about getting more to the matter? What about what I am so proud to say about my country when I travel? About how multicultural we are. About how my peer group is composed of people of every ethnicity. About how diversity is not only embraced but encouraged.

Implicit in such a view on Canada, however, is my acknowledgement and understanding that my Canada is indeed quite different from that of someone who grew up in North Battleford, Saskatchewan, or Chibougamau, Quebec, or Truro, Nova Scotia.

I was born in Toronto, and attended university in Montreal. Aside from short weekend trips to Ottawa, Quebec City, Vancouver, and a couple random towns in Ontario and Quebec—those two cities comprise my Canada.

Over the years my privilege has enabled me to travel, and provided experiences that have further driven home what I love about Canada and why I am so proud to be Canadian. I suppose this may be, in fact, the very reason for the newfound patriotism that I always seem to discover when away from home soil.

Recognizing the factors that play a role in understanding something is sometimes almost as important as the understanding itself. The perspective that my travels at home and abroad have provided me, have and continue to serve as a reminder of how much I love my country, and perhaps more accurately, my hometown. "I Am Torontonian" just don't have the same ring to it though, does it?

Essentially, living, learning, working, and playing in an ethnically, racially, and religiously diverse society presents complex and difficult challenges that individuals must confront. As the experiences and reflections of students in this chapter indicate, the tension and conflict found in culturally diverse societies suggests to them that multiculturalism is not working, at least for them. Their problems with multiculturalism, evidently informed by their respective identities and experiences, are, in various ways, a result of variations in political perspectives, a lack of recognition of—and respect for—differences, a lack of access to political and economic resources, and our society's seeming inability to accommodate and adjudicate these differences. Canada is not unique in the difficulties that arise between its various ethnocultural groups (for example, the French–English tensions). Similar tension and conflict can be observed in other nations; in fact, as we discussed earlier, we are constantly faced with international news stories recounting the tragic results of ethnic tension and even worse, ethnic conflict. How we address these issues and tensions reflects how we understand and accept our cultural diversity and cultural differences, as well as how we accommodate our immigrant and minority populations.

ON THE FUTURE OF "OFFICIAL" MULTICULTURALISM IN CANADA

On Canada Day in 2008, the *Toronto Star* published an article by noted social researcher Michael Adams exploring the state of Canada and the issues most concerning to Canadians (July 1, 2008, AA6). It noted that in the early 1990s, the issue concerning most Canadians was Quebec nationalism and fears of Quebec sovereignty, but in 2008 there was a much different focus. As Adams puts it, "Today, immigration and multiculturalism are most often held up as the pressing threats to the national identity." He points out that polls reveal an interesting contradiction or divide amongst Canadians: "Most Canadians are comfortable with this country's high levels of immigration, but some (especially our pundits) feel that Canada needs to do more to encourage newcomers to integrate into the Canadian cultural mainstream." As the article suggests, it seems that while immigration is seen as "all fine and well," multiculturalism is no longer considered an effective "framework for addressing unprecedented levels of ethnocultural diversity." And while multiculturalism was always praised as "fair-minded" and "idealistic"—something that Canadians should be proud of—Adams also suggests that it is increasingly being blamed for a variety of social concerns, such as "civic apathy among immigrants, dilution of national identity, and even racism itself." Those who espouse this argument hold that "multiculturalism encourages immigrants to maintain their cultures at the expense of participation in mainstream Canadian life, leading not just to the isolation and alienation of minority ethnic groups but also to a weak and divided Canada."

Similarly, a 2007 series in the *Globe and Mail* featured a two-page exploration of multiculturalism in Canada entitled "Cracks in the Mosaic." The newspaper investigated "how multiculturalism is failing Canada's visible minorities." Author Marina Jiménez focused particular attention on various ethnic enclaves (or "ethno-burbs") that have arisen in some of Canada's largest cities (February 8, 2007, A8). According to Allan Gregg, chairman of marketing research firm the Strategic Counsel, "In Canada, we may live in a multicultural society, but the evidence suggests that fewer and fewer of us are living in multicultural neighbourhoods" (A8). He adds, "We spend so much time congratulating ourselves on tolerance and diversity that we have allowed it to slide into self-segregated communities, isolated along ethnic lines." The article draws attention to the growing South Asian community in Brampton, Ontario, as well as the increase in Chinese families in Markham, Ontario, and Richmond, British Columbia. With reference to the growth in "ethnic enclaves"[18] as contributing to greater marginalization of differences, the *Globe and Mail* asks: "What are the long-term consequences of this explosion in ethnic enclaves? Does self-isolation impede integration? Will the children of these immigrants eventually blend into Canadian society like previous generations, or will their status as visible minorities block their progress no matter where they live?" (A8). While it's generally agreed that it is too soon to determine the answers, the article concludes that "multiculturalism isn't working that well for visible-minority newcomers." (See Chapter 6 for further discussion of this issue.)

Questions about the efficacy of multiculturalism continue to be a concern, not only among members of Western societies, but more importantly, to their political leaders. It is a concern to Europeans and North Americans, especially in those societies with explicitly (and not so explicitly) articulated multicultural policies or programs. But many people, including American scholar Walter Benn Michaels (2006), argue that a focus on diversity, and subsequently the accommodation of differences, distracts us from concrete issues of equity. In his 2006 book, *The Trouble with Diversity: How We Learned to Love Identity and Ignore Inequality*, Michaels argues that we need to "move beyond diversity—to make it clear the commitment to diversity is at best a distraction and at worst an essentially reactionary position" (17). For Michaels, the matter of importance should not be discrimination based on characteristics such as hair colour, skin colour, gender, sexuality, religion: "No issue of social justice hangs on appreciating hair color diversity ... [or] on appreciating racial or cultural diversity" (15). These characteristics—"our identity"—argues Michaels, are "the least important thing about us," yet they are the things to which "we have become most committed to talking about." Michaels sees this as a "profound mistake," alleging that the identity discussion (about religious, racial, sexual and other identifiers) omits and ignores the importance of other issues, such as "economic inequality." But what Michaels—and others who are quick to dismiss diversity—fails to acknowledge is that we cannot separate these identity characteristics from social systems, institutions, and structures, and the resulting economic inequality because they are all inextricably linked. For instance, women face persistent economic inequality, despite the advancement of women's rights over the last few decades and countless equity initiatives. Some argue that overcoming this inequality requires a fundamental shift in our society's attitudes surrounding motherhood.

If indeed there is a commitment to addressing inequity—not just inequality[19]—then multicultural policies and practices cannot simply be about acknowledging or responding to "identity" differences as unitary and independent characteristics, nor should it be about "celebrating" differences—or "celebrating diversity," as the popular mantra goes. Further, a multicultural approach that addresses inequity does not posit culture as a set of static, uncomplicated, and observable items and practices that can be identified, displayed, easily communicated, and represented. Neither should it reify "culture as the most salient factor in intergroup dynamics, deflecting attention from the disquieting legacy of white supremacy and casting people of color as culturally problematic" (Thobani 2007, 162). Rather, culture must be understood and recognized as something that is dynamic and that people make together. Hence, immigrants and minority members cannot continue to be marked as "outsiders" or "foreigners"—thereby re-inscribing their "immigrant-for-life" status. They must be considered *Canadians* for they too contribute to the shaping and reshaping of the culture, or cultures, that exist in Canada. If multiculturalism is to live up to its promise then, there must be a recognition and critical examination of the overt and covert pressures toward conformity. The hegemony of a particular ethnic group (as discussed in Chapter 2) exists within the state apparatus, managing the differences and dissension that are to be expected in any society, and, of course, any diverse society (Foster 2005; James 2005). How else but through some form of conformity or some level of assimilation will immigrants and minority group members be able to "fully participate?"

Some ethnic and racial group members may reside in "enclaves" in and around large urban centres—or even on reserves—and some members practice versions of their ancestral cultures in varying degrees, but this does not mean that their cultures remain the same. Even though they may appear to reside in homogeneous communities or to socialize largely with ethno-racial group members, ultimately, these groups are still subjected to the same legal, political, economic, social, and cultural structure as everyone else in our society. In reality, they do not exist apart from, or outside of, the mainstream of society. Hence, the natural or inevitable process of cultural integration, conformity, and in some cases, assimilation, in terms of values, customs, and behaviour is sure to take place. In one way or another, the mainstream will also have changed because of the population's diversity. Whether they live in "enclaves" or not, minority group members attend educational institutions where the curriculum is directly and indirectly informed largely by the dominant values, norms, and expectations of the society. Ultimately, through the textbooks used, the languages spoken, and the daily routines of educational institutions, minority group students, just like other Canadians, are socialized into the elements of Canadian culture.

The powerful role of education in helping to integrate the young, new members of society cannot be overestimated. Susanna's experience and appeal for an education curriculum that is inclusive of her background is instructive.

Susanna: As I reflect on the person I am today, I realize just how much I have changed. Growing up I attended a small Catholic elementary school located in a predominantly Italian neighbourhood and I was usually embarrassed to say where my parents came from. None of my classmates were familiar with the Dominican Republic and I often felt left out because of this. This is just proof of how important it is to have multicultural communities—this way people, especially children, do not feel left out and can relate to others as opposed to feeling different because of where they are from.

If multicultural education is to enable learners to take advantage of the opportunities provided, attain their aspirations, and participate fully in society, then the differences and cultural resources that these learners bring to the educational process must be taken into account. To ensure equality and equity, educational programs—curriculum content and pedagogical approach—must address the inequities, racism, and discrimination that operate as barriers to participation within the education system and society as a whole. Multicultural education will have to be conceptualized in ways that are inclusive of all students, beginning by addressing Aboriginal peoples and recognizing how Canada's colonial legacy informs the issues facing them today.

Multicultural education also needs to help students understand the complex, unstable, and relational nature of culture, and how characteristics such as class, gender, ethnicity, and race structure and affect educational and occupational opportunities. Ultimately, student success will be determined by the extent to which the school environment, curriculum content, and school practices reflect and acknowledge the diverse cultural backgrounds represented within their classes and society as a whole. The promise that multicultural education can therefore provide equal opportunity, address problems of educational underachievement, and improve individuals' self-image will not be realized within the current context, which ignores the hegemonic nature of the dominant culture, based as it is on compounded privileges accrued from class, race, and gender (Sleeter and Delgado 2004). Subject matter may change (such as in the study of history), but this does nothing to address the traditional pedagogy that continues to fail minority young people.

As I discussed earlier, current multicultural practices have been ineffective in helping today's young, minority Canadians see themselves as Canadians. A 2007 *Globe and Mail* article by Marina Jiménez titled "How Canadian Are You?" which referenced a study by Jeffrey Reitz and Rupa Banerjee,[20] reported that "for some immigrant groups and their children, living in Canada longer does not necessarily lead to a greater sense of belonging or a higher degree of social integration on their part" (January 12, 2007, A1). This trend was shown to be particularly "profound" among Canadian-born racial minority members, who increasingly felt a strong sense of exclusion or less attachment to Canada than their immigrant parents. In comparison to their white counterparts, these young people were also less likely to vote. Furthermore, that racial minority members were less likely to identify as "Canadians" was said to contribute to their diminished sense of trust, and signalled a failure on society's part to address their experiences and needs in order to engage them as full members of the society. The study also suggests that while Canada has, in the past, served as a model of integration, it is not immune to, nor can it, "avoid the violence and social disruption that has plagued some European countries" (A1). Given the trend identify by Reitz and Banerjee, it is clear that we must address the root of problems such as racism and discrimination that plague young people if we want to avoid such crises.

THE CHALLENGES AHEAD

In June 2006, seventeen members of an alleged Islamist terrorist cell were arrested and charged with participating in a group with the intention of carrying out terrorist activity in Ontario between March 1, 2005, and June 2, 2006. The seriousness of the charges notwithstanding, what is significant about the arrests was how initially the "immigrant" backgrounds of those charged were used as part of their identities. But, as Canadians soon found out, none of the men arrested were recent immigrants and many were Canadian-born. As Joshua Hergesheimer, a Canadian columnist based in the United Kingdom, wrote for *Aljazeera.net*:

> If these arrests are really an indication that Canada is under threat, then it is clear that the problem is home-grown, not imported ... Multiculturalism and the acceptance of diversity is not the problem. But unless Canadians defend their social policies by living them out every day, in direct defiance of people who blame multiculturalism for the current problems, there may soon be nothing left to champion. (June 27, 2006)

Hergesheimer identifies the existing disconnect between talking about a commitment to diversity and multiculturalism, and real action to resolve the challenges facing immigrants and minority groups in our society.

In claiming that multiculturalism provides opportunities for integration, while still holding tight to white, Anglo-Franco traditions, we ultimately reinforce, protect, and grant legitimacy to the existing hegemonic structure. Consequently, the racism and discrimination that are barriers to minority groups' integration and full participation in our society remain in place. By providing programs and policies (which by their nature are destined to fail) we allow members of society to conceptualize racism as a "problem" of individuals and not a structural issue. The political, social, and cultural messages that all Canadians need to receive through multiculturalism should not be ones that contribute to the homogenization of "visible minorities," "foreigners," or "cultural groups" based on "likeness" or "sameness." Such cultural relativism is based on an assumption that minority people, having been socialized in the "same" culture, act in similar ways and are motivated by similar values and concerns (Benhabib 2002, 89). These assumptions, with their emphasis on ethnic identities, negate intra-group differences and issues related to gender, class, sexuality, and other differences. This multicultural approach to knowing or learning about ethnic groups does little to ensure that their particularities and differences are understood and addressed. As cultural analysts, we must resist essentialist stereotyping of people, but it does not follow that we should ignore how race, ethnicity, and immigrant status operate in the lives of individuals.

In considering the future of multiculturalism, we must reconsider the uniquely Canadian term "visible minority." Developed in the 1960s and 1970s and codified in the 1995 *Employment Equity Act,* the term has become part of the multicultural discourse. Used to identify people who are not white, or who are visibly different from the dominant group, some critics suggest that the term is preferred because it maintains a "colour-blind" perspective and eliminates the use of the word "race." However, the term "visible minority" has come under much criticism, particularly by the very people that it seeks to identify. In 2007, the United Nations Committee for the Elimination of Racial Discrimination (CERD) criticized Canada's use of the term, suggesting that it is "problematic not because of malevolent intent but because of the unintended consequences of unconscious racist assumptions" (cited in Fleras 2008, 6–7).

In a panel presentation at the 2008 National Metropolis Conference in Halifax, Nova Scotia, Augie Fleras explained that there were two main elements to the CERD's criticism:

> First, by problematizing visibility, reference to visible minorities was thought to normalize whiteness at the expense of "whitewashing" racial minorities; hence the nomenclature was deemed discriminatory because of its racial connotations. Second, by normalizing invisibility under a singular typology, specific minority experiences and identities were glossed over, in effect perpetuating the very racism under challenge. (7)

In the discussion that followed, the panel presentation, participants, some of them racial minorities who were concerned with having no alternative term to represent employment equity target group members, argued for retaining the term. Others disagreed, noting that, as Brydon (2008) proffers, "it assumes, without questioning, an invisible white hegemony with the power to define, and subordinate, what deviates from its assumed norm" (1). In moving forward, as Fleras noted, we need to establish the source of our concern: which of the words—"visible" or "minority"—presents the problem? Should we be naming or focusing on physical appearance? How do we address the problems of racism and discrimination without having a way of naming their targets? Can an equity program avoid positioning whiteness as the norm and using some kind of "us" and "them" construction?

CONCLUSION

Of course, cultures evolve. Human populations migrate and adapt. Cultures do not and cannot remain the same, so we should not expect them to. When we think of Western societies today compared to fifty years ago, we see the significant impact that civil rights, the women's movement, the sexual revolution, and advances in art, music, design, architecture, and technology have had on our cultures. What is clear is that individuals adapt, conform, acculturate, integrate, and assimilate to the changing circumstances of their societies. As Peter Li suggests,

> Academics' general acceptance of the multicultural ideal has sometimes tarnished their ability to distinguish between the force of assimilation as a social fact and the social expectation of their doing so as an ideology. The multiculturalism policy may have created an ideal of incorporating diversity, but this in itself is no assurance that immigrants in Canada are not expected to succumb to the forces of assimilation, especially when the actual forces of conformity remain compelling. (Li 2003, 329)

In other words, regardless of any official government policy, is it really possible to stop the children of immigrants from adopting the cultural values and customs of their surroundings? Some level of assimilation or acculturation is inevitable, whether it expected at an explicit (as in the United States) or implicit (as in Canada, as Li argues) level. However, young members of ethno-racial minority groups might argue that it is not assimilation they seek, but respect and recognition—similar to that received by young members of the dominant group.

Some newcomers move into "ethnic communities," generating a concern among some members of the society about their commitment to Canada. But the reality is that the culture of the "old country" changes in ways unknown even to the **diaspora**, which tries hard to "hold on" to an imagined history and culture. Therefore, identifying with a particular culture (ethnicity or nationality) in Canada is not necessarily the same as it may be or may have been in the country of origin. Consider, for example, the large population of people with Scottish heritage in Cape Breton and other areas of the East Coast, which maintains many traditional cultural practices and continues to teach them to their children. This cultural maintenance can have intriguing benefits; for example, Canadian experts in Highland folk dance have returned to Scotland to teach dances lost to the community there. Certain practices, dialects, and vocabulary that are often used in North American Italian and Portuguese communities are no longer used in the country of origin because immigrants often hold on to words, linguistic forms, and "old country" thinking that may be forgotten over time. Immigrants have, over many years, held on to that which they remember as the culture that was brought to Canada, not recognizing that the culture they have left behind has been constantly transforming and shifting. What we are suggesting is that multiculturalism, and what is constructed as the culture of people from other countries is sometimes a misrepresentation. When members of such group cultures visit their "old country" they are sometimes seen as "foreigners" and clearly North American.

Religious beliefs and practices continue to pose particular problems in the integration process of immigrants and minority Canadians,[21] despite other compromises that are made in the accommodation process. Referring to the resulting challenges, Biles and Ibrahim (2005) explain that

> the most pressing at the moment is the relentless treatment of Canadian Muslims as an un-integratable mass of illiberal individuals who pose a threat to Canadian society—a problem that predates the 2001 terrorist attacks that have merely intensified with what some term "Islamophobia"... This erroneous and bigoted attitude is widely held, is extremely unhelpful in building an inclusive Canada, and results in some serious illiberal behaviours on the part of other Canadians and Canadian institutions. (68)

Demographic projections indicate that the population of those who follow non-Christian religions will continue to grow in Canada, and "only a commitment to real religious pluralism will ensure that the Canadian commitment to a 'shared citizenship' model undergirded by a multicultural ideology will flourish in the 21st century" (Biles and Ibrahim 2005, 69). The concerns of these faith traditions "cannot be ignored ad infinitum without serious issues of exclusion emerging" (69).

To conclude, multiculturalism purports to be creating a kind of Canada in which immigrants and minorities can be integrated while maintaining their heritage and becoming proud Canadians who participate in mainstream public life. However, many criticize Canada's multiculturalism because of the belief that, as in countries such as Britain,[22] this type of policy socially fragments populations and facilitates "separateness," which in turn "ghettoizes" minorities and increases tensions between groups and communities, making possible the organization of extremist groups. Nevertheless, in spite of these criticisms, multiculturalism has generally been celebrated as one of the principles that defines us as Canadians. While this multiculturalism has not produced the same sorts of extremism or rioting and violence in Canada, as we have seen in London, Paris, and other European cities, "there are disturbing signs of cracks in the mosaic" (Friesen, *Globe and Mail*, August 20, 2005, F8). These cracks are evidenced in the recent debates on reasonable accommodation in Canada, and specifically in Quebec. Such debates provide examples of how multiculturalism is and can be taken up by Canadians, many of whom are finding it difficult to reconcile their understandings of what it means to be Canadian—their own privileges and way of life, values, culture—with those that are different or believed to pose a threat to an understood way of life. Indeed, as Brydon (2008) declares:

> What is at stake here is the nature of Canadian democracy and whether we can transform a colonial and unjust society into a better home. Part of making that shift will involve changes in how we understand culture, and the relationship among culture, community, identity and citizenship. The policy implications are serious (9).

The accommodation debates also reveal how multiculturalism, when understood as the maintaining of separate cultural groups, can become positioned as the "fall guy" for various cultural and social challenges and fears about change.

NOTES

1. While the terms are often used interchangeably, it is important to distinguish between multiculturalism, multicultural or multiculturalism policy, and the *Multiculturalism Act*. Canada maintains what many refer to as "Official Multiculturalism," which began with the adoption of the principles of multiculturalism in 1971 by an all-party policy agreement in Parliament. These principles were further codified in the drafting of the *Canadian Charter of Rights and Freedoms* in 1982 and were finally enshrined in the *Multiculturalism Act,* passed in 1988. See page 136.

2. For more discussion, see Bunar 2007; as well as Bideke and Bideke's report on protests in Malmo, Sweden (2007).

3. Recall that in September 2005, a series of twelve cartoons were published in one of Denmark's largest daily newspapers, *Jyllands-Posten*. The cartoons, regarded as racist and Islamophobic because of their caricature depictions of the Prophet Muhammed, spurred protest (at times violent) in many North American and European communities. Many in the West saw the protest as evidence of Islam's incompatibility with the Western values of freedom of expression and modern concepts of democracy, which further served to separate the Muslim population as the "other."

4. Ayaan Hirsi Ali was also an elected member of the Dutch House of Representatives, and resigned her parlimentary seat following the political scandal over the allegation that she gave false information to secure asylum in the Netherlands.

5. Writing of the situation in Britain, Tariq Modood (2007, 12) notes, "In 2004, a swathe of civil society for a [forums] and institutions of the centre-left or the liberal-left held seminars or produced special publications with titles like 'Is Multiculturalism Dead?', 'Is Multiculturalism Over?', 'Beyond Multiculturalism,' etc. This critical, sometimes savage, discourse reached a new peak with the London Bombings of 7 July 2005 (7/7) and the abortive bombings of '21/7.'"

6. While civil conflict in Canada has never reach the level seen in American history (as with the Civil War in the 1860s), some class and cultural conflicts did lead to armed rebellions in the nineteenth century. More recently, Aboriginal peoples continue to protest their treatment in Canada; usually by occupying land to prevent development or exert sovereignty. These occupations sometimes lead to violence, as with the shooting death of a law enforcement officer in Oka, Quebec, in 1990 or the death of a protestor in Ipperwash Provincial Park, Ontario, in 1995. However, the most violent cultural conflict in modern Canada is the 1970 October Crisis, which represented the violent expression of the centuries-old conflict between French and English. After years of detonating bombs in Quebec, the extremist *Front de libération du Quebec* (FLQ) kidnapped two government officials, killing one and releasing the other in exchange for safe passage to Cuba. During the crisis, the federal government employed the *War Measures Act*, virtually declaring martial law.

7. The 1970s saw significant movement of people around the world, particularly from so-called developing countries to North America and Europe; with the global economic and technological boom, it was necessary for Canada to compete for its share of immigrants. Multiculturalism became a viable brand for Canada's image—something that was not to be had in the United States.

8. "Integration" here describes the process by which immigrants and minorities are able to participate fully in the society and realize their aspirations. (See the definition by the Standing Committee on Multiculturalism, 1987.)

9. The earliest incarnations of the *Indian Act* declared that all Indians who married non-Indians or who received an education in a Christian residential school would be recognized as "civilized" and "fit for white society." All of these "enfranchised" Indians and their families would then be required to leave the reserve. For decades, Aboriginal children were taken from their families and placed in residential schools to isolate them from Native culture and language and to Christianize them. Today, there are few Aboriginals alive who have not been influenced by the enormous impact of European culture on their traditional way of life (Dion 2002). See also Monture-Angus 1995 and Haig-Brown 1988.

10. But the commission noted that "it would be absurd to want to extend this rule of neutrality" to everything, since symbols such as crosses on buildings exist because of the history they represent. Hence, the report concluded that "'Quebeckers' common sense will surely prevail in this respect" (Bouchard and Taylor 2008a, 49).

11. It is worth noting that when the RCMP commissioner approved Sikh's wearing of turbans, the Association of Retired RCMP went to court to contest the decision on the basis of religious freedom. They claimed that the wearing of the turban as a visible religious sign violated the religious freedom of others. The court rejected the claim and was further confirmed on appeal. Grant v. Canada (Attorney General) [1995] 1 F.C. 158 (Federal Court—Trial Division. 125 D.L.R. (4th) 556 F.C.A.

12. See also *Pandori v. Peel Board of Education* 1990, *Peel Board of Education v. Ontario Human Rights Commission and Pandori* 1991, and Sweet 2005. With reference to early Canadian religious history, in her article "Accommodating Religious Difference," Sweet (2005) writes about how religious dress, religious teachings, and holy days have been accommodated in

Canadian schools and other institutions, and how these issues have been "battled out in Canadian courts." She also notes: "Certainly, there is a tension between accommodating religious minorities and a liberal political culture that emphasizes individualism, majority rule, integration and secularism" (152).

13. This argument is not limited to the realm of public safety. In November 2007, safety was used as the reason for a Calgary referee's refusal to allow a fourteen-year-old girl to play indoor soccer while wearing a religious head scarf. The referee and the representative of the governing body for soccer in Alberta reasoned that the hijab poses a risk or threat to the safety of players. The referee's decision was upheld, despite the fact that the girl had been playing all season while wearing the head scarf "without incident." Earlier the same year, two other girls' soccer teams (one in Nepean, Ontario, and another in Ottawa) forfeited their games when one of their players was ordered to remove her hijab (*The Gazette*, November 26, 2007, A12).

14. In March 2009, the Ontario Human Rights Commission intervened in the case, arguing that the woman should be allowed to testify without removing her niqab, and appealed to the Ontario Superior Court. In May 2009, Superior Court Justice Frank Marrocco ruled there is no blanket right for a Muslim woman to wear a niqab while testifying in court. He suggested that judges should determine on an individual basis whether or not wearing a niqab is acceptable in their courtroom, weighing societal interests, freedom of religion, and the right to cross-examine. Marrocco instructed Judge Weisman to conduct another hearing to explore the reasons the woman is wearing the niqab, after which he will have the right to determine whether or not she may testify while her face is covered (Kari 2009). The issue of face covering also gained attention during the 2007 election, when concerns were raised about allowing women who cover their faces to vote without confirming their identity.

15. One side effect of the debate over the issue of religious arbitration was the narrow focus on sensationalizing Islam and Sharia Law, which often included stereotypes and extreme examples of Muslim practices.

16. Biles and Ibrahim (2005, 86) report that there have been other accommodations of religious differences. Specifically, the Chaplaincy Service of the Correctional Service of Canada (CSC) provides halal and kosher meals to inmates, and in 2005 the Quebec Correctional Service hired a full-time imam. In 2003, the Canadian military appointed the first Muslim to serve as chaplain. Also, in 1996 the first covered woman began serving in the Armed Forces and eventually becoming an officer. By her own account in various Canadian media outlets, her experience has been positive and the military has been most accommodating of her dress and dietary restrictions at both the institutional and individual level, from official approval of not just a hijab but a loose-fitting uniform, to food services personnel ensuring there's always something she can eat in the galley.

17. See Bannerji 2000; Dei and Calliste 2000; Fleras and Elliot 2002; Foster 2005; James 2005; James and Shadd 2001; Thobani 2007; Walcott 2003.

18. It seems that in the public discourse "ethnic communities" are acceptable, but "ethnic enclaves" are not. The latter seems to be associated with segregation, while the former represents the communities of minority or immigrant groups that we are accustomed to. We tend to think of "ethnic communities" as quaint—places where we go to enjoy cuisine and "ethnocultural" performances.

19. There is a difference between *equity* and *equality*; equality is concerned with equal shares of a given thing, such as rights (for example, in a democracy, all people are equal under the law), but equity is concerned with ensuring people are able to experience the equality afforded under the law. While providing opportunities for minorities in relation to their representation in the population is a matter of equality, equity calls for accommodating the needs of minorities based on the ethos of social justice, thereby giving attention to historical and systemic barriers that have operated to affect their social and economic situation. The

concepts of equality and equity are often used in education—equality calls for all children to be educated by the state; equity requires that children be given what they need to obtain that education. For example, a system based on equity helps ensure that students with learning disabilities get the differentiated instruction they need to be successful.

20. The study, *Racial Inequality, Social Cohesion, and Policy Issues in Canada*, which used Statistics Canada's Ethnic Diversity Survey, was published by Montreal-based Institute for Research on Public Policy, www.irpp.org.

21. The observance of religious holidays is one example of traditions that pose particular problems—Christian holidays are the foundation of civic holidays in Canada. However, many countries, such as Trinidad and Tobago and Singapore, have incorporated multiple faiths' holidays into their national calendar (Biles and Ibrahim 2005, 69). In Canada, individuals of other faiths must often work or use vacation or sick days to observe their holy days.

22. Tariq Modood, a Bristol University sociology professor, explains that multiculturalism has been less successful in Britain because it entered into public discourse differently than it did in Canada (i.e., as federal policy in 1971). In the United Kingdom (and I would add Sweden), multiculturalism was applied mainly to education (*Globe and Mail*, August 20, 2005, F8).

ASSESSING THE MERITS OF IMMIGRATION

The significance and merits of immigration are ongoing questions for Canadians, as they are in almost every immigrant-receiving country. And while Canadians often concede—even if on only a superficial or sentimental level—that "except for Aboriginal people, we're all immigrants," we cannot underestimate or dismiss the value of new immigrants and refugees to the social, economic, and political existence and prosperity of Canada. In fact, our individual successes are directly related to the presence and contributions of immigrants who came before and after every one of us. Understanding this relationship is part of any cultural analysis. Such analysis gives attention to the social and historical context of diversity in Canada, beginning with the Aboriginal peoples of Turtle Island, and moving to the early European settlers or colonists who, with the ideology of *assimilation*, structured early immigration policies and practices. Such an analysis helps bring about an understanding of how issues of racism, xenophobia, Islamophobia, and discrimination have emerged and are embedded in Canadian society.

The first part of this chapter presents an overview of Canadian immigration, including an historical perspective, which provides context for understanding Canada's project of settling people from Europe and elsewhere in the territory that many Aboriginal peoples refer to as Turtle Island. This program of settlement was, in part, a reflection of ethnically and racially based immigration policies established by early governments—with the necessary justification—to exclude or control the entry and settlement of particular immigrant groups. And as I have argued elsewhere, how and when immigrant groups are permitted to enter a country—and the ways in which they are accommodated and expected to participate economically, politically, socially, and culturally—sets the stage for how they come to be perceived and treated by members of the ruling elites of that society. Similarly, "mythologies and 'overgeneralized truths' help to construct social images or stereotypes" that justify the treatment immigrant group members receive and the position they come to occupy in the economic and social structure of the society (James 1997b, 310).

The second part of the chapter examines some commonly made claims about immigration and immigrants, as expressed by some of the young people with whom I have worked over the last few decades. These claims reflect the young people's attempts to make sense of their employment opportunities, their access to social services, a perceived increase in criminal activities, and what they see as a "changing" of Canadian culture. Much of the misinformation and many of the myths evident in their common claims underlie the prevailing attitudes and positions that are so often evident in our society. These ideas are perpetuated by major socializing institutions such as the media, schools, governments, and others. How immigrant young people and the children of immigrants respond to these is taken up in the latter part of this section.

The final part of the chapter discusses Canada's need for immigrants and the implication that has for the economic and social welfare of all Canadians.

Canadian Immigration: An Overview

Before proceeding, it is useful to clarify the difference between an *immigrant* and a *refugee*; confusion between these two terms is reflected in everyday comments. An **immigrant** is a person who takes up permanent residence in Canada and is admitted only after meeting strict criteria, either on their own or by their relationship to other Canadian citizens or permanent residents. A **refugee**—also known as a "Convention refugee" according to the United Nations' definition adopted by all member countries, including Canada—is:

> Any person who, by reason of a well-founded fear of persecution for reason of race, religion, nationality, membership in a particular social group or political opinion, (a) is outside the country of his (her) nationality and is unable or, by reason of such fear, is unwilling to avail himself (herself) of the protection of that country, or, (b) not having a country of nationality, is outside the country of his (her) former habitual residence and is unable, or by

reason of such fear, is unwilling to return to the country.
(Ministry of Employment and Immigration 1978, 11)

According to Citizenship and Immigration Canada, refugee protection is available to "people in Canada who fear persecution or whose removal from Canada would subject them to a danger of torture, a risk to their life or a risk of cruel and unusual treatment or punishment" (Citizenship and Immigration Canada 2009). However, it should be noted that people do not simply enter Canada and claim refugee status. Canada must first recognize an applicant's country of citizenship as a refugee-producing country, with reference to the United Nations' definition. Individuals from non-refugee producing countries may also claim refugee status as "persons in need of protection"—for example, journalists or activists from countries that do not afford their citizens the right to free speech. And in very rare circumstances, individuals denied refugee status can apply to stay in Canada on humanitarian or compassionate grounds—for example, non-residents who are caring for a sick family member or with Canadian-born children.

Until recently, Canadian immigration was separated into three classes: refugee class, which is described above; family class, which requires sponsorship from a closely related Canadian citizen or permanent resident; and the economic class, which assigned points for various qualifications and characteristics, such as education, language fluency and the market need for an individual's skills. Most immigrants to Canada have qualified through the economic class and a points system first introduced in 1967.[1] Now, in addition to the traditional refugee and family sponsorship categories, there are five main paths to becoming a permanent resident of Canada under the umbrella of the old "economic class." Within these categories, either a modified points system or other economic factors are used to determine eligibility. These paths are business immigrant; skilled worker and professional; Quebec-selected skilled worker; Canadian experience class; and provincial nominee.

Under the *family class*, Canadian citizens or permanent residents may sponsor close family members, such as spouses, parents, grandparents, and dependent children. Other related children who are orphaned and under the age of eighteen, such as grandchildren, siblings, nieces, and nephews may also be sponsored under family class; independent adult children may not be sponsored. However, immigrants applying under the skilled worker class may earn extra points for adaptability if they have a close Canadian relative. Sponsors must have the financial means to support their family member for three years or more, depending on that relative's age, and in Quebec, which administers its own immigration program, sponsors must sign a contract to that effect. Sponsorship now extends to same-sex spouses and partners, reflecting how changes in cultural values, norms, and attitudes of society have influenced shifts in immigration polices and practices. According to Citizenship and Immigration Canada (2009) a person can apply to sponsor his or her same-sex partner as a spouse if they were married and issued a certificate by a Canadian province, or other jurisdiction that has made same-sex marriage legal, such as Spain, the Netherlands, and American states such as Massachusetts, Vermont, and Iowa.

Within the *business immigrant class*, there are three sub-classes, each of which is intended to contribute to the Canadian economy: investors, entrepreneurs, and self-employed. Investors are expected to make a $400,000 investment; entrepreneurs are expected to start and manage a business that creates a specified number of jobs; and the self-employed category is reserved for artists, entertainers, athletes, and individuals with experience in agriculture. Those in the investor and entrepreneur classes must also have a minimum net worth of C$800,000 and C$300,000 respectively.

The traditional points-based system is still used within the *skilled worker and professional class*. Immigrants in this category are selected based on education, work experience, fluency in an official language, and other qualifications that will help them to be economically secure in Canada. Individuals who can apply under this category are foreign nationals living legally in Canada as temporary foreign workers, international students, and newcomers with offers of employment. Applicants must also receive a minimum of 67 points according to the points system. See **Table 6.1** for a breakdown of the current points system.

The remaining paths for immigrants to Canada that are not subject to the points system include the *Canadian experience class, provincial nominee*, and *Quebec-selected skilled worker* programs. Individuals who have been working in Canada on temporary work visas for two years, or foreign students who graduate from Canadian post-secondary institutions may qualify under the experience class; it is assumed they have knowledge of French or English, are familiar with the society, and have demonstrated their ability to transition from temporary to permanent residents. Under an agreement with the federal government, provinces may also nominate individuals who wish to live and work in that province; while not subject to the skilled worker points system, provincial nominees are expected to fulfill an immediate economic need in the province in question. The *Canada-Quebec Accord on Immigration* allows Quebec to administer its own immigration program; individuals who wish to immigrate there must meet the standards of the Quebec-selected skilled workers category, which does not employ the same system as the federal program.

TABLE 6.1 — IMMIGRATION SELECTION CRITERIA FOR
SKILLED WORKERS AND PROFESSIONALS

Criteria	Maximum Points	Example
Education	25 points	Graduate degree = 25 points High school diploma = 5 points
Ability in English and/ or French	24 points	Points awarded by level of proficiency in both languages
Experience	21 points	5 years or more = 21 points 1 year = 15 points
Age	10 points	21 to 49 years = 10 points Fewer points given to youths and people over 50 years
Arranged employment in Canada	10 points	Temporary workers and those with certified job offers = 10 points
Adaptability	10 points	Any previous experience in Canada or family members in Canada = 5 points, with maximum of 10 points Spouse or partner's level of education = 3 to 5 points
Total	100 points	
Pass mark	67 points	

Source: Adapted from Citizenship and Immigration Canada. 2009. <www.cic.gc.ca>

HISTORICAL OVERVIEW OF CANADIAN IMMIGRATION

Since Confederation, the majority of immigrants to Canada have come from the United States and the United Kingdom. As immigrants began to arrive from "other" areas, authorities attempted to control, monitor, and regulate immigration (or those who "got in"). Historically, those who were allowed in without difficulty were those who belonged to preferred groups or nationalities, such as American citizens or British subjects.[2] Factors such as race, ethnicity, nationality, and social class were used to control the quality and character of immigration, and to ensure that those who entered would assimilate (Kalbach and McVey 1971, 37). This meant that white Europeans (specifically Western Europeans) were initially the preferred immigrants, after Americans and white citizens of Commonwealth countries. Successive governments, and parliamentarians in general, debated the necessity of and their commitment to keeping Canada white. For example, in 1908 Robert Borden, then the minister responsible for immigration, bluntly stated that "the Conservative Party stands for a white Canada." The Liberal government that later came to power, keeping with that same policy, introduced an Order in Council in 1911 that was designed to "stem the tide" of some 1,300 Black American homesteaders who were immigrating from Oklahoma to Alberta (Shepard 1997). While Americans were classified as "preferred immigrants," this referred only to white Americans.

Canadians' prevailing attitudes regarding those who would best qualify as immigrants at that time are well represented in the writings of J. S. Woodsworth—a Methodist minister, father of the Social Gospel Movement, and founder of the Co-operative Commonwealth Federation (CCF), the precursor to the New Democratic Party (NDP). In his seminal work, *The Vertical Mosaic* (1965), John Porter reminds us of Woodsworth's views by quoting from his 1909 book, *Strangers within Our Gate*. While remembered for his service to the poor and vulnerable, Woodsworth's own words remind us of the attitudes of the time; he wrote that the "orphans and pauper children" of Britain, the main country of Canada's early immigrants, were an unwelcome group because of their "inherited tendencies to evil." In fact, Woodsworth felt that "any large immigration of this class" of people would "lead to degeneration of our Canadian people" (cited in Porter 1965, 65). Paraphrasing Woodsworth further, Porter continues:

> The Scandinavians, "accustomed to the rigours of a northern climate, clean-blooded [sic!], thrifty, ambitious and hard-working" would be certain of success. The Bohemians "constitute no peculiar 'problems' as they readily adapt themselves to American or Canadian conditions." But the Slovaks of northern Hungary, "closely akin to the Bohemians," were "distinctly a lower grade." The capacity to do certain kinds of work was attributed to centuries or generations of breeding. "Much of the rough work of the nation-building in Western Canada is being done by the despised Galician ... working with a physical endurance bred of centuries of peasant life." Of the southern Italian, who "usually lands here almost destitute," it was thought that "his intelligence is not higher than one could imagine in the descent of peasantry illiterate for centuries." (65)

Syrians and Armenians were said to have "wits" that were "sharpened by generations of commercial dealings." However, as "parasites from the far East," they were thought to be "detrimental and burdensome," hence would not be welcome (Porter 1965, 65). According to Clifford Sifton, the minister of immigration in 1922, the individual judged as making the best immigrant was, "a stalwart peasant in sheep-skin coat, born on the soil, whose forefathers had been farmers for generations, with a stout wife and a half-a-dozen children" (cited in Porter 1965, 66). Referring to these views and attitudes, Porter writes: "Reputed biological qualities were thus used for and against the immigration of particular groups, for it was these qualities which suited them for particular tasks" (65).

TABLE 6.2 – TOP TEN COUNTRIES OF BIRTH FOR IMMIGRANTS TO CANADA, 2001 CENSUS

	Immigrated before 1961		Immigrated 1991 to 2001	
1	United Kingdom	894,465	China	1,830,680
2	Italy	217,175	India	197,360
3	Germany	147,320	Philippines	156,120
4	Netherlands	96,770	Hong Kong	122,010
5	Poland	79,170	Sri Lanka	118,385
6	United States	44,340	Pakistan	62,590
7	Hungary	34,810	Taiwan	57,990
8	Ukraine	27,425	United States	53,755
9	Greece	21,240	Iran	51,440
10	China	20,755	Poland	47,080

Source: Statistics Canada. 2002. *Canada's Ethnocultural Portrait: The Changing Mosaic.* Cat. No. 96F0030XIE2001008 <www.statscan.gc.ca>

Essentially, until the second half of the twentieth century, Canadian governments sought to ensure that Canada remained largely white (see **Table 6.2**). This served to restrict the entry of those who were not European. For example, beginning in 1885, a fifty-dollar head tax was levied against Chinese immigrants, and this tax was increased to one hundred dollars in 1900, and to five hundred dollars in 1903 (Bolaria and Li 1988). The government also maintained control of Chinese immigration through various bans and other restrictions, such as quotas. Not only did these measures serve to limit the number of Chinese men who could afford to come to Canada (mainly to work on the railroad), but it also impeded family unification, as many were unable to raise the funds. It was expected that after the work was done, migrant workers would return to China. We now know that many of the men grew old and died in Canada without ever reuniting with their families.

The number of Japanese immigrants allowed into Canada was similarly restricted. For example, in 1920, this number was limited to 150 per year (Kalbach and McVey 1971). And, while the devastating internment of Japanese Canadians during World War II is well known, the way the Canadian government handled Japanese immigration after the war may not be. Prime Minister Mackenzie King's statement to the House of

Commons in 1947 is representative of the government's attitude towards Asian immigrants:

> Canada is perfectly within her rights in selecting the persons whom we regard as desirable future citizens. It is not a 'fundamental human right' of any alien to enter Canada. It is a privilege. It is a matter of domestic policy … The people of Canada do not wish, as a result of mass immigration, to make a fundamental alteration in the character of our population. (House of Commons 1947)

Mackenzie King added that "large-scale immigration from the Orient would not be permitted to change the fundamental composition of the Canadian population." As Jansen (1981) explains, Canadian immigration policy before World War II was based "purely on ascribed characteristics of prospective immigrants, in particular race and national origin" (19). Yet even after the war, "the racial aspect played an important role—and was considered more 'threatening' to Canadian society than national characteristics" (Jansen 1981, 19). Like the Germans and Italians, the Japanese were considered enemy aliens during the war, so they were not allowed to immigrate to Canada in the post-war period (see Berger 1987). While the label was lifted for the Germans in 1950, it was not lifted for the Japanese until two years later.

In Canada's early years, entry by Asians from the Indian subcontinent was also restricted. Bolaria and Li (1988) point out that Canada, not wanting to take direct action against South Asians because of British interests in India, introduced "indirect" measures that functioned to limit immigration from the Indian subcontinent. One such measure was increasing the amount of money that immigrants were required to have upon arrival from twenty-five to two hundred dollars—most people in India earned 10 cents a day at the time. Most telling, however, was legislation that required immigrants to have made a "continuous voyage" to Canada. According to this measure, immigrants to Canada were required to arrive via a continuous voyage from their country of origin, on a ticket purchased in that country. At that time the only company able to offer a continuous journey from India to Canada was the Canadian Pacific Railroad, and the Government of Canada issued a directive that they were not to sell any through tickets to Canada (Bolaria and Li 1988, 170).

This legislation was tested in 1914 by an Indian businessman who chartered a Japanese ship called *Komagata Maru* to make the voyage. The ship, originating in Hong Kong arrived in Vancouver on May 23 with 376 South Asian, mostly Punjabi Sikh, passengers. The few passengers who were dependants of earlier immigrants were allowed to enter the country, but most were denied entry and remained on the ship for two months. During this time, the ship was guarded by police, and upon leaving, it was escorted out to sea by a Canadian naval ship (Bolaria and Li 1988; Nayar 2004). The media referred to the ship's passengers as "Hindu invaders" and accused them of "preaching sedition and treason" (Kelley and Trebilcock 1998, 152). The British Columbia Court of Appeal upheld the government's immigration policy, which required continuous passage from the country of origin; the *Komagatu Maru*'s passengers had not departed for Canada directly from their homeland, but from Hong Kong. The court's ruling included the statement that "the laws of this country are unsuited to them, and their ways and ideas may be a menace to the well-being of the Canadian people" (cited in Kelley and Trebilcock 1998, 144).

Like other non-Europeans, Africans were deemed an inadmissible group, despite having settled in Canada as early as the 1620s (initially as slaves); in the late 1700s during the resettlement of Jamaican Maroons[3] in Nova Scotia; and as a result of immigration through the Underground Railroad to Ontario. In fact, the Census of 1901 indicates that some 17,437 "Negroes" were residing in Canada (Government of Canada 1937, 162). As previously mentioned, some Blacks who tried to emigrate from Oklahoma in 1911 were barred from doing so. However, a limited number of people from the Caribbean had come to Canada during the late 1800s and early 1900s. Calliste (1994) reports that, by the end of the eighteenth century, a small number of Black Caribbean males, who paid Canadian schooner captains a transportation fee, were able to come to Canada on the schooners. Most of these men settled in Nova Scotia and worked in the coal mines and the coke ovens of steel plants, not only because of discriminatory labour practices, but "because of the myth that blacks could withstand the heat better than whites" (Calliste 1994, 135). In the early 1900s, Caribbean women were also allowed into Canada as domestic servants based on the Caribbean Domestic Scheme, the result of an agreement between Canada and various Caribbean governments (Calliste 1994; Satzewich 1992; Silvera 1984).

The immigration policies pertaining to Blacks were consistent with Canada's attitude toward non-European immigrants. Simply put, Blacks were restricted well into the twentieth century because they were considered unassimilable. As the deputy minister of immigration explained on January 14, 1955:

> It is from experience, generally speaking, that coloured people in the present state of the white man's thinking are not a tangible asset, and as a result are more or less ostracized. They do not assimilate readily and pretty much

> vegetate to a low standard of living ... many cannot adapt
> themselves to our climatic conditions. (Calliste 1994, 136)

It is humbling to remind ourselves that such comments were
commonplace a mere six decades ago—even though some in the
academic community had argued otherwise. As Jean Burnet (1984)
writes, politicians continued to advance arguments against allowing
Blacks to immigrate that we now consider "nonsensical."

> As late as the 1950s, one federal minister of immigration
> after another had to defend regulations on allegedly
> scientific grounds that most natural and social scientists
> regarded as nonsensical. For example, the restrictions
> on Black immigration were said to have been imposed
> because it had been "scientifically proven" that Blacks
> could not endure cold climates. (19)

The immigration policies that served to construct who was best suited
to become a citizen of Canada created entry barriers for those considered
"unassimilable;" these barriers remained in place even when Canada was
called upon to demonstrate a humanitarian spirit, such as with Jewish
refugees escaping Nazism before and during World War II (Burnet 1984,
19). Preference was given to refugees from Europe at this time, but due
to prevailing anti-Semitism, European Jews did not qualify. In 1989 the
Globe and Mail reprinted an article from January 25, 1939, concerning
the issue of Jewish refugees from Europe:

> Opposition to immigration in general and to the
> admission of Jews to Canada, was voiced in the House of
> Commons tonight by H. E. Brundle (Lib., Champlain).
> He said he believed Canada's natural resources should be
> developed by and for Canadians. "I object strongly to the
> entry of Jews en masse or otherwise into Canada," he said.
> "I have no brief against the Hebrew race, but since they
> have, justly or unjustly, created great difficulties in other
> countries, we should be careful. They nearly always live
> in the cities, and that means they will be on relief or take
> jobs from other workers." (reproduced in the *Globe and
> Mail*, January 25, 1989, A15)

IMMIGRATION TODAY

Over the years, Canadian governments have always sought to admit
immigrants who would benefit Canada economically (Satzewich 1992;
Jakubowski 1997). And under current immigration criteria—the point

system—in addition to work experience and expertise, educational qualifications,[4] age, and demand for the potential immigrant's skill, there are points given for what is termed "personal qualities" or "personal suitability." These points are awarded by immigration officers—one can only to guess on what basis the officers assign these points. However, given this policy, one might say that immigrants to Canada are "hand-picked," with the intention that they will not only survive but thrive in Canadian society.

The profile of today's immigrant population has much to do with the point system that was introduced in the 1960s. For instance, over three-quarters (77 percent) of all immigrants admitted to Canada during the 1980s were under the age of forty; over half (57 percent) were under thirty (Logan 1991, 11). Between 2001 and 2006 Canada's foreign-born population rose by 13.6 percent—from 3.3 percent to 19.8 percent, four times faster than the overall population growth—making this increase in growth the highest in seventy-five years (Statistics Canada 2007b). And among the 1.1 million immigrants arriving in Canada between 2001 and 2006, 58 percent were from Asia, including the Middle East, and only 16 percent from Europe, formerly the main source of Canada's immigrants. Statistics Canada also reported that while English and French are still the dominant languages of Canadians, about 20 percent of the population reports a first language that is neither French nor English (Statistics Canada 2007b). Statistics Canada also estimates that in 2006 approximately 1,034,000 people in Canada spoke one of the Chinese languages or dialects as their first language, which makes the combined Chinese languages Canada's third most common first language after English and French.

Educational attainment data includes the levels attained by preschool and school-age children, and still a full 33 percent of new immigrants in the late 1980s had some post-secondary education; among refugees, 28 percent had some post-secondary education (Employment and Immigration 1992b, 22). Adjusted for age, the 1986 Census shows that 28.2 percent of immigrants, compared to 22.3 percent of native-born Canadians, had some university education (Jansen and Richmond 1990, 6). Data from the 2006 Census released in March 2008 by Statistics Canada reveals that about one-third of Canada's population born outside of the country holds a university degree, compared to only one-quarter of the general working-age population. This means that immigrants tend to be better educated than the general population, and that the increasing proportion of the overall Canadian population with post-secondary education can be attributed in part to recent immigrants. Further, close to half, or 49 percent, of the Canadians who hold doctorate degrees are immigrants, as are 40 percent of those who have master's degrees (Church 2008). Unfortunately, as we will discuss later, these credentials do not easily translate into employment in one's skilled or professional field.

Despite the high skill levels and qualifications of immigrant applicants, a 1989 National Film Board documentary, *Who Gets In,* reveals that country of origin, life circumstances, relative wealth, and responses to the questions of immigration officers often determined who got into Canada. Specifically, the film demonstrates that Vietnamese refugees in Hong Kong and Filipino women working in Hong Kong and wishing to immigrate to Canada as domestic workers were not treated or questioned in the same manner as the Hong Kong entrepreneurs, who were expected to bring thousands of dollars to invest in Canada. For example, in the film, an entrepreneur with an untested business idea and three million dollars seems to undergo a very easy interview and, before long, is given permission to immigrate. In some cases, individuals within this "investor class" of immigrants were represented by immigration lawyers and consultants, some of whom were Canadians working in Hong Kong.

The film also demonstrates that Africans and South Asians in Kenya did not receive the same respectful treatment that the Chinese entrepreneurs of Hong Kong received. In Kenya, applicants are largely dependants of Canadian citizens and permanent residents, and refugees seeking asylum. One case is particularly telling. A former prison guard, Mr. Tulumba of Zaire (now the Democratic Republic of Congo), assisted political prisoners in escaping incarceration. He fled to Kenya because he believed his life was in danger. Even though Mr. Tulumba impresses the immigration officer, as the officer himself says, and demonstrates his courage, determination, ambition, and tenacity (illustrated, among other things, by the fact that he was able to learn English in six months while in a refugee camp), he is refused entry to Canada. As the officer explains, "He is very, very bright. A remarkable man under any circumstances. But it doesn't necessarily mean that we want him in Canada. I would rather have him spend a couple of years growing tomatoes or something, and kind of get that sharp edge off him before we can think of introducing him into our society." As a refugee applicant, Mr. Tulumba failed the "personal suitability" test because, according to the officer, he did not seem like a person who could "move in next door to my mom," or live in a small community in Canada. This film clearly demonstrates that it is not the unmotivated and unambitious who typically get into Canada, it is individuals who are either financially secure or willing to work hard to become economically and socially successful.

According to Peter Li (2000), a "racial subtext," is a consistent feature of Canada's discourse of immigration policies. This subtext is evident in the framework, assumptions, and vocabulary of immigration as contributing to the country's "diversity problem"—a problem which is simplistically and conveniently used by some Canadians to explain their opposition to higher levels of immigration. Li also mentions:

> The discourse reifies "race" by recognizing the legitimacy of evaluating superficial physical differences of people, and by casting "non-white immigrants" and "Canadians" as opposites based on socially constructed immutable differences. Over time, the discourse makes it socially acceptable to consider immigrants on racial grounds; in turn, physical and cultural characteristics of "non-white" immigrants become socially significant, since they represent convenient markers by which they can be distinguished and problematized. (2000, 12)

So despite Canada's multiculturalism claims, specific ethnic, racial, national, and cultural differences of immigrants are used to signal whether or not they are likely to be "threats to Canada's core values"—the implication, then, is that immigrants are expected to "fit in" (Li 2003, 321).

In establishing preference in terms of race, ethnicity, class, and assumed inherent or genetic qualities, Canada's historical immigration policies have determined who would eventually become "Canadian." These policies explain, not only why the majority of racial minority citizens came to Canada within the last half of this century, but also how—the multiculturalism policy notwithstanding—some immigrant or ethno-racial groups have become socially constructed as "Canadian," and others have not. The requirement that immigrants must be able to assimilate into an Anglo- or Franco-Canada (that is, a white Canada) indicates the extent to which the ideology of racism has framed the stereotypes and the racialization of some Canadians as "others." These individuals are perceived as unable or unwilling to assimilate or conform to Canada, and are therefore seen as less likely to become "good citizens."

It is in this context that today's young people seek to make sense of their lives, particularly in relation to their educational and occupational aspirations and the opportunities that are available as they enter the competitive job market. In the section that follows, I first engage some students' ideas and claims about the impact of immigration and immigrants on the social, economic, and cultural resources and welfare of Canada, and then go on to discuss how some students of immigrant background (either having been born outside of Canada or having immigrant parents) talk about their lives and opportunities in Canada.

PERCEPTIONS OF IMMIGRANTS AND THEIR IMPACT ON SOCIETY

For most students, the prism through which they view the impact of immigration has to do, in part, with their career goals, as well as their understanding of the job market. Many young people—white males in particular—see immigration, multiculturalism, and employment equity as impediments to obtaining the jobs to which they aspire. Immigrants are often perceived to be "taking jobs away from Canadians," "a drain on our social services," the "cause [of] an increase in crime," and "coming into our country and changing our culture." Multiculturalism is seen as facilitating or encouraging changes to the "Canadian way of life," and individuals often speak of this as causing unneeded tension and frustration among "Canadians." In this and other chapters, the student comments and excerpts are used to illustrate the thinking of some young people and particular groups within society; in some cases, I have included a substantive portion of the young person's essay in an effort to capture his or her thought process. While some excerpts were written by students ten, fifteen, and even twenty years ago, it is instructive to note how much has remained unchanged since the close of the twentieth century.

IMMIGRANTS, EMPLOYMENT, AND SOCIAL SERVICE

In discussions pertaining to the impact of immigrants on the economic and social welfare of Canadians, participants often claim that immigrants "take away jobs" from Canadians. The idea of competing for a job with immigrants seems to cause some young people much dissension, especially after they have obtained a college or university education with the belief that such a qualification operates as a surety, if not a guarantee, to a job. Take for example Bill, who thought it was unfair that immigrants—or people with names that he "couldn't pronounce"—were getting access to the same education for employment as him.

> **Bill:** I thought this was unfair. This negative attitude was formed when I was out of work and looked into upgrading my education through the unemployment office. The waiting list was long, and what infuriated me was that the names of those waiting to enrol were ones that I couldn't pronounce. All these people were ahead of me, and I resented the fact that a Canadian didn't come first. It has taken a bit of attitude adjusting to come to terms with it.

While immigrants are found in significant numbers, and in some cases are overrepresented, in certain industries and businesses in comparison to Canadian-born workers (for example, in service, construction, skilled trades, and engineering), this is certainly not the case in the labour force as a whole. In fact, in 2006, the national unemployment rate for immigrants was 11.5 percent compared to 4.9 percent for the Canadian-born (Statistics Canada 2007a). Based on her research on issues faced by immigrant professionals in the job market, Jelena Zikic (2009) contends that immigrant workers face longer periods of unemployment than Canadian-born workers, [and] when they are employed, they are often underemployed, working in positions below their skill levels and earning lower wages. Their foreign credentials and experience are also discounted, which makes it very difficult for them to gain employment in positions that suit them. (1)

An experimental study by Philip Oreopoulos (2009) designed to examine why immigrants are allowed into Canada on the basis of skill, education, and professional qualification, yet still have such low economic outcomes, found that high unemployment among immigrants and ethnic minority Canadians was a result of "considerable employer discrimination." Oreopoulos sent out six thousand resumés with Chinese, Indian, and Pakistani names (representing the backgrounds of most of today's immigrant groups) in response to online job postings across multiple occupations in the Toronto area. He found that employers "substantially discriminate" based on the names of applicants, because they value "Canadian experience far more than Canadian education when deciding to interview applicants with foreign backgrounds" (24). Moreover,

applicants with English-sounding names who also had Canadian education and experience received callbacks 40 percent more often than did applicants with Chinese, Indian, or Pakistani names who had similar Canadian education and experience. Conditional on listing four to six years of Canadian experience, being foreign-educated (whether at a highly ranked school or not) did not affect callback rates substantially. But changing only the location of the applicant's job experience, from Canadian to foreign, lowered the callback rate further from about 10 percent to 5 percent. Adding more language credentials, additional Canadian education, or extracurricular activities had little impact on these overall results. The effects were almost the same regardless of whether the jobs applied to required more or fewer social or language skills. Callback differences mostly went away when comparing Canadian-born applications to British immigrants. (Oreopoulos 2009, 7)

Oreopoulos further explains that the disappearance of the differences in callbacks between individuals with British and Canadian resumes suggests that applicants with "foreign" names are assumed to have "inadequate language and cultural skills for the job," whereas it is assumed that those with British resumés "arrive fluent in English and with similar cultural background to those from Canada" (26).[5]

According to a 2008 *Toronto Star* article by Lesley Ciarula Taylor, recent Statistics Canada data indicate that university-educated women who immigrated to Canada from Asia or Africa have more difficulty than other university-educated individuals. The 2008 Statistics Canada labour survey reported that almost half of all the university-educated individuals who immigrated to Canada in the last five years were women. But these women were much less likely to have jobs or be looking for jobs than male immigrants with university degrees. "Only 62.7 percent of the 86,000 university-educated recent immigrants from Asia and 38 percent of the 9,700 from Africa were working or looking for jobs" (*Toronto Star*, July 19, 2008, A19).

Immigrants tend to have difficulty finding employment—and once employed tend to be in low-wage jobs—making them likely candidates for social assistance. This further feeds the misplaced resentment that some individuals develop toward immigrants—they feel that not only do immigrants take jobs away from Canadians, but they become users (and abusers) of social services. Bill expressed this idea in his reflections on immigration: "I used to resent immigrants and refugees. I always looked at them as taking from the Canadian social services system." But as Fleras (2010) writes, "despite financial and social costs related to initial settlement in Canada, immigrants are the same people who will keep the economy afloat so that Canadians can retire comfortably" (264).

Moreover, as will be seen in the sections on life in ethnic communities (or enclaves) and on immigrants' aspirations, newcomers' aspirations and desire for success means that immigrants' use of social services tends to be lower than native-born Canadians. In fact, according to Fleras (2010) immigrants actually "pay more in taxes than they accept in social services" (263). They tend to turn to their sponsoring relative or community for social and financial assistance rather than to government. In fact, as part of the family class system, sponsors are obligated to support newcomers for at least three years. Consider also that immigrants generally aspire to be self-sufficient, and this can only be achieved through their own work efforts. Their lack of experience with government assistance programs (particularly those from developing nations) often causes newcomers to feel that accepting such assistance is an admission of failure and contrary to the reason they immigrated in the first place—to achieve success independently. As one immigrant commented in a 1991 *Toronto Star* article: "You have to understand that back home, we don't have social insurance or anything of that kind ... Everyone's social insurance policy is [their] relatives and friends. If you grow older, or you are somewhat poor, you always rely on the people you know and your relatives. We always depend on each other" (Watson, *Toronto Star*, September 27, 1991, A11).

WHEN IN ROME: LANGUAGE, CUSTOMS, AND EXPECTATIONS

While early immigration debates focused on race and maintaining a white society, Canadians have moved beyond the issue of skin colour and now focus on the issue of assimilation. Those who expect immigrants to assimilate often employ the popular maxim: When in Rome, do as the Romans do. In Chapter 5, we discussed the issue of accommodation and assimilation; now we examine the role of immigration when considering Canada as the proverbial Rome.

Findings from a ten-year study of 5,366 young immigrants in thirteen countries, reported by N. Keung in the *Toronto Star*, suggest that "young immigrants who successfully plant a foot in both their own culture and the adopted one tend to feel better about themselves and have fewer social problems than those who become either totally assimilated or stick to their own kind" (*Toronto Star*, December 9, 2006, L7). The study's lead author, John Berry, a Queen's University psychology professor, explains that youth fare better when they have a strong sense of their heritage, as well as ties to their new country. He says that the youth riots that occurred in Paris[6] did not happen in Canada because of Canada's multicultural policy, which encourages ethnic groups to maintain their identity while participating in Canadian life (*Toronto Star*, December 9, 2006, L7).

Despite such evidence, and a social and legal commitment to accommodation (see Chapter 5), the general feeling in Canada has been—and continues to be—that immigrants should assimilate or be made to assimilate "into Canadian culture." In Ryan's words, "individuals who do not wish to assimilate ... can leave."

> **Ryan:** I am in some ways prejudiced. I feel that individuals who do not wish to assimilate and abide by our society's rules and regulations can hop back on the boat and leave. We live in a country where individuals need to work as a team, as one mass—we don't need sore thumbs ... We need people who will work as Canadians. We need people who will work with Canadians. We need people who will work to be Canadians. We need people who will fight for Canada ... Individuals who wish to come to Canada are welcome if they possess qualifications that are in demand. As part of a growing society, it is up to all these new individuals to assimilate and conform so that we, the people around them, can relate to them and they can relate to us.

Ryan advocates for complete assimilation. Many Canadians, such as Jane, see immigrants' facility with English (in English Canada) and their wearing of "traditional clothes" as important measures of their efforts to assimilate.

> **Jane:** One issue I find irritating is that immigrants come to Canada, an English- and French-speaking country, and apparently make little or no effort to speak English or even to get involved in English as a Second Language classes (ESL). They continue to wear traditional clothes, and also want to wear their traditional clothes at their place of employment.

Immigrants' use of languages other than English or French and their decision to wear "traditional clothing" are often interpreted as reluctance or resistance "to adopt the customs held by the majority" Canadians. But many Canadian-born individuals rely on superficial observations and lack an understanding of the complexity of being an immigrant in a new country. Lisa provides a perfect example of such a perspective.

> **Lisa:** I always held the firm belief that immigrants arriving in Canada should learn English and should adopt the customs held by the majority; [to not] do so is a snub to all Canadians and implies the attitude, "Although I am here now, I shall carry on as I did before." Nothing infuriated me more than seeing "immigrants," especially of college or university age, conversing in their mother tongue while ignoring the language that surrounded them—English. I figured that, when in Rome, you should do as the Romans do. This belief included dress, attitude, and especially language…
>
> I realize that assimilation does take time and that there is security in conversing in one's mother tongue among friends. I also realize that culture is an integral part of one's sense of being. Without it, an essence of the self is lessened. Although I still feel my old sense of ire stir whenever I am riding on public transit and am seated near others who are using a foreign language, I can now at least comprehend some of the troubles they might have functioning in what may be a different society and why they continue to maintain their old behaviour.

Even though Lisa acknowledges that assimilation takes time and that "conversing in one's mother tongue" gives an individual a sense of security, she nevertheless sees the use of languages other than English as somehow wrong. This begs the following questions: Is bilingualism not a valuable skill or asset? Would most English-speakers practise their second language on public transit? Is speaking a language such as French, Mandarin, Greek, Urdu, Arabic, or Tagalog on the subway or bus tantamount to ignoring English? What does Lisa's "ire" really demonstrate? Does the fact that an individual has resided in Canada for many years, yet does not speak English or French, mean that he or she is not Canadian?

For the most part, individuals who do not speak English or French circulate within communities where they are able to do business, shop, bank, and interact primarily with members of their own ethnic group.

In some cases, employees of schools and other government institutions will communicate with them in "their" language. Yet, implicit in Ryan, Jane, and Lisa's comments is the idea that non-English people should not be catered to, and in providing translation services or information in languages other than English or French, we are allowing non-English speakers to retain their own language and condoning their failure to become truly "Canadian." This insensitivity to non-English speakers reflects, in some cases, an ethnocentric attitude. Consider also attitudes such as Ria's, who in the following comment argues that if she was able learn English, so can all other immigrants.

> **Ria:** Are they really trying or do they want to keep to themselves and not assimilate into the Canadian society? If people come from another country with a different language and are unable to understand people in their new country, they should make an effort to learn the new language so they can be understood, feel more at home and become a part of the majority of the people. I feel very strongly about this as I went through it when I came to Canada thirty-four years ago. I did not understand or speak the English language. I took English lessons and worked among English-speaking people because I wanted to learn our new language. I also kept up my Dutch language.

While it is understandable that individuals will evaluate others based on their own experience and situation, it is important to recognize the limitations of doing so. What is true of one person or one group's experience cannot be generalized to another—consider, for example, that Ria's efforts to learn English would have been greatly assisted by the common European root of her first and second languages. But what might be evident in these students' viewpoints, is not so much a resentment of foreign language use, but their difficulty owning their language chauvinism, ethnocentrism, and racism. Some people do recognize or understand that language is intimately linked to a person's cultural identity. Sue, for example, does understand the significance of language to a person's identity, and recognizes her own biases.

> **Sue:** I have to recognize the feelings of frustration and impatience I experience with those who do not speak English fluently. And perhaps most difficult to acknowledge is my insensitivity towards these people, when it is this very attitude I abhor in others who do not understand sign language as part of a deaf person's culture.

To understand why some people would speak in or try to retain their first language while residing in Canada, we must bear in mind that language not only enables us to send messages and exchange ideas with each other, it also plays a key role in the development, maintenance, and evolution of a culture (Avison and Kunkel 1987, 51). The symbols that are defined in a language mirror the items, world views, and values considered important to that culture. As such, language is symbolic and an integral part of cultural identity. In the case of minority groups, the first language enables them to communicate and maintain contact with relatives, as well as deal with pragmatic concerns such as economic, social, and familial issues (Schecter et al. 1996). Also, for some, depending on age, familial responsibilities, learning experiences, expectations, and cultural similarity, learning a new language can be a very difficult process. While some members of groups that speak minority languages may embrace English, the social, familial, and psychological cost of doing so might limit other individuals' success at learning the new language.

Research tells us that despite the efforts of first- and second-generation immigrants, minority languages cannot survive in a context that does not favour their maintenance (Schecter et al. 1996). We can look to the extremely low number of French speakers in historically French areas of the United States, such as Louisiana and Maine, as well as the dominance of English in more recently established European settlements across Canada. Consider, for example, the Waterloo region of Ontario, which was a destination for German immigrants in the second half of the1800s, following the earlier settlement of Mennonites relocating from the United States. While the German influence is still obvious in family names and cultural activities (such as the popular Oktoberfest), residents now speak English almost exclusively. Many Mennonites still retain their original German dialect, but they also speak English with those outside their communities. Their ability to maintain their language is attributed to their simple rural life, which separates them from mainstream society.

It would probably help for us to think of Canada as multicultural and multilingual, thereby allowing us to appreciate the many languages we hear on the streets and in the media. Being Canadian, then, in a multicultural context, would suggest that there is room for more than one language as well as a respect and appreciation for the many cultural customs and practices that we see around us. Hence, contrary to Raj's claim below, visitors to Canada should expect diversity in our dress, languages, accents, and behaviours:

Raj: People coming to Canada should be informed or enlightened about what to expect when they arrive here … I respect people's cultures, traditions, and beliefs, and I expect people to respect mine. Many Westerners complain of the treatment they receive in many Middle Eastern countries if they dress "disrespectfully," (i.e., in Western clothing), especially women. They are often not allowed to commute or to live in certain areas, because it is felt they will corrupt the natives with their culture. Yet people from these very countries come to Canada and expect us to accept them in their traditional garments, and to work side by side with them. That is not fair. Canada is a sovereign nation with an identity.

I wonder what foreigners would say if they arrived in Canada to find people in various modes of dress—some with turbans, working as police officers; some with daggers, attending schools; others wearing kimonos or saris. They would obviously be confused. I don't believe that Canadians should wear a national uniform or dress, but I disagree with immigrants coming to Canada and insisting on wearing their traditional dress on the job. The world must be able to recognize Canadians for who they are; Canadians should have an identity. I believe this is one of the many reasons that white people are viewed as Canadians, and most non-whites are seen as immigrants. I am not saying that we non-whites should try to conform to the ideals and mould of whites, but the integration process is one of blending in. It is expected that many traditional habits and practices will be muted; for the immigrant, Canada is a new country, a different culture and a new way of life.

When considering Canada as the proverbial Rome, we are faced with the question of what we, as Canadians, *do*. Raj, in his adherence to the doctrine of assimilation, compares Canada to Middle Eastern countries that require Westerners to dress and live a certain way, arguing that it is unfair that newcomers from those same countries may do as they please in Canada. In employing a cultural analysis, we cannot ignore the absurdity of such an argument. The fundamental difference between Canada and many parts of the world, especially immigrant-producing nations, is that Canadians are permitted to do as they please and generally consider the dress and behaviour codes of other countries to be oppressive. One might argue that when immigrants to Canada choose to dress a certain way and speak a different language, they are in fact doing as Canadians do—exercising their freedom to choose.

ETHNIC ENCLAVES: CHOICE, SEGREGATION, CULTURAL DESIGN, OR SOCIAL MOBILITY?

The employment and financial situations of immigrants, as well as expectations that they "speak English" and conform to the cultural norms, values, customs, habits, and dress of Canadian society—in short, assimilate—have an effect on their settlement or residential patterns and situations. In reality, the communities or neighbourhoods in which people live are built on solidarity, as well as shared interests, aspirations, and identities (Crow and Maclean 2000); as such, they are a source of social capital, mutual support, and "ethnic economies" (Kumar and Leung 2005, 2). But in the following comment, Nancy, like many of her peers, considers it counterproductive for immigrants or ethno-racial minorities to live in the same community.

> **Nancy:** The issue that I wish to discuss involves the immigrants who come to Canada and settle with their own ethnic group. I realize that when someone comes to a new country they feel safe in a community that is similar to the one they left behind. However, I feel that this only forces people of different cultures further apart rather than bringing them closer together. I am not saying that it is wrong for people to be actively involved in their cultural community—I feel that it is important to maintain your heritage and pass it down to future generations—but I think that heritage is something that should be shared with others and not kept to yourself.
>
> I am an active participant in a Ukrainian dance group and have been for eight years. Within this time I have seen how these people interact with non-Ukrainians. It seems as though they want nothing to do with people that are not of their ethnic background. They all belong to Ukrainian churches, schools, sports teams, camps, country clubs. They have relatives in Ukrainian rest homes, and on their vacations, they drive up to their Ukrainian community cottages…
>
> When people of the same ethnicity cling together, they become so involved in their own culture that they are not willing to open their eyes and experience what other cultures have to offer. It becomes impossible for them to do so because they have spent so much time in their own community that they cannot communicate with anyone outside of it. For example, I knew someone who had been in this country for sixty years. He could hardly speak a word of English and, therefore, how was he supposed to communicate with anyone outside his ethnic community? He had trapped himself inside it.

In reality, each of us selects a neighbourhood for the same reason—because it meets our needs. Young people choose neighbourhoods that are affordable and conveniently located to social activities; families choose neighbourhoods that offer amenities for children—schools, parks, and other families; artists often choose neighbourhoods that provide access to convenient and affordable studio space. Immigrants are no different—they choose communities that meet their economic and social needs.

As Qadeer (2003) argues, within the context of Canada's multiculturalism, **ethnic enclaves**[7] can be seen as representative of individuals' right to maintain their attachment to their culture and of "the groups' right to build communal institutions and maintain its heritage and language within the limits prescribed by the Canadian constitution and Charter" (2). For instance, in the case of Muslim immigrants, researchers observed that religion plays a significant role in creating important social networks that help them deal with the stress related to settlement in their new environments (D'Addario et al. 2008; Jedwab 2008). In their study of the "residential segregation" of Muslims (using a case study of one mosque), D'Addario and others (2008) established that proximity to places of worship or living near a religious establishment provided recent newcomers with the "mutual aid and … social support" of religious groups with which they affiliated. The resulting "residential concentrations that are segregated from other ethnic and religious groups in the community" are not necessarily indicative of "a turning away from the rest of the society in which immigrants are settling" as they are often interpreted (2). "By locating around a mosque," D'Addario and others continue, "Muslim immigrants seek to signify their presence in Canada and their willingness to engage, at least on their own terms, with other Canadians" (2008, 2). Furthermore,

> even in an official multicultural society, such as Canada, the residential concentration of an immigrant group may arise for a variety of reasons that include the imperative to sustain religious, cultural, and social practices, the desire to mark the presence of Muslims in a hostile and discriminatory environment, and the commitment to develop facilities and activities that will allow Muslims to inform the larger public about Islam. (D'Addario et al. 2008, 25)

Apart from seeking social and cultural supports and shared interests, aspirations of upward social mobility—the "immigrant dream"—also inform the residential patterns that we find among immigrant groups. Take for example the desire of immigrants to demonstrate that they have "made it" in the new society, and that their move to Canada was "worth it." A tangible demonstration of this aspiration is home ownership; for many, this entails owning a new house, rather than one of the historic homes preferred by many urban dwellers. Given that they have generally low incomes,[8] most immigrants can only afford houses in the less expensive suburbs (Bauder and Sharpe 2002). For this reason, many recent immigrants are found living in suburban areas that DeWolf (2004) refers to as "ethnoburbs," which are "home to a wide variety of ethnic groups and income levels" (2). DeWolf writes that in Canadian cities,

> suburbia is becoming increasingly diverse. More and more middle-class immigrants are skipping traditional [urban] ethnic enclaves and heading straight for the boonies, where strip malls are now filled with ethnic businesses, bubble-tea parlours dot the landscape and schools fill up with kids from any number of different backgrounds. Forget suburbia; this is ethnoburbia. (3)

Ethnoburbs also emerge through a dynamic of migration, with residents of older established suburban communities—many of whom are long-time, white Canadian residents of European backgrounds—moving to new outer suburban areas and immigrants moving in to replace them (Phelan and Scheider 1996).

Then again, access to housing and communities is often influenced by the discriminatory practices of home sellers, real estate agents, landlords, and building managers, resulting in the concentration of some immigrant or ethno-racial minority groups in particular suburban areas of metropolitan cities (Preston and Wong 2002, 33). Today's ethnoburbs do not represent the affluent, homogeneous, middle-class neighbourhoods of the past; instead, they are socially and culturally diverse, and the conditions within them are much like the inner city in terms of poverty, social marginalization, conflict, and high housing density (see Phelan and Scheider 1996). In fact, in Toronto, DeWolf explains, one suburban area located in "the far northeastern side of the city" is, as one newspaper columnist contends, "culturally diverse but very poor." This situation is considered to be "part of an alarming trend of ghettoization and systemic poverty. You can meet kids who've never been downtown. They expect to stay there for the rest of their lives ... We've unwittingly created large pockets of suburban underclass" (quoted in DeWolf 2004, 3).

Essentially, the residential patterns of immigrants in the suburbs are related to both voluntary and involuntary factors, and a combination of "the processes of economic and residential decentralization" (Bauder and Sharpe 2002, 207). That immigrants reside in racially, ethnically, and economically diverse or homogeneous suburban communities is a product of the complex interrelationship of choice, affordability, social, economic, and cultural factors, as well as racist and classist structures that not only enable or limit their integration and participation in the society, but also their aspirations for themselves and their children. That some immigrants choose to live in "ethnic enclaves" or "ethnoburbs" is, in part, related to their wish for social support; as DeWolf points out, this choice is also a way for parents to manage the acculturation of their children, thereby helping them to maintain their ethnic culture and language.

THE QUESTION OF CITIZENSHIP, PROTESTS, AND DUAL RELATIONS

Just as language use and residential patterns are used as a measure of immigrants' commitment to Canada and their willingness to "be Canadians" (i.e., to conform to the values, customs, and political expectations of society) so too are their actions. One example is the staging of protests relating to their countries of origin. Does protesting the political situation or social conditions in the countries from which individuals emigrate reflect their lack of commitment to Canada? And what of those who hold dual citizenship—does this mean that they are not "fully" Canadian? Is their well-being a concern for Canada when they are in their countries of origin? The following comments by Dave and Ryan no doubt capture the sentiments of many Canadians over the last few decades.

> **Dave:** I would like to see these people protesting about Canadian issues … I cannot understand why immigrants who come to Canada, after making the choice to leave their place of birth and adopt Canada as their new home, would protest in the streets of Canada about issues back in their home country. Canada is filled with problems, and the country needs people who will come here and contribute to the welfare, progress, and development of this country. I would like to see these people protesting about such Canadian issues as the lack of jobs … taxes and other social issues that affect them, because this is where they are living.

> **Ryan:** These individuals [immigrants] need to realize that they are part of the Canadian society. If they refuse to conform, they will not last very long. They are in a new country now and are called Canadians. I don't want to hear all about their country's problems, because they ran away from their country's problems.

Dave and Ryan argue that immigrants should not "protest in the streets of Canada about issues in their home country," and that they should "protest about Canadian issues." While they are responding to events that took place several years ago, cultural groups and ethno-racial minorities continue to engage in public demonstrations in Canada; recent examples include the controversy over the Danish newspaper cartoons of Muhammad and the ongoing conflict between Tibet and China. Consider also the extensive series of Tamil protests against the civil war in Sri Lanka.[9] In the winter and spring of 2009, thousands of Canadians of Tamil and other ethnic backgrounds protested the Sri Lankan government's human rights abuses against Tamil civilians. The protestors formed human chains in downtown Toronto, disrupting commuters and urban traffic; protested outside embassies and at Queen's Park for long periods of time; and in the most talked-of action, walked on to the Gardiner Expressway, stopping traffic for hours on a Sunday afternoon. The height of the protests coincided with the most aggressive action on the part of the Sri Lankan government, which ultimately led to the de facto end of the civil war and thousands of civilian deaths.

Approximately 200,000 Canadians of Sri Lankan background live in the Toronto area, and the city is home to one of the largest Tamil populations outside Sri Lanka. However, public response to the protests reflected deep discomfort and even anger. As one individual wrote on the CBC website after one of the initial demonstrations: "This protest was nothing more than a complete nuisance and no one has the right to force their ideologies [upon] complete strangers."[10] While most agreed that the reason for the protest was justified, and governments all over the world condemned Sri Lanka's efforts, many associate the Tamil cause with terrorism or were offended by the extreme and persistent nature of the protests in Toronto.

Objections to protests and activism raise an important question: Should all Canadians not have the freedom to exercise their rights as citizens, including the right to express their political positions about local, national, and international issues? When members of the society generally, and dominant group members in particular, protest about issues outside of Canada, the same objections are not raised. Such a double standard implies that protests by immigrants or minority group members are out of self-interest, rather universal human concern and empathy. While the motivation to protest always has some link to personal interest and political beliefs, one would think that protests by any group are related to concern for the welfare of the offended group.

Political activism is not a measure of an individual's commitment to Canadian society, even if individual protestors might hold dual citizenship. However, in addition to questions about the loyalty of individuals with dual citizenship, there is also ongoing concern about our government's responsibility for such individuals, especially when they are living in their country of origin or citizenship. While thousands of Canadians hold dual citizenship and live abroad, this issue became the subject of public debate during the Israel-Lebanon War of 2006. Israel agreed to cease its attack on Beirut for short periods of time to allow foreign nationals to evacuate, usually with the help of their own governments, and (in the case of Canada) at great expense. However, there was much controversy surrounding what the government should do about evacuating Canadians of Lebanese origin who had been living in Beirut or had gone there to visit relatives. As Luiza Savage reported in *Maclean's* magazine, many argued that some of the evacuees were living and working in Beirut and treating their Canadian citizenship as insurance; they felt that the government should not be obligated to help "Canadians of convenience" (August 7, 2006). As one Ontario Member of Parliament questioned: "If they don't live here and don't pay taxes, and may never be coming back, what is the responsibility of the government of Canada supported by the Canadian taxpayer?" (cited in Savage 2006, np).

While it was the evacuation of Lebanese Canadians that sparked the debate about dual citizenship, the *Maclean's* article also noted that, according to the Census, more than 500,000 Canadians at that time held two or more passports—the majority were European Union citizens, and of those, most were British-Canadians. During the same time, more than 250,000 Canadians (dual and non-dual Canadian citizens) were reported to be living in Hong Kong, and nearly a million Canadians were living in the United States (Savage 2006). More recent Statistics Canada figures indicate that only 2.8 percent of the population (or 863,100) people have dual citizenship. And the largest group among those held citizenship with the United Kingdom (14.7 percent), followed by Poland (6.6 percent), and the United States (5.4 percent) (Siddiqui, *Toronto Star*, April 10, 2008, AA6).

The issue of dual citizenship was explored again when the Canadian Parliament passed an amendment to the citizenship law in April of 2009, which effectively changed the 1977 legislation that allowed individuals to hold citizenship in another country. According to a CBC News article, the law, while intended to grant citizenship to those who had been stripped of their citizenship or told they weren't eligible (including war brides who married Canadian soldiers after 1947), prevents Canadian citizenship from being passed beyond first-generation Canadians in some cases (CBC News 2009). For example, a Canadian citizen born in Canada but living abroad can have a child in a foreign country and that child would still be granted citizenship automatically. However, should the children of that individual (who is a Canadian citizen) also be born outside of Canada, they would not be granted Canadian citizenship. Previously, Canadian citizens could pass on their citizenship without limit. While designed to protect the value of Canadian citizenship, it also puts in jeopardy the citizenship of a future generation—especially for those who study or work abroad. It may also affect the children of individuals adopted from abroad.

THE GEOGRAPHY OF IMMIGRATION

The student reflections in this chapter generally indicate that a distinction is not made between immigrants and racial and ethnic minorities. In fact, visible minorities are often constructed as immigrants, perceived as having "come to our country," settling within "their own ethnic groups," and then protesting "in the streets of Canada about issues back in their home country." Some suggest that Canada's multicultural policy is responsible for immigrants (or minority group members) "taking advantage of our liberalism" to the extent that they try to change "our identity," "our laws," and "our culture." However, an honest examination of our demography demonstrates that the "ethnic" neighbourhoods throughout the country have existed for many, many generations. The established communities of Italians in the Niagara Region of Ontario, the Finnish community in Thunder Bay, Ontario, and the Icelandic community in Winnipeg, Manitoba, are lively and protective of their cultures. No one accuses these communities of being isolationist or "un-Canadian." The same cannot be said for the long-standing communities of South Asians and East Asians in British Columbia, both of which date back to Confederation and the construction of this country.

Neighbourhoods populated by people of similar background—based on shared language, social class, ethnicity, race, nationality, or sexual orientation—provide members of that community with a support system. The associations, organizations, and businesses located in these neighbourhoods strengthen individual and group identity, nurture community spirit, and foster economic self-sufficiency and productivity. Insofar as immigrants must adjust to a new environment and are likely to experience barriers to full participation in the society, particularly as racial and ethnic minorities, it is inevitable that they would seek alternative ways of participating. It is within these communities that they find the space and the voice to experience life as they wish. Furthermore, all members of a democratic society have the right to live where and with whom they choose, as well as to participate in the ways they want. Hence, where immigrants live and the ways in which they participate in society should remain individual choices and rights, rather than prescribed options.

Facing the Challenges and Weighing the Possibilities for Successful Life

As noted earlier, immigrants come to Canada with dreams of "better lives" for themselves or their children. And for the most part, this aspiration is effectively communicated to their children, many of whom live their lives and construct aspirations that are in concert with their parents' desires and wishes. Susanna relates how she has come to appreciate the sacrifices of her parents, and the inspiration that she gained from their sacrifices. Susanna is the daughter of immigrant parents and a "minority," but still sees the possibilities and social capital that her background affords "to succeed in life."

Susanna: Thousands of immigrants come to Canada each year to start new lives. In 1984 my mother was one of them. I usually find interest in those brave individuals who leave their homelands to permanently live in Canada. Whenever I ask why they immigrated, the answer is usually the same or very similar—they did it for a better life. I understand what they mean but at the same time it is not clear; I have concluded that this is just one of those questions you never figure out because you would have had to experience it for yourself in order to understand...

I have always felt a little pressure to excel and I know it is because my parents are immigrants. I always feel that because [my mother] sacrificed so much and went through so much in this country, the only way to repay her is to do well in school and make her proud. I know for a fact that I am not the only immigrant offspring who feels this way. I use this and the fact that I am considered a "minority" as my inspiration to prosper.

The colour of your skin does make a difference with everything. And only those living in denial would oppose [me]. Although there has been a drastic change and the situation has definitely improved from times in the past, racism does still exist. You notice at school [and] when you walk into certain stores—it is everywhere and this is something you cannot change. Many immigrants are portrayed as uneducated and below the average white person, especially if they do not speak English fluently and they are often taken advantage of because of this.

I will never forget a time when I visited the house of one of my elementary school friends and when I met her parents, both of whom were Canadian [read western European], they questioned me as to what my parents did for a living. When I informed them my father worked with computers as a technician, they were amazed that my father did not work for a cleaning company, and that he was even computer literate. At that time I did not really pay any mind to their comments or even their reactions, but now I understand why they reacted in the way they did. I have also experienced a few similar scenarios since then, but I do not get offended, I simply do not let it bother me. You cannot change the ignorance of others, but what you can change is what you make of yourself.

Being classified as [a member of a] minority group has given me a lot of motivation. I would love to succeed in life and know that everything I own I provided for myself through my work [and that] nothing was given to me. [This dream] is an inspiration. Just to prove to the ignorant people in the world, who think that because you look a certain way or because you come from a certain area you are predestined to follow the negative trends. We are so fortunate in this country and many of us do not even realize it; we take many things for granted when we should be taking advantage of what is given to us. If not for ourselves, then for our parents who sacrificed so much for our futures.

But despite the optimism alluded to by Susanna, and the drive to succeed that is shared by most immigrant parents and their children, attaining middle-class status has never been easy. In *The Vertical Mosaic*, John Porter identified significant variations in immigrants' movement from their entrance-class status to the middle-class status they endeavour to attain. Indeed, as Castles (2000) contends, social class plays a role in the migration decisions individuals make, including whether to migrate, and to which countries they will migrate. Initially lacking the economic capital required to access material resources; the cultural capital to adequately read crucial sources of information and take advantage of opportunities; and the social capital for social networking (Castles 2000), immigrants and their children, as Susanna describes, work hard to navigate the cultural, employment, economic, and social systems to attain their dreams of success. As is to be expected, there are variations in the social and economic outcomes of immigrants and their children, so it is misleading to generalize about how well members of "visible minority" or immigrant populations are doing.

Recent Statistics Canada reports indicate that the children of Asian and South Asian immigrants (1.5 and second generation[11]) tend to be more successful, in terms of economic mobility, than children of Blacks, Filipinos, and Latin Americans. As Marina Jiménez writes in a 2008 *Globe and Mail* article, "second- and third-generation Chinese and Japanese Canadians surpass all other groups of newcomers including whites, while for blacks and other groups, there is little or no economic mobility across generations" (October 6, 2008, A1). As Jiménez reports, Census figures regarding income levels suggest that Blacks experience more discrimination and barriers in the labour market than others. With reference to this research, sociologist Jeffrey Reitz of the University of Toronto clarifies that immigrants from the Caribbean and Africa tend to fare far worse in employment outcomes than other newcomer groups, despite the fact that they tend to be well-educated or as educated as other immigrant groups. "Blacks do fairly well in terms of education," says Reitz, "but black men especially stand out with strikingly lower incomes. They report experiences of discrimination on a much higher level than other racial groups" (cited in the *Globe and Mail*, October 6, 2008, A10). And in their research on homelessness among Black Caribbean youth in Toronto, Springer and others (2007), report that negative changes in government and education policies such as income support, tenant protection, and school expulsion "seem to have combined with discrimination, racism, and economic restructuring to push immigrants, and immigrant youth in particular, closer to the margins of society" (6).

Aasha, a Black Ethiopian who immigrated as an adolescent, writes about her experiences growing up in Canada. She compares her early years in Ethiopia to her experiences with racism and discrimination in Canada, and discusses how these experiences affected her optimism about her life in this country.

Aasha: Growing up in Ethiopia until my teen years has moulded my view of the world. The school I attended is where most of my memories and my view of the world were sculpted. It was a school that was made up of children from all over the world. They were usually there because their parents were working for the United Nations or the African Union. I was surrounded by students who came from all sorts of backgrounds and different family dynamics, such as some [who] had two moms or two dads, or one of each, or even [just] one of the two. I grew up looking at these things as normal and with the notion that what constitutes a family is different for all people.

However, when I came to Canada, my flowery view of the world collapsed and I had to rebuild it again with a foundation of truth. I grew up believing that if I worked hard I would succeed and that there is no such thing as discrimination based on your colour. This is false. I still do believe that if you work hard you can succeed, but if you are of a race besides the white race then you face more obstacles and struggles and you have to work even harder.

My race was something I never questioned or discussed because I looked at it as though God created us all differently to make the world more colourful. But then living in Canada has made my colour a constant thought. Is the shopkeeper keeping an eye on me because of my colour? Did the teacher say I cannot be a doctor because I am black? Questions that made life a little pessimistic. Questions that almost made me give up. Who would not, if you are constantly being told by society and through education that you are worthless and that you need to be the superior race (white) to survive, and that throughout history you did not accomplish anything. That ought to bring you down and keep you down. I was lucky I had an encouraging childhood that, unrealistic as it seems, was not based on colour but what was in your mind.

Notwithstanding the difficulties that immigrants and their children experience, studies for the most part bolster immigrants' hopeful, determined confidence and their belief that education and hard work can make possible the realization of their dreams for a better life. In a longitudinal study that my colleagues and I conducted between 1993 and 1998 (Anisef et al. 2000), we compared the educational and occupational achievements of children of foreign-born parents from non-Western countries with those of children of Canadian-born parents. The initial study of the educational and occupational aspirations of Ontario Grade 12 students, first done in 1973 by professor Paul Anisef of the Department of Sociology at York University, found that the children of foreign-born parents, who in some cases were themselves foreign-born, tended to have high educational and occupational aspirations (Anisef 1975). This finding is similar to many other studies that report that the high aspirations of immigrant children tend to be supported by their parents and their respective communities, who place confidence in education as a means to success (James 1990; Lam 1994; Larter et al. 1982).

Our follow-up study of the class of 1973, who in the late 1990s were in their early forties, reveals that many managed to fulfill their aspirations. Specifically, the findings showed that, while the children of foreign-born parents were disproportionately more likely to come from working-class family backgrounds here in Canada, they sought out and acquired the education—in some cases with the financial support of their parents—

necessary to attain the careers and occupations to which they aspired. Noteworthy is the fact that, when compared to their female counterparts of Canadian-born parents, female respondents of foreign-born parents were less likely to be unemployed and twice as likely to be self-employed.

> As newcomers, the foreign-born are challenged to question conventional strategies for achieving success and may lack the social capital available to Canadians. Yet … foreign-born parents are made more reflexive by their migration experiences, and aspire to do well in Canada by actively supporting the ambitions of their children. Canadian-born parents might well learn from the experiences of … the foreign-born in helping broaden the life experiences of their children and preparing them to deal effectively with the 21st century. (Anisef et al. 2000, 260)

In another study (with York University's Celia Haig-Brown), we examined the educational experiences of immigrant and refugee students currently in university who had graduated from an ethnically and racially diverse school in a working-class area of Toronto. Apart from the educational and social ambitions demonstrated by the students in the interviews, we also noted their strong desire to contribute to both their geographic and ethnic communities, which they agreed had contributed much to their educational success. Most striking were the comments of Nguyen, who came to Canada with his parents as a refugee from Vietnam at a young age. Nguyen expressed his indebtedness to his community, school, teachers and, most of all, to Canada for the opportunities he has had. Contrary to his parents' wishes that he go into business, where it might be "easier to get jobs … and [he would] probably make more money," Nguyen was thinking of going into teaching, where he could more directly "pay back" his community and society.

> But also, I'm thankful to be here, so I'm paying, well it's not really paying back, but I want to return my dues, so if I'm going into teaching, I'm probably going to go into some service field … It's very silly but it's deep-rooted in me that I'm thankful to be here … so this is why business is not for me … I think you're in business for yourself … not the community or the country, whatever. (James and Haig-Brown 2001)

In another study, professors Jansen, Plaza, and I investigated the employment experiences and social mobility patterns of Caribbean immigrants to Canada, specifically those of African and South Asian (or Indian) origin. Of the 328 individuals surveyed, 92 percent were born in the Caribbean, most arrived as children and 82 percent are now citizens of Canada. Eighty-two percent reported having completed some post-secondary education; approximately 50 of the men and women with post-secondary education reported that institutional and systemic discrimination in their workplaces operated as barriers (or as a "glass ceiling") that prevented them from reaching their potential and attaining their occupational or professional aspirations. Despite these barriers and their failed dreams, most, relying on their own initiative (and, to a lesser extent, family and friends), persevered and found work largely in the service area. And, in keeping with their strong will and determination, slightly more than three-quarters (78 percent) said that they were satisfied or very satisfied with Toronto as a place to live; two-thirds (66 percent) felt that Toronto was a good place to raise their children; and only about one-third (32 percent) said that they would return to the Caribbean if conditions were right (James, Plaza, and Jansen 1999).

By and large, immigrants to Canada have managed to confront the limitations before them and have applied themselves to take advantage of the opportunities and possibilities for success in Canada. And, if they do not succeed in the ways they wished, they hope that their children will. In effect, immigrants have made good use of their energies and resources in reaching their goals. It is this drive, ambition, and determination that immigrant-receiving countries have long recognized; they therefore have supported (though in the case of some immigrants, reluctantly) the idea of immigration.

RESOURCEFUL RESOURCES: CANADA NEEDS IMMIGRANTS

> We are resistant to change and anything foreign. What we don't understand, we destroy. The cold, hard fact is that we need immigrants more than they need us. (College student)

It is generally understood that Canada would experience a serious decline in population if we were to significantly reduce the number of immigrants and refugees entering the country. In fact, it is expected that by 2012, due to the aging workforce, declining birth rate, and growing labour shortages, immigration will account for virtually all labour force net growth in Canada. This means that there will be a high need to attract talented workers from abroad (Canadian Press 2008a)—something that has always been a important feature of Canada's immigration policy. As a result, between 2001 and 2006, as Statistics Canada reports, 57.3 percent of the nearly 1.1 million recent immigrants in Canada were of working age, and while unemployment among immigrant groups remained relatively high, it was found that their employment rate increased 3.6 percent—from 63.4 percent in 2001 to 67 percent in 2006. Of note is that the increase in immigrants entering the labour force is greater than that of the Canadian-born population, which in turn led to a decrease of 2.1 percent in the employment gap between the Canadian-born and recent immigrant population (*Statistics Canada* 2008a).

According to Statistics Canada (2008b), between July 1 and October 1, 2008, Canada's population grew more than it did in any third quarter since 1990. This growth across the country is attributed mostly to immigration and the efforts of individual provinces to attract skilled workers. The reality is, the Canadian birth rate is low, and while the rate has increased in recent years, in 2000 it reached a level not seen since World War II (Hanes, *National Post*, September 22, 2007, A1). The Canadian population is also aging; there are more Canadians dying than are born each year. Because of this situation, the Canadian government, despite many Canadians' opposition to immigration, continues to give entry to approximately 250,000 applicants or as much as 1 percent of the Canadian population. Many demographers and statisticians claim that we need this number of immigrants to enter Canada each year if we are to have a viable economy and social stability. The aging of our population is of particular importance. It is estimated that by 2036, one in every four Canadians will be sixty-five years of age or older (Gauthier 1994). As the post-war baby boom generation grows older and drops out of the labour force, there will be an increased need for immigrants to meet labour force demands, which in turn will provide a steady tax base to fund the high quality health and social service needs of that generation.

To sustain population levels and meet labour force demands, Canada's immigration policies have traditionally sought to attract the youngest, healthiest, best-educated, and most resourceful people.[12] But while the current points system and categories give significant preference to newcomers with particular educational skills, because of discriminatory employment practices, immigrants with extensive credentials are often forced to work in jobs for which they are overqualified.[13] When we think about immigration, many Canadians do not consider that Canada depends on immigration to not only supplement the country's skilled labour, but also its unskilled labour, needs. Indeed, a successful economy does not only require skilled workers, but also a considerable number of unskilled workers. Unskilled workers do not pass Canada's points system; therefore, immigrants with professional qualifications and skills who do "get in" to the country take jobs cleaning houses, delivering pizza, and driving taxi cabs.

Also relevant here, and often unaddressed, is that when you select immigrant workers, you are also selecting their family. This means that issues of family reunification are an important aspect of immigration and, accordingly, is one of the largest categories of immigration across the globe. For example, in Germany and France the majority of official immigration has been classed as family reunification, totalling hundreds of thousands of individuals each year. However, as Doug Saunders reports in a 2007 *Globe and Mail* article, "France is trying to restrict family reunification, through mandatory DNA tests on applicants and other harsh policies" (November 3, 2007, F3). Canada has one of the lower percentages of family-class immigrants, and many countries have started to model their selection system on Canada's; nonetheless, in 2007, 40 percent of Canada's immigrants were still within the family class (*Globe and Mail*, November 3, 2007, F3).[14] On this question of family migration, Saunders writes: "The idea that you can allow a worker to enter, as if he were a machine part, without allowing his mother or children is pure mythology" (2007, F3).

Reporting on the housing demands created by immigrants, a July 2009 Scotiabank release noted that according to 2001 Census data, 68 percent of the immigrant population, compared to 73 percent of Canadian-born population, "lived a dwelling owned by a household member" (Warren 2009, 2), and by 2006 the percentage increased by 4 percent for immigrants compared to only 2 percent for Canadian-born individuals. This increased rate in home ownership between 2001 and 2006 included "all immigrant groups, regardless of how long they had resided in Canada," with the biggest increase "among those living in Canada less than 10 years" (2). The trend in home ownership contradicts the idea that new arrivals first settle in rental accommodation and, over time, become homeowners. As the report indicates, immigrants "make the move to homeownership, at rates similar to the Canadian-born population." Hence, as Scotiabank's Adrienne Warren suggests, "as recent immigrants make the transition from renter to owner, they will increasingly drive housing demands" (2).

What is clear is that immigration has always been and continues to be essential. In fact, Statistics Canada projects that not only will immigration form an important role in the Canadian economy, but that immigration will ultimately become Canada's sole source of growth (Martel and Caron-Malenfant 2006). But the current number of immigrants entering Canada still does not meet the country's labour or economic needs. In this regard, governments—both federal and provincial—have responded by introducing guest workers, also known as migrant workers, who temporarily move to another country to work. Canada has long had guest-worker programs that "borrow" people from their home countries and send them back when their utility has expired. Ontario recently lobbied the federal government to bring in more immigrants on work permits to satisfy labour shortages in the food industry, especially in places such as Tim Hortons. Lesley Ciarula Taylor reported in a 2008 *Toronto Star* article that while the population is aging, and there will be relatively fewer and fewer young adults and teenagers, the food services industry expects to need 181,000 more workers by 2015. This need for "unskilled" workers is exacerbated by the decrease in the traditional labour pool (*Toronto Star*, October 29, 2008b, A20).

Immigrants on short-term work permits have satisfied many of these labour gaps in Alberta, British Columbia, and Saskatchewan. The jobs most commonly filled on these kinds of work permits include those in the areas of construction, fast food service, or hotel cleaning. The number of these short-term migrants far surpasses the number of individuals who enter as permanent residents. This need for unskilled workers challenges the points system, which tends to privilege doctors, engineers, and other high-skilled immigrants without considering the true economic needs of the country (*Toronto Star*, October 29, 2008b, A20).

Furthermore, a guest-worker mindset, which treats workers more as commodities than human beings, does not address the reality that people who come to Canada to work are likely to develop ties, have conjugal relationships and children, and participate in various degrees in the broader Canadian society. Saunders's comment that "the inconvenient thing about immigrants is that they happen to be people" is well taken (*Globe and Mail*, November 3, 2007, F3).[15] Advocates for workers' rights express concerns over the expansion of temporary-worker programs for low-skilled workers, fearing that such programs might lead to human rights abuses. Specifically, they fear that low-skilled workers, whose work permits are tied to a single employer, are vulnerable to exploitation, in part because of "language barriers, poor education and unfamiliarity with Canada's labour laws" (Brennan, *Toronto Star*, March, 15, 2008, A19). A case in point is that of Jamaican migrant workers in the Okanagan. According to an article in the *Kelowna Capital News*, Jamaican workers were expected to follow strict rules, which included an eleven o'clock curfew on work nights and restrictions on overnight guests of the opposite sex. Workers were also told not to drink on work nights (*Kelowna Capital News*, September 23, 2007, 23).

According to the Citizenship and Immigration Canada website, in 2008 the federal government passed legislation that would place more emphasis on job skills. The government's change to the immigration system is intended to more closely connect migration with job skills by selectively choosing skilled new permanent residents, increasing the number of temporary foreign workers, and allowing higher skilled temporary workers and visa students who already have Canadian experience to stay in Canada permanently (see pages 170–173). The Harper government's *Budget Implementation Act*, introduced March 14, 2008, included a section that amends the *Immigration and Refugee Protection Act* to guarantee that "processing of applications and requests" is carried out in a manner that "will best support the attainment of immigration goals" determined by the government (Brennan, *Toronto Star*, March 15, 2008, A19). Many immigration advocates consider this legislation to be dangerous because it creates competition that may make it even more difficult for earlier immigrants who already struggle to find jobs in their fields of expertise despite their "foreign" credentials. As an Afghani immigrant who came to Canada in 1999 contends: "Tying immigration so tightly to jobs risks letting the government forget the thousands of underemployed, skilled immigrants in low paying survival jobs ... Being an immigrant myself, I understand the frustration. Many newcomers are in debt and live in poverty" (Taylor and Keung, *Toronto Star*, October 24, 2008, A17). There is also the fear that under the new legislation the government will pay less attention to sponsoring refugees from danger zones and may limit or delay family sponsorship.

But, according to Les Linklater, director general of Citizenship and Immigration Canada's Immigration Branch, such legislation is intended to "allow us to better manage to respond to immediate labour market needs" (Campion-Smith, *Toronto Star*, March 29, 2008, A27). This means is that if the immigration minister determines that Canada needs skilled tradespeople, applicants fitting this profile will be privileged in the application process. Those who possess whatever skills are in demand will be given priority, a change from the first-come, first-served system previously in place. The changes would also allow the immigration minister to reject applicants who have already been approved by immigration officials, and would allow the minister to place limitations on the types of immigrants whose applications could be processed.

In the following essay, Zena, while certainly not representative of all immigrants, articulates a perspective that should always be borne in mind: immigrants and refugees are not poor, uneducated people who enter Canada seeking handouts and who avoid actively participating in the larger culture. Zena considers herself an insider—a "Canadian"—and expects the rights, respect, privileges, and acceptance that this citizenship entails.

ZENA: "I CONSIDER MYSELF A CANADIAN ISMAILI."

An immigrant Canadian, I am a part of the much-talked-about Canadian ethnic mosaic. I epitomize the diversity of this mosaic: an East Indian by race, born and raised in East Africa (a second-generation African), a practicing Shiite Ismaili Muslim, and with a working knowledge of three languages (East Indian,[16] Swahili, and English). A Tanzanian national by birth, I left my country in 1971 as a result of political considerations for a four-year stay in the United Kingdom prior to immigrating to Canada in 1975.

It was during the 1960s that Tanzania (then Tanganyika) and the other countries in the region attained independence from Britain. The colonial affiliation meant that, until 1970, the school system, the judiciary, and other institutions were modelled along the lines of those in Britain. For example, the medium of instruction in schools and the predominant language of commerce and government was English. I was therefore brought up with an understanding and appreciation of British culture—the predominant culture I subsequently found in the U.K. and in Canada.

A strong part of what I am is formed by the Ismaili community to which I belong. The Ismaili faith, one of the seventy-two sects of Islam, takes the Islamic concept of religion as a way of life (i.e., unlike the strict Augustinian distinction between material and spiritual, Islam considers both to be equally important) even further. The community encourages and has developed major programs in education and social and economic development. Higher education, and excellence in commerce and in the professions are put on par with prayer, as is enterprise with a conscience and self-help. My faith has instilled strongly in me the existence of God, and a balance between the pursuit of material things and prayers for the soul.

Culturally, I consider myself a Canadian Ismaili. This would not change if I were asked this question on a visit to Tanzania or at Jamatkhana (the Ismaili prayer/community house). As minorities in all the countries they reside in, Ismailis' first loyalty is to their country of residence. There is no Ismaili code of conduct; they adopt the language and dress code of the respective countries. As an "unhyphenated" Canadian, I see myself as a citizen, sharing the same future with other Canadians, all equal and without special privileges.

As someone who left her country of origin because of political reasons, I am able to appreciate the stable political environment, democratic values and institutions, and the various freedoms (of expression, religion, and so on) far more than Canadians who were born and raised here. This is reflected in my active participation in, and support of, civic affairs; for example, [my voting] in all elections, my membership in a political party, my open-mindedness in accepting various differing opinions, my interest in reading newspapers—in particular, editorials and opinion pieces—and my support and respect for law and authority.

Similarly, I am able to appreciate the high standard of living in Canada after having lived in a Third World country, where electricity and running water are considered luxuries. I place a high premium on education. It was a luxury back home, both in terms of user fees and availability—Tanzania, with a population of twenty-five million, has only one university. Although I was born and raised in relative luxury, the poverty of, and lack of opportunities for, most Tanzanians are permanent reminders that, to most of the people in the Third World, getting three meals a day remains a major preoccupation.

These "backgrounds" have also given me a high regard for the work ethic and self-help. Social security programs (medicare, pensions, and so on) [as we know them] do not exist in Tanzania or India (the country of my great-grandparents' birth), and therefore this dependence on government is an alien concept to me. Although as a liberal-minded, social democrat, I support [social assistance], I would find it difficult to collect from these programs. The work ethic, pursuit of excellence, and self-help are reinforced by all of my background influences (nationality, ethnic, and religious). As a parent, I expect to pass along these values to my children, [as well as the] related ones of thrift and of carrying as little debt as possible.

My being a member of a visible minority that is frequently negatively stereotyped is another major influence. The ignorance of my fellow Canadians as to the many different peoples generalized as East Indians (a Tanzanian Ismaili like myself has as much in common with a Tamil from South India as a WASP[17] would have with a Ukrainian—they are both white) is disappointing. I am frequently drawn into the role of educator, explaining different Eastern cultures and religious backgrounds.

Unfortunately, the only thing many Canadians know about the world's second largest religion is the political violence and terrorism in the Middle East. This is like equating Christianity with violence because of the struggle in Ireland between Catholics and Protestants. People lose sight of the fact that Muslims, like everyone else, can be poor or rich, tolerant or intolerant, honest or dishonest, illiterate or scholarly. In personal terms, this has cultivated a tolerance in me for other cultures, a desire to learn more about them, and a sympathy for the negative stereotyping to which they might be subjected.

Another effect of this is that I try very hard to be a model citizen, because, as a member of a visible minority, I feel that my shortcomings will be attributed to my race, ethnicity, and so on. A beneficial result of this (sort of a "backward compliment") is that this makes me a winner, since I try harder than I would have otherwise.

CONCLUSION

Contrary to some Canadians' perceptions that immigration is largely unnecessary, a hindrance to economic advancement, and a threat to positive social relations—particularly during times of high unemployment and social tension due to economic recession—the evidence indicates differently.

The racial, ethnic, religious, and class differences and the related cultural values, customs, and beliefs associated with immigration do not contribute to disharmony and a loss of "Canadian identity." The energy, optimism, and "drive" that immigrants bring into society make them an important and viable addition to our economic and cultural structures. Indeed, the multilingual, multicultural, and multi-skilled character of today's Canada has much to do with the kinds of immigrants and refugees that we accept into the country. Not only does this diversity contribute to a dynamic society, it also enables Canada to more effectively compete economically around the changing world. But many of today's immigrants face considerable barriers to having their educational credentials and work experience recognized, making the time it takes them to adjust to their new home longer than it once was.

Compared to some forty years ago, when immigrants were largely from Europe, many of today's immigrants struggle to be seen as Canadians. As racial minorities—people largely from Asia, Africa, and the Caribbean—their colour signals them as, or is used to construct them as, foreigners—seemingly, they are "immigrants for life." It does not help matters when critics attempt to identify a correlation between an increase in crime and an increase in immigration. Such a claim is not supported by evidence; it is irresponsible to suggest that immigrants and refugees bring with them "violent and lawless tendencies" and behaviours that have become the "root cause" of problems in Canada. Such a stereotypical assertion is in opposition to the reality that individuals are not hard-wired with cultural values and behaviours. As previously argued, culture is not static, and individuals' behaviours and beliefs are structured or informed by the environment in which they live their lives.

Furthermore, the *Immigration Act* stipulates that persons convicted of or suspected of criminal offences, and persons who would constitute a danger to national security are inadmissible. A study by Samuel (1989) showed that the criminality rate of immigrants from source areas such as Africa, Asia, and the Caribbean was less than one-third that of immigrants from the United States and Europe. Further, Weinfield (1998) identifies evidence that indicates "criminality, measured by incarceration in federal penitentiaries, is less for the foreign born than for the native born."[18] Our perception of immigrants as criminals is more accurately attributed to the connection between crime and poverty. Generally, the criminal behaviours of any population must be examined in relation to that group's access to opportunities. We need to examine how, as the host society, our accommodation or integration practices provide immigrants with access to the necessary employment and education opportunities.

Peter Li (2003) contends that integration relies on society being open to immigrants on an institutional, community, and individual level. This openness would require "policy-makers, immigration critics, and academics to abandon an ethnocentric complacency," and to start evaluating how Canada as a nation does on the "two-way street" of integrating immigrants (330). Successful integration can't happen without Canadians being willing to make some changes as well. In this regard, Canadians will need to recognize that culture is not static—just as

Canadian culture without immigration would change with time, so too will it change with new people participating in it. Cultural and ethnic differences are not absolute or static; cultural identity is not a primordial or singular identity that immigrants bring with them that cannot be merged with what is understood to be a Canadian identity. Integration, then, cannot be considered successful until immigrants—regardless of their colour and the language they speak—are considered to be Canadian and are granted all the rights of citizenship, including the same democratic rights and freedoms that we hold dear, such as the right to disagree, the right to be different, to be assertive, to live in the communities of our choosing, and to protest. Integration, as Li writes, "is about incorporating newcomers into a democratic process of participation and negotiation that shapes the future, and not about conforming and confining people to pre-established outcomes based on the status quo" (2003, 330).

In summary, this chapter draws attention to the fact that Canada—with the exception of Aboriginal peoples—is a society of immigrants. The comments by students and others considered thus far demonstrate less about their dislikes, frustrations, distrusts, or sentiments regarding immigration (although these are significant), but more about how their views are structured by the racism, xenophobia, and systemic discrimination inherent or embedded in our multicultural existence.

NOTES

1. The Law Union of Ontario (1981) gave the following three reasons for introduction of the point system: (1) racist ideologies were under attack and the government no longer wanted to appear exclusionary; (2) employers wanted a criteria-based system that would identify and admit people with specialized skills; and (3) immigration from Europe was dwindling and Canada needed to look elsewhere for immigrants (40). According to Oreopoulos (2009), as the international competition for skilled immigrants increases, countries such as the United Kingdom, Spain, and Germany are considering, or are in the process of introducing, a point system as an "approach to evaluate the desirable characteristics of prospective immigrants" and to "shift their immigration policies more towards a skill-based focus" (3).

2. Apart from people born in Britain (as spelled out in the policy), those from Ireland, Newfoundland, Australia, New Zealand, and the Union of South Africa were also considered British subjects. Of note is the fact that people from other African countries under British control, as well as India, Pakistan, Ceylon (now Sri Lanka), the Caribbean, and other "Commonwealth" countries were not included in the list of "subjects."

3. Maroons are Africans who were transported to Jamaica as slaves and later escaped. They were considered by the British colonialists to be unlawful and a threat to the social stability of the island. In an attempt to rid the island of them, they were shipped to Nova Scotia in 1796 as a form of punishment (Walker 1980).

4. Because of these criteria, about 60 percent of immigrants to Canada have undergraduate degrees compared to only 20 percent of Canadian-born population (Statistics Canada 2008a).

5. Interestingly, admitting the anecdotal nature of the results, Oreopoulos also observed that "evaluators with Asian or Indian accents or names are *less* likely to call back resumes with Asian or Indian names" (27).

6. See Chapter 5, page 134 for discussion of the Paris riots.

7. Ethnic enclaves are residential areas "where a particular ethnic group numerically dominates," with corresponding symbols, institutions (e.g., social, religious, cultural, linguistic, commercial), and services that cater to the needs of the group. Enclaves are distinct from "geographic concentration" of an ethnic group where members of the particular group might live "side by side without any community bonds and shared sentiments" (Qadeer and Kumar 2006, 2).

8. Whereas in 1980, recent immigrant men with some employment income earned 85 cents for each dollar received by Canadian-born men, in 2005, that ratio dropped to 65 cents. For immigrant women, the numbers dropped from 85 cents to 56 cents (Statistics Canada 2008d).

9. The protests surrounding the results of elections in Iran in July 2009 might not have garnered the same reaction from Dave and Ryan because, both at home and abroad, these were reported as attempts by Iranian youth to uphold the rule of democracy, which is a hallmark of Western ideology.

10. Reader comment from "Sri Lankan protesters form human chain at Toronto's Union Station," CBC News. Friday, January 30, 2009, http://www.cbc.ca/canada/toronto/story/2009/01/30/tamil-toronto.html?ref.

11. As previously explained in Chapter 4, note 2, when *first generation* is used to refer to Canadians who immigrated as adults, and *second generation* denotes the Canadian-born children of first-generation immigrants, *1.5 generation* is used to identify those who immigrated to Canada before starting high school.

12. See Anisef and Lamphier 2003; Jakubowski 1997; Li 2000; Satzewich 1991.

13. Tony Fang (2009) notes that the points system presents new challenges as it more heavily weighs education in its choice of newcomers.

14. The *Toronto Star* reported that more than 10 percent of new immigrants were schoolchildren between the ages of five and sixteen years, and more than half spoke a language other than English and French at home (December 5, 2007a, AA6).

15. See also Deshaw 2006.

16. While "East Indian" is not a language (the term is generally used to designate ethnic communities originating from the Indian subcontinent, where hundreds of languages are spoken), Zena is likely using it as a common term for one of the widely spoken languages in India, such as Gujarati or Urdu, in much the same way the term "Chinese" is used to designate any of the variety of languages spoken in China (e.g., Cantonese, Mandarin, etc.).

17. It is important to understand is that while many contributors to this text use the term **WASP**, not all white people, even whites from the United Kingdom, are "so-called" WASPs—or white Anglo-Saxon Protestants—and that this term is often used, even by other white people, as a derogatory or derisive term. Few Canadians today still fit this category, and the dominant white power structure is not limited to Anglo-Saxons or Protestants. What is more, some white European immigrant communities are still affected by racism, language barriers, and exclusion.

18. See also the *Report of the Commission on Systemic Racism in the Ontario Criminal Justice System: A Community Summary*, 1995.

RACISM, IDENTIFICATION, AND EQUITY

> Our commitment to address racism must not paralyze us.
> We should not be afraid to question, to make mistakes,
> and above all to learn. We should all commit ourselves to
> rights literacy for ourselves, our families, and our clients.
> The process of naming racism is not an indictment, it is an
> opportunity for change. (St. Lewis 1996, 119)

In many of the stories that students and aspiring professionals who
are ethno-racial minorities tell about their lives in Canada, they make
reference to experiences with racism and discrimination. They submit
that racism and discrimination—as well as ethnocentrism, xenophobia,
stereotyping, etc.—have informed their understanding of the opportunities
open to them in Canadian society, as well as the construction of their
identities as Canadians with particular ethnic and racial heritages. While
majority group members may not similarly attribute their identification,
experiences, and opportunities to these factors, their lives are no less
informed by racism and discrimination; for these factors are structurally
embedded in society and affect everyone, though admittedly in different
ways in relation to gender, social class, citizenship, immigrant status,
sexuality, and other demographic factors. The stories that individuals
tell are of their own personal experiences and encounters, but these
experiences, and the values, ideas, and attitudes that individuals express
do not occur or develop in isolation.

In this chapter, we seek to demonstrate that individuals' experiences with racism, and the values, attitudes, and ideas they express, are not merely a product of their encounters with other individuals, but are structured by the prevailing ideologies, ethics, and practices of the institutions and society around them. In particular, we focus on how racism operates at the individual, institutional, and structural levels to frame the self-identification and experiences of individuals, as well as their perceptions of the possibilities offered to them in Canadian society. Indeed, as Hier (2007) argues, it is important to begin with the assumption that "racism is a fact of Canadian social life," and that documenting the different manifestations of racism is necessary if we are to gain a "full understanding of racism in Canada" (21). To the extent that racism (or racisms) operate in relation to discrimination, ethnocentrism, xenophobia, prejudice, Islamophobia, stereotyping, and racial profiling, we will also examine and define these concepts and discuss their operation. Our focus, therefore, is on racism at the *institutional* and *structural levels*, for as Hughes and Kallen (1974) suggested thirty years ago, it is structural racism that is particularly relevant when examining racism and discrimination in Canada. According to Hughes and Kallen (1974), it is because of institutional and structural racism that minority group members are denied access to the qualifications, education, and skills necessary for full participation in society (106); we see from the personal stories included in this book and from current media coverage that this remains true today. In the final section of the chapter, we explore the ways in which equity programs are taken up by individuals as viable measures to address inequities, racism, and discrimination.

MECHANISMS THAT SUPPORT IDEOLOGIES OF INEQUITY AND SOCIAL DIFFERENTIATION

It is a commonly held notion that racism results from ignorance. It is typically understood in terms of an individual's lack of awareness, knowledge of, or exposure to the racial group under consideration, as one white female university student wrote:

> Racism for me is a lack of awareness of other cultures, or a lack of sensitivity for differences—not appreciating and not having that sense of appreciation for other cultures and different knowledge that you can get from just talking or being friends with or conversing with people from other cultures … in a sense it is ignorance, I think. Again, it's a lack of knowledge of what is out there and what is different.

One white, male university student wrote that racism is "based on ignorance towards issues like colonialism and how that affects people even today." Ignorance is also perceived in the choice individuals make not to become informed about other ethnic groups; and, since people are more likely to have information about the mainstream ethno-racial group, ignorance is largely about the minority group. In explaining a white male's "ignorance" of her, a South Asian student had this to say:

> When I was on the bus, a guy said: "Oh, so you're from India, so how come you don't have an accent?" I turned to him and in all humour, I said, "Well I guess I lost you on the boat ride home—boat ride to Canada. Sorry." So I tackled it and I let him know that it wasn't something I appreciated ... Yes, out of ignorance, he asked me how come I don't have an accent, but not everyone has an accent ... I guess it has to do with ignorance. Once you tackle ignorance in a humorous way, or even in a strong way and say, "Hey dude, I don't appreciate what you're saying"—educate them—the world will definitely be a better place.

But as Pasha Malla explained in his 2008 *Globe and Mail* article, "Self-portrait of a racist," "We often hear that racism is largely a result of ignorance—but I live in Toronto, with regular exposure to all races. If my journal is any indication, exposure to other cultures doesn't necessarily allay racist tendencies" (March 22, A1). Malla reported that he kept a journal over a twelve-month period and noted every time he "made an assertion, had a thought or acted on an attitude based on race" (A1). In his journal, Malla described the following occurrences: "Today I was sitting on the subway beside a black man. When he got off at his stop, I instinctively checked my pocket for my wallet," and "At the movies I noticed a Middle Eastern-looking guy in line, wearing a backpack. For a moment, I second-guessed going into the theatre." In reference to these observations, Malla noted:

> This proved useful in recognizing how I think and interact with people of other races, and brought into shocking relief how often my behaviour is based in prejudice or stereotype. My racism journal has revealed that, although I conduct myself publicly in a way that conforms to Canadian political correctness, what I'm often thinking, and occasionally doing, is often very racist indeed. (A1)

What then is racism? **Racism** is the set of beliefs or the ideology that constructs groups—typically identified by physical characteristics—as culturally or biologically lacking in certain abilities, skills, and characteristics that are necessary for their participation in a group, community, or society, thereby leading to subordination, colonization, and discriminatory or unequal treatment of such identified groups. Stated differently, it is an ideology that considers race as immutable and directly linked to the biological, intellectual, emotional, and behavioural characteristics of a racial group. Fleras (2010) defines racism as "those ideas and ideals (ideology) that assert or imply the normality or superiority of one social group over another, together with the institutional power to put these perceptions into practice in ways that control, exclude, or exploit those defined as culturally different or racially different" (68).[1] Salient to the way in which racism is conceptualized, is not the arbitrarily selected characteristics— such as skin colour, intelligence, and temperament—based on biological or physical differences between groups, but "the public recognition of these differences as being significant for assessment, explanation, and interaction" (Fleras and Elliott 2003, 55). A key component of racism is power, not in terms of the "everyday" influence one individual might have over another, but in terms of influence that is supported and held in place by power, based on ideological, cultural, economic, political, and social factors and exerted by one racial group over another. This power, evident in the unequal distribution of scarce resources, is sustained by established laws, regulations, policies, conventions, and customs that contribute to normalized and taken-for-granted ways of thinking and behaving. Racism operates at different levels, a point that we will return to later.

Social scientists make a distinction between racism and ethnocentrism. **Ethnocentrism** refers to the tendency to see things from the perspective of one's own ethnic group culture, to have a preference for one's own group cultural symbols, and to think that what is true of one's ethnic group culture is also true—or should be true—of others (Carroll 1993). Ethnocentrism, then, is often an uncompromising allegiance and loyalty to one's own cultural values and practices, which are viewed as natural, normal, and necessary. The idea that the culture of one's own ethnic group is preferable may appear harmless; however, problems arise when established expectations based on this assumption lead to cultural "standards" as a frame of reference for interpreting and evaluating the behaviours of other groups. Not surprisingly, other ethnic groups (or outgroups) tend to be rated inferior and untrustworthy. As Elliott and Fleras (1992) write, "although favouritism towards one's own group can promote cohesion and morale, it can also contribute to intergroup tension and hostility... [and] to a proliferation of stereotypes about outgroup members" (55).

As in the case of racism, ethnocentrism tends to have a more detrimental effect on the more vulnerable ethno-racial groups in society. The internment of Italians during World War II is illustrative. As the National Film Board's *Barbed Wire and Mandolins* (Zavaglia 1997) shows, after Mussolini declared war on England and France on June 10, 1940, Italian Canadians came to be regarded as untrustworthy. They were seen as "enemy aliens" as per the *War Measures Act*, and some seventeen thousand people, many of them Canadian citizens, including women and children, were fingerprinted and ordered to report regularly to the RCMP. About six hundred were arrested, and seven hundred were interned without being charged—some for as long as two years. In his apology to the Italians in 1990, Prime Minister Brian Mulroney stated, "Sending civilians to internment camps without trial simply because of their ethnic origin was not then, and not now, and never will be accepted in a civilized nation that purports to respect the rule of law." Harney (1978) reports that Canadians had turned against Italians, smashing their store windows, refusing to work with them, and withholding job opportunities. (See also Jansen 1988.)

Racism, ethnocentrism, and prejudice are often used interchangeably. But it is important to pay attention to their difference. **Prejudice** is understood to mean an unfavourable attitude based on a premature, hasty, or uninformed judgment of, or an unreasoning predilection toward, a person or group, or having preconceived opinions that are assumed to be true before having been tested (Dalrymple 2007; Driedger 1989). Elliott and Fleras (1992) define prejudice as a set of biased and generalized beliefs (or stereotypes) about outgroups derived largely from inaccurate and incomplete information. Prejudice involves that "attitudinal component of identity formation, boundary maintenance, and intergroup relations" (335). These faulty and inflexible generalizations contribute to a frame of mind that makes it difficult to interact with and relate to outgroup members—especially members of minority groups—in an impartial and objective manner, Essentially, prejudice is not simply a question of attitudes or emotions among individuals about different groups; rather, it is a socially constructed representation of group members that is influenced by social processes and modes of communication and dominant discourses.

The word *bias*, which is a particular inclination and predisposition toward objects or people, is often substituted for prejudice (as well as other "isms" and phobias). In fact, the *Oxford Shorter Dictionary* lists "bias favourable or unfavourable" in its definition of prejudice (Dalrymple 2007). While bias may be either negative or positive, ethnic prejudice, particularly that directed at marginalized or racialized groups, is usually negative. It is an unfounded, irrational, rigid judgment involving emotions, attitudes, and subjective evaluation. Typically, such attitudes, predispositions, or prejudgments are not reversed or changed—even when new information is revealed.

The tendency to categorize and make prejudgments is considered necessary to some extent, as the human mind needs to organize the stimuli with which it is bombarded. As such, we select and store only some of the many experiences and facts available to us in order to effectively react or respond to them. And as we acquire new experiences and information, we tend to assimilate them as much as possible into the categories that already exist. This enables us to identify related objects and retrieve information in ways that allow us to make sense of our experiences or what we see. But there are inevitable drawbacks to this. Consider, for instance, Naomi's experience.

> **Naomi:** People whom I meet frequently ask, "What are you?" as a way of determining my racial background. I then proceed to tell them that I am Canadian. They then ask me, "Where are your parents from?" I tell them Poland, and they then look confused … And when they learn that I am Jewish, their responses always amaze me. People express surprise and say, "You are Jewish!" as if I had a disease or something. And some people think that they are paying me a compliment by saying, "We do not think of you as Jewish; you are different than most Jewish people we know." This is an outright insult to my ethnicity, of which I am proud. Another typical comment is that I "do not look Jewish." I do not understand what it means to "look Jewish" considering that there are Jewish people from all over the world.

The reaction to Naomi is part of the larger concept of *anti-Semitism,* which in the extreme is defined as "hostility directed at Jews solely because they are Jews … and is the result of attitudes and behaviour that arise regardless of what Jews do or believe" (Mock 1996, 120). Karen Mock writes, "while most Jews would acknowledge what can be called their 'white privilege' in a racist society, I believe that there has been, and is currently, a powerful racist component in anti-Semitism" (120). Much of this is evident in the "antagonism" directed at Jews, as Mock submits, for who they are and for what they represent, both historically and contemporarily. This antagonism seems to come through in the "insults" to which Naomi refers, and in Mark's statement: "Yes, I am Jewish. Is there anything wrong with that?" (see Chapter 3).

Anti-Semitic sentiments were one of the catalysts that led to the establishment of the Bouchard–Taylor Commission (2007) to examine "reasonable accommodation" in Quebec (see Chapter 5). In addition to setting out its "standard of behaviour" for migrants who considered settling in their town, noting that there was no separation of boys and girls and eating was for nourishment of "the body, not the soul," the town council of Hérouxville signalled to Jews (and Muslims) that their cultural practices would not be welcomed. In fact, as was reported by D. Moore in the *Globe and Mail* (January 30, 2007, A19), "the Herouxville officials have said the standards are in response to recent culture clashes, including at a Montreal gym where windows were obscured to block the view of exercising women from a nearby Hasidic Jewish synagogue and school."

Similar hostility is evident in the beliefs held about, and the treatment of, Muslims. In other words, Islamophobia, a fear and hatred of Muslim people and Islam as a religion, is fostered by the presumption that Muslims do not integrate into society—Western society, that is—by insisting on maintaining their different religious practices, wearing their different religious attire, and having their own faith-based schools. Particularly since 9/11, Muslims are associated with extremist views and even terrorist activity, making them a threat to the stability of Western societies. This leads to the common notion that they must be closely policed. Writing in the *Asians News*, Martin Jacques (2007) notes that in addition to the significant amount of discrimination that Muslims face, they are "stalked by a constant sense of distrust and suspicion."

In their recently published book, *Islamophobia: Making Muslims the Enemy*, Peter Gottshalk and Gabriel Greenberg (2008) write that the publication of twelve images depicting the Prophet Muhammad in the Danish newspaper, *Jyllands-Posten*, in September 2005, is a notable example of how Islamophobia operates in Western societies to bring about and maintain intolerance toward Muslims. The images at issue were twelve editorial cartoons that were commissioned by the cultural editor of the newspaper. Offended by the use of the Prophet's image, which is forbidden in Islam, a Dutch Muslim approached the newspaper and the Danish government seeking redress, but none was granted. And when an attempt by ambassadors of Muslim-majority nations to meet with the Danish government was turned down, scholars at al-Azhar University in Cairo and the secretary general of the Arab League in Lebanon condemned the images and actions of the newspaper. These actions contributed to global protest when Muslims around the world learned of the cartoons through news from the Islamic conference held in Mecca (Gottshalk and Greenberg 2008, 1).

Commenting on the protests, some peaceful and others violent, Gottshalk and Greenberg write:

> Once more the familiar pattern unfolded, as some Muslims reacted violently to apparently an insignificant event that seemed the latest battlefront in the West's holding action to preserve inalienable rights against ever threatening Islamic intolerance. Although the Muslims involved never represented more than a fraction of a fraction of the world's more than one billion Muslims, their vociferous fury only confirmed a western image of Muslim intolerance and Islamic otherness. (1)

The images were also featured in Canadian media, whose publishers justified doing so under the guise of freedom of speech and freedom of religion.[2]

Further, the Western image of Muslims undoubtedly played a role in the treatment of Maher Arar, the Canadian citizen who was detained at a New York airport and sent to Syria by the United States (in consultation with Canadian authorities), where he was tortured, while never having been charged with a crime. Consider also the "standard of behaviour" that was set out by the town council of Hérouxville. Through the policy, the council was communicating to Muslims that their lifestyle, dietary practices, cultural values, and religious practices would not be tolerated, much less accepted, by the people of the town, should any Muslims happen to come there; the most insipid aspect of this incident is the fact that the town was acting preemptively.

The town council's position, which operated to maintain a system of differentiation among members of society, was also informed by *xenophobia*—a fear, dislike, and/or aversion to strangers or foreigners. The term comes from the Greek words *xenos*, meaning "stranger" or "foreigner," and *phobos*, meaning "fear." While it is typical to be reserved or careful when interacting with people that one does not know, this reservation becomes xenophobia when the interaction is based on an exaggerated fear or dislike toward people constructed as foreigners or immigrants, merely on the basis of "visible" or presumed characteristics such as race, ethnicity, accent, language, religion, origin, cultural practices, etc. Again, if we consider the situation of Muslims, Sikhs, and Jews, whose religious and cultural practices were seen as unacceptable by the town council of Hérouxville, it should be clear that these groups were not rejected on the basis of being immigrants or newcomers to Canada. Indeed, such groups have been in Canada, and in Quebec, for generations, but they were constructed as different and "foreign," hence the insistence that they must assimilate and become a part of the mainstream community if they are to be trusted.

These mechanisms—ethnocentrism, prejudice, anti-Semitism, Islamophobia, xenophobia, and others—function with racism to maintain the system of differentiation and racialization. Recall that *racialization* is a process by which individuals, by virtue of their racial difference (from dominant group members) are constructed as having immutable cultural values, beliefs, behaviours, personality traits, political ideas, and social practices related to their race. Evident in this construction of individuals' difference is a tendency toward *essentialism*, which is a perception of individuals' characteristics and patterns of behaviours as inalterable. Dominguez (1994) notes that racialization "is produced and reproduced through ideological, institutional, interactive and linguistic practices that support a particular construction of Difference" (334). Any examination of how the mechanisms of social differentiation operate must take into account individuals' attitudes and behaviours, as well as how the various institutions and structures in society operate to maintain a system or ideology that produces racialization and the resulting intolerance, indifference, and exclusion of individuals on the basis of race. Attitude refers to individuals' thoughts (or beliefs) and feelings about particular people, objects, or issues. While *attitude* is about the psychological or the cognitive and affective component of people's relationships with others (Rubin and McNeil 1987), *ideology* represents the social, economic, and political factors that structure thoughts and feelings. The behaviours or actions and practices that result from ideology, beliefs, and attitudes are discrimination, which will be defined later.

In what follows, I discuss the different levels of racism, particularly focusing on institutional and structural racism. Afterward, I return to the mechanisms of social differentiation, and using examples, note how they operate in unison with racism at institutional and societal levels.

RACISMS

As mentioned earlier, racism operates in different forms, at different levels, and has different expressions, which can be willful, deliberate, and conscious, or indirect, unintentional, reflexive, and unconscious. According to Hall (1978), there are "different racisms—each historically specific and articulated in a different way" (26).[3] And as **Figure 7.1** illustrates, there is an interlocking relationship between individual, institutional, and structural racisms, but it is individual racism that is often taken up and reflected in the general public discourse and understanding of social differentiation and behaviour patterns toward racial minorities. **Individual racism** is structured by an ideology or set of ideas and beliefs that frames individuals' negative attitudes toward others, and is reflected in the willful and conscious, or unconscious, indirect, and reflexive conjectures of individuals. Dobbins and Skillings (1991) explain that racism operates in cases where individuals, because of their membership in a particular racial group, have access to power and are able to enforce their racial prejudices. In this sense,

> although people of color ... frequently hold prejudices about members of the dominant group, as a group they lack power to enforce or act on these prejudices. For this reason, it is said that people of color do not act in racist ways unless they are acting as agents for the dominant power structure. (Dobbins and Skillings 1991, 41)

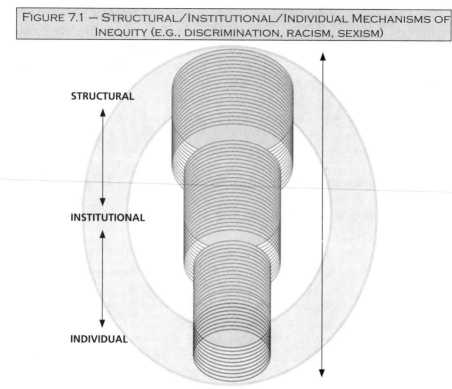

FIGURE 7.1 – STRUCTURAL/INSTITUTIONAL/INDIVIDUAL MECHANISMS OF INEQUITY (E.G., DISCRIMINATION, RACISM, SEXISM)

STRUCTURAL

INSTITUTIONAL

INDIVIDUAL

The extent to which an individuals' attitudes and ideologies are informed by, or related to, the rules, policies, and regulations of institutions, and contribute to a particular construction of individuals based on race, is referred to as **institutional racism**. In other words, institutional racism exists in organizations or institutions where the established rules, policies, and regulations systemically reflect and produce differential treatment of various groups based on race. In such cases, it is individuals who, because of their training and allegiance to the organization, put in place and implement racist policies and regulations. These policies and regulations help to maintain a system of social control, as well as a situation that favours the dominant groups in society, meaning that the status quo is maintained (Fleras 2010, 76–78). Further, the principles, norms, and values upon which institutions operate and which are enacted by individuals, are sustained by society's ideology, which serves to justify the allocation of racial groups to particular positions within institutions. Hence, on the basis of socially selected physical characteristics, racial minority group members gain access to, participate in, or are excluded from, institutions.

As indicated earlier, institutions exist within societies, and the ideologies and legislations of society function to structure those upon which institutions operate. This level of racism is referred to as **structural**

racism or sometimes as cultural or systemic racism. It represents the ways in which the rooted inequities of society produce the differentiation, categorization, and stratification of members of society on the basis of race, and in turn their participation in economic, political, social, cultural, judicial, and educational institutions. Scholars agree that it is fundamental in any examination of racism to give particular attention to structural racism.[4] This is necessary to understanding the complex, interlocking, and multi-layered characteristics of racisms at all three levels and the reciprocal relationship among them. It also means recognizing that racism—as a system of privileges and advantages—is about power, and that expressions of racism vary in relation to historical and social contexts and specificity, taking into account factors such as ethnicity, class, religion, gender, and immigrant status. As Stuart Hall reminds us:

> Racism is not a static ideology or set of social practices, but takes on specific meaning in different circumstances. The forms, expressions and meanings of racism vary on the basis of those who articulate and put into practice racist ideas, as well as on the basis of those who are the particular targets of those ideas and practices. (cited in Satzewich 1998, 22)

With reference to majority/minority power relations based on race, Kallen (2003) writes, "racist ideologies are transposed into potent political instruments wielded by dominant ethnic [or racial] authorities to oppress (deny political rights), neglect (deny economic rights), diminish (deny social rights), and deculturate (deny cultural rights) members of ethnic [or racial] minorities" (89).

The social situation in which minority groups find themselves also has to do with colonialism (a term sometimes used interchangeably with structural racism). *Colonialism* refers to the "political control of a society and its people by a foreign ruling state." According to the *Blackwell Online Encyclopedia of Sociology*, the term comes from the Latin *colonia*, meaning "the settlement of people from home," and is associated with the term "colonization" which refers to "the transplantation or settlement of peoples from one territory to another" (Go 2007). We should all be familiar with the process of colonization, as evident in the displacement and resettlement of Aboriginal peoples on reserves and the existence of the *Indian Act*, as well as the movement of African peoples to colonies in the West, including Canada. This history helps to frame the ways in which colonialism operates today as part of the ideology of social differentiation, in which there is a persistent and sustained political, economic, social, and cultural domination and construction of one racial group by another, and where the latter is deemed inferior to the former and kept in a subordinate and exploited position. This is also considered racialization.

Scholars also identify other types of racism. One is known as *redneck racism*, or sometimes *old-fashioned racism*. This type is characterized by its overt consciousness, and deliberate and highly personal attacks, including derogatory slurs and name-calling toward those who are perceived to be culturally and biologically inferior (Elliott and Fleras 1992, 58). Another type of racism is *polite racism*—often used to identify Canadian racism (Philip 1992; Henry 1978)—which refers to "the deliberate attempts to disguise racist attitudes through behaviour that is non-prejudicial or discriminatory in appearance" (Elliot and Fleras 1992, 59). With reference to the various types and expressions of racism that people of colour experience in their everyday lives, Essed (1990) uses the term *everyday racism*. She explains that it is "racism from the point of view of people of color, defined by those who experience it (Essed 1990, 31).

In 1983, Benjamin Chavis Jr., a religious leader, coined the term *environmental racism*, which refers to the process by which enacted policies, regulations, and legislations pertaining to the environment result in people in communities populated by particular racial group members being exposed to environmental hazards or contaminants. It is also

> the deliberate targeting and placing of noxious facilities in particular communities; environmental blackmail that arises when workers are coerced or forced to choose between hazardous jobs and environmental standards; segregation of ethnic minority workers in dangerous and dirty jobs; lack of access to or inadequate maintenance of environmental amenities such as parks and playgrounds; and inequality in environmental services such as garbage removal and transportation. (D. Taylor n.d., 2)

Evidence of environmental racism in Canada can be seen on Canadian reserves, particularly in terms of poor housing conditions, lack of access to medical facilities, lack of nutritious food, etc. One recent example is the disproportionately high rate of H1N1 (swine flu) cases among people living on reserves in western provinces in 2009. Another well-referenced site of environmental racism in Canada is Africville, a community that was located on the shores of the Bedford Basin in Halifax, Nova Scotia. Established in the 1850s, Africville came be to characterized as "one of the worst slums in Canada." This was due in part to environmental conditions—among other things, there was no running water, sewage system, or paved roads (even though the residents paid taxes)—and its historical proximity to hazards and blights such as "Rockhead Prison (1853), the city's night soil disposal pits (1858), an infectious disease hospital (during the 1870s), a trachoma hospital (1905)," an incinerator, and an open city dump located three hundred metres from the nearest home (in the early 1950s), fertilizer plants, and a slaughterhouse (Ward 2002).[5]

Henry and Tator (2006a) propose that living in a democratic society with both egalitarian values and racist attitudes that are recognized to be socially unacceptable has contributed to our development of a set of justificatory arguments and mechanisms that allow us to make congruent these two contradictory value systems. These arguments and mechanisms are premised on the ideology of *democratic racism*, which is defined as the justification of the inherent conflict between the egalitarian values of justice, equality, and fairness coexisting "with attitudes and behaviours that include negative feeling about minority groups, differential treatments, and discrimination against them" (Henry and Tator 2006a, 22). A related form of racism is *aversive racism*, which involves "well-intentioned" individuals, despite their claim to have a commitment to egalitarianism, fairness, and democracy, nevertheless holding negative attitudes and perceptions of racial minority people that are revealed when confronted with a personal situation that tests their claim. Such individuals tend to engage in tolerant, polite, and token behaviours, as well as other gestures that show them as liberals; they are not blatant with their discomfort, and disgust with, or distrust of minority people—they merely avoid them (Henry and Tator 2006a; Kawakami et al. 2009).

Social scientists are also increasingly using the term *new racism* to refer to "contemporary expression[s] of racial hostility towards racial minorities that go undetected by conventional measures" (Elliott and Fleras 1992, 62). Elliott and Fleras go on to say that within Canada, this form of racism is seen to be "an ambiguous and disguised response to the growing presence of increasingly assertive racial minorities" whose activities and demands are criticized as a threat to national identity and social harmony (62). Central to new racism is a belief in *colour-blindness*, a claim that an individual's race has nothing to do with their experiences, successes, failures, privileges, or disadvantages, but does have an effect on the choices they make and the advantages they take of the opportunities presented to them. Differences in people's achievements and levels of participation in society are also explained in terms of culture as related to one's racial, ethnic, or national origin. Seen from this perspective, culture is taken to be immutable and therefore incompatible with that of mainstream society. In this way, racism is not overt, but is packaged as an attempt to preserve "Anglo-European heritage," which majority ethnic group members fear is being "lost" through an untamed mix of cultures and identities (Lee 2006). "This new color-blind racism," Ferber (2007) writes, "is less overt and less biologically based than the racism and legally enshrined inequality and segregation of the past" (14).

Related to new racism[6] is *liberal racism,* which is understood to be premised on individuals' notions of their own and society's colour-blindness, commitment to democracy, and sense of equality and social justice, while at the same time remaining indifferent to (or choosing not to acknowledge) the structural character of racism into which they have been socialized, and as such unwittingly maintain. In the report of a workshop session from a conference in the United Kingdom called "London Schools and the Black Child," it was noted that liberal racism is "a form of racism exhibited by white middle-class liberals who expound anti-racist sentiments but are unaware of their own racism." One finds such racism in "the indignation shown by white professionals at any accusation of responsibility for institutional racism." As a consequence, white professionals tend to "pay more attention to their own feelings and to trivialise black people's experiences, and to react to black people's concerns rather than act proactively with black people" (Mayor of London 2003, 28).

A CTV report entitled, "Quebec Radio Shrink Sparks Complaints of Racism," (September 29, 2005) is an excellent illustration of the multilevel interlocking relationship of racisms. The report indicated that in his French-language Sunday program on radio station CKAC, Dr. Pierre Mailloux commented on-air on the inferior intelligence of Aboriginal and Black people. He suggested that the current circumstances of Black people are related to their physical, mental, and intellectual aptitude, which also played a role in their survival of slavery. Mailloux claimed—in an unorthodox application of evolutionary principles—that slaves who showed great aptitude would have been killed by their owners, therefore artificially selecting for less intelligent individuals to pass on their genes to subsequent generations.

Challenged by members of RDI, another French-language radio station, for his racist comments, Mailloux declared: "No, I'm not racist at all. I have black people who are friends. I'm no racist," and he defended his remarks by saying, "We must remain open to studies of human groups and behaviours." He further suggested that the emotional response people had to his comments "prevents us from seeing reality," which he claimed was found in scientific studies and data, none of which he could specifically identify.[7]

Our typical response to such incidents is disgust at the individuals who utter these comments. We tend to focus on the individual, though we also expect organizations to discipline or dismiss members. However, we rarely consider the organizational environment—the policies, philosophy, and politics, and the diversity of members—and its role in facilitating or enabling such remarks. If an organization establishes rules against racism, hires a racially diverse staff that provides opportunities for the offender to challenge racist ideas, and puts in place a management team that ensures that diversity among employees and management is maintained, it is possible that people like Dr. Mailloux will be much more aware, and with organizational support, will maintain the principles of anti-racism. Consider also the society and the structures that maintain racism and discrimination—people do not develop and maintain ideas and opinions in total isolation.

In making the distinction between prejudice and racism in his book, *The Sociologically Examined Life*, Michael Schwalbe (2005) raises the question as to whether racial minorities can be racist against whites. Using the notion of a "false parallel," Schwalbe mentions that when he talks about "white racism, someone will invariably say, 'yeah, but blacks can be racist too.'" When he questions how that can be, the response might be, "'you see it all the time. Like in the cafeteria, Blacks sit by themselves and exclude white students. They also make disparaging remarks about whites, just like some whites do about blacks. That's racism.'" However, according to Schwalbe, in sociological terms, "while this behavior might reflect prejudice, it is not racism ... Accusing blacks of racism—for keeping to themselves or for satirizing whites—is a false parallel" (213–214). Schwalbe goes on to say that we must be sociologically mindful in examining such situations and take into account the history, context, and power relationships that have contributed to oppression, exploitation, and disrespect of one group (in this case, whites) toward the other (in this case Blacks). In taking these things into account, Schwalbe explains: "It was not Africans but Europeans who invented the racial categories 'black' and 'white' to justify colonization and slavery. If any group is racist, it is the group that invents and imposes such categories. It makes no sense to call the victims racist ... Blacks have suffered, not benefited, from the idea of 'race' and the social arrangements built on this idea" (214).

DISCRIMINATION AND STEREOTYPING

We have established that ethnocentrism, anti-Semitism, Islamophobia, xenophobia, and racism are based on ideologies rooted in the economic, political, and social systems of society. The corollary to these social mechanisms or ideologies is *discrimination*, which is the actions or practices resulting from the attitudes of individuals, the policies of institutions or organizations, and the laws and legislation of the state that produce differential and unequal treatment and opportunities for individuals in areas such as education, housing, employment, health care, social services, and participation in society generally. In other words, discrimination is when racism and other mechanisms of social differentiation "are translated into action and political policy, the subordination of minorities and deprivation of their political, social, and economic rights" (Kinloch 1974, 54). As seen with racism, discrimination operates at the individual, institutional, and societal levels—all of which are interconnected. For example, when individuals who meet all the necessary requirements for employment or a particular educational program are denied the opportunity, it is the action of the individual responsible for administering the process, the policies of the institution or business, and the ideology of inequity inherent in the society that make this discrimination possible. In fact, as Henry and Ginzberg (1985) indicated with reference to their study of individual discrimination—in which it was shown that whites were three times more likely to land a job than an equally qualified Black person—discriminatory acts are not performed by an isolated "handful of bigots." They are found, not only in the actions of individuals, but also in the social barriers that deny certain people access to opportunities.

We have already discussed some of social mechanisms (racism, anti-Semitism, xenophobia, etc.) that have operated historically in the discrimination of immigrants and other members of our society:

○ The segregation or apartheid[8] and annihilation of Aboriginal peoples

○ The enslavement of African peoples until 1834, when Britain abolished the institution throughout its empire

○ The assimilation of Aboriginal and other minority and immigrant students through education (sometimes through segregated schooling)

○ The head tax that Chinese immigrants were required to pay to enter Canada

○ The continuous voyage requirement that negatively affected non-European migrants, particularly South Asians

○ The refusal of entry to Jews fleeing Nazi persecution in Europe

○ The internment of Japanese and Italians during World War II, and Ukrainians during World War I

○ The legislative restrictions on non-white immigration until the late 1960s

There was also, as George Elliott Clarke (1998, 103) writes, "the numerous legislation 'Black Codes' enacted by various levels of government to control where Chinese, Japanese, Native, and African citizens could work, live, be buried, and even, in some cases, vote." In these cases individuals were denied equal access and opportunity to participate in our democratic society, as well as the rights and rewards to which they were entitled.

Today, other forms or expressions of discrimination occur, for example, when ethnic and racial group members are abused verbally, when they are the targets of ethnic or racial jokes, when they are subjected to literature which represents them in a hateful and derogatory manner; and when they are harassed, their property is vandalized, or they are attacked physically. This is referred to as disadvantageous treatment. It is defined as the treatment which occurs when individuals are placed at some disadvantage that is not merited by their own misconduct. It may be characterized as the "effective injurious treatment of persons on grounds rationally irrelevant to the situation" (Driedger 1989, 351).

In her *Royal Commission on Equality* report, Judge Rosalie Abella (1984) explained that discrimination

> means practices or attitudes that have, whether by design or impact, the effect of limiting our individual group's right to the opportunities generally available because of attributable rather than cultural characteristics. What is impeding the development of potential is not the individual's capacity but an external barrier. (58)

Basically, discrimination is the unequal treatment of individuals or groups through the granting or denying of certain rights. In the case of minority groups, this treatment is often based, not on an individual's abilities and skills, but on other characteristics such as skin colour, language, accent and physical (or "visible") traits. Discrimination involves differential treatment where restrictions are placed on the activities and aspirations of some members of society, such as their desire to live where they choose, to work at any job for which they are qualified, or to have an education geared to their interests. Through discrimination, certain groups of people are able to maintain their positions of privilege, largely at the expense of other groups that are deliberately and inadvertently excluded from full and equal participation at their jobs or in society, or are denied the rights to which they are entitled.

Consider the case of Ms. Muse as reported in the *National Post* (November 20, 2007, A1 and A11). Muse, a baggage screener at Toronto Pearson International Airport and an observant Muslim, was suspended after six years of employment for lengthening the skirt on her uniform an extra twelve inches in order to comply with her religious practices. She had changed the length of the skirt after more than five years of being uncomfortable in slacks. She worked with the lengthened skirt for seven months before an operations manager discovered it and suspended her. Ms. Muse filed a complaint with the Canadian Human Rights Commission claiming discrimination. She explained that: "I practice my religion and I have to wear a skirt because it's a religious issue ... it's not that I like it. I have to—it's my religion" (A1). She also added that she did not understand why lengthening her skirt was such a big issue, when some of her co-workers hemmed their skirts shorter, and while others were allowed to wear religious garb such as turbans, kirpans, and head scarves as part of their uniforms.

The Canadian Air Transport Security Authority (CATSA) argued that it should not have to make accommodations for Muse because, as spokeswoman Anna-Karina Tabunar said, "It's important to stress the importance of the uniform and uniformity. The reason it was rolled out was to have a credible and professional corporate identity." She added, "We're treating it not just as an issue of a new skirt, we're treating it as a broader issue, a policy issue, and as such CATSA has to gather all the facts to evaluate the different aspects of the request and the impact it's going to have on CATSA's uniform and uniform policy" (A11). Mihad Fahmy, a human rights lawyer, explains that the issue over whether Sikhs could wear turbans on the job was current a decade ago, and that today the issue is how Muslim women dress. This has much to do "with the public's perception about Muslim women and about the hijab," explained Fahmy. "A lot of it is not about safety concerns or business interests. I think a lot of the reaction has to do with assumptions about whether [the] hijab fits within modern society" (A11).

In the following essay, Kulsoom Anwer, a young adult of Muslim background explains what she considers the significance of the hijab, and offers her views on the current media attention and criticisms associated with women, religious rights, and Islam.

KULSOOM: "THERE IS A VERY LIMITED PUBLIC UNDERSTANDING OF THE HIJAB."

The hijab is the most public symbol of Islam and in the wake of 9/11 some Muslim women put it on for the first time as a mark of defiance and identity consolidation. Not wearing it, of course, protected you from harassment in that time. I've never worn hijab myself because my mother didn't and in the country I come from, it's not common practice. A head scarf is kept handy but it's usually not worn on the head. The mosque is the only place it's mandatory. It is, however, good Islamic practice to wear it publicly.

The hijab functions as a potent marker of difference in Canada or any non-Islamic society. Young girls who wear it because their families require it are very ambivalent about it, proud but also resentful. They often remove it on special occasions like when they perform in assemblies or at prom, which defeats the very purpose of the hijab, which is modesty always, particularly when all eyes are on you. Correct wearing of the hijab requires you to wear it at all times except in the company of women, or at home with men like one's father, brother, or husband. The removal of the hijab by these teenagers is certainly understandable. The teenager's desire is to be like everyone else, to be viewed as attractive, and to get positive attention. The hijab prevents all that.

I don't like the way non-Muslims watching this very public struggle with religion, assimilation, and identity decide that whether a girl wears or takes off her hijab gives them license to judge her Islam. The complexities of Islamic orthodoxy and orthopraxy are many; to have those who know very little about these feel that they can make decisions about someone's religiosity [based on] the wearing of the hijab is highly presumptuous. Furthermore, there is almost no consideration of the fact that young hijabi girls are at a very vulnerable time in their lives, only further exacerbated by their membership in a minority religion. There is a very limited public understanding of the hijab; many think it is easily doffed, partly probably because of the young women who take it off and on, but I don't find this to be an excuse for making judgments or more importantly, for involving oneself in this personal religious issue.

Supporting or maintaining discrimination, the mechanisms of differentiation, and the structures of inequity are the *stereotypes* that are held of individuals. As a concept in social science, "stereotype" was first used by Lippmann in 1922 to refer to the manner in which ideas, images, and habits are accumulated, shaped, and hardened. The term originated from the printing industry, where a "stereotype" was a metal plate with a uniform matrix of type that was molded so that printing was standard and unchanging. For the social scientist, *social stereotype* refers to "a highly exaggerated picture, the intervention of supposed traits, and the formation of incomplete images leaving little room for change or individual variation" (Driedger 1989, 343). D. M. Taylor (1981) described stereotypes as people's perceptions or beliefs about others rather than ideas based on factual information. **Stereotypes** are characterized by shared beliefs—a set of characteristics believed by large numbers of a group to be true of another. They are flawed judgments of others, since applying characteristics to entire groups involves over-categorization and over-generalization. This tendency to categorize, evaluate, and generalize racial and ethnic minority groups is often accompanied by a strong belief in the "correctness" or "truth" of the stereotype and a disregard for fact. Stereotypes sometimes emerge from a person's encounters and experiences (good or bad) with members of other ethnic or racial groups (see Paul 1998).

> Stereotypes serve first to categorize, organize, or simplify the amount of complex information that we receive in order to reduce it into units. And when little or nothing

is known about a group or person, stereotypes "fill in" the missing information, thus providing an organized perception of the group or person. For example, Bethlehem—whom we met earlier in Chapter 3—recalls being "read" as Muslim because that is the stereotype that exists regarding people from the Horn of Africa. Although she would, sometimes in frustration, correct people by explaining that she is Christian, they would often insist on that initial identifier, showing not only their ignorance of the area from which her parents emigrated, but also denying her complex identity.

One reason individuals might hold on to stereotypes is to satisfy their need to see themselves in a positive light. Moreover, to the extent that stereotypes refer to individuals' perceptions of and beliefs about others, and contain a "kernel of truth," they serve a purpose, especially when used to understand cultural differences and similarities. They are often used as guides to behaviour and play a role in inter-group relations. Indirectly, stereotypes operate in defining one's self and social status (D. M. Taylor 1981, 155). When stereotypes refer to a group's attributes in a positive way, the consequences may be socially desirable insofar as "the particular inter-group stereotypes satisfy the desires of both groups involved, and where inter-group interaction is not characterized by destructive forms of conflict" (D. M. Taylor 1981, 163). But as Driedger reminds us,

> the assumption that when we know the facts about another person or group, that we will act on those facts is not necessarily true. Reason does not always prevail: emotions often impose positive and negative evaluations. When images of others become rigid, like the printer's stereotype, and when they produce the same reaction automatically without further examination, then we have a social stereotype. (1989, 344)

Writing about stereotyping in *Psychology Today*, Annie Murphy Paul (1998) quotes professor John Bargh as saying that "stereotypes are categories that have gone too far." He suggests that, when we use stereotypes, we take into account the gender, age, race, and skin colour of a person or people and ascribe to them the attributes we learned from society. These socially constructed attributes, according to psychology professor Margo Monteith, are learned from early childhood ("by age five") when "children don't have a choice about accepting or rejecting these concepts, since they are acquired well before they have the cognitive abilities or experiences to form their own beliefs" (Paul 1998, 55). Further,

Bargh points out that "stereotypes emerge from what social psychologists call in-group/out-group dynamics" (53). This refers to the fact that

> humans, like other species, need to feel that they are part of a group, and as villages, clans and other traditional groupings have broken down, our identities have attached themselves to more ambiguous classifications, such as race and class. We want to feel good about the group we belong to—and one way of doing that is to denigrate all those who aren't in it. And while we tend to see members of our own group as individuals, we view those in the out-group as undifferentiated—stereotypes—mass. The categories we use have changed, but it seems that stereotyping itself is bred in the bone. (In Paul 1998, 53–54)

Another term for stereotyping is racial profiling, described in Chapter 1. The term originated in the United States, where it is largely used in law enforcement to refer to the practice of acting on "erroneous assumptions about the propensity of African American, Latino, Asian, Native American, and Arab people to commit particular types of crimes" (ACLU 2010). You might be familiar with the statements: "Driving while Black" or "Flying while Arab;" both are plays on the offence "driving while intoxicated" (DWI), a common reason for police to stop motorists. These phrases are meant to convey how these ethno-racial groups are categorized and essentialized based on their differences, without regard for their complex, varied, and multiple identities and related experiences. Racial profiling is also about how institutional and societal structures help to construct and sustain the mindset that frames people's "difference" on the basis of race, ethnicity, religion, and national origin (or birthplace) as outsiders, and unknown entities or strangers. As such, questions often exist about their allegiance or sense of belonging and commitment to the society in which they live, and their likelihood to be troublemakers (or lawbreakers). In the practice of racial profiling, race as a social construct is not simply a matter of skin colour or race, but also encompasses religion, ethnicity, national origin, and/or birthplace.

Stereotyping or racial profiling as expressed through discriminatory acts, sometimes takes the form of what is termed a **hate crime**. Statistics Canada defines hate crimes as:

> Criminal offences that are motivated by hate towards an identifiable group. The incident may target race, national or ethnic origin, language, colour, religion, sex, age, mental or physical disability, sexual orientation or any other similar factor, such as profession or political beliefs. These

types of offences are unique in that they not only affect those who may be specifically targeted by the perpetrator, but they often indirectly impact entire communities. (In Dauvergne, Scrim, and Brennan 2008, 7)

According to a 2006 Statistics Canada report, Canadian police services covering 87 percent of the population reported 892 hate-motivated crimes, the majority of which were motivated by race/ethnicity (61 percent), religion (27 percent), and sexual orientation (10 percent). Half of the racially motivated hate crimes reported by police in 2006 were targeted at Blacks and two-thirds of the religiously motivated hate crimes were targeted at Jews. Among census metropolitan areas, Calgary (at a rate of 9.1 incidents per 100,000 people), Kingston (8.5 per 100,000), London (5.9 per 100,000), and Toronto (5.5 per 100,000) had the highest reports of hate crimes (Dauvergne, Scrim, and Brennan 2008).

Research on the effects of racial discrimination has found that there is a direct relationship between a person's physical and mental heath and their experiences with discrimination. For instance, in a study that followed 59,000 African American women for six years found that the more incidents of racial discrimination that were reported, the greater the risk for breast cancer. Explanations offered by the study included: "perceived racial discrimination can take a toll on a person's health" and "unjust treatment serves as a source of chronic stress, which itself has been linked to poorer physical health" (Paradies 2006). This means that race is a significant factor in understanding not only one's identity and experiences with racism, but that perceptions resulting from an understanding of race in society can have significant effects on one's quality of life and mental and physical health (Paradies 2006). A team of researchers led by Dr. Teletia R. Taylor at Howard University in Washington, D.C., similarly found that when women were asked how frequently they experienced "everyday" discrimination (such as feeling that people fear them or are superior to them; receiving poorer service than others in shops; being treated unjustly in a job, etc.), those who said they frequently encountered these experiences had a higher risk of developing breast cancer—the risk was 32 percent higher among women who experienced prejudice than for those who did not (T. R. Taylor et al. 2007). Experts have also noted that the medical problems, such as hypertension, diabetes, cardiovascular disease, that Aboriginal and Black people and other minority group members experience in larger percentages than the wider population are not merely a product of genetics or lifestyle, but are related to the environmental (as mentioned above), social, cultural, economic, and employment conditions in which people live.

LIFE WITH RACISM, OTHER MECHANISMS OF DIFFERENTIATION, AND DISCRIMINATION

> **Ramish**: Racism has affected me personally ever since I can remember. I lost opportunities, I felt, because of my skin colour and nationality. I love hockey and have been playing since I was young. I remember the name-calling and repeatedly being told that I couldn't play hockey because I was not white. I was made fun of and laughed at, and I was usually the last one picked for teams. I grew up in a white neighbourhood, and as all the kids played hockey, I began practising the game in the hope that one day I could play with everyone else. After a couple of months of practise I became a better player, as I was faster and much smarter than the rest of the guys. I was asked to play for higher calibre teams because I excelled in the sport. I was always working hard but was still being made fun of by the opposing teams. My teammates learned to accept me. However, when [there was a] minority [player] on another team, they taunted him with the same names used against me by the other team members. All I wanted was the opportunity to play and to be treated like everyone else. I finally learned to work harder and shield myself from the comments. Unfortunately, I would go home and feel the effect of the cruelty and meanness of some people.

In the above comment, Ramish contends that racism is responsible for his lack of equal opportunity to play hockey, a sport he loved. He declares that despite his hard work and the acceptance of his teammates, his "skin colour and nationality" were factors that limited the extent to which he excelled at the game. Surely, Ramish's experiences cannot be explained away as being in the wrong place at the wrong time. Neither can his lack of success in hockey be attributed to his efforts and skills alone. Indeed, Herb Carnegie (1997) has provided good historical evidence of the extent to which, and the ways in which, skin colour has operated to limit the presence of racial minorities in the game of hockey, Canada's "national sport" (Gruneau and Whitson 1993).[9] Ramish is alerting us to more than peer group taunts and coaches' oversights and preferences, but to systemic practices and values that exist, not only in hockey or in sport generally, but in society as a whole. After all, why would Ramish's teammates understand that the "names" they used in their taunts against opposing minority team members produce the results they expected? And isn't it likely that they understood that the same "names" would affect Ramish in similar ways?

That Ramish's teammates would taunt minority players without being challenged by other teammates is reflective of individuals' indifference when faced with an act of racism. This explanation is substantiated by a 2009 study, "Mispredicting Affective and Behavioral Responses to Racism," by Kerry Kawakami and her colleagues, which explored how people imagine they would feel and behave upon hearing a racist comment, as opposed to how they actually feel and behave. The study found that individuals were less likely to be distressed or to take action when they witnessed an act of racism than they claimed they would be. The researchers placed 120 participants into roles of "experiencer" and "forecaster." The experiencer was put into a room with a Black individual and a white individual who, unknown to the experiencer, were acting as part of the study. After the Black individual gently bumped the white individual's knee and left the room, the experiencer witnessed one of three different responses from the white individual: no comment about race, a "moderate" racial comment, and an "extreme" racial comment (276). Later, the experiencer was asked to select a partner for a subsequent task from among the two individuals. Forecasters were given a description of the situation and asked to write about how they would respond after witnessing an act of racism and then being asked to choose a partner.

The results of the study indicate that a racist comment did not provoke distress or social rejection toward the white individual. While the forecasters had predicted choosing the white individual who made a racist comment only 17 percent of the time, the actual experiencers chose the white individual over the Black individual 63 percent of the time (277). The study draws attention to the fact that, while we live in a society where acts of racism are broadly and generally condemned, and while there is a strong "stigma" attached to being labelled racist, racism still occurs "with alarming regularity" (276). Researchers suggest that, "racism may persevere in part because people who anticipate feeling upset and believe that they will take action may actually respond with indifference when faced with an act of racism" (Kawakami et al. 2009, 276). Although people may have good intentions and suggest that they would take action in cases of "overt acts of racism," they tend not to censure those who utter racist remarks; hence, they are not as genuinely committed to the amelioration of racism and discrimination as would be expected. This reveals an important paradox in race relations—people condemn racism but rarely do anything about it.

The indifference to racist incidents that Kawakami and her colleagues found among their research respondents—corroborated by Ramish's experiences—is also evident in Keisha's story. Keisha, a student of South Asian background, refers to the racism she experienced when she first went to university as a "big shock:"

> **Keisha:** I came to university with a big mind and an open mind and I was here to learn and it was an environment where my fellow peers, I had hoped, would have the same stand or the same understanding of a lot of things. So walking into lecture one day, I was a little bit late, so I

just turned around to one of the girls and I asked what was happening, and she turned to me and said something that was very awful and I will quote. She said: "Don't talk to me, filthy Paki." She was pretty loud, and the girls in front of me and behind me kind of heard and there were a couple of guys who heard and they turned around … I was so shocked that I couldn't respond because I couldn't fathom that someone my age, someone in the same society that I grew up in or at least at the level of education system that we were in, would not have an open mind and would say something like that … I couldn't respond because I'm a person who is very naïve … I didn't say anything. But I was hoping, I guess, that the people who were sitting in front of me or behind me would've said something. That's what hurt me a little bit.

Keisha and Ramish's expectations that people would recognize racism and act against it is also represented in Luis's account of his conversation with someone from whom he expected, not only validation of his experience with racism, but also agreement about the existence of racism.

Luis: I had gotten into a heated discussion with [Tom], the white husband of a colleague from my school. It started because of a comment I had made about discrimination. I was relating my experiences about apartment hunting in the city [in 2002] to others. I spoke of the various (and some nefarious) landlords that I came across. I said that, here in Ontario racial discrimination is still ongoing but it is not "in your face," but rather more subtle and hidden. He responded by saying that that was simply not true. There was no racism anymore. I responded by relating an incident where I had called to look at a place that was well within my budget. On the phone the woman said that the apartment was still available and that I could come down and look at it. As I was literally right around the corner I asked if I could come immediately to which she replied, "Sure."

Five minutes later, I am at her office door. Upon seeing me, her look told me I should introduce myself as the person that had just called. Inviting me in, she proceeded to interview me as to what my intentions were for the apartment. I did not know what she meant, so she explained that it was only a one bedroom and she didn't want me trying to move in with a bunch of people. I politely explained that I did have children but that they only see me on the weekends. She asked what I did and then reframing the question, asked me again, and then later in the conversation again rechecked that I had indeed told her I was a teacher. I then asked if I could see the apartment. She replied that the apartment that I had asked about was just taken but there might be another one. To my next query she replied that it was not ready because the workers were fixing it and I couldn't even look in the door.

I then asked [Tom], as he himself is a landlord, if he could explain this story to me as anything other than racial discrimination. The landlord must have had another reason, he said. His explanation was to relate a story about how he had been looking for a tenant for an apartment that came with one parking space. He had received an application from a "Black guy." Everything was in order; he had a good job, he appeared clean, he was a non-smoker, he had excellent references, and his finances were in order. The only problem was that he had a car and he [Tom] wanted to save that parking spot so he did not rent the apartment to him. He did rent the apartment to a woman who happened to be white because she did not have a car. It had nothing, he said, to do with race. Interestingly, she did get a car once she was accepted as a tenant so he did lose the parking space after all. I looked at him incredulously, but he truly did not realize what he had just said to me. Racism has been so thoroughly cultivated that it is no longer distinguishable from everyday living. He assessed my explanation as wrong because he had never experienced racism himself, nor did he feel he practiced it. As he said, "I work with Black people all the time and we all get along." So to him there was no racism anymore, yet has he walked in my shoes? Could he ever? Most likely his attitude is related to not seeing the cultural dominance he was born into and the privileges he was born with.

The experience of Luis, who is of Black and white mixed race, is not unlike that of many other Canadians who have reported encountering discrimination in relation to housing. A 2009 report, *Sorry, It's Rented: Measuring Discrimination in Toronto's Rental Housing Market* by the Centre for Equality Rights in Accommodation (CERA), explained that racial minorities, and Black single parents in particular, experienced moderate to severe discrimination when they inquired about renting available apartments. The following scenario is typical: A racial minority person calls a landlord enquiring about an apartment that was advertised for rent in the newspaper; if the caller's accent is identified as "foreign," the response is likely to be: "It's been rented," but an identified "Canadian-accented" caller is likely to be invited to see the apartment. People take different actions to find out if they were lied to in these situations. Here is how one South Asian man reacted:

> [When] I called to book an appointment ... I used a Canadian accent and the superintendent gave me the interview and was quite cordial and even went the extra mile. Once I showed up for the viewing with my family, the superintendent was making various excuses, which seemed quite unusual at that particular time. He claimed that the apartment was already rented out. Later in the week I had my white friend call and go in for a viewing and it turned out to be the same apartment that I was supposed to view. My white friend was successful in viewing and applying for the apartment. (CERA 2009, 19)

Evelyn Myrie (2009) of Hamilton, Ontario, also shares her story of showing up "less than fifteen minutes" after calling about an apartment and being told that it was no longer available. When her white college mate later called about the same apartment, she was invited to see it and was able to make a deposit.

In 2004, white Montreal journalist Stéphane Alarie engaged in an exercise much like American author John Howard Griffin did in 1959 in the Southern United States—he disguised himself as a Black man for seven days and tried to rent an apartment, hunt for jobs, hire taxis, hang out at bars, and hock merchandise at a pawnshop. In his article, he concluded that "the vast majority of people are tolerant, and don't mind what colour of skin you have. In some situations, racism is so flagrant it's amazing. I think that the differences make people afraid" (in Scott 2004; see also Alarie 2003a). Alarie went through the exercise alone (and not with a Black person).[10] In a commentary on Alarie's project, Scott suggests: "There's no way a man with a thousand dollars worth of shoe polish on his face could really grapple with this stuff." And Canadian scholar George Elliott Clarke, whom Scott interviewed, argued that "in our society ... black reality is not palatable coming from blacks, but the white person who takes on the black voice, or wants to explore black reality, is celebrated as being daring, courageous, liberal and humanistic ... I can agree and say, yes, this is offensive ... Doing this kind of reportage and coming back saying, 'Gee whiz, there is racism,' and then passing it off as news is upsetting" (Scott 2004).[11]

Despite Alarie's good intentions, what is important here is that racism and discrimination are not merely the result of individual attitudes, and verbal and non-verbal expressions and behaviours, but of institutional policies and practices as informed by the ideological structure of society. So we cannot simply rely on Alarie's experience with, as Scott writes, a "little bit of makeup, an afro wig and a Fubu shirt;" for racism is not just about skin colour and clothing, but is a vast system that structures our relationships, interactions, and institutions (Vaught and Castagno 2008). Indeed, as Alarie writes in one of his journal reports:

> The vast majority of Montrealers proved to be just as courteous or otherwise behaved properly towards a journalist in incognito, either of white or black skin. However it took only a week in the skin of a Black person to acquire a handful of examples of mistrust, intolerance, or even blatant racism ... even in 2003! ... Imagine such a thing over one year, over an entire life. (translated from French, Alarie 2003b)

Juan, a first-generation Latino Canadian and first-year PhD student from one of Toronto's low-income neighbourhoods, writes about how a lifetime of dealing with racism and discrimination affected him.

Juan: Throughout my high school years, I experienced racism. One of the ways this manifested was in the particular preferences some teachers gave to white, middle-class students. These teachers took the time to help them with their work, but more importantly, they were perceived to be their equals. In my experience, however, teachers were not supportive; in fact, on one occasion, a teacher told me it was unlikely that I would amount to anything in life. As such, I should do my best to graduate and find a job. This is contrary to the experiences of white middle-class students; it appears that teachers are complicit in perpetuating particular statistics in relation to which groups in society graduate from high school and advance to post-secondary education.

Dealing with this reality was very difficult for me. I felt powerless and that my efforts were futile. In spite of [most teachers'] efforts to make me feel hopeless, there were two teachers that provided me with inspiration and support. They were crucial factors in my pursuit of [excellence] and thereby pursuing post-secondary education. While I experienced this advantage, I wondered why I had this privilege, while other racialized minorities did not. More broadly, I wondered about the extent to which other racialized minorities in other schools were being betrayed by the myth that education is for everyone. I was deeply angered by my experience …

After high school I pursued an undergraduate degree. The first two years were pivotal because for the first time, I did not directly feel that I would not amount to anything. I was just another number in the university system; but at least no body was telling me "I can't." I returned to my high school to serve as a mentor for racialized students. Returning to the school surprised my former teachers, especially when they discovered that I was a university student. They inquired about my studies and what my plans were upon completion of my degree. I told them that I intended to pursue [a master's] and thereafter a doctoral degree. I was obviously not taken seriously by them. They said it was next to impossible to obtain. Some told me how they attempted to attain the same goals, but had not done so as yet.

One of the factors that pushed me to succeed is the educational injustice I experienced as a high school student. This has also propelled me to return to my roots and try to mentor and inspire other people in the area. When I returned to my high school as a graduate student I receive a host of royal treatment from teachers. For the first time, I was treated with respect. Some teachers actually took the time to speak to me, treat me to lunch, and interact with me as a worthy human being. Their "benevolent" gestures bewilder me, however, because when I was a high school student, who was hungry and did not have money to purchase

> lunch, they did not take the initiative to help ... Perhaps what is most ironic in this scenario is that when I needed food they were insensitive to me; now that I can purchase my own food, they want to treat me.
>
> At face value, it appeared as if my relationship with the teachers was harmonious and collegial. Some of them even attributed my success to their efforts and influence. This is false. Now they treat me as equal to mask the fact that we are not equal ... By doing this, they are trying to conceal and therefore deny that a racialized minority has surpassed them. What is more, I have succeeded in an education system that is structured to keep racialized minorities oppressed and disenfranchised.

One of the paradoxes of Juan's life is how his experiences with racism, as well as classism, "pushed" him to pursue post-secondary studies with a determination to succeed. In doing so, he became an activist working with students from his old high school trying to address what he sees as "educational injustice." In a similar way, Abdi talks of his commitment and determination to pursue law school and become a lawyer.

> **Abdi:** In the end, all of the hatred that I have experienced, both subtle and overt, has greatly influenced my career aspirations. It has led me to the realization that I need to continue to commit myself to social justice initiatives and not succumb to the numerous problems that are commonly associated with being a racialized student in law school ... There is very little representation of racialized people and those who are from racialized groups tend to be unwilling to discuss issues related to race due to a lack of interest or for fear of being pigeonholed as "too political" or a "troublemaker." It is simply not enough that I have become more socially aware of race and its intersection with other tools of oppression, namely class, gender, ethnicity, sexuality, and ability. I have to ensure that I am doing my part to expose these constructs for what they are: poisonous, ignorant lies. The goal of such work will be to educate as many young people as possible about other ethno-racial communities beyond the superficial education that multiculturalism programs currently provide
>
> ... It is also about implementing systemic change that creates situations where the various equity policies currently in place at institutions of higher learning and in other spaces—both public and private—go from being mere rhetoric to the catalysts for wholesale, meaningful change. Then and only then will I feel as though I belong in this society as a Black man.

This activism and resolve to challenge stereotypes and demonstrate that they are able to succeed in the system as it exists, often earns racialized young people like Juan, Abdi, and others the label "model minority." Ironically, they come to represent the idea that it is possible for minorities to attain the educational and career goals to which they aspire if they apply themselves. Here, racism and discrimination is not considered a structural barrier, for individuals are able to meet people such as teachers, as Juan did, who will help them succeed. This discourse of constructing role models is considered a form of new racism (see page 224) in which an individual, as a "representative" member of a particular ethnic group, is ascribed "positive stereotypes" such as a high achiever and hard worker, reinforcing the idea of meritocracy and a "fair playing field."

More common, however, is ascribing positive stereotypes to a particular ethno-racial minority group—one to which other ethno-racial minority groups are judged or compared. Such stereotypes are used to hold one group up as model citizens. Gordon Pon (2000) explains that the identity of "positive role model" is often attributed to Asians (see also Lee 2005). In discussing his experience with the "model minority" stereotype, Pon writes that during high school his English teachers often queried about whether or not he had done his essay assignments himself, and despite his assuring them that it was his work, they seemed unconvinced. Because of his teachers' continuing suspicions, he never received a grade higher than an A- in English. He continues:

> It took me years beyond high school to figure out that my essay-writing skills, which were strong for my grade level, ruptured the dominant stereotypes of Chinese students, particularly the belief that we are all math whizzes. Stereotyping particular groups—such as Chinese—places limits on what is expected of them and inhibits an understanding of the complex differences among the members of the group. Thus, the stereotypes my English teachers held of Chinese people resulted in an expectation that I was supposed to be good at math, not English. (Pon 2000, 224)

Tara, a white first-year university student, recalls the effect that this stereotype of the Asian as "good at math" had on her and the other members of her class.

Tara: The high school that I went to was very "WASPY"—which I guess is a racist term in itself. But I was friends with several people who weren't Caucasian and they were segregated. Most of them were from India and Asia and they were always thought to be the smart ones in the class, even by the teachers. I remember once in my calculus class my friend, who is actually very smart in math—and she goes to university for math—was singled out straight away [because she was Asian], when the class was asked: "How do you guys feel about calculus?" And she raised her hand and the teacher said to her, "Well of course, you would feel good about calculus." I remember thinking "Wow! That's so inappropriate." The school

I went to was very culturally diverse. We had lost of assemblies celebrating that … But it was almost shocking when stuff like that happened.

Consider here the effect of the teacher's comment on Tara and her non-Asian classmates. It is important to remember that racism affects everyone—indeed, *racism is everybody's business*—not just the students who are perceived to be "naturally gifted" at math and science; for it means that those who struggle in these subjects might not get the attention they need from teachers. These "positive" constructions are not likely to be seen as racism; rather, it is likely they will be dismissed and seen as unfounded.

Similarly, as L. Taylor (2000, 2008) notes, mixed-race individuals—particularly those whose physical appearance is increasingly celebrated as "cool," "beautiful," or coveted—may find that their racialized experiences, frustrations, and challenges are either overlooked, ignored, or seen as an overreaction or over-sensitivity (L. Taylor 2000, 2008). The experience of Tanika, also a first-year university student of mixed-race (Black and white) background, is illustrative.

Tanika: The only time I encountered racism was at a club and I was dancing with some white guy and we were just dancing and he was like, "Oh you're black, I know you can do better then that." I was like, "Oh my God." I was so shocked, I just stopped dancing and walked away, but I wish I had said something … I don't know if I would've felt more satisfied if I had reacted to that but I was totally blown away.

Such comments about "positive" attributes are, in fact, racialization and racism. Donovan recalls his experience with this stereotype of Blacks—"Blacks are born with natural rhythm and are really good dancers."

Donovan: I was not always that good a dancer and to this day I am still not that great. Because of my lack of dancing ability, I was made to feel inferior as a Black person. This made it seem to me that I was not truly a Black person because of my inabilities.

Further, Black students are often stereotyped as having innate superior athletic skills and abilities, despite the fact that there is little evidence to support such claims. Educators continue to encourage Black youth to participate in sports, thinking that by doing so they are supporting Black students in their schooling. But the result is often a lack of similar support for the students' academic interests and aspirations. In some cases, not only do Black students come to believe or internalize these stereotypes, but they give priority to their athletic role at the expense of their academic performance and educational achievements. For example, Kai James

(2000, 54) writes: "Gym teachers are perhaps the most overt in their interpretations of the stereotypes. I remember the track coach coming into my Grade 9 class and asking all the Black students if they would be participating in the track meet." Drawing attention to the different ways in which students were treated by teachers, James, who was about six feet tall at the time, goes on to write: "I was recruited by a coach who had no knowledge of my athletic ability or my interests. At the same time, an Asian friend was being encouraged by the math department to write the math contests." Describing another instance involving a tall Black student who was a friend, James says: "On the first day of school his social studies teacher, a complete stranger to the student, greeted him [saying]: 'I hope you are not one of those basketball players that's gonna show up for class once a week, because if you do you can just leave right now." Donovan also experienced this stereotype; as with his lack of skill as a dancer, Donovan was not an athlete: "I felt inferior and embarrassed. I felt as if I had to play sports because it was expected of me. When it was discovered that I was not as good as 'every other Black person,' I felt that I was less than them."

What is wrong, some might ask, with thinking of someone as a good student, a good athlete, or a good dancer? Gordon Pon (2000) points out that the seductive nature of such "positive stereotypes" masks racism and structural inequalities that exist in society, and as such "is often quite harmful." The fact is, even after nearly forty years of an official multiculturalism policy in Canada, racism and other mechanisms of social differentiation remain in existence, seriously affecting the lives of all Canadians. This suggests that the policies, legislations, laws, and numerous government-led diversity and equity programs have done little to change the inequitable and discriminatory condition of racial minorities and Aboriginal people. This also suggests that these programs are not effective in addressing the institutional or structural aspect of racism and discrimination. In the following section, we take a brief look at the effect of employment equity and educational access programs on the lives, opportunities, and achievements of some Canadians.

EQUITY PROGRAMS AND QUESTIONS ABOUT QUALIFICATION AND FAIR TREATMENT

The headline on the front page of the *Toronto Star* for May 14, 2009, read: "Racism in Canada: Darker the skin, less you fit" and featured a photograph of a Kenyan woman, Kirunda, and her ten-year-old son, who immigrated to Canada six years ago. The accompanying article by reporter Lesley Ciarula Taylor described Kirunda as "poised, articulate, educated, and confident," but upon arrival in Canada she was sent to an adult learning centre for language classes even though English is her first language. She also recalled "getting passed over for a college spot in favour of a white friend" (A1). The story was meant to build on an April 2009 study, *Multiculturalism and Social Cohesion: Potentials and Challenges of Diversity*, by University of Toronto professor Jeffrey Reitz and his colleagues. The study found discrimination to be most common in applying for jobs and at work. Based on data from Statistics Canada's 2002 Ethnic Diversity Survey, Reitz and his colleagues also found that skin colour—not religion, not income—was the biggest barrier to employment opportunities for minority Canadians. Their findings also indicated that among recent immigrants, about one-third of Chinese, South Asians, Filipinos, and Southeast Asians, 40 percent of Koreans and Japanese, and 50 percent of Blacks reported experiencing discrimination in the previous five years, compared to only 19 percent of whites. But for racial minority children of immigrant parents, the rate of reported experiences with discrimination was 42 percent, and for Blacks it was over 60 percent, whereas among whites the rate was about 10 percent (Reitz et al. 2009).

THE MYTH OF REVERSE RACISM

Governments, agencies, institutions, and businesses have introduced equity programs for Aboriginal peoples, women, persons with disabilities, and "visible minorities" (or people of colour) in response to the experiences of minority group members and inequitable access to, and participation in, employment and education. It is logical that these programs are introduced at an institutional level because discriminatory practices are not merely a product of individuals' attitudes or individual racism, but are to be found in the policies of these establishments.

Critics claim that these equity initiatives are violations of the "merit principle," which supposes the "best" will get the job or access to educational institutions. The general criticism of individuals, and white males in particular, tends to characterize equity and access programs as examples of "reverse racism." In fact, in response to the newspaper article mentioned above, one reader wrote this comment:

> I am a white male and I am discriminated against all the time. Faced with trying to get jobs that have been reserved for minorities and not the best candidate. There is racism in Canada and as a white male I feel lots of it is aimed at myself. There was an article here not long ago that Toronto police want to hire more minority police. I think that comment in itself is racist. We don't want the best person for the job anymore?

This sentiment is not new—it was first expressed in the early days of equity programs. In the first edition of this book, one student, Randy, writing as a member "of the 'white male' group" noted:

Randy: I think the phrase "employment equity" should be changed to "employment inequity" ... Equality should mean that everyone has the same chance of being hired. If the top ten applicants are Black, they should be hired; if they are white males, they should be hired; if they are female, the same. Forget about balancing the numbers. Give the job to the person who best deserves it. That's equal!

I'm a firm believer in the saying "Two wrongs don't make a right," but this is what's happening now with employment equity ... Will employment equity benefit society as a whole? I don't think so. If anything, it has created greater tension between the white applicants and the [designated] groups. It has brought our society into a state of disrepute ... Even the minorities state that they want to be hired because they are the best, not because they are a minority. On the other hand, if some recruiter told me I was wanted because I was white and they were short of whites, I wouldn't think twice about the so-called "equity."

Similarly, Roger's story reflects his lack of understanding of how racism affects everyone and of the inherent privilege experienced by members of the dominant group.

Roger: I come from an Irish-English family (three-quarters Irish, one-quarter English), and was raised in a white, middle-class household. My family has never been overly rich, but we have never starved. I was born in Toronto, but raised in the suburbs, so in essence I have lived a rather sheltered life.

Even though I grew up in a good, financially stable home, I don't consider this fact to be an advantage created by my race or ethnicity. Through school and social clubs, I've had many friends from different races and ethnic backgrounds from homes of equal or greater financial stability. Like many others, my parents are both fairly uneducated by today's standards. Yet, through hard work and determination, they have managed to make a success of themselves.

While talking with other people, I've been trying to think of an instance where my race or my ethnicity has been an advantage to me, and I haven't been able to think of one. Sure, there is the fact that I come from a stable home, but this has nothing to do with my race. It has to do with loving parents who have shown genuine concern with what I do. The fact that I am fairly well-educated could be considered an advantage, but my race didn't put me through school. My parents' guidance, my own drive to better myself, and my desire to reach a certain goal are what completed my education. Perhaps my always having money in my pocket could be considered an advantage, but even this fact is not a result of my race; I have always had a part-time job and I work hard to earn the money.

So even after listening to other people's stories and points of view, I have found no situation where my being white is an advantage. I have always been a believer in the human spirit. I believe that what a person is, not what a person looks like, determines his or her future.

Just as I have not been able to think of a past experience or incident in which my race or ethnicity has been an advantage, I am not able to think of an incident in which my race or ethnicity has been a disadvantage. That is, until recently.

As my graduation quickly approaches, I am becoming more and more frustrated by the tough, uphill battle I will have to undertake. My future goal is to become a police officer, a profession that has been drastically affected by special-interest groups, pathetic government policies, and government-appointed "overseers"... Through the media and schools, we are constantly bombarded with messages and slogans denouncing racism and discrimination. We are told that these will no longer be tolerated by society, and they will be slashed through government policies and public awareness. In our tireless search for racism and discrimination, two very interesting and disturbing phenomena have appeared: everything has become a "racial issue," and [we are now engaging in] "reverse discrimination."

This government's employment equity program and the *Multiculturalism Act* have, in essence, turned my race and my ethnicity into a disadvantage. The fact that I am a high school and college graduate no longer carries any significant merit when I apply to a police force or any other government agency. The prime qualification has become skin colour.

Many "experts" and government officials will deny the existence of reverse discrimination and hiring quotas ... [and] many people talk about instances when they have been denied jobs because of their race. Well, in the near future, I too will be able to relate to these people ...

How does this make me feel? Quite simply put, nauseous. The fact that I am qualified and possess more than sufficient skills to perform my job has little to no bearing. I may now be forced to sit back and watch less qualified and less educated persons pass by me in line because they are members of a race targeted by employers ... If a person is more qualified because of English skills, education, and experience, he or she should get the job. This is not necessarily true with the implementation of employment equity.

An example of how the government has gone overboard with this [hiring] program is an incident that took place during the summer. I had to go to the OHIP building to straighten out a problem I had with my health card. As soon as I entered the office, I was taken aback. Not only was I the only white in the office, I was the only one capable of speaking English at an understandable level ... My point here is that, if these jobs are posted publicly, there would have to be applicants for them who possess good

English skills. Did these people just not show up during the interviews for these jobs? In these economic times, I find that very hard to believe. Also, if the purpose of employment equity is to show an equal representation of the community, someone obviously made a mistake.

The ways in which Roger, Randy, and the public generally articulate and understand equity programs represents the new racism that we discussed earlier. Recall that, as Baker (1981) puts it, such racism "is expressed in a language of innocence which disguises its insidious intent by framing its message in a way that endorses 'folk' values of egalitarianism, social justice, and common sense" (cited in Kallen 1995, 30); and according to Sleeter (1994), racism is often "couched in expressions of unfairness and reverse discrimination." Further, racism is conceived of as something that is based on individual belief and action (rather than as an ideology), thus disavowing or diminishing its structural and systemic significance in our "democratic" society (Henry and Tator 2006a; Kallen 2003).

The claim that reverse racism, or reverse discrimination, operates to prevent access to educational and occupational opportunities is premised on the notion that our society is meritocratic, egalitarian, and democratic, and as such, through individual efforts, appropriate educational preparation, and possessing the "right" qualifications (including the ability to speak English—as Roger infers) individuals are able to attain the occupations to which they aspire irrespective of factors such as race, language, social class, gender, ethnicity, and disability. What is most often misunderstood, however, is that our educational and employment structures are inherently unequal, and that minority group members are systemically excluded from accessing educational and occupational opportunities.[12] In other words, critics of equity programs usually fail to recognize that our education and employment systems were designed by and for the very population that claims to be punished by equity programs.

EQUITY: RECOGNIZING AND VALUING DIFFERENCE

Randy argues that "equality should mean that everyone has the same chance of being hired." Indeed, this should be the case, but equity can only be attained if "the same chance" involves taking differences into account, for as Judge Abella stated in her 1984 Royal Commission report, *Equity in Employment*:

> Ignoring differences and refusing to accommodate them is denial of equal access and opportunity. It is discrimination. To reduce discrimination, we must create and maintain barrier-free environments so that individuals

can have genuine access free from arbitrary obstructions to demonstrate and exercise their full potential. (3)

These differences are not only related to the racial, ethnic, linguistic, and gender experiences of individuals or applicants, but also to how individuals' experiences are mediated by inequitable social, economic, political, educational, and cultural structures. It is necessary, therefore, to recognize that an individual's outcome or attainment is not merely a result of his or her personal qualities or failings, but is related to the structural barriers over which he or she has little or no control. In addition, equity programs are also strengthened by the notion that when such individuals attain the qualifications needed to apply for jobs, it represents not only their motivation, determination, and capacity to work against the odds, but also a particular perspective that should prove to be a valuable additional resource for any job.

The experiences that marginalized individuals bring to a job are often overlooked. But, if such individuals are to have "the same chance," we must value the differences—and related experiences and perspectives— that they bring to the job or educational situation. We must also revisit the "standards," traditions, and the "ways things have been done"—even when such standards have been perceived to have worked over the years. Doing so involves re-interpreting, re-adjusting, or simply abandoning the criteria that might have been set out without due consideration to historical and structural barriers and the diverse pool of experiences that can be called upon in today's society.[13] In this regard, it is necessary to acknowledge that obtaining a job or obtaining a particular level of education cannot be the "same" for everyone when race, gender, class, ethnicity, and other factors operate in structural or systemic ways to enhance or limit opportunities. Hence, as Judge Abella also points out, differences should not be ignored—individuals must be *treated differently if they are to be treated equally.*

> Formerly we thought that equity only meant sameness and that treating persons as equals meant treating everyone the same. We now know that to treat everyone the same may be to offend the notions of equality ... To create opportunity we have to do different things for different people ... The process is an exercise in redistributive justice. (3)

FAIRNESS AND QUALIFICATION

It cannot be that race, or as Roger says, "skin colour," has become the "prime qualification" for a job. Contrary to Roger's statement, which is influenced by his overarching frustration, the OHIP office where he was "the only white," and "the only one capable of speaking English at an understandable level," could not have been staffed by "unqualified" individuals; and skin colour could not have been the only reason for employment—no employer can afford to have a workforce that is incapable of doing the job. While the government did indicate that particular groups should be targeted under the equity programs, nowhere was it said that the ability to competently execute the job would be compromised. If such a compromise takes place, we need to question the motives of those who do the hiring and the situation into which minority employees are placed.[14] Similarly, in the case of educational access programs, we should expect that those given the chance to pursue their university or college education are able and ready to engage in the educational process. Providing employment or educational access to a member of a minority group who does not meet specified qualifications on the basis of stereotypes (for example, "this is the best that can be expected from a member of this particular group") would be disingenuous and is itself tantamount to racism.

Interestingly, issues of fairness and qualification are often raised when minorities are perceived to be entering areas of employment from which they have been traditionally excluded. If hiring practices are fair, then how do we explain employment situations that have been exclusively or largely homogeneously white for many years? Indeed, as one student quite correctly pointed out some time ago, "if there were equitable hiring practices in effect, there would be people of all races occupying power positions." Certainly minorities have long been "qualified" for many of the jobs for which they have applied; however, they have been excluded partly because of recruiters' subjective interpretation of who is "best qualified." Henry and Ginzberg found in their 1985 Toronto study, "Who Gets the Work: A Test of Racial Discrimination in Employment," that in cases where job applicants had similar resumés, white applicants were three times more likely to be offered a position than non-whites, and evidence suggests that very little has changed since. Reitz and Weiner (2005) explain that while employment equity has been adopted across the Canadian labour market, competing business concerns can get in the way. Also, many of the barriers to employment still exist, leading to a lack of qualified applicants from target groups, and stereotypes and discrimination in the workplace are still problems for visible minority workers. Such discrimination is "often expressed as concerns about lack of Canadian experience or the presumed inadequacy of foreign-born education and training" (9).

In a well-publicized incident of denial of access to employment, the *Toronto Star* reported the experiences of Evon Reid, who was denied an internship position in the office of Ontario premier Dalton McGuinty. After Reid was contacted and told that he was not selected for the position, an email (not meant for external circulation) referring to Reid as a "ghetto dude" was sent by an employee in the office. At the time, Reid was enrolled in university and by all accounts was an excellent student. The employee was dismissed; however, as Phyllis Kumi pointed out in an article entitled, "Lessons from 'Ghetto Dude' Affair," that "while the public was understandably outraged, the narrative lacked a definitive discussion about the underlying racism that allowed a 'low level' [employee] to comfortably air her thoughts. Many people in the African Canadian community, in particular, have identified discrimination in hiring practices as a significant barrier to employment" (*Toronto Star*, January 22, 2008). She continues, "thus this is a systemic problem, not an issue involving any specific individual in the public service." What the "ghetto dude" affair reveals is that by attaining a higher level of education an individual will not necessarily successfully change the attitudes and stereotypes that may act as a barrier to their aspirations. While the employee who used the term "ghetto dude" was not the decision maker in the hiring process, her use of such a phrase is indicative of a systemic issue.

In a seven-year study I conducted with twenty African Canadian youths about their employment experiences in 1993, respondents reported that racism and discrimination were "challenges" with which they had to contend, both in terms of obtaining a job and while they were on the job. Participants in the study also indicated that "who you know" is even more important than education, particularly when competing against a white person for a job. As one respondent stated, "while education can help, I have seen that who you know gets you further" (James 1993, 10). In 2006, I completed a follow-up study with seven of the original participants some twenty-one years after my first interview with them. Participants reiterated many of the same things—that as Blacks they have to work "twice as hard to get half as far," and that their work is "examined under a microscope." As a result, they "work really, really hard" because they understand that they are "representing" their race, especially when they are the first Blacks to be employed by an organization. One participant, who was a manager of a tool and die shop—one of very few Black people to work in that occupation—indicated that he has had difficulty being a "Black manager." For example, he explained: "If I hire a Black kid, everyone says ... that he's related to me. But if I hire a white, Chinese, or Indian ... they never say a word" (from interview with the author in Toronto, August 2006).

In a 2002 Canadian Labour Congress research report, *Is Work Working for Workers of Colour?*, Jackson explores the issues of employment, pay gaps, poverty, and economic security in relation to workers of colour, noting that while "some racialized workers with high levels of education" have managed to attain stable, professional jobs, there are many others with good qualifications who are "trapped in low-pay, insecure, no-future jobs." Many argue that the gap between qualification and job attainment can be attributed to many racialized workers being relative newcomers to Canada. However, the Labour Congress report demonstrates that the "catch-up" theory does not hold; even those with more Canadian experience have difficulty securing good jobs. Racialized workers today, unlike previous white European immigrants, are still "disproportionately employed in jobs requiring lower levels of skills and education, despite higher than average qualifications" (1). Jackson argues that systemic racism is still very present in the Canadian job market: "Racialized workers are paid less, enjoy less security, and are much more vulnerable to poverty than other workers" (18). And the labour market in Canada continues to be stratified along racial lines, with racialized group members overrepresented in low-income, under-regulated occupations such as retail, and under-represented in higher income, unionized sectors (Galabuzi 2001).

The concern that "the white male is being discriminated against for something beyond his control" is an understandable one. But it should be understood that we have all inherited the history of racism and discrimination and, with it, the consequences. These consequences constitute barriers to employment and educational opportunities for some and the privilege of access to employment and education for others. It is this inherited race privilege that makes it possible for Roger not to notice instances where his "race or ethnicity has been an advantage." The hard work and determination of both Roger and his parents, as well as the guidance he received from them, have not been mediated by the racism that racial minorities experience in their drive to educational and employment opportunities and success. And the "human spirit" that Roger is convinced is critical to success exists in raced, classed, abled, and gendered bodies and, as such, is subject to the social, political, economic, and cultural contestations in society. Just as the earned and unearned privileges described by McIntosh (1995) are accepted, so too must be the responsibility for how those privileges were acquired in the first place. Furthermore, as Stanley Fish (1993) argues in an article, "Reverse Racism or How the Pot Got to Call the Kettle Black," such programs are "not intended to disenfranchise white males" (136). Rather they are meant to remove barriers that have traditionally advantaged some groups and disadvantaged others. When the playing field is levelled, it does not disadvantage white males, it merely takes away their long-time advantage, thereby increasing competition.

THE PARADOX OF EQUITY PROGRAMS

Back in the early 1990s, Randy made the point that "even the minorities state that they want to be hired because they are the best, not because they are a minority." This is a common argument against equity programs, or affirmative action, as it's known in the United States. As Arina explains, members of minority groups must contend with the many questions, expectations, and challenges related to equity policies.

Arina: As a visible minority woman, I feel that my teaching experience thus far has been one that is focused on my skin colour. I am not just a teacher; I am a coloured teacher. This has benefits and drawbacks, but in general, it is inescapable, whereas, white [teacher candidates] and teachers, it seems, have the option of being advocates of minorities or else simply being "mainstream" teachers. This is not even an option for me in a school with a large population of students of South Asian background, some of whom, for a number of reasons, look to me as a role model.

Role models are important for children and young adults. They provide guidance and a real-life example of how a young person could turn out. But in my own experience, this idea of identifying based on a common sense of difference from the mainstream not only pulls people together, it also has its disadvantages. For example, in a school where I was a student teacher, because the mentor teacher had heard about my interest in equity issues, he interpreted this as my wanting to participate in the school's Asian Heritage Day. He went further to suggest that I start up the school's first South Asian club. I agreed, realizing that this might really help out some students in this school, as South Asians were highly represented but there was no club. However, I thought it interesting that these options were presented in a way that assumed I would be ready and willing to take on the role, simply because I am of South Asian heritage. My own schedule and level of commitment at this point in my program were not discussed, and I had to make a point of reminding him that my time at the school was limited.

Similarly, I have spent some time looking for a job as a teacher in Ottawa. At one of the schools, the vice-principal sat down to talk to me and give me strategies on applying. She talked to me about my resume and my strengths and weaknesses. Then she went on to tell me that I should not have much of a problem getting a job, as I am a visible minority. According to her, this would be especially helpful to me in a school such as hers, which has a high South Asian population. Basically, she assumed that I was interested in becoming a role model for South Asian students, and she obviously saw me as a "coloured teacher," not just as a teacher.

As a role model, I am held up as someone who represents success in mainstream society and, hence, models ways of achieving success. I am held up as an "ethical template" (Allen, as cited in Solomon 1997), and as someone who knows how to reconcile roles and responsibilities that are conflictual between the mainstream culture and the South Asian ones. Also I am expected to be a symbol of achievement in my community, as well as a nurturer of South Asian students' needs in a mainstream school. There are a number of problems with this. First of all, there is enormous social and psychological stress in carrying this responsibility (Solomon 1997, 405). Secondly, taking on this role takes the dominant group teacher off the hook for teaching an inclusive curriculum (406). I am seen as the "expert;" therefore, any issues or program units in my "area of expertise" would be directed to me.

Finally, another major problem arises if I accept this position of "role model." In his study, Carl James asks, "Whose version of morality, identity, and aspiration will be privileged?" (James 1997, 168). The answer is, the "mainstream's." Essentially, I have been able to adopt the morality, identity, and aspirations that are considered valuable in this society. Therefore, am I really being a good role model, or merely an instrument of the mainstream culture and state to "convert" those who identify with me because of our similar racial backgrounds?

All of these questions are problems that are difficult to grapple with as a beginning teacher. On the one hand, I am highly committed to serving my community and reaching at-risk students. If this means that I serve as a role model to them, I am happy to take on that role. However, I believe that much reflection will be needed when I do decide to follow that path. I need to remind myself of the issues, and to try to provide a multi-dimensional view into my life as a role model. This means exploring my own background and achievements within my community, as well as the Canadian mainstream one. It means asking myself if I am doing these students justice by having them look up to me.

So while employment equity provides welcome access to employment opportunities, it presents difficulties or problems for some people, like Arina, who have to contend with expectations, stereotypes, and stressful situations that often become burdensome—a paradox indeed.

ENCOURAGEMENT IS A TWO-EDGED SWORD

BY ALISON BLACKDUCK

Please don't take exception to the fact that I'm a young aboriginal woman who finished her undergraduate degree.

Since I've started writing on this page, I've received emails from a few readers congratulating me on being in university.

"It's good to see that you're in university," is the general sentiment that's expressed, although one reader advised me that I must finish my studies in order to enhance my professional credibility as a journalist.

Now you're probably wondering why I'm bringing this up. It's good to have one's achievements and hard work recognized, right? Encouragement is desirable, isn't it? Well, of course, but what's undesirable are the implicit assumptions underlying the "encouragement" I've received.

If I weren't a young aboriginal woman who's finishing her undergraduate degree, would any reader pick up on it and make a point of telling me what a fine example I'm setting? Would somebody tell me that I'd hurt my professional credibility as a journalist if I failed to complete my degree requirements? I doubt it; nobody seems to question the professional credibility of Avril Benoit and Naomi Klein, two celebrated, young Canadian journalists who openly admit they're university dropouts. In fact, judging from biographical profiles of both women that I've read in the popular press, both regard their failure as a sign of their journalistic gifts; they were simply too much in demand as journalists to finish their studies. So what gives?

My aboriginal background and some people's perceptions of what it means to be an aboriginal in Canada today is what gives. To some, I'm an exception to the rule, which then begs the question: The rule of what? If I'm exceptional because I'm an aboriginal person who has dedicated the past few years of my life to my studies, then those who write me to congratulate me don't expect such behaviour from an aboriginal person. The implicit assumption is that I'm doing really well for an aboriginal person, because we're perceived widely as being incapable of attaining certain levels of success as defined by non-aboriginal society.

This reasoning usually follows through to one of two predictable conclusions: Those aboriginal people who are "successful" must either be exceptional to escape their pathetic circumstances or they were raised with middle-class values in assimilated middle-class families, therefore, they're privileged, inauthentic representatives of aboriginal society.

Both conclusions are false and damning.

According to Plains Cree Métis writer and academic Emma LaRoque, being "exceptional is another rung on the ghettoization ladder."

Those who are deemed "exceptional" are perceived as belonging to neither aboriginal society nor non-aboriginal society. They don't belong to aboriginal society because many Canadians assume that there's nothing inherent in contemporary aboriginal society that fosters excellence and success, only despair. (You've no idea how many non-aboriginal people who, upon meeting me for the first time, decry the pain I must have experienced, what with the high suicide rate and all those homeless aboriginal people living on the street!)

And they don't belong to non-aboriginal society because they're, quite frankly, aboriginal. In either case, they're suspect and must be segregated into another category known as the Aboriginal Intellectual Elite, which by its very moniker smacks of self-service.

The other extreme assumption, which is the question of privilege, is countered brilliantly by Cree/Métis writer Kim Anderson in her book, *A Recognition of Being: Reconstructing Native Womanhood*. Anderson is the daughter of an upper-middle-class woman of predominantly English Protestant ancestry and a man of mixed Scottish, Cree, French, and Saulteaux ancestry, who is often taken to task by aboriginal and non-aboriginal people for her relatively privileged upbringing, which includes a university education, and her lighter skin. She admits she's never experienced the overt violent prejudice, poverty, abuse, and family breakdown that is accepted as the lot of the aboriginal majority. But she then turns this around by asking why these basic human rights are taken for granted as commonplace for most non-aboriginal Canadians yet deemed as privileges for aboriginal people?

Why, indeed. For my part, I don't see much about my life or my choices that's exceptional, nor do I feel I'm breaking free from a predetermined life script that's dictated and imposed by cultural stereotypes about aboriginal people. I write, I study, and I work for the same reasons everybody else does—their own—and fortunately I have the opportunity to do so. My only hope is that everybody has such freedom, because freedom isn't an exception to the rule, it is the rule we should all uphold, for your sake and mine.

Source: *Toronto Star*, March 6, 2001, A21. Alison Blackduck is a Dogrib writer and was a full-time student at Concordia University in Montreal when she wrote this article.

Toward Equity that Makes Opportunities Possible for All

There should be no question or doubt about the significance of providing equal employment and educational opportunities for *all* Canadians; it is part of what democracy is about, and as the Conference Board of Canada argues, the importance of an inclusive, diverse workforce cannot be overstated. But research shows that while there has been an increase in the hiring of racial minority people over the years, their level of representation in employment has yet to be achieved; and at the senior levels in Canadian institutions and businesses, racial minorities are under-represented. This situation, according to the Conference Board of Canada survey, has to do with the fact that individuals still have difficulty getting their foreign credentials recognized, and the general under-funding of diversity initiatives. It was observed that companies with successful diversity initiatives usually have executive-level involvement in such programs. In their report, *The Value of Diverse Leadership* (2008), for the Conference Board of Canada, Tim Krywulak and Ashley Sisco write:

> Canada professes to embrace diversity, yet there is a striking lack of inclusiveness at the top of its public, private, and non-profit organizations—especially in our largest organizations. For example, visible minorities comprise 16.2 percent of the Canadian population, but hold only 5.2 per cent of senior management positions in large companies and 1.6 per cent of executive management positions in the public sector. In 2006, only 24 visible minority candidates were elected to the 308-seat House of Commons, representing but 8 per cent of the total number of seats. (3)

That we are yet to include minority members of our society into the mainstream of employment and education likely has to do with the myths, misinformation, and half-truths that characterize much of the discussion about employment equity; this type of misinformation also characterizes our knowledge of immigration and immigrants. On one hand, these myths are based on a lack of acknowledgment of the inherent economic and social inequities within our society, a fear of social change, and an anticipated loss of political, economic, and social power and privilege. On the other hand, the multicultural, meritocratic ideology of Canada has so structured the ideas of individuals that they have difficulty critically reflecting on these issues or recognizing the myths. The claims that equity programs are misguided and unnecessary embody the "new racism" to which Kallen (2003) refers. Little wonder, therefore, that individuals might fail to see the role played by prejudices, stereotypes, and racism directed toward the "benefactors" of equity programs. If we are to build a democratic and equitable society in Canada, then we must be critically reflexive, prepared for social change, and play a part in initiating and fighting for that change. It is indeed inevitable that, in the words of one discussion participant, "corrective measures" in the form of equity programs must be taken if equal employment and educational opportunities are to be realized. And while it seems simplistic to say, as one participant did, that such programs "would definitely help" because having co-workers from "all racial backgrounds can and will benefit a multicultural society," it is still something worth striving for.

CONCLUSION

Racism is generally understood at the level of individual attitudes, and as acts of discrimination. But it is more than this. It must be understood in terms of historical and structural factors, and in terms of the rules, policies, and practices that have been the prevailing norm in institutions that have operated for years in favour of those by whom and for whom they were constructed in the first place. If racism is seen merely in terms of the attitudes and actions of individuals against other individuals, based on individual ignorance, then the claims, challenges, and criticisms raised by individuals based on their experiences with racism will continue to be ignored and denied. To change things, equity programs must be seen as attempts to undo the effects of arbitrary and racist policies and practices that have operated historically as barriers to access and opportunity. The difference between equity programs and the ways in which individuals have traditionally gained access to educational and occupational opportunities is "not in the outcome but in the ways of thinking that have led to the outcome. It is the difference between an unfairness that befalls one as an unintended effect of a policy rationally conceived and an unfairness that is pursued as an end in itself" (Fish 1993, 136). Stated differently, equity programs are not intended to prevent males or whites from employment opportunities, but to remove structural barriers that have limited minority participation.

If current equity programs are to be seen as useful and appropriate for addressing racism and building a productive and inclusive society, then members of society must collectively and critically reflect, as Mario does in the following excerpt:

Mario: So, are we ignorant bigots? Is our collective frustration with the perils of inclusivity and equity borne of our inability to understand, on a personal level, the travails of being alienated? Having been raised in the comfort of dominance, do we neglect, consciously or unconsciously, the fact that the "other" is constantly glancing at us and our wealth (relative, of course)? We have opportunities, they have few. We have the connections, they do not. We win, they lose.

So, how is it that we say that we owe our success, such as it is, to our personal diligence and efforts? We can't. The root of the issue is not a personal bias or a lack of knowledge with regard to the "other." It is systemic, institutionalized, and therefore an integral part of the power relations and politics of our white male dominance. We have the tools of dominance: laws, regulations, social custom, ownership of the means, and we use them to our ends.

What better way to inculcate those grand ideas than through the institution we call school? Schools are lily white at their very core, although on the surface they are multicoloured (not just skin colour, but class and culture as well). We preach inclusivity and opportunity for all because our official values demand it. The reality is somewhat different. It is no great revelation that those of colour, those who are different, those who must be shunted, are in fact shunted (or tracked, or streamed, or whatever you want to call it) into programs, schools, and catchment basins where opportunity is simply an untaught five-syllable word.

Indeed, it is important to have an education program in which *all* Canadians are able to learn what it means to be inclusive and equitable, as well as how we are influenced by structures. We must all learn and understand that as long as equity programs are not accompanied by systemic changes that dismantle the structures (e.g., legislation, policies, procedures, and practices) that have traditionally operated as barriers to educational and employment opportunities, these programs will remain ineffective. Nevertheless, if we are to address the educational and employment situation of those citizens who are, and have been in the past, disadvantaged by structural inequalities, there is a need for equity programs. If not now, when?

NOTES

1. See also Henry and Tator 2006.

2. It is of note that, as Gottshalk and Greenberg report, "three years before this controversy the same editor for *Jyllands-Posten* turned down cartoons satirizing the resurrection of Jesus," claiming that they would "'provoke an outcry' among Christians" (2). He reasoned that his different reactions to the two sets of cartoons had to do with the fact that he did not commission those featuring Jesus.

3. See also Frejute-Rakauskiene 2006.

4. See Dua et al. 2009; Fleras 2010; Henry and Tator 2006; Hier and Bolaria 2007.

5. See also Clairmont and Magill, 1999. The location of Africville was named an "historic site" in 2002 by the federal government, but in the 1960s, Halifax's City Council expropriated the land and bulldozed the houses, destroying the community. While most residents opposed the move, they were nevertheless relocated by the city to public housing in areas within Halifax. The residents, many of whom were uncertain about their legal right to the land due to a lack of formal record keeping, were given less than $500 compensation for their home and property. City workers in garbage trucks moved residents and their possessions from the site. Now, more than thirty years later, the site of the community of Africville is now known as Seaview Park (Clairmont and Magill, 1999).

6. The term *neo-racism* is also used in place of new racism.

7. It's worth noting that the application of the science of evolution to human social history is generally considered to be specious and there is a long tradition of manipulating the public's understanding of evolution to racist ends. One could also argue that the Africans held as slaves developed strategies and coping mechanism to survive such a horrid period in history, and that the existence of a rich cultural, spiritual, and artistic tradition from that period is testament to those who did survive and were able to influence future generations.

8. In an article entitled "The Canadian Origins of South African Apartheid," Michèle DuCharme (1986) compares the treatment of Aboriginals in Canada and the then-apartheid situation of Blacks in South Africa. Noting the parallel colonial situation, DuCharme writes that, according to information obtained from government documents in the Public Archives in Ottawa, a "South African government official visited Canada at different times... [between] 1948 and 1963 in order to tour Indian reserves and industrial schools in the West. For example, as late as July 1962, the South African High Commissioner W. Dirkse-van-Schalkwyk visited selected Indian reserves in Western Canada." DuCharme

goes on to speculate about the establishment of the apartheid policies of South Africa in the early 1960s that came "around the same time that the South African high Commissioner was touring Canadian reserves" (3).

9. See also James 2005.

10. At one time, Alarie did return to a bar in the Montreal area with a Black man who had earlier been refused service, because the bar claimed it had a no-Black policy and that the presence of Black individuals would hurt business. The Human Rights Commission later fined the owner sixteen thousand dollars.

11. Clarke went on to say:

Why is it news? Because he's white. Just like when John Howard Griffin went to the Deep South in the '50s. Black people had been talking and complaining about racism since before slavery, and it really didn't get a lot of attention. All those civil rights marchers, sit-downs and sit-ins, people who were falsely charged, jailed, beaten, shot, executed, assassinated and lynched—didn't their black bodies testify to the racism in the south? All of it doesn't matter, because it was Griffin's book that propelled the civil rights movement forward. *Black Like Me* helped people in Middle America know that the civil rights movement was justified and necessary. Believe it or not. (in Scott 2004)

12. Access here means not only getting into a place of education or employment, but also encountering conditions that enable one to participate fully and effectively without constraint.

13. For example, in the case of police officers, many of us would agree that the standard height requirement—historically, it was based on the average height of white North American males and for years it was used as a standard requirement —seems unnecessary, and it has been appropriately discontinued, thereby making policing accessible to a more diverse number of Canadians, both male and female.

14. Obviously, the situation in which individuals are employed ought to enable them to perform their tasks effectively. Anything less might indeed lead to, as Roger (a student quoted in this chapter) indicates, horror stories resulting from what may be perceived as resistance to "government-imposed, 'hiring-of-minorities-at-all-costs' tactics." While individuals might be "well qualified" for the job, their effectiveness at and success in the job is very much dependent on the support they receive from employers and colleagues.

IDENTITY, PRIVILEGE, AND DIFFERENCE

Scott: For better or worse, and perhaps without even actually realizing the possible consequences, most people wrap themselves in their protective cocoon of self-concept. Unlike nature's irrevocable cycle of life, however, humans often choose to remain with the familiar and forsake the butterfly-like flight into the unknown. I believe this protective cocoon of self-concept spans the racial, ethnic, and cultural difference gap and is a defense mechanism that is hard to penetrate.

Being asked to instigate the penetration of oneself can be a traumatic experience for some. For others, it can be an uplifting and enlightening experience. For the dominant group members, however (and I place myself in this category), the racial, cultural, and ethnic influence has never really come into play —in a conscious sense—in relation to values and behaviour. Therefore, it is initially rejected as a concept better left to intel-lectual discussion or, more to the point, left until the wells of discussion on sex and sports have run dry.

When the enforced impetus of academic requirement is applied and more than the perfunctory scratching of the shell of self-concept occurs, the supposedly well-rounded individual can appreciate just who, why, and what was involved in the molding. He or she can better understand and accept the final product.

That whites like Scott "wrap themselves in their protective cocoon of self-concept" and do not consciously explore the extent to which race and ethnicity play a role in their experiences, values, and behaviours, may indeed be considered "a defense mechanism." But a defense against what?

According to Scott, it is a defense against the "traumatic" consequences of having to deal with the "difference gap"—in terms of race, ethnicity, and culture—between whites and non-whites. This "gap" seemingly refers to the power difference between whites and non-whites. Scott seems aware of the power and privilege that accrue to him as a result of racism, yet his preference is to stay "with the familiar." In other words, he prefers to pretend ignorance (of what he refers to as "the unknown"), maintaining his privilege and avoiding the "trauma" that might come with acknowledging his role in maintaining the structures of racism.

Scott's insightful comments are consistent with the findings and arguments of Carr and Lund (2007), Kendall (2006), Kobayashi and Peake (2000), Phoenix (1997), Rosenberg (1997), Sleeter (1994), and Wise (2005). Scott indicates—as do the arguments of these scholars—that he and other "dominant group members" have difficulty talking about themselves in racial terms. When they do so, they tend to justify and defend their privilege. In concluding this text, I reflect on how dominant and minority (or racial or ethnic marginalized) group members take up privilege in their discussion of identity and related experiences. I demonstrate that, contrary to Scott's hypothesis—and as we have seen throughout this book—many white participants, particularly those who identify as having British roots, seem hesitant (or less likely) to recognize the role that race plays in the privileges they enjoy as members of Canadian society. Those who acknowledge their privileges indicate that it takes a level of critical awareness or consciousness to see, understand, and appreciate the role that race plays in their cultural, as well as social, political, and economic existence. Some individuals, in turn, seem determined to use that privilege in their role as advocates for social change.

On the other hand, people of colour (with exceptions, of course) seem more willing to acknowledge the extent to which their opportunities in society are structured, mediated, and circumscribed by the constructed meaning of race. In so doing, they tend to acknowledge the significance of race in the selves or the identities they constructed. This is likely related to their recognition that—compared to whites—they have to continually expose the extent to which social structures, rather than factors inherent in themselves or the ethno-racial group with which they identify, mediate their experiences. The narratives of minority group members are likely to reflect their attempts to understand how the prevailing structures of society inform and affect their situations and their wish to avoid blaming themselves for their lack of success. Alternatively, whites habitually tend to indicate that there is no requirement or need for them to know, identify, or articulate how social structures operate to provide them with privileges. For example, as James explains in the following excerpt, while he was able to negotiate and navigate the various social and cultural structures and groups with which he interacted, he still did "not know" how his privileges were related to his whiteness.

James: I don't think of myself as having a "colour," and I guess that is because society does not highlight or stress this message to me every waking moment, as it does to a person whose skin is not white. The message sent by our First World society is that the "civilized world" is white; I can't imagine how that impacts on a person who is not white …

I am an immigrant. I was born in Glasgow, Scotland, and my family immigrated to Canada when I was four. This would be my ethnicity, but I have no specific, conscious attachment to the culture of my place of birth. Coming to Canada at a young age, I had not fully absorbed the culture of Scotland, and so it was not very difficult for me to assimilate into Canadian culture. I did not have to suffer the potentially painful effects of acculturation, because Canada was, and continues to be, in many respects very similar to Scotland. The neighbourhood that I first lived in consisted of white, working-class families, and I can't recall any people of different cultural backgrounds who lived there.

While as a child I was never bombarded with messages of my Scottish ethnicity, I was still very much socialized into that culture. The friends of my parents were mostly Scottish (i.e., first generation here in Canada) and all were white. And I grew up conscious of some of the negative perceptions that were associated with being Scottish, such as being cheap, wearing a kilt, eating porridge, and speaking with an accent. When I was young, there were occasions when I would not acknowledge my ethnicity because of the stereotypes associated with being Scottish. Certainly the impact of what I perceived to be negative characteristics pales in comparison with stereotypes that people of other cultures are subjected to …

My identity is never questioned. People automatically assume that I am Canadian, born and raised here. I am almost never asked where I was born; in fact, many people are often surprised when I tell them I was born in Scotland. I am also never asked what kind of an accent I have, although when I visit Scotland I am often asked if I am American (to which I take great offence).

As a white person, I am never asked to be the spokesperson for all white people, a position that many minority people find themselves in. I guess this is because most white people know that all white people do not think alike, but those same white people assume that people of other racial groups think alike.

Have I had privileges because of the fact that I am white? Well, because I understand how society works, I would have to say "yes." A more difficult question to answer is: What were those privileges that I received, aside from not being followed around in stores by a sales clerk, or receiving better service in a restaurant? I don't know. Did I ever get a job because I am white? I don't know. Perhaps this is the crux of the problem that whites have in accepting equity programs. It is that we honestly don't believe that we have *ever.* had any special privileges purely because we are white. This demonstrates the urgent need for societal re-education.

James provides very good insights into the privileges that he has enjoyed. Even though he is an immigrant, he has not suffered "the potentially painful effects of acculturation;" he has always felt a sense of belonging to and acceptance in Canada; he could often ignore his ethnicity altogether; and his identity is never questioned because people automatically assume he is "Canadian, born and raised." Although James alludes to the possibility of having benefited from white-skin privilege, he goes on to say that whites "honestly don't believe that we have ever had any special privileges purely because we are white." James's seeming unwillingness to concede that he and other whites benefit from their whiteness is a very important point. All members of society experience life—its privileges and its disadvantages—in relation to their position in the social hierarchy, which, among other variables, is built on ethnicity, race, citizenship, immigrant status, and language, and operates to structure their identities, sense of belonging, participation in society, and their social outcomes.

Individuals' cultural identities become linked with their geopolitical and historical experiences, values, ways of life, and the social patterns that are part of their group life. However, acquiring an ethnic and racial identity and a dominant–minority identification, is not simple in our contemporary, pluralistic, Canadian society. Take the case of Doreen, who was born and raised in Newfoundland. In the previous edition of this book, Doreen wrote of "relocating" to Canada, and constructed herself as a "newcomer" who, in light of her cultural differences, was subject to feelings of alienation as an immigrant to Canada. So while Doreen might have white privilege, the privilege is mediated by the fact that she is a Newfoundlander. In her article: "Provincially Speaking: You Don't Sound Like a Newfoundlander," Susan Tilley (2000) similarly wrote: "Meeting fellow Canadians supported and strengthened my developing provincial identity while educating me about the stereotypical notions of Newfoundland embedded in the national psyche" (236). Another student, Daniella, who identifies as Italian, did not see herself as "white," because she saw whiteness as referring to someone who is Canadian— and Canadian as referring to someone of British background.

Consider also Claudia, who, while not denying her whiteness and related privileges, writes that she does not fit the social-class profile of most university students. She writes of being working-class with a class-consciousness and anti-racism values, which, from her perspective, make her different from many other white students. Similarly, Loretta, who identifies herself as a "queer woman," indicates that because of her sexuality, she has to constantly negotiate the oppressive homophobic structures of society that contribute to how she feels about herself, and to the treatment that she can expect from others around her, even from her family members.

Clearly, privileges are mediated by gender, place of birth (or province of origin), social class, sexuality, and demographic characteristics, as well as experiences in schools, churches, synagogues, workplaces, and with other major institutions such as the media. Sometimes it is through encounters with these institutions that individuals come to recognize the privileges they have as racial and ethnic group members. Dominant group members may come to realize that they have a privileged and prestigious position in society, and, as a result, access to all of the social, political, and economic institutions within that society. They might even come to realize that they can "get ahead" without compromising their identities. According to Peggy McIntosh (1995) the phenomenon of white privilege is "denied and protected, but alive and real in its effects." (See also Carr and Lund 2007.)

Clearly, whiteness—like Blackness and other racial and ethnic identities, such as being Italian—is not monolithic, and the experiences, ideas, responses, and value systems of individuals within groups are correspondingly heterogeneous. Hence, neither privileges, limitations, nor disadvantages will be experienced in the same way by members of any one group (James 2007, Jensen 1998). Instructive here are the experiences of "mixed-race" or "biracial" individuals (such as Andrew and Leanne whom we met in earlier chapters) whose identities are ambiguous—they do not neatly fit into any of the racially or ethnically constructed groups of society. For these biracial individuals, their "whiteness"—especially for individuals who have the privilege of "passing" (see Lazarro 1996; Shrage 1997)—or their "in-between-ness," hybridity, or as one student puts it, "raced identity," is very much related to the context (that is, the neighbourhood, country, and school setting) in which they were operating. But in a race-conscious society such as ours, and one in which racism structures everyday interactions, it is likely that mixed-race or biracial individuals will be questioned about their identity. This is a form of racialization premised on racism; it is a challenge to whatever privileges that they might seek to enjoy in the society.

Minority group members often come to realize that to get ahead they may have to compromise their ethnic identities. They learn that "if they wish to enjoy the rewards of employment, education or social contact with higher-status groups, it will be necessary to forsake their language and many other cultural attributes of their ethnic [or racial] groups" (Agocs 1987, 170). This could also mean denying their ethnicity or race because these characteristics identify them as "different" or "inferior." They may reject their ethno-racial group experiences or, alternatively, they may embrace what they consider to be the cultural values of their ethnic or racial group and work hard to change the negative perceptions of their group. Through socialization, an individual learns about their position in society, which in turn is likely to influence their identity and behaviour.

Several of the narratives of minority group members illustrate that, despite their efforts, they did not manage to attain the privilege of feeling a sense of belonging to Canada. They were not seen as "Canadians"— they were seen as different, the "other." Even "without [a foreign] accent" or "marked dialect," their Black or brown skin constructed them as foreign and different. Their appearance prompted the questions "Where are you from?" and "What's your background?" and the statement, "You have an accent." These questions and statements are all forms of the racialization process. Interestingly, even though some people of colour do not perceive themselves as having an accent, an accent is nevertheless projected onto them or integrated into constructing their difference; they are unable to escape these perceptions. Some immigrant individuals found that contributed to the questioning and negative reactions among the people with whom they interact.

For example, Winsome, a young Black Jamaican woman, writes:"When I tell people that I am Jamaican, I get a very different reaction than when I say that I was born in the United States. People seem more accepting of American Blacks than they do of Blacks from the Caribbean, particularly Jamaica." This is an example of the role that nationality plays in the racialization and marginalization of Black people. As I discuss elsewhere (James 2008), there is a tendency in the racialization and marginalization processes of Blacks generally, and Caribbean people in particular, to criminalize and "Jamaicanize" them; in other words, to construct them as criminals who are mainly from Jamaica. Despite their efforts to "fit in," the racialization process will continue to construct people of colour as different until the privilege of Canadian identification goes beyond those who are white and Anglo-Saxon to include those who are Italian, Black, brown, yellow, and mixed race.

People often ask how it is that some individuals who live in racially and ethnically diverse cities or communities know so little about minority Canadians, or have had such limited interaction with them? When people do interact with those of other racial and ethnic groups, they report that they are "awakened to the reality of others." However, it is also true that members of the majority group often feel a sense of fear or nervousness during interracial or inter-ethnic interactions, particularly when encounters with racial minority group members place them in a minority position. Kallen (1995) tells us that when confronted with racially diverse environments, the most common response of whites is to withdraw. The fact is, while admitting to having "preconceived notions" or "bias" and being "theoretically aware" of "other" Canadians and their experiences and living conditions, whites often tend to be indifferent to race differences. This undoubtedly enables them to avoid dealing directly or constantly with the issues and treatment of racial minority people, including their friends. It is possible that through their interactions with racial minority group members some white individuals are indeed "awakened" to the experiences of "other" Canadians, as they may be on occasions when they are forced to acknowledge their race privileges. However, it is not generally true that whites are unaware of their privileges, but that their privileges are so much a part of their existence that they take them for granted.

Nevertheless, it should be evident in our discussion that whether one has or exercises privilege is related to context—both when and where. For example, individuals can have privilege in one country, but not in another. As well, the exercise of, or the capacity to exercise, privilege is related to an individual's resources and his or her willingness to do so given the context and circumstances in which they live. The power and privilege that individuals possess or are able to exercise depend upon their agency to legitimate their heightened status in the community and the world. Essentially, as the individual reflections and discussions in this text indicate, privilege is not simply related to the colour of a person's skin, or his or her gender, class, or sexuality, but to a whole host of factors operating in relation to his or her position in the society and the context in which he or she functions or exists. Privilege is complex, fluid, and alterable. What should become clear in our discussion is the way in which subjectivity and agency operate in the definition or construction of identity and the related power and privileges that individuals enjoy. As the various narratives indicate, identities and their associated privileges and disadvantages are complex, contextual, contingent, and relational, operating in different ways for different people.

A CONVERSATION

The following conversation with my friend and colleague, Carol Geddis, first appeared in the 1999 edition of the book. It is included in this volume because it contains ideas and issues that continue to be relevant.

C. G. You talk about things like self-awareness and increased understanding of others (in fact, largely, the "other") as being central and important to any kind of individual change as well as social change, over time, towards a more equitable society. Why do you believe that? Why do you think that if I understand myself better and increase my understanding of people who are racially and culturally different, somehow that will all accrue to the good?

C. J. I don't think that it necessarily follows that because I am more aware of myself I will be much more active in social change. But I do think that personal awareness is a critical and crucial aspect in the whole issue of social change. If you are going to be involved in social change, you have to understand yourself—and understanding yourself involves understanding how structures have impacted on you; how they have affected your life; and consequently how you can influence the structures in order to bring about change. So personal awareness is an important starting point in the process of social change.

C. G. It seems to me that something more than self-knowledge and understanding of others is required in order for substantive change to come about. Or do you believe, in your heart of hearts, in the "perfect-ibility of human kind?" That you can take anyone from anywhere, teach them some things, and this will turn them around?

C. J. I believe, like you do, that more than self-knowledge is required. It is a matter of how we move people towards collective action. We can move towards collective action if we have a common understanding of the forces that shape all of our lives. These forces impact on racial minori-ties differently from the racial majority. In knowing that, a person—either racial minority or racial majority—will understand the role she or he will have to play individually and collectively in bringing about change.

C. G. Whether or not they accept that role is another thing, though, isn't it?

C. J. Oh, yes. But some will accept the role and others will reject it.

C. G. Yes, that is true. You did not answer my question directly. I asked you if you believe in the perfectibility of human kind. I think that at some level you must, if you believe what you are saying to me now. Let me respond to you as a white person. If I accept the fact that racism as we know it in Canada is a white problem, given the historical forces such as colonialism that have helped to shape this society, then, as a white person, I also need to clarify my responsibility—or the role that I could be playing to help make society more equitable.

When I interact with other white people around that issue, it seems to me that it comes down to the big question of power and privilege. I am too often left with the question of what it will take to have white people share, relinquish, or somehow modify our power and privilege. Or even to have us realize that we have such things as power and privilege. Even when there is recognition of white power and privilege, then the issue often becomes one of, once I know that I have it, why should I give it up? It seems to me that it is not only a matter of us white folk holding tight to our power and privilege because it is to our advantage to do so, but sometimes it is also a matter of risk and fear. I have had white people say to me, for example, that if they challenge racism among family or friends by defining it as an expression of white power, they are putting themselves in some jeopardy. By this they mean that they run the risk of damaging their relationships by setting themselves apart from their group. That is a powerful combination—self-interest in wanting to maintain power and privilege, on the one hand, and not wanting to pull away from the group, on the other. I would like to know what is it going to take to get us beyond those major roadblocks.

C. J. It is going to take a lot of effort and struggle. While you were talking, I was thinking about the students whose experiences are documented in this book. Most are white and are twenty-one, twenty-two, and up to twenty-four years of age. Their understanding of their own power and privilege, and of the impact of social structures on individuals and groups, is limited. They seem to believe that they don't have any power. For example, when employment equity was being discussed, the assumption was that racial minorities have all the power now and are taking over. So much work remains to be done in terms of bringing people to an understanding of their power and privilege. There is nothing wrong with recognizing one's personal power. One has it because of his or her skin colour and because of the meaning given to such things by our society. Understanding the structural aspect of power would hopefully lead to an understanding of how one can use her or his power for social change.

C. G. I think the employment equity issue moves the discussion of power, and the recognition and acceptance of differential power as part of the problem, past the academic level of discussion. It is true that the notion of unearned power and the part it plays in advantaging the lives of those that have it is a complex and difficult issue for some people to come to grips with. Not only twenty-years-olds, but also forty- and fifty-year-olds find the notion of power difficult to understand. They have trouble perceiving of themselves as having power, of understanding power as a factor of how things are structured, as something that works in some people's favour and to the disadvantage of others. They have difficulty relating this understanding of power to their own experience. My concern is that, as we try to lead people through this type of analysis of power, too often the discussion remains academic. Employment equity is going to take it beyond the academic. People, for the first time, are going to experience what it feels like to have a system or structure that does not automatically work in their favour. Employment equity is going to be a "test case" for this society and for those of us who see ourselves as agents of change …

C. J. A sense of guilt also emerges as a result of such discussions.

C. G. I am less patient with guilt than I used to be. I find it is self-defeating; and too often it can become a ploy to prevent people from getting beyond a certain point to a deeper analysis and, ultimately, to action.

C. J. Guilt is not a productive consequence of these exercises. It is important to present this kind of material and manage these kinds of discussions in a way that does not produce feelings that are counterproductive in terms of moving towards action.

C. G. You mentioned that many of the students you worked with were in their early twenties. Presumably many of them have gone through the school system here, up to the college and university levels. The fact that they approached course material as if it were the first time they had been exposed to the issues is, for me, an indictment of the school system in general. One should not have to wait until the post-secondary level before one is given the opportunity to contend with the major issues that are central to the health of this society.

C. J. Yes. And as our society becomes even more multiracial, multi-faith and multicultural, we are going to have to do a better job in the schools to prepare students to live and work in our diverse society. If social change is going to take place, if education is to liberate and be meaningful to the students, then we must educate our students early about issues of classism, sexism, racism, and other oppressive mechanisms.

C. G. You realize that you are talking about a big change?

C. J. Certainly; and a re-education of the teachers who are responsible for educating the students.

C. G. Yes, re-education of existing teachers and a re-conceiving of teacher training programs.

CONCLUSION

We have discussed culture as a dynamic, contradictory, and conflictive force upon which everyone has an impact and that has an impact upon everyone. To understand culture, one has to recognize its colonizing effects and the role that the mechanisms of differentiation—racism, stereotyping, prejudice, sexism, classism, and other factors—play in defining, enabling, and maintaining culture as we know it. Individual and group resistance to the effects of cultural hegemony or colonization (in Canada's case, Anglo-conformity) produces tension and conflicts that give meaning to race and ethnicity within a particular context. Our identities, then, insofar as they are a social construct and not only an individual production, are related to the social construction of race and ethnicity in Canada. We are a part of the dynamic production and reproduction of culture, inclusive of our race, ethnicity, gender, class, and so on.

For instance, while I may have cultural practices that are sometimes attributed to my racial group (Black), they are not independent of Canadian culture; rather, they are part of it. My various identities (immigrant, male, middle class, parent, son, friend, etc.) and behaviours are just as Canadian as those of any other Canadian person, for I am a product of, and I respond to, the Canadian social structure. My behaviours are, in part, informed by my understanding of, and interaction with, Canada's institutions and the values and norms that have been communicated to me. My behaviours are also related to how I perceive my situation contextually in terms of power and privilege in society, and they are influenced by my capacity to participate and influence social, political, and economic structures and events.

The educational and socialization processes through which we come to understand and identify ourselves are political. They provide insights into the structures that determine the relationships between racial and ethnic groups, between the dominant and subordinate, and between individuals. As a result, we can expect individuals to react in both positive and negative ways to these processes, and to their interactions with various members of the society based on social status. It is possible that discussions of race, ethnicity, and culture can inspire the understanding and sensitivity necessary to confront these issues, as can individual engagement in self-criticism and the admission of one's own negative qualities. However, this is only the beginning of what will be for many, a long, difficult, and sometimes painful lesson in race and ethnic relations. Without nurturing, coaching, and encouragement, initial insights and the commitment and determination to take up the challenge of dealing with these societal issues might be lost.

Despite awareness, sensitivity, and understanding, there are some issues that we as individuals still find difficult to discuss—racism is an important example. However, if we are to meaningfully discuss prejudices based on race, and the power factor that accompanies racial prejudices, then we must talk of racism and its related painful and negative conditions. This talk must include the history of racism and its colonial construction, because to attribute the problems of racism and its inherent tensions and conflicts to our individual experiences with cultural differences is to misrepresent difference. Difference is not what contributes to tension and conflict in diverse settings; rather, it is the value, understanding, and interpretations of difference and how we, in turn, use these to inform our actions that lead to conflict.

I can only hope that the issues discussed in this text have brought into focus many of the issues that must be discussed if we are to move to a more equitable society. It is time for a more critical approach to education, for the current multicultural and cross-cultural approaches have not helped to alleviate the social and educational problems we experience today. The issues we currently identify as being rooted in cultural differences— due to a large minority population mainly consisting of "immigrants,"— will remain beyond the first decade of this millennium. As time goes on, many more members of racial minorities will be born, socialized, and will reach adulthood here. According to the 2006 Census, one-sixth of Canada's population consisted of racial minorities (CBC News 2008). Most estimates suggest that in just a few years the racial minority population will be well over 20 percent of the total Canadian population. Already racial minorities make up over 40 percent of Toronto's population, and more than one-quarter of the city's racial minority population was born in Canada (Canadian Press 2008b).

We must equip ourselves to work and live in a multiracial and multicultural society where social justice and equity are actively sought:

○ It is appropriate and important to begin with our education system. Curricula and materials must reflect our diverse population and present all groups as Canadian. We must rid education of its largely Eurocentric approach and include the contributions that all groups have made to the historical, political, economic, social, and cultural development of Canada today. We must strive to inculcate in students the critical thinking and analytical skills that are necessary for living in a diverse society.

○ We need to commit to "knowing" our identities or selves, as knowing and understanding ourselves is an important part of the process of coming to understand others. We must recognize that we are all cultural, racial, and ethnic beings (just as we are gendered, classed, sexual, and ability beings); we produce and reproduce culture, and are affected by culture. As Canadians, the "differences" between us are based on interpretations related to our various social locations in society and the social conditions under which we exist.

○ Racism and discrimination, as social mechanisms that are rooted in our Canadian history, must be acknowledged and addressed directly. We are all affected by them. Issues and situations that are racist and discriminatory must be explicitly identified as such. These issues and events must be named. We need to use language that allows us to act together while recognizing each other's individuality.

○ With the appropriate awareness, knowledge, skills, and language, we must proceed to engage in advocacy and action for social change. Engaging in social change activities means accepting that we all have varying degrees and sources of power. When combined, they can be used to transform the system that provides advantages or privileges to some and disadvantages to others.

○ Both self-discovery and social awareness are necessary if we are to gain an understanding of each other. Only then can we work toward building a society where all members have equal opportunity and access.

Abbott, J. 2006. *Report of Meetings with Representatives of the Indo-Canadian Community.* Ottawa: Citizenship and Immigration Canada. www.cic.gc.ca/multi/publctn/ichr/indo-eng. asp.

ACLU (American Civil Liberties Union). 2010. "Urge Congress to Stop Racial Profiling." https://secure.aclu.org/site/Advocacy?id=113 (retrieved February 18, 2010).

Abella, R. 1984. *Equality in Employment: A Royal Commission Report.* Ottawa: Ministry of Supply and Services.

Abraham, C. 2005. "The New Science of Race." *Globe and Mail.* June 20. F1.

Adams, M. 2008. "Is Multiculturalism Really Keeping Canadians Apart?" *Toronto Star.* July 1. AA6.

Adler, P. S. 1977. "Beyond Cultural Identity: Reflections Upon Cultural and Multicultural Man." In R. W. Brislin (ed). *Cultural Learning.* Honolulu: East-West Center.

Agocs, C. 1987. "Ethnic Group Relations." In J. J. Teevan (ed). *Basic Sociology.* Scarborough: Prentice-Hall.

Akwani, Obi. 2006. "Racism Against Blacks Is a Growing Trend in Europe." *IMDiversity.com: Global News Digest.* www.imdiversity.com/villages/global/civil_human_equal_rights/RacismagainstBlacksinEurope.asp.

Alarie, S. 2003a. "Je veux pas de trous dans les murs—le proprio; retour au dossier." Canoë—Général. September 6. www2.canoe.com/cgi-bin/imprimer.cgi?id=121491 (retrieved September 22, 2009).

———. 2003b. "Sept jours dans la peau d'un Noir." *Journal de Montréal.* October 10.

Anisef, P. 1975. "Consequences of Ethnicity for Educational Plans Among Grade 12 Students." In A. Wolgang (ed). *Education of Immigrant Students: Issues and Answers.* Toronto: Ontario Institute for Studies in Education. 122–36.

Anisef, P. et al. 2000. *Opportunity and Uncertainty: Life Course Experiences of the Class of '73.* Toronto: University of Toronto Press.

Anisef, P., and M. Lamphier. 2003. *The World in a City: Settlement and Integration of Immigrants in the Greater Metropolitan Area.* Toronto: University of Toronto Press.

Apple, M. (ed). 2003. *The State and the Politics of Knowledge.* New York: Routledge.

Armstrong, J. 2009. "In Vancouver, dozens of boat migrants await their fate." *Globe and Mail.* October 18.

Armstrong, J., and J. Ibbitson. 2009. "Seeking a safe haven, finding a closed door." *Globe and Mail.* October 20.

Avison, W. R., and J. Kunkel. 1987. "Socialization." In J. J. Teevan (ed). *Basic Sociology.* Scarborough: Prentice-Hall. 49–79.

Bagnall, J. 2004. "Citizen of Convenience? So What?" *Montreal Gazette.* April 23. A23.

Bakht, N. 2005. "Arbitration, Religion and Family Law: Private Justice on the Backs of Women." Ottawa: National Association of Women and the Law.

Bamshad, M. J. and S. E. Olson. 2003. "Does race exist?" *Scientific American.* December. 78–85.

Bannerji, H. 2000. *The Dark Side of the Nation: Essays on Multiculturalism, Nationalism, and Gender.* Toronto: Canadian Scholars' Press.

Barlund, D. C. 1988. "Communication in a Global Village." In L. A. Samovar and R. E. Porter (eds). *Intercultural Communication: A Reader.* New York: Wadsworth.

Barnhill, D. L. (ed). 1999. *At Home on the Earth: Becoming Native to Our Place.* Berkeley: University of California Press.

Bauder, H. and B. Sharpe. 2002. "Residential Segregation of Visible Minorities in Canada's Gateway Cities." *Canadian Geographer* 46(3): 204–222.

Bell, S., M. Morrow, and E. Tastsoglou. 1999. "Teaching in Environments of Resistance: Toward a Critical, Feminist, and Antiracist Pedagogy." In M. Mayberry and E. C. Rose (eds). *Meeting the Challenge: Innovative Feminist Pedagogies in Action.* New York: Routledge. 23–46.

Benhabib, S. 2002. *The Claims of Culture: Equity and Diversity in the Global Era.* Princeton: Princeton University Press.

Benzie, R. 2008. "MPPs to Hear Lord's Prayer and Many Others." *Toronto Star.* June 13. A1.

Berger, T. 1987. "The Banished Japanese Canadians." In L. Dreidger (ed). *Ethnic Identities and Inequalities.* Toronto: Copp Clark Pitman Ltd. 374–394.

Bideke, M., and M. Bideke. 2007. "Racism in Sweden." *ENAR Shadow Report.* European Network Against Racism. www.enar-eu.org.

Biles, J., and H. Ibrahim. 2005. "Religion and Public Policy: Immigration, Citizenship and Multiculturalism—Guess Who's Coming for Dinner." In P. Bramadat and D. Seljak (eds). *Religion and Ethnicity in Canada.* Toronto: Pearson Education Canada. 154–177.

Blatchford, C. 2004. "Judge Lashes Police for Racial Profiling." *Globe and Mail.* September 17. A1.

Bolaria, B. S., and P. Li (eds). 1988. *Racial Oppression in Canada.* Toronto: Garamond Press.

Bouchard, G., and C. Taylor. 2008a. *Building the Future: A Time for Reconciliation, Abridged Report.* Commission de Consultation Sur Les Pratiques D'Accommodement Reliees Aux Differences Culturelles. Gouvernement du Québec.

Brennan, R. 2008. "Immigration Changes Pose Risk Critics Say." *Toronto Star.* March 15. A19.

Brown, L. 2008. "Yes to Black-Focused School." *Toronto Star.* January 30. A1.

Brydon, D. 2008. "Negotiating Citizenship in Global Times: the Hérouxville Debates." Paper presented at Voice and Vision: Situating Canadian Culture Globally. International Colloquium. Centre d'Etudes Canadiennes Sorbonne Nouvelle, Paris. May.

Bunar, N. 2007. "Hate Crimes against Immigrants in Sweden and Community Responses." *American Behavioral Scientist.* 51(2): 166–181.

Burnet, J. 1984. "Myths and Multiculturalism." In R. J. Samuda, J. W. Berry, and M. Laferriere (eds). *Multiculturalism in Canada: Social and Educational Perspectives.* Toronto: Allyn and Bacon, Inc.

Calliste, A. 1994. "Race, Gender and Canadian Immigration Policy: Blacks from the Caribbean, 1900–1932." *Journal of Canadian Studies.* 28(4): 131–147.

Campbell, N. D. 2009. *"She tries her tongue:" A Case for Interrupting Homophobia and Heterosexism in Black Communities in Canada.* Unpublished paper. York University, Faculty of Education.

Campion-Smith, B. 2008. "Immigration Proposal 'Dangerous:' Arab Group." *Toronto Star.* March 29. A27.

Canadian Press. 2008a. "Dubious Moves on Immigration." *Toronto Star.* March 17. AA6.

————. 2008b. "Almost Half of Torontonians Visible Minorities." CBC News. April 2. www. cbc.ca/canada/toronto/story/2008/04/02/census-toronto.html.

Carnegie, H. H. 1997. *A Fly in a Pail of Milk: The Herb Carnegie Story.* Oakville, ON: Mosaic Press.

Carr, P., and D. Lund. (eds.). 2007. *The Great White North? Exploring Whiteness, Privilege and Identity in Education.* Rotterdam: Sense Publishers.

Carroll, M. P. 1993. "Culture." In J. J. Teevan (ed.). *Basic Sociology: A Canadian Introduction.* Scarborough: Prentice-Hall Canada Inc. 23–53.

Castles, S. 2000. "International Migration at the Beginning of the Twenty-First Century: Global Trends and Issues." *International Social Science Journal.* 52: 277–281.

CBC News. 2009. "As Many 'Lost Canadians' Gain Citizenship, Others Are Left in Limbo: Children Born Abroad to Canadian Parents or Adopted Abroad May Lose Rights." April 17. www.cbc.ca/canada/story/2009/04/16/lost-canadians.html.

————. 2008. "1 in 6 Canadians is a Visible Minority: StatsCan. South Asians Top Chinese as Largest Visible Minority Group." April 2. www.cbc.ca/canada/story/2008/04/02/stats-immigration.html.

CERA. 2009. *"Sorry, It's Rented:" Measuring Discrimination in Toronto's Rental Housing Market.* Toronto: Centre for Equality Rights in Accommodation.

Church, E. 2008. "Nearly Half of PhDs in Canada Are Immigrants: Census." *Globe and Mail.* March 4. A1.

Citizenship and Immigration Canada. 2009. Ministry website. www.cic.gc.ca. Ottawa: Citizenship and Immigration Canada.

Clairmont, D. H., and D. W. Magill. 1999. *Africville: The Life and Death of a Canadian Black Community*. Toronto: Canadian Scholars' Press.

Clarke, G. E. 1998. "White Like Canada." *Transition*. 73: 98–109.

Commission on Systemic Racism in the Ontario Criminal Justice System. 1995. *Report of the Commission on Systemic Racism in the Ontario Criminal Justice System: A Community Summary*. Toronto: Government of Ontario.

Conway, J. K. 1999. *When Memory Speaks: Exploring the Art of Autobiography*. New York: Random House.

Crampton, T. 2005. "Behind the Furor, the Last Moments of Two Youths." *New York Times*. November 7. www.nytimes.com.

Crow, M., and C. Maclean. 2000. "Community." In G. Payne (ed). *Social Divisions*. Basingstoke: Macmillan. 223–241

CTV. 2005. "Quebec Radio shrink sparks complaints of racism," September 29. www.ctv.ca/servlet/ArticleNews/story/CTVNews/20050928/mailloux_defends_050928/20050928.

D. A., Adebe. 2008. "In the Mix: Race, Identification and Diversity." *Excalibur: York University Community Newspaper*. February 1. 5. www.excal.on.ca.

D'Addario, S., J. Kowalski, M. Lemoine, and V. Preston. 2008. "Finding Home: Exploring Muslim Settlement in the Toronto CMA." *CERIS Working Paper #68*. 1–26.

Dalrymple, T. 2007. *In Praise of Prejudice: The Necessity of Preconceived Ideas*. New York: Encounter Books.

Dauvergne, M., K. Scrim, and S. Brennan. 2008. *Hate Crime in Canada 2006*. Canadian Centre for Justice Statistics Profile Series. Cat No. 85F0033M, No. 17. Ottawa: Statistics Canada.

Davis, F. J. 1991. *Who Is Black? One Nation's Definition*. Philadelphia: Penn State University Press.

Dei, G. S., and A. Calliste (eds). 2000. *Power, Knowledge and Anti-racism Education*. Halifax: Fernwood Publishing.

Del Gobbo, D. 2009. "The SCC's distressing decision in *Alberta v Hutterian Brethren*; mandating photographic driver's licences." *The Court*. July 29. www.thecourt.ca/2009/07/29/snapshot-of-a-distressing-result-in-alberta-v-hutterian-brethren (retrieved October 10, 2009).

Deshaw, R. 2006. "History of Family Reunification in Canada and Current Policy." *Canadian Issues: Immigration and Families*. Spring: 9–16.

DeWolf, C. 2004. "Keeping Up with the Dosanjhs: The Rise of North America's Ethnoburbs." *Cultures Canada*. October 25. www.culturescanada.ca (retrieved March 1, 2006).

diCarlo, C. 2006. "We are all African: Four words that can change the world." *Humanist Perspectives*. 39(156): 10–16.

Dion, S. 2002. "Braiding Histories: Responding to the Problematics of Canadians Hearing First Nations' Post-contact Experiences." Unpublished doctoral dissertation. Ontario Institute for Studies in Education.

Dobbins, J. E., and J. H. Skillings. 1991. "The Utility of Race Labelling in Understanding Cultural Identity: A Conceptual Tool for the Social Science Practitioner." *Journal of Counseling and Development*. 70(1): 37–44.

Dominguez, V. R. 1994. "A Taste for 'the Other.'" *Current Anthropology*. 35(4). 333–338.

Driedger, L. 1989. *The Ethnic Factor: Identity in Diversity*. Toronto: McGraw-Hill Ryerson Ltd.

Dua, E. 2009. "On the Effectiveness of Anti-Racist Policies in Canadian Universities: Issues of Implementation of Policies by Senior Administration." In F. Henry and C. Tator (eds). *Racism in the Canadian University: Demanding Social Justice, Inclusion and Equity*. Toronto: University of Toronto Press. 160–195.

DuCharme, M. 1986. "The Canadian Origins of South Africa Apartheid?" *Perspectives*. Summer: 2.

Effron, D. A., J. S. Cameron, and B. Monin. 2009. "Endorsing Obama Licenses Favoring Whites." *Journal of Experimental Social Psychology*. 45(3): 590–593.

Elliott, J. L., and A. Fleras. 1992. *Unequal Relations: An Introduction to Race and Ethnic Dynamics in Canada*. Scarborough: Prentice-Hall Canada.

Employment and Immigration Canada. 1992b. *Managing Immigration: A Framework for the 1990s*. Ottawa: Public Affairs Branch, Ministry of Supply and Services.

Errande, A. 2000. "'But sometimes you've not part of the story:' Oral Histories and Ways of Remembering and Telling." *Educational Researcher*. 29(2): 16–27.

Essed, P. 1990. *Everyday Racism: Reports from Women of Two Cultures*. Claremont: Hunter House.

Fang, T. 2009. "Workplace Responses to Vacancies and Skill Shortages in Canada." *International Journal of Manpower*. 30(4): 326–348.

Ferber, A. L. 2007. "The Construction of Black Masculinity: White Supremacy Now and Then." *Journal of Sport and Social Issues*. 31(1): 11–24.

Fish, S. 1993. "Reverse Racism or How the Pot Got to Call the Kettle Black." *The Atlantic Monthly*. November: 132–36.

Fleras, A. 2008. "The Politics of Renaming: International Typologies, a Canadian Conundrum." Paper prepared for the Department of Justice, presented to the Metropolis Conference. April.

———. 2010. *Unequal Relations: An Introduction to Race and Ethnic Dynamics*, 6th ed. Toronto: Pearson Education Canada.

Fleras, A., and J. L. Elliott. 2002. *Engaging Diversity: Multiculturalism in Canada*, 2nd ed. Toronto: Nelson Thomson Learning.

———. 2003. *Unequal Relations: An Introduction to Race and Ethnic Dynamics in Canada*. 4th ed. Toronto: Prentice Hall.

———. 2007. *Unequal Relations: An Introduction to Race and Ethnic Dynamics in Canada*. 5th ed. Toronto: Pearson Education Canada.

Foster, C. 2005. *Where Race Does Not Matter: The New Spirit of Modernity*. Toronto: Penguin Canada.

Frankenberg, R. 1993. *White Women, Race Matters: The Social Construction of Whiteness*. Minneapolis: University of Minnesota Press.

Freeze, C. 2007. "Why U.S. Won't Remove Arar from No-fly List." *Globe and Mail*. October 20. A1.

Frejute-Rakauskiene, M. 2006. Contemporary Phenomenon of Racism and its Manifestations in Public Discourse. *Filosofija Sociologija*. (4): 13–19.

Frideres, J. S. 1993. *Native People in Canada: Contemporary Conflicts*. Scarborough: Prentice-Hall.

Friesen, J. 2005. "Blame Canada (for Multiculturalism)?" *Globe and Mail*. August 20. F8.

Galabuzi, G-E. 2001. *Canada's Creeping Economic Apartheid*. Toronto: Canadian Social Justice Foundation for Research and Education.

Gauthier, P. 1994. "Canada's Seniors." In C. McKie and K. Thompson. *Canadian Social Trends*. Vol. 2. Toronto: Thompson Educational Publishing.

Gereluk, D., and R. Race. 2007. "Multicultural Tensions in England, France and Canada: Contrasting Approaches and Consequences." *International Studies in Sociology of Education*. 17 (1/2): 113–129.

Gibney, M., R. E. Howard-Hassmann, J-M. Coicaud, and N. Steiner (eds). 2007. *The Age of Apology: Facing up to the Past*. Pittsburgh: University of Pennsylvania Press.

Gilroy, P. 1993. *The Black Atlantic: Modernity and Double Consciousness*. Cambridge: Harvard University Press.

Globe and Mail. 1989. "50 Years Ago." January 25. A15.

Globe and Mail. 2007. "Cracks in the Mosaic." News series. February.

Globe and Mail. 2008. "Don't Panic, Remain Seated." May 21. A16.

Go, J. 2007. "Colonialism (Neocolonialism)." In G. Ritzer (ed). *Blackwell Encyclopedia of Sociology Online*. Blackwell Publishing. www. sociologyencyclopedia.com/subscriber/ tocnode?id=g9781405124331_chunk_ g9781405124331_ss1-72.

Gotanda, N. 2000. "A Critique of 'Our Constitution is Color-blind.'" In R. Delgado and J. Stefancic (eds.). *Critical Race Theory: The Cutting Edge*. Philadelphia: Temple University Press. 35–38.

Gottshalk, P., and G. Greenberg. 2008. *Islamophobia: Making Muslims the Enemy*. Lanham, MD: Rowman and Littlefield Publishers, Inc.

Government of Canada. 1937. *Racial Origins and Nativity of the Canadian People*. Ottawa: Dominion Bureau of Statistics, King's Printer.

———. 1998. *Canadian Multiculturalism Act*. Ottawa: Queen's Printer.

Greenwald, B. (director). 1989. *Who Gets In?* Documentary film. Toronto: National Film Board of Canada.

Gregg, A. 2006. "Identity Crisis. Multiculturalism: A Twentieth-century Dream Becomes a Twenty-first-century Conundrum." *The Walrus*. March. 38–47.

Griffin, J. H. 1961. *Black Like Me*. New York: Houghton Mifflin.

Gross-Stein, J. 2005. "Image, Identity and the Resolution of Violent Conflict." In M. Evangelista (ed). Peace Studies: Critical

Concepts in Political Science. New York: Routledge. 364–389.

Gruneau, R., and D. Whitson. 1993. Hockey Night in Canada: Sport, Identities and Cultural Politics. Toronto: Garamond Press.

Haig-Brown, C. 1988. Resistance and Renewal: Surviving the Indian Residential School. Vancouver: Arsenal Pulp Press Ltd.

Hall, S. 1978. "Racism and Reaction." Five Views of Multi-racial Britain. London: London Commission for Racial Equality.

———. 1990. "Culture Identity and Disapora." In J. Rutherford (ed). Identity, Community, Culture and Difference. London: Lawrence Wishart.

———. 1996. "The Question of Cultural Identity." In S. Hall, D. Hubert, and K. Thompson (eds). Modernity: An Introduction to Modern Societies. Cambridge.: Blackwell Publishers. 595–634.

———. 2003. "The Whites of Their Eyes: Racist Ideologies and the Media." In G. Dines and J. M. Mumez (eds). Gender, Race, and Class in Media: A Text Reader. Thousand Oaks: Sage Publications. 89–93.

Hamilos, P. 2007. "The Worst Islamist Attack in European History." The Guardian. October 31.

Hanes, A. 2007. "Older Mothers Leading Miniboom: Statistics Canada; For First Time, More Babies Born to Women Over 30." National Post. September 22. A1.

Harney, R. F. 1978. Italians in Canada. Toronto: Multicultural History Society of Ontario.

Harris, C. I. 1993. "Whiteness as Property." Harvard Law Review. 106: 1707–1791.

Henry, F. 1978. The Dynamics of Racism in Toronto: Research Report. Toronto: York University.

Henry, F., and E. Ginzberg. 1985. Who Gets the Work: A Test of Racial Discrimination in Employment. Toronto: Social Planning Council.

Henry, F., and C. Tator. 2006a. The Colour of Democracy: Racism in Canadian Society, 3rd ed. Toronto: ITP Nelson.

———. 2006b. Racial Profiling: Challenging the Myth of a "Few Bad Apples." Toronto: University of Toronto Press.

Hepburn, B. 2007b. "What It Means to Be Canadian." Toronto Star. December 8. AA6

Hergesheimer, J. 2006. "Canada's Multiculturalism a Threat or Grace?" June 27. www.aljazeera.net.

Hier, S. 2007. "The Status of Research on Race and Racism in 21st Century Canada." In S. Hier and B. Singh Bolaria (eds.). Race & Racism in 21st Century Canada: Continuity, Complexity, and Change. Peterborough, ON: Broadview Press. 15–30.

Hill Collins, P. 1998. Fighting Words: Black Women and the Search for Justice. Minneapolis: University of Minnesota Press.

Hinchey, P. H. 2008. Finding Freedom in the Classroom: A Practical Introduction to Critical Theory. New York: Peter Lang.

Hirsi Ali, A. 2005. "Unfree Under Islam: Shariah Endangers Women's Rights, from Iraq to Canada." The Wall Street Journal. August 16. www.wsj.com.

Holt, T. 2002. The Problem of Race in the 21st Century. Cambridge: Harvard UP.

hooks, b. 2003. Teaching Community: A Pedagogy of Hope. New York: Routledge

Hoopes, D. S., and M. D. Pusch. 1981. "Definition of Terms." In M. Pusch (ed). Multicultural Education. Pittsburgh: Intercultural Network.

House of Commons Debates. 1947. Vol. 3, 2644–2647.

Howard, L. A. 2002. "From Ivory Tower to Town Hall: Using Dialogic Inquiry as a Critical Pedagogy." American Behavioral Scientist. 45(7): 1125–1134.

Hughes, D. R., and E. Kallen. 1974. The Anatomy of Racism: Canadian Dimension. Montreal: Harvest House.

Hunter, M. 2005. Race, Gender and the Politics of Skin Tone. New York: Routledge.

Jackson, A. 2002. Is Work Working for Workers of Colour? Research Paper #18. Toronto: Canadian Labour Congress.

Jackson, A. P., and F. B. Meadows. 1991. "Getting to the Bottom to Understand the Top." Journal of Counseling and Development. 70(1): 72–76.

Jacques, M. 2007. "Islamaphobia—The New Face of Racism." Asian News. February 15. www.theasiannews.co.uk/community/heritage/s/523/523551 (retrieved September 7).

Jakubowski, L. M. 1997. Immigration and the Legalization of Racism. Halifax: Fernwood Publishing.

James, C. E. 1990. Making It: Black Youth, Racism and Career Aspirations in a Big City. Oakville: Mosaic Press.

———. 1993. "Getting There and Staying There: Blacks' Employment Experience." In P. Anisef and P. Axelrod (eds). *Transitions: Schooling and Employment in Canada.* Toronto: Thompson Educational Publishing. 3–20.

———. 1997. "Contradictory Tensions in the Experiences of African Canadians in a Faculty of Education with an Access Program." *Canadian Journal of Education.* 22(2): 158–74.

———. 2001. "Making Teaching Relevant: Toward an Understanding of Students' Experiences in a Culturally 'Different' Sweden." *Pedagogy, Culture and Society.* 9(3): 407–426.

———. 2004. "Stereotyping and its Consequence for Racial Minority Youth." *Canadian Diversity/Diversité Canadienne.* 3(3): 40–42.

———. 2005. *Race in Play: Understanding the Socio-cultural Worlds of Student Athletes.* Toronto: Canadian Scholars' Press Inc.

———. 2007. "Who Can/Should Do this Work? The Colour of Critique." In P. Carr and D. Lund (eds). *The Great White North: Exploring Whiteness, Privilege, and Identity.* Rotterdam: Sense Publishers. 119–124.

———. 2008. "'Armed and dangerous'/'Known to police': Racializing Suspects." In B. Schissel and C. Brooks (eds). *Marginality and Condemnation: An Introduction to Criminology.* Halifax: Fernwood Publishing. 378–403.

James, C. E., and C. Haig-Brown. 2001. "'Returning the dues': Community and the Personal in a University/School Partnership." *Urban Education.* 36(3): 226–255.

James, C. E., D. Plaza, and C. Jansen. 1999. "Issues of Race in Employment Experiences of Caribbean Women in Toronto." *Canadian Women's Studies Journal.* 19(3): 129–133.

James, C. E., and A. Shadd (eds). 2001. *Talking About Identity: Encounters in Race, Ethnicity and Language.* Toronto: Between the Lines.

James, C. E., and M. Wood. 2005. "Multicultural Education in Canada: Opportunities, Limitations and Contradictions." In C. E. James (ed). *Possibilities and Limitations: Multicultural Policies and Programs in Canada.* Halifax: Fernwood Publishing. 93–107.

James, K. 2000. "A Letter to a Friend." In C. E. James (ed). *Experiencing Difference.* Halifax: Fernwood Publishing.

James, M. 2007. "Wrestling with the Past: Apologies, Quasi-apologies and Non-apologies in Canada." In M. Gibney, R. E. Howard-Hassmann, J-M. Coicaud, and N. Steiner (eds). *The Age of Apology: Facing up to the Past.* Pittsburgh: University of Pennsylvania Press. 137–153.

Jansen, C. J. 1981. "Problems and Issues in Post-war Immigration to Canada and their Effects on Origins and Characteristics of Immigrants." Paper presented at Meetings of The Canadian Population Society, Dalhousie University, Halifax.

———. 1988. *Italian in a Multicultural Canada.* Lewiston, NY: The Edwin Mellen Press.

———. 2005. Canadian Multiculturalism. In C.E. James (ed). *Possibilities and Limitations: Multicultural Policies and Programs in Canada.* Halifax: Fernwood Publishing. 32–33.

Jansen, C. J., and A. Richmond. 1990. "Immigrant Settlement and Integration." Paper presented at the Symposium for Immigrant Settlement and Integration, Toronto, May.

Jedwab, J. 2008. "Knowledge of History and National Identity in Quebec and the Rest of Canada." *Canadian Issues.* Fall: 7–13.

Jensen, R. 1998. "White Privilege Shapes the U.S." *Baltimore Sun.* July 19, 1998. C1.

Jiménez, M. 2007. "How Canadian Are You?" *Globe and Mail.* January 12. A1.

———. 2007. "Do Ethnic Enclaves Impede Integration?" *Globe and Mail.* February 8. A8.

———. 2008. "Immigrants Face Growing Economic Mobility Gap." *Globe and Mail.* October 6. A1.

Jones, S. 2006. *Antonio Gramsci.* London and New York: Routledge Taylor and Francis Group.

Kagawa-Singer, M., and R. C. Chung. 1994. "A Paradigm for Culturally-based Care in Ethnic Minority Population." *Journal of Community Psychology.* 22: 192–208.

Kalbach, W. E., and W. W. McVey. 1971. *The Demographic Bases of Canadian Society.* Toronto: McGraw-Hill Co., Ltd.

Kallen, E. 1995. *Ethnicity and Human Rights in Canada.* 2nd ed. Toronto: Oxford University Press.

———. 2003. *Ethnicity and Human Rights in Canada: A Human Rights Perspective on Ethnicity, Racism and Systemic Inequality.* 3rd ed. Toronto: Oxford University Press.

Kari, S. 2009. "Veiled Testimony of Ontario Woman left to Judges' Individual Discretion." *National Post.* May 1. www.canada.com/story_print.html?id=1554194&sponsor=.

Kawakami, K., E. Dunn, F. Karmali, and J. Dovidio. 2009. "Mispredicting Affective and Behavioral Responses to Racism." *Science.* 323(5911): 276–278.

Kelley, N., and M. Trebilcock. 1998. *The Making of the Mosaic: A History of Canadian Immigration.* Toronto: University of Toronto Press.

Kendall, F. E. 2006. *Understanding White Privilege: Creating Pathways to Authentic Relationships Across Race.* New York: Taylor and Frances Group.

Keung, N. 2006. "Our Immigrant Youth on Right Track, Study: Research Finds Canadian Approach Yields Best Results." *Toronto Star.* December 9. L7.

Kinloch, G. C. 1974. *The Dynamics of Race Relations: A Sociological Analysis.* Toronto: McGraw-Hill.

Kobayashi, A., and L. Peake. 2000. "Racism Out of Place: Thoughts on Whiteness and an Antiracist Geography in the New Millennium." *Annals of the Association of American Geographers.* 90(2): 392–403.

Kohli, R. 2009. "Critical Race Reflections: Valuing the Experience of Teachers of Color in Teacher Education." *Race, Ethnicity and Education.* 12 (2): 235-251.

Kondo, D. K. 1990. *Crafting Selves: Power, Gender, and Discourses of Identity in a Japanese Workplace.* Chicago: University of Chicago Press.

Korgen, K., and E. O'Brien. 2006. "What's Race Got to Do With it? Close Black/White Friendships in a 'Color-Blind' Society." In D. L. Brunsma (ed). *Negotiating the Color Line: Doing Race in the Color-Blind Era and Implications for Racial Justice.* Boulder: Lynne Rienner Publications.

Krywulak, T., and A. Sisco. 2008. *Report: The Value of Diverse Leadership.* Ottawa: The Conference Board of Canada.

Kumar, S., and B. Leung. 2005. "Formation of an Ethnic Enclave: Process and Motivations." *Plan Canada.* June.

Kumi, P. 2008. "Lessons from 'Ghetto Dude' Affair." *Toronto Star.* January 22. www.thestar.com/article/296054.

Laing, L. 2006. "Black and White Twins." *Daily Mail Online* (UK). February 21. www.dailymail.co.uk/news/article-377839/Black-white-twins.html.

Lal, B. B. 2001. "Learning to Do Ethnic Identity: Transracial/Transethnic Adoptive Family as Site and Context." In D. Parker

and M. Song (eds), *Rethinking "Mixed Race."* London: Pluto Press. 154–172.

Lalande, J. 2006. "The Roots of Multiculturalism—Ukrainian-Canadian Involvement in the Multiculturalism Discussion of the 1960s as an Example of the Position of the 'Third Force.'" *Canadian Ethnic Studies.* XXXVIII(1): 7–64.

Lam, L. 1994. "Immigrant Students." In P. Anisef (ed). *Learning and Sociological Profiles of Canadian High School Students.* Queenston: Edwin Mellen Press. 121–130.

Larter, S., M. Cheng, S. Capps, and M. Lee. 1982. *Post-Secondary Plans of Grade Eight Students and Related Variables.* Toronto: The Board of Education for the City of Toronto. 165.

Law Union of Ontario. 1981. *The Immigrant's Handbook.* Montreal: Black Rose Books.

Lazarro, J. 1996. *Beyond Whiteness of Whiteness: Memoir of a White Mother of Black Sons.* Durham: Duke University Press.

Lee, J. 2006. "International Student Experiences of Neo-racism and Discrimination." *International Higher Education.* (44): 3–5.

Lee, J., and J. Lutz (eds). 2005. *Situating "Race" and Racisms in Space, Time, and Theory: Critical Essays for Activists and Scholars.* Kingston, ON: McGill-Queen's University Press.

Lee, S. J. 2005. *Up Against Whiteness: Race, School, and Immigrant Youth.* New York: Teachers College Press.

Leger Marketing. 2007. *Sun Media: Racial Tolerance Report.* www.legermarketing.com/documents/spclm/070119ENG.pdf.

Lenk, H. M. 2000. "The Case of Émile Ouimet: News Discourse on Hijab and the Construction of Québécois National Identity." In A. Calliste and G. S. Dei (eds). *Anti-racist Feminism: Critical Race and Gender Studies.* Halifax: Fernwood Publishing. 73–90.

Leslie, K. 2005. "McGuinty Rejects Ontario's Use of Shariah Law and All Religious Arbitrations." Canadian Press. September 11. www.canadianpress.com.

Leung, R. 2005. "Born In USA; Adopted In Canada: Lesley Stahl Reports On Controversial New Trend In Adoptions." CBS News. February 13. http://www.cbsnews.com/stories/2005/02/11/60minutes/main673597.shtml.

Lewontin, R. 2002. "A Question of Biology: Are the Races Different?" In E. Lee, D. Menkart, and M. Okazawa-Rey (eds.).

Beyond Heroes and Holidays: A Practical Guide to K–12 Anti-racist, Multicultural Education and Staff Development. Washington: Network of Educators on the Americas. 316–320.

Li, P. S. (ed). 1990. *Race and Ethnic Relations in Canada.* Toronto: Oxford University Press.

———. 2000. "The Racial Subtext in Canada's Immigration Discourse." University of Saskatchewan and Prairie Centre of Excellence for Research on Immigration and Integration.

———. 2003. "Deconstructing Canada's Discourse of Immigrant Integration." *Journal of International Migration and Integration.* 4(3): 315–333.

Logan, R. 1991. "Immigration during the 80s." *Canadian Social Trends*. Ottawa: Statistics Canada. 9–13.

London Assembly. 2006. "Report of the 7 July Review Committee." Greater London Authority. www.london.gov.uk.

Lull, J. 1995. "Hegemony." In G. Dines and J. M. Mumez (eds). *Gender, Race, and Class in Media: A Text Reader.* Thousand Oaks: Sage Publications. 61–66.

Lum, L. 2006. "Internationally-educated Health Professionals: A Distance Education Multiple Cultures Model." *Education & Training*. 48(213): 112–126.

Mahtani, M. 2002. Interrogating the Hyphen-nation: Canadian Multicultural Policy and 'Mixed-race' Identities. *Social Identities*. 8(1): 67–90.

Makin, K. 2003. "Court Grants Blacks Special Sentencing." *Globe and Mail*. February 13. A1.

Malla, P. 2008. "Self-Portrait of a Racist." *Globe and Mail*. March 22. M1, M4.

Martel, L., and E. Caron-Malefant. 2006. *Portrait of the Canadian Population in 2006.* Ottawa: Statistics Canada.

Martin, J. R. 1994. "Methodological Essentialism, False Difference, and Other Dangerous Traps." *Signs: Journal of Women in Culture and Society*. 19(3): 630–657.

Martin, N. 2008. "Acting White/Acting Black is Still an Issue." *Excalibur.* February. 7.

Mayor of London. 2003. *Towards a Vision of Excellence: London Schools and the Black Child—2002 Conference Report.* London: Greater London Authority. www.london.gov.uk.

McDermott, R., and H. Varenne. 2006. "Reconstructing Culture in Educational Research." In G. Spindler and L. Hammond (eds). *Innovations in Educational Ethnography: Theories, Methods and Results*. New York: Routledge.

McIntosh, P. 1995. "White Privilege and Male Privilege: A Personal Account of Coming to See Correspondences Through Work in Women's Studies." In M. L. Andersen and P. Hill Collins (eds). *Race, Class and Gender: An Anthology*. Belmont: Wadsworth. 70–81.

Michaels, W. B. 2006. *The Trouble with Diversity: How We Learned to Love Identity and Ignore Inequality.* New York: Metropolitan Books.

Mills, C. W. 1956. *The Power Elite.* New York: Oxford University Press.

Miner, H. 1956. "Body Rituals Among the Nacirema." *American Anthropologist*. 58.

Ministry of Employment and Immigration. 1978. *New Directions: A Look at Canada's Immigration Act and Regulations*. Ottawa: Ministry of Supply and Services.

Mock, K. 1996. "Anti-Semitism in Canada: Realities, Remedies and Implications for Anti-Racism." In C. E. James (ed). *Perspectives on Racism and the Human Services Sector: A Case for Change.* Toronto: University of Toronto Press. 120–133.

Modood, T. 2007. *Multiculturalism: A Civic Idea.* Cambridge: Polity Press.

Montreal Gazette. 2007. "Ridiculous Ruling." Editorial. February 27. A20.

Montreal Gazette. 2007. "Hijab and Soccer: Another Red Card." November 26. A12.

Monture-Angus, P. 1995. *Thunder in My Soul: A Mohawk Woman Speaks.* Halifax: Fernwood Publishing.

Moore, D. 2007a. "Accommodation Hearings Mostly Civil, Spokesman Says." *Globe and Mail*. November 26. A19.

———. 2007b. "Quebec Town Bans Kirpans, Stoning Women." *Globe and Mail*. January 30. A12.

Municipalité de Hérouxville. 2007. "Publication of Standards." 2007. Municipalité de Hérouxville, Québec. http://municipalite. herouxville.qc.ca.

Myrie, E. 2009. "Housing Discrimination Must be Fought." *Hamilton Spectator.* September 10. www.thespec.com/article/631859.

National Post. 2007. "Muslim Woman Takes Uniform Complaint to Human Rights Commission." November 20. A1, A11.

Nayar, K. 2004. *The Sikh Diaspora in Vancouver.* Toronto: University of Toronto Press.

Ng, R. 1993. "Racism, Sexism, and Nation Building in Canada." In C. McCarthy and W. Chrichlow (eds). *Race, Identity and Representation in Education.* New York: Routledge. 50–59.

Nieoczym, A. 2007. "Jamaican Workers Arrive in Okanagan." *Kelowna Capital News.* September 23. A4–A5.

Offman, C. 2008. "The Nasty Side of Fishing." *National Post.* May 14. A3.

Omi, M., and H. Winant. 1993. "On the Theoretical Status of the Concept of Race." In C. McCarthy and W. Crichlow (eds). *Race, Identity and Representation in Education.* New York: Routledge. 3–10.

Ontario Human Rights Commission. 2003. *Paying the Price: The Human Cost of Racial Profiling.* Toronto.

Oreopoulos, P. 2009. "Why Do Skilled Immigrants Struggle in the Labour Market? A Field Study with Six Thousand Resumés." Paper presented at the Coming and Goings Conference, Ottawa Research Data Centre. May.

Palmer, H. 1975. *Immigration and the Rise of Multiculturalism.* Vancouver: Copp Clark.

Paradies, Y. 2006. "A Systematic Review of Empirical Research on Self-reported Racism and Health." *International Journal of Epidemiology.* 1–14.

Parker, D. and M. Song (eds). 2001. "Introduction." *Rethinking Mixed Race.* London: Pluto Press. 1–22.

Paul, A. M. 1998. "Where Bias Begins: The Truth About Stereotypes." *Psychology Today.* May/June: 52–56.

Peritz, I. 2006. "Find Prayer Space, School Told." *Globe and Mail.* March 23. A13.

Phelan, T. J., and M. Scheider. 1996. "Race, Ethnicity, and Class in American Suburbs." *Urban Affairs Review.* 31(5): 659–680.

Phoenix, A. 1997. "'I'm White! So What?' The Construction of Whiteness for Young Londoners." In M. Fine, L. Weis, L. Powell, and L. M. Wong (eds). *Off White: Readings on Race, Power, and Society.* New York: Routledge. 187–97.

Philip, M. N. 1992. *Frontiers: Essays and Writings on Racism and Culture.* Stratford: Mercury.

Pitter, K. 2008. *Dark Days: The Story of Four Canadians Tortured in the Name of Fighting Terror.* Toronto: Penguin Canada.

Pon, G. 2000. "Beamers, Cells, Malls and Cantopop: Thinking Through the Geographies of Chineseness." In C. E. James (ed). *Experiencing Difference.* Halifax: Fernwood Publishing. 222–234.

Porter, J. 1965. *The Vertical Mosaic: An Analysis of Social Class and Power in Canada.* Toronto: University of Toronto Press.

Powell, B. 2009. "Order to Take Off Niqab Pits Law Against Religion." *Toronto Star.* February 2. A1.

Preskill, S. L., and R. S. Jacobvitz. 2001. *Stories of Teaching.* Upper Saddle River: Merrill Prentice Hall.

Preston V., and M. Wong. 2002. "Immigration and Canadian cities: Building inclusion." In C. Andrew, K. A. Graham, and S. D. Phillips (eds). *Research on Community Safety: From Enforcement and Prevention to Civic Engagement.* Toronto: Centre for Criminology, University of Toronto. 203–214.

Q Blog. 2008. "When Is Talking Sex Sensationalist?" December 12. www.cbc.ca.

Qadeer, M. 2003. *Ethnic Segregation in Toronto and the New Multiculturalism.* Centre for Urban and Community Studies. Research Bulletin No. 2.

Qadeer, M. and S. Kumar 2006. "Ethnic Enclaves and Social Cohesion." *Canadian Journal of Urban Research.* 15(2): 1–17.

Rattansi, A. 2005. "On Being and Not Being Brown/Black-British: Racism, Class, Sexuality and Ethnicity in Post-Imperial Britain (With Postscript 2004: The Politics of Longing and (Un)Belonging, Fear, and Loathing)." In J. Lee and J. Lutz (eds). 2005. *Situating "Race" and Racisms in Space, Time, and Theory: Critical Essays for Activists and Scholars.* Kingston: McGill-Queen's University Press. 46–76.

Reitz, J., R. Breton, K. Dion, and K. Dion. 2009. *Multiculturalism and Social Cohesion: Potentials and Challenges of Diversity.* New York: Springer.

Reitz, J. G., and N. Weiner. 2005. *Review of Employment Policies, Programs and Practices Designed to Achieve Employment Equity for Aboriginal Peoples and Visible Minorities.* Report prepared for the Labour Program. Ottawa: Human Resources and Skills Development Canada.

Rockquemore, K. A., T. Laszloffy, and J. Noveske. 2006. "It All Starts at Home: Racial Socialization in Multiracial Families." In D. Brunsma (ed). *Mixed Messages: Multiracial Identities in the "Color-blind" Era.* Boulder: Lynne Rienner Publishers. 203–216.

Rodriguez, R. 2002. *Brown: The Last Discovery of America*. New York: Viking Penguin.

Rosaldo, R. 1993. *Culture & Truth: The Remaking of Social Analysis*. Boston: Beacon Press.

Rosenberg, P. 1997. "Underground Discourses: Exploring Whiteness in Teacher Education." In M. Fine, L. Weis, L. C. Powell, and L. M. Wong (eds). *Off White: Readings on Race, Power, and Society*. New York: Routledge. 79–89.

Rubin, Z., and E. B. McNeil. 1987. *Psychology: Being Human*. New York: Harper and Row.

Salek, S. 2007. "BBC Delves Into Brazilians' Roots." *BBC News*. July 10. http://news.bbc.co.uk/2/hi/americas/6284806.stm.

Samuel, J. T. 1989. "Visible Minorities and Immigration." *Currents: Readings in Race Relations*. 5(2): 3–6.

Satzewich, V. 1991. "Social Stratification: Class and Racial Inequality." In B. S. Bolaria (ed). *Social Issues and Contradictions in Canadian Society*. Toronto: Harcourt Brace Jovanovich.

——— (ed). 1992. *Deconstructing a Nation: Immigration, Multiculturalism and Racism in 90s Canada*. Halifax: Fernwood Publishing.

———. 1998. *Racism and Social Inequality in Canada*. Toronto: Thompson Educational Publishing.

Saunders, D. 2007. "Why Our Thinking About Immigration Remains Borderline." *Globe and Mail*. November 3. F3.

Savage, L. 2006. "O Canada, Do We Stand on Guard for Thee? What Does the Government Owe Dual Citizens Who Live Elsewhere?" *Maclean's*. August 7. www.macleans.ca/article.jsp?content=20060814_131837_131837.

Scering, G. E. S. 1997. "Themes of a Critical/Feminist Pedagogy: Teacher Education for Democracy." *Journal of Teacher Education*. 48(1): 62–68.

Schecter, S. R., D. Sharken-Taboada, and R. Bayley. 1996. "Bilingual by Choice: Latino Parents' Rationales and Strategies for Raising Children with Two Languages." *The Bilingual Research Journal*. 20(2).

Schwalbe, M. 2005. *The Sociologically Examined Life: Pieces of the Conversation*. New York: McGraw Hill.

Scott, C. 2004. "Race and Black Faces." *Montreal Mirror*. March 4–10. 19(37). www.montrealmirror.com (retrieved March 9, 2008).

Shepard, R. B. 1997. *Deemed Unsuitable: Blacks from Oklahoma move to the Canadian Prairies in Search of Equality in the Early 20th Century Only to Find Racism in Their New Home*. Toronto: Umbrella Press.

Shephard, M. 2007. "New Security Certificate Law to Be Unveiled Today." *Toronto Star*. October 22. A15.

———. 2009. "Almost Home." *Toronto Star*. August 15. A1.

Shrage, L. 1997. "Passing Beyond the Other Race or Sex." In N. Zack (ed). *Race/Sex: Their Sameness, Difference and Interplay*. New York: Routledge. 183–90.

Siddiqui, H. 2008. "Political Messages in Census Data." *Toronto Star*. April 10. AA6.

Silvera, M. 1984. *Silenced: Talks with Working Class West Indian Women About Their Lives and Struggles as Domestic Workers in Canada*. Toronto: Sister Vision Press.

Simich, L., M. Beiser, M. Stewart, and E. Mwakarimba. 2005. "Providing Social Support for Immigrants and Refugees in Canada: Challenges and Directions." *Journal of Immigrant Health*. 7(4): 259–268.

Simpson, J. S., A. Causey, and L. Williams. 2007. "'I Would Want You to Understand It:' Students' Perspectives on Addressing Race in the Classroom." *Journal of Intercultural Communication Research*. 36(1): 33–50.

Sleeter, C. 1994. "White Racism." *Multicultural Education*. Spring.

Sleeter, C. E., and D. B. Delgado. 2004. "Critical Race Theory, and Antiracist Education: Implications for Multicultural Education." In J. A. Banks and C. A. McGee Banks (eds). *Handbook of Research on Multicultural Education*. San Francisco: John Wiley and Sons. 240–258.

Small, P. 2003. "Police Union Sues *Star* Over Race-Crime Series." *Toronto Star*. January 18. A6.

Smardz Frost, K. 2006. "The Birth of Black History Month." *Heritage Matters*. Vol. 4, Issue 1. 17

Smith, E. J. 1991. "Ethnic Identity Development: Toward the Development of a Theory Within the Context of Minority/Majority Status." *Journal of Counselling and Development*. 70(1): 181–188.

Smolicz, J. J. 1981. "Culture, Ethnicity and Education: Multiculturalism in a Plural Society." In *World Yearbook of Education (1981): Education of Minorities*. London: Kegan Page Ltd.

Solomon, P. R. 1997. Race, Role Modelling, and Representation in Teacher Education and

Teaching. *Canadian Journal of Education.* 22(4): 395–410.

Spice, B. 2002. "Genetics and Race: Researchers Explore Why Rates of Diseases Vary from One Population to Another." *Pittsburgh Post-Gazette.* www.postgazette.com/healthscience, May 7.

Spivey, M. 1998. "Identity Politics of a Southern Tribe: A Critical Ethnography." Unpublished doctoral dissertation. Toronto: York University, Department of Sociology.

Springer, J., T. Roswell, and J. Lum. 2007. "Pathways to Homelessness Among Caribbean Youth Aged 15–25 in Toronto." *Policy Matters.* CERIS. 30: 1–12.

St. Lewis, J. 1996. "Race, Racism, and the Justice System." In C. E. James (ed). *Perspectives on Racism and the Human Service Sector: A Case for Change.* Toronto: University of Toronto Press. 104–119.

Standing Committee on Multiculturalism. 1987. *Multiculturalism: Building the Canadian Mosaic.* Ottawa: Supply and Services Canada.

Statistics Canada. 2007a. *The Canadian Immigrant Labour Market in 2006: First Results From Canada's Labour Force Survey.* Cat. No. 71-606-XIE. Ottawa: Statistics Canada.

———. 2007b. *Immigration in Canada: A Portrait of the Foreign-born Population, 2006 Census.* Cat. No. 97-557-XIE. Ottawa: Statistics Canada.

———. 2008a. "Canada's Changing Labour Force. 2006 Census: The Provinces and Territories." *2006 Census Analysis Series.* Ottawa: Statistics Canada. www12.statcan.ca/english/census06/analysis/labour/ov-cclf-27.cfm.

———. 2008b. "Canada's Population Estimates." *The Daily.* December 19. Ottawa: Statistics Canada. www.statcan.gc.ca/daily-quotidien/081219/dq081219b-eng.htm.

———. 2008c. *Earnings and Incomes of Canadians Over the Past Quarter Century.* Cat. No. 97-563-X. Ottawa: Statistics Canada.

———. 2008d. "Report on 2006 Census: Earnings, Income and Shelter Costs." *The Daily.* May 1. Ottawa: Statistics Canada.

Supreme Court of Canada. 2009. *Alberta v Hutterian Brethren of Wilson Colony.* 2009 SCC 37.

July 24, docket 32186. http://csc.lexum.umontreal.ca/en/2009/2009scc37/2009scc37.html (retrieved October 8, 2009).

Sweet, L. 2005. "Accommodating Religious Difference: The Canadian Experience." In

C. E. James (ed). *Possibilities and Limitations: Multicultural Policies and Programs in Canada.* Halifax: Fernwood Publishing. 130–153.

Szepesi, K. 2001. "I Want to Call Myself Canadian." In C. E. James and A. Shadd (eds). *Talking About Identity: Encounters in Race, Ethnicity, and Language.* Toronto: Between the Lines. 33–34.

Taylor, D. n.d. "Environmental Racism." *Pollution Issues.* www.pollutionissues.com.

Taylor, D. M. 1981. "Stereotypes and Intergroup Relations." In R. Gardner and R. Kalin (eds). *A Canadian Social Psychology of Ethnic Relations.* Toronto: Methuen. 151–71.

Taylor, L. 2000. "Black, White, Beige, Other? Memories of Growing up Different." In C. E. James (ed). *Experiencing Differences.* Halifax: Fernwood Publishing. 59–70.

———. 2008. "Looking North: Exploring Multiracial Experiences in a Canadian Context." In K. A. Renn and P. Shang (eds). *Biracial and Multiracial Students.* (123): 83–91. San Francisco: Jossey-Bass.

Taylor, L., C. E. James, and R. Saul. 2007. "Who Belongs: Exploring Race and Racialization in Canada." In G. F. Johnson and R. Enomoto (eds). *Race, Racialization and Antiracism in Canada and Beyond.* Toronto: University of Toronto Press. 151–178.

Taylor, L. C. 2008a. "Degrees Don't Ensure Jobs for Female Immigrants." *Toronto Star.* July 19. A19.

———. 2008b. "Immigrants Sought to Fill Vacancies in Food Industry; Work Permits Seen as Way to Ease Ontario Shortage." *Toronto Star.* October 29. A20.

———. 2009. "Racism in Canada: Darker the Skin, Less You Fit." *Toronto Star.* May 14. www.thestar.com/news/gta/article/634117.

Taylor, L. C., and N. Keung. 2008. "New Criteria Alarm Immigrants: Radical Changes to Immigration Process Are Dangerous, Say Some Educated Newcomers." *Toronto Star.* October 24. A17.

Taylor, T. R., et al. 2007. "Racial Discrimination and Breast Cancer Incidence in US Black Women: The Black Women's Health Study." *American Journal of Epidemiology.* 166(1): 46–54.

Thiederman, S. 1992. *Profiting in America's Multicultural Marketplace.* Lanham: Lexington Books.

Thobani, S. 2007. *Exalted Subjects: Studies in the Making of Race and Nation in Canada.* Toronto: University of Toronto Press.

Tilley, S. 2000. "Provincially Speaking: You Don't Sound like a Newfoundlander." In C. E. James (ed). *Experiencing Difference.* Halifax: Fernwood Publishing. 89–98.

———. 2006. "Multicultural Practices in Educational Contexts: Addressing Diversity and the Silence Around Race." In D. Zinga (ed). *Navigating Multiculturalism, Negotiating Change.* Newcastle: Cambridge Scholars Press. 142–159.

Todorov, T. 1993. *On Human Diversity: Nationalism, Racism, and Exoticism in French Thought.* Cambridge: Harvard University Press.

Toronto Star. 2002. "Singled Out: Star Analysis of Police Crime Data Shows Justice is Different for Blacks and Whites." October 19. A1.

Toronto Star. 2005. "The Way We'll Be: Visible Majority By 2017." March 23. A1.

Toronto Star. 2007a. "Diversity Defines Modern Canada." December 5. AA6.

Toronto Star. 2008a. "How It All Went Down." April 6. A9.

Toronto Star. 2008b. "Why the Apology Matters to Us All." Editorial. June 11. AA6.

Treasury Board of Canada Secretariat. 2009. *Employment Equity in the Public Service of Canada 2006–2007 and 2007–2008.* Ottawa: Treasury Board of Canada Secretariat. www.tbs-sct.gc.ca.

———. 2007. *Employment Equity in the Public Service of Canada, Annual Report to Parliament, 2005–2006.* Ottawa: Treasury Board of Canada Secretariat. www.tbs-sct.gc.ca.

Twine, F. W. 2000. "Racial Ideologies and Racial Methodologies." In F. W. Twine and J. W. Warren (eds). *Racing Research, Researching Race: Methodological Dilemmas in Critical Race Studies.* New York: New York University Press. 1–34.

Valpy, M. 2005. "Could It Happen Here?" *Globe and Mail.* November 12. A1.

Van de Perre v. Edwards, 2000 BCCA 167. B.C. Court of Appeal. March 9. www.courts.gov. bc.ca/jdb-txt/ca/00/01/c00-0167.htm.

Vaught, S. E., and A. E. Castagno. 2008. "'I Don't Think I'm Racist:' Critical Race Theory, Teacher Attitudes, and Structural Racism." *Race Ethnicity and Education.* 11(2): 95–113.

Walcott, R. 2003. *Black Like Who?: Writing Black Canada.* 2nd ed. Toronto: Insomniac Press.

Walker, J. W. 1980. *History of Blacks in Canada: A study guide for teachers and parents.* Ottawa: Minister of State for Multiculturalism.

Wallace, A. 2009. "Africentric Schools: Segregation, Self-determination, the Solution to Alarming Drop-out Rates among Black Youth." *This Magazine.* January/February: 18–22.

Ward, L. 2002. "Africville—The Lost Town." CBC News Online. July 8. As posted on Halifax Regional School Board Teacher Webspace. http://hrsbstaff.ednet.ns.ca/waymac/African%20Canadian%20Studies/Unit%208.%20Afro-Canada/africville.htm.

Warren, A. 2009. *Global Economic Research: Real Estate Trends.* July 9. www.scotiabank.com.

Watson, K. 1991. "Somalis Find Home in Etobicoke." *Toronto Star.* September 27. A11.

Weinfield, M. 1998. "Immigration Facts." *Transition—Newcomers: Immigrant Families Adapting to Life in Canada.* September.

Weis, L., and M. Fine. 1996. "Notes on 'White as Race.'" *Race, Gender & Class: An Interdisciplinary and Multicultural Journal.* 3(3): 5–9.

Wieringa, S. 2002. "Essentialism versus Constructivism: Time for a Rapprochement?" In P. Mohammed (ed). *Gendered Realities: Essays in Caribbean Feminist Thought.* Kingston, JA: University of the West Indies Press. 3–21.

Williams P. J. 1997. *Seeing a Color-blind Future: The Paradox of Race.* New York: Farrar, Straus and Giroux.

Williams, R. 1983. *Keywords: A Vocabulary of Culture and Society.* London: Fontana Paperbacks.

Winant, H. 2000. "Race and Race Theory." *Annual Review of Sociology.* 26: 169–185.

Wise, T. 2005. *White Like Me: Reflections on Race from a Privileged Son.* New York: Soft Skull Press.

Wortley, S., and J. Tanner. 2004. "Discrimination or 'Good' Policing? The Racial Profiling Debate in Canada." *Our Diverse Cities.* (1): 197–201.

Yakabuski, K. 2007. "Young, Diverse Quebec is Curiously Attracted to its Ancestors." *Globe and Mail.* November 3. A19, A21.

Yi, S. 1992. "An Immigrant's Split Personality." *Globe and Mail.* A20.

Yon, D. 2000. *Elusive Culture: Schooling, Race, and Identity in Global Times.* Albany: State University of New York Press.

Zavaglia, N. 1997. *Barbed Wire and Mandolins.* Documentary film. National Film Board of Canada and Canadian Broadcasting Corporation.

Zikic, J. 2009. "Breaking Down Barriers for Immigrant Professionals." *YFile: York's Daily Bulletin.* Online newsletter. May 15.

cultural analysis—An approach that requires us to appreciate and respect the experiences of other people by understanding how they live, struggle, and exist in the world; this theory of culture better enables us to see and understand the complex ways in which individuals lead their lives (see McDermott and Varenne 2006).

cultural hegemony—*Hegemony* is the dominance of one group or state over all others. *Cultural hegemony*, as described by Marxist philosopher, Antonio Gramsci, is the cultural dominance of one class or group over others within a culturally diverse society. Cultural hegemony ensures that certain power relations are embedded in the social order and seem so normal and such a part of our everyday lives that we do not question their existence or operation.

culture—The way in which a given society, community, or group organizes and conducts itself, as distinguished from that of other societies, communities, or groups. Culture consists of a dynamic and complex set of values, beliefs, norms, patterns of thinking, styles of communication, linguistic expressions, and ways of interpreting and interacting with the world that help people understand and thus survive their circumstances.

diaspora—This term is used to describe any population of people that has been dispersed from their homeland. A diaspora differs from simple migration of populations, as it implies the retention of an identity associated with the homeland in some way.

essentialism—The notion that certain traits or behaviours of racial, ethnic, cultural, or even gendered groups are both fixed and universal, hence not allowing for variations among individuals, within groups, or over time. This perspective also tends to assume behaviours to be inherent or biological.

ethnic enclaves—Residential areas "where a particular ethnic group numerically dominates," with corresponding symbols, institutions (e.g., social, religious, cultural, linguistic, commercial), and services that cater to the needs of the group. Enclaves are distinct from "geographic concentration" of an ethnic group where members of the particular group might live "side by side without any community bonds and shared sentiments" (Qadeer and Kumar 2006, 2).

ethnicity or **ethnic group**—Groupings of people who are identified as, or identify themselves as, having a common historical, cultural, and ancestral origin. Like race, ethnicity is a social construct based on historical, social, religious, geographical, and political elements. As such, it is subject to the ambiguities, inconsistencies, and contradictions found in societies, with meanings that change over time and in relation to context. In Canada, one of the ways in which ethnicity is constructed is by ancestry or by national or regional origin. Understandings of ethnicity or ethnic groups are, in part, informed by existing multiculturalism discourses.

ethnoburbs—Suburban ethnic enclaves that have resulted from the migration of long-term residents out of established suburban communities into new outer suburbs and immigrants moving in to replace them (see Phelan and Scheider 1996). Ethnoburbs are also the result of traditional urban reception areas undergoing gentrification; given their relatively low incomes, most new immigrants can only afford houses in what have become less expensive suburbs (see Bauder and Sharpe 2002).

ethnocentrism—The tendency to see things from the perspective of one's own ethnic group culture, or to have a preference for your own group's cultural symbols, and to think that what is true of one's ethnic group culture is also true of others (Carroll 1993). Ethnocentrism is considered to be an uncompromising allegiance and loyalty to one's own cultural values and practices, which are viewed as natural, normal, and necessary.

group culture or subculture—A group of people within a larger society or culture that shares distinctive cultural traits that clearly distinguish them from others within the larger culture; such traits may include language, dialect, religion, and ancestry (see Hoopes and Pusch 1981).

hate crimes—Crimes motivated by hate toward people because of their membership or perceived membership in identifiable groups. Such crimes or incidents may target race, national or ethnic origin, language, colour, religion, sex, age, mental or physical disability, sexual orientation, or other factors, such as profession or political beliefs (see Dauvergne, Scrim, and Brennan 2008, 7).

immigrant—A person who takes up permanent residence in a country other than that of their birth or national origin. Typically, immigrants are admitted only after meeting strict criteria, either on their own or by their relationship to other citizens or permanent residents of the country.

individual racism—An ideology or set of ideas and beliefs that frames individuals' negative attitudes toward others and are usually reflected in the willful, conscious or unconscious, direct or indirect, and reflexive actions, words, and opinions of individuals.

institutional racism—Exists wherever the established rules, policies, and regulations of institutions, businesses agencies, etc., systemically reflect and produce differential treatment of various groups and individuals based on race.

integration—A process by which individuals and groups are able to fully participate in society's political, cultural, economic, and social life. In contrast to assimilation, integration assumes a coexistence of multiple cultures within the society and accommodation of all ethnic groups.

Islamophobia—A term used to denote anti-Muslim sentiment; according to Fleras (2010), it is a fear of Islam and the racialization of the Muslim religion, leading to the belief that Muslims are incapable of integrating into society and that their existence poses a threat to security.

multiculturalism policy—In Canada, also known as Official Multiculturalism, this policy began in 1971 with an all-party agreement in Parliament and was included in the 1982 *Canadian Charter of Rights and Freedoms*, and became law—the *Multiculturalism Act* of 1988. The policy outlines a framework for the coexistence of diverse cultures within Canada; it sets principles, values, and ideas, which are then expressed through programs.

prejudice—An unfavourable attitude based on a premature, hasty, or uninformed judgment of a person or group; having preconceived opinions that are assumed to be true before having been tested (see Dalrymple 2007).

race—A socially constructed classification of human beings based on identified or perceived characteristics such as colour of skin and informed by historical and geographic context; it is not a biological classification. It is often the basis upon which groups are formed, agency is attained, social roles are assigned, and status is conferred.

racial profiling—The stereotyping of individuals or groups based on "difference" related to such things as race, religion, or ethnicity, or more generally, culture. Racial profiling usually involves the policing of racial, religious, or ethnic groups allegedly for reasons of safety and security, resulting in the singling out of an individual for different treatment or for an assumption of culpability based on racialized identifiers. Common examples are when law enforcement agents stop minority individuals without probable cause or at a more frequent rate than what is considered random.

racialization—The process by which personality traits, behaviours, and social characteristics are ascribed to minority people because of their race, and are seen as permanent and inalterable (see Tanovich 2009).

racism—An ideology that constructs groups, usually identified by physical characteristics, as culturally or biologically lacking in certain abilities, skills, and characteristics deemed necessary, thereby leading to subordination, colonization, and discriminatory or unequal treatment of such identified groups. Racism operates at different levels—individual, institutional, and structural or systemic reasonable accommodation—Adjustments made by institutions to accommodate the needs of minority groups with the intention of facilitating full participation. Initially a concept developed within labour law to address the needs of persons with disabilities in the workplace, reasonable accommodation was extended through the *Canadian Charter of Rights and Freedoms* to address religion and sex (Brydon 2008). Current debate over Canada's multiculturalism often focuses on the issue of what is considered "reasonable."

refugee—A person who is forced to leave their country or region of residence due to an extreme situation. Convention refugees are those who meet the United Nations' definition of refugee. Such refugees leave or are prevented from returning to their country of origin due to a well-founded fear of persecution for reasons of race, religion, nationality, or membership within social or political groups.

social stratification—The hierarchical system in which segments of the population are ranked on the basis of their power and thereby gain access to material resources, wealth, and prestige. One's ranking in the system is determined by a complex interplay of wealth as related to property ownership, income, education, and occupation—in other words social class—as well as factors such as gender, ethnicity, race, length of residency, and citizenship status.

stereotype—A set of characteristics believed to be true distinctive features of a group. Stereotypes are based on perceptions or beliefs rather than factual information, and involve over-categorization and over-generalization.

structural racism—Also known as systemic racism, this refers to the laws, legislations, rules, and ideology upon which the state operates and which tends to privilege the dominant group members and prevent minority group members from fully participating in society. Structural racism is difficult to overcome as it can be hard to identify and is often seen as the norm. Systemic discrimination is often hidden within seemingly objective and democratic systems.

Turtle Island—The English translation of a term used for North America by many Aboriginal peoples. In his book, *At Home on the Earth*, David Landis Barnhill (1999) argues that this term—made popular by Gary Snyder in his 1974 book of poetry—serves to shift the conception of North America from a space that was "discovered" and colonized by Europeans to one looked after by diverse groups of indigenous peoples.